Ship Routes . . . . ———————
Alternate Tanker Routes . . . . . - - - - - - - - - -

Sovereignty for Sale

THE ORIGINS AND EVOLUTION OF THE PANAMANIAN AND LIBERIAN FLAGS OF CONVENIENCE

Rodney Carlisle

NAVAL INSTITUTE PRESS
Annapolis, Maryland

Library of Congress Cataloging in Publication Data

Carlisle, Rodney P.
Sovereignty for sale.

Bibliography: p.
Includes index.
Supt. of Docs. no.: D 201.2:So8/4
1. Ship transfers to foreign registry—History.
2. Ships—Registration and transfer—Panama—
History. 3. Ships—Registration and transfer—
Liberia—History. I. Title. II. Title: Flags of
convenience.
HE736.C37   386'.224   81-607020
ISBN 0-87021-668-6   AACR2

Printed in the United States of America

For Anna, Nathan, and Bonnie
and in memory of a merchant officer
Henry G. Wilson, Jr., 1921–80

If the grant of a maritime flag is the function of government, the flying of the flag on the high seas or the territorial waters of the maritime states of the world is an undoubted attribute of sovereignty.

Nagendra Singh
Maritime Flag and International Law

Suddenly it seems the sovereign states are feeling naked. Concepts such as national sovereignty and national economic strength appear curiously drained of meaning.

Raymond Vernon
Sovereignty at Bay

Contents

Illustrations

Tables

Acknowledgments

In the course of researching and writing this book, the author has accumulated a number of obligations. Foremost among those entailed by this work are those to archivists at several repositories, especially Thomas Thalkin, Don Wood, and Dwight Miller at the Herbert Hoover Presidential Library, West Branch, Iowa; David Haight at the Dwight D. Eisenhower Presidential Library in Abilene, Kansas; Erwin Mueller at the Harry S Truman Presidential Library, Independence, Missouri; Rich Berger of the Research Department of the National Maritime Union in New York; John Taylor and Ken Hall at the National Archives, Washington, D.C.; Frederick Coker of the Library of Congress Manuscript Division; George Leet of the National Labor Relations Board; Mary Jane Harvey of the Maritime Administration; and Dean Allard at the Naval History Division, Navy Yard, Washington, D.C. Each of these able scholar-archivists directed the author to resources and documents which proved invaluable.

Readers and commentators on parts of the manuscript whose suggestions proved insightful and useful included colleagues Jeffrey Dorwart, Robert Horowitz, Warren Kimble, and Allen Woll of Rutgers University; L.F.E. Goldie of Syracuse University; Tony Muldoon of the Camden *Courier-Post* newspaper; and Richard Hewlett, Jack Holl, Joe Pratt, and Philip Cantelon at the Historian's Office of the Department of Energy.

Financial aid for various stages of the research came from the Rutgers Research Council, the American Philosophical Society, the Hoover Presidential Library Association, and the Department of Energy Visiting Scholar program.

The staff of the Rutgers University Computer Center, Camden, New Jersey, including David Gwalthney and Joseph Sowers, assisted in preparing a computer-accessible data base of Panamanian-registered ships.

Special thanks go to Judie Zubin, free-lance editor and graphic designer, whose excellent editorial assistance and suggestions were invaluable in the preparation of the manuscript for publication.

Personal interviews with participants and observers, including former United States Solicitor General Archibald Cox, the Liberian Maritime Commissioner Gerald Cooper, and Fred Lininger and Frank Wiswall of the International Trust Company, all added insights, anecdotes, and excellent suggestions for further research.

Acknowledgment is gratefully made to the Curator of Manuscripts, University of Virginia Library, for permission to use documents in the Edward R. Stettinius, Jr., Papers. For permission to republish elements of my article, "The American Century Implemented: Stettinius and the Liberian Flag of Convenience," thanks are due to the editorial board and to Albro Martin of *Business History Review*, in which the article appeared in the Summer 1980 issue.

A personal note of thanks is due my wife Anna for her comments, support, typing diligence, and for her indefatigable good nature which made the research in Massachusetts, Virginia, Washington, D.C., Iowa, Missouri, and Kansas an exciting adventure rather than simply a set of tiring chores.

Notwithstanding all this able and excellent assistance, the author of course must take responsibility for any conclusions, omissions, and errors that remain in the work. None of the opinions or interpretations expressed in the book should be regarded as representing those of the U.S. Naval Institute or the U.S. Department of Energy.

Abbreviations Used in the Text

ACFN   American Committee for Flags of Necessity
AOTC   American Overseas Tanker Corporation
API   American Petroleum Institute
Bapico   Baltisch-Amerikanishe Petroleum Import-Gesellschaft, mbH
CIO   Congress of Industrial Organizations
CNO   Chief of Naval Operations
DAPG   Deutsch-Amerikanische Petroleum-Gesellschaft
EPA   Environmental Protection Agency
ESSO   Standard Oil Company of New Jersey
FACS   Federation of American-Controlled Shipping
FCN   Friendship, Commerce, and Navigation
ILO   International Labor Organization
IMCO   Intergovernmental Maritime Consultative Organization
IMWU   International Maritime Workers Union
Intertanko Independent Tanker Owners' Association
ITF   International Transport Workers Federation
JCS   Joint Chiefs of Staff
JMTC   Joint Military Transportation Committee
MarAd   Maritime Administration
NATO   North Atlantic Treaty Organization
NLRB   National Labor Relations Board
NMU   National Maritime Union
ONI   U.S. Office of Naval Intelligence
OPEC   Organization of Petroleum-Exporting Countries
SIU   Seafarers' International Union
VLCC   Very Large Crude Carrier
WSA   War Shipping Administration

Introduction

A SHIP OWNED IN ONE COUNTRY while it is registered in another for purposes of commercial or legal advantage sails under a "flag of convenience." The term has been in use since 1950, but registry under a foreign flag had precedents in the nineteenth century and even earlier. Some American merchant vessels flew the flag of Portugal during the War of 1812 to evade the American and British restrictions. From the 1830s through the 1850s, slave-trading ships owned by Latin American and American citizens used a variety of flags to avoid slave-trade suppression treaties, which allowed Britain to police the high seas against ships registered with signatory states. In 1905, the Permanent Court of Arbitration at the Hague decided, in the *Muscat Dhows* case, that the flag and registry of a ship, rather than its ownership, certified the nationality of the ship. In the first decade of the twentieth century, as iron, steel, and steam took over from wood and sail, American companies purchased and registered ships in Britain to avoid the high costs of construction in American shipyards required for registry in the United States.[1]

This book is not concerned with establishing the early conceptual roots of such precedents of flags of convenience. Indeed, its writing was stimulated after the author, whose training is that of historian, read a series of excellent law review articles and legal treatises on the subject that adequately explained those concepts, but left untold the essential part of the story, from an historical point of view. Who stood to gain by this practice? Why was it allowed? What political ideas were behind flag of convenience registry? Why should American shipping have registered in Panama—why *that* particular country, at a particular time? Why should the Liberian flag, of all merchant flags of the world, have attracted the tankers, supertankers, "Very Large Crude Carriers," and "Ultra Large Crude Carriers" of the

1960s and 1970s? The legal treatises skirted these subjects and demonstrated the legislative, judicial, diplomatic, and conceptual principles that *allow* for the practice, but left unexplained the more down-to-earth questions of just how and why the system began, evolved, and grew to take over the bulk of the world's shipping

Once research was initiated on the project, the author discovered rich and virtually untapped primary documentation in the National Archives, the Library of Congress, presidential libraries, and other document collections. The wealth of data available presented an intimidating task—how to sort the material out and present it in a reasonable narrative. Since the question had not previously drawn historians, the author had to make a number of arbitrary decisions about arrangement and definition of the topic. First, of all, I begin the story, not with the nineteenth- or eighteenth-century precedents, but with the first foreign-owned ship registered in Panama—the *Belen Quezada*, in 1919. Thus, this book narrates the story of the *modern* flags of convenience, primarily Panama's flag and Liberia's flag, and the uses to which these flags have been put by American and European shipowners. The growth of the fleets of these two "nonmaritime" tropical states is told in the interplay of economic, political, and strategic issues behind the individual ships sailing under those flags.

While Panama and Liberia both were regarded by the traditional maritime states as upstarts in the world of shipping, both had had minor maritime traditions of their own. Indeed, Liberia's sailing fleet in the mid-nineteenth century was a striking achievement, since many of her 300 sailing ships were constructed and wholly owned in Liberia and became an important, if temporary, factor in the West African economy. Yet, that fleet had nearly vanished by 1900, as steam took precedence over sail and as large German and British firms competed for the coasting trade of the region. Small, locally owned sailing vessels and steamers had provided Panama's only connection to Colombia during the nineteenth century when it had been a province of that republic. For such reasons, it is not quite fair to call either Liberia or Panama "nonmaritime" nations. But the characteristic of both fleets in recent decades has been the fact that among the thousands of large ships registered in both countries, less than ten or twelve individual vessels are owned by true nationals of the countries. While ownership of ships through a corporation, itself formed in Panama or Liberia, has been common, nearly all of those corporations are wholly owned by foreigners—Americans, Europeans, or Asians.[2]

At times, other small nations, including Honduras, Costa Rica, Nicaragua, Lebanon, Cyprus, Somalia, and Singapore, have emulated the maritime codes of Panama and Liberia, in attempts to attract shipping and its registry revenue. None of these efforts has approached the success of either Panama or Liberia, and they are discussed in passing, at appropriate

Liberia, like Panama, depended upon sea transport in its early period. This lithograph shows the capital, Monrovia, in the 1840s. At this period, sailing vessels registered in Liberia were owned by merchants, leaders of the Afro-American settlers who founded the republic. Such ships engaged in local coasting trade. (Library of Congress)

points in the narrative. Therefore, this work is limited arbitrarily to the story of the merchant flags of Panama and Liberia, in the period from 1919 to the present.

I have further limited the focus of the book by concentrating primarily upon the American use of these flags, and on the political issues surrounding those uses. Even with such limitations, the story is a lengthy one, for the issues surrounding American maritime policy and the registry of American-owned ships under both of these flags are intricate, previously little-explored, and yet vitally important to the modern world economy.

At times American maritime policy was front-page news. In the years immediately prior to United States entry into World War I, Americans awoke to the fact that seamen were among the most exploited laboring classes in the nation, and legislation was passed to improve their lot. The Great War revealed the need for massive construction of troop transport and cargo vessels. By the time the shipbuilding effort moved into production, the war ended; but the program continued as contracts ran their course. Thus, through the 1920s, Republican administrations faced the task of disposing of a huge surplus government-owned fleet. That job was politically explosive. To dispose of the ships was to strip the country of an important military asset, yet to maintain the fleet was expensive, wasteful, and represented governmental involvement in business to an extent that ran counter to ideas of the superiority of private enterprise to public operation, ideas that were deeply rooted in American ideological perceptions.

Another shipping problem of the 1920s was smuggling by rumrunners. As groups of international criminals flaunted the law, some sensed that their crimes were widely supported by the American public in the name of personal liberty. As Prohibition divided the nation, a tolerance for finding loopholes and practical ways around the law became entrenched in American ideas.

The depression set back reforms initiated by Herbert Hoover in the late 1920s. The Roosevelt administration, faced with growing threats of war in Europe, restructured maritime policy with primary emphasis on national defense and security. World War II brought an unprecedented maritime effort in the United States, as the nation built a forty million ton fleet with which to supply the war fronts. In the postwar period, the disposal of the World War II surplus fleet went forward rapidly, without quite the soul-searching of the 1920s. But the late 1940s saw serious labor-management crises, which wracked the American maritime industries.

Through the 1950s and 1960s, the cold war brought a concern with maintaining in peacetime a strong merchant fleet that would be available in time of war. In the 1970s, environmental concerns and the energy crisis brought shipping once again to the front pages as wrecked oil tankers spilled millions of tons of Arabian crude oil into the sea.

While such issues as surplus ships, liquor smuggling, national defense, German torpedoes, labor conflict, cold war, and environmental and energy crises put ships on the front pages and in the forefront of American public consciousness, the system of flags of convenience quietly evolved. The evolution went unnoticed, except as it now and then bore on the issues of the time. Public ignorance of the system's evolution was matched by the ignorance of policy makers. Each generation of leaders had to learn again the logic that allowed American ships, by an act of documentation and registry, to be transformed for legal purposes into foreign ships, yet to continue to earn money for their American owners. Since policy makers had little historical awareness of the process, Panama's procedures and systems developed largely without conscious planning in the period from 1919 to 1949. In 1949, a group of American business and political leaders set out to improve on Panama's haphazard and self-evolved system, and created, through an amazing example of corporate-dictated international political action, the Liberian registry system. Because the Liberian system was tailor-made to modern American shipping necessities, it was far more efficient, effective, and responsive to business and governmental pressures than the accidentally formed Panamanian system. Within a few years, the new maritime flag system surpassed Panama's, until Liberia's flag flew over the largest merchant fleet in the world.

The consciously created and conscientiously administered system of Liberian registry attracted public attention as its ships created a number of international problems in the 1950s, 1960s, and 1970s. Yet, the publication of information about Liberia's system remained topical—often prepared from the viewpoint of the "policy sciences" in legal treatises, technical reports, congressional investigations, and naval assessments. Such literature rarely probed questions of origin and evolution. Policy makers and the public alike seemed to lose sight of their power to control events when confronted with such massive documentation of particular aspects of an established system.

Topical studies and technical reports have examined flags of convenience in the light of the crises of each period. In the early 1980s, issues such as petroleum supply, environmental protection, and national defense bring once again a need for information about this system and its peculiar logic. At the United Nations, the Conference on Trade and Development has debated plans for "phasing out" flags of convenience. But, it is this book's purpose to go beyond the issues of the present and to probe the roots of the institution. It is an element of the historian's faith that while knowledge of the past is valuable in itself, it is only with a thorough understanding of the origins of present institutions that we can hope to shape their future evolution.

1

The Evolution of Convenience, 1919–25

In the years immediately following World War I, a few unpublicized vessels owned in the United States quietly began to fly the flag of Panama. Within ten years, this practice had evolved into a system with marked advantages for shipowners. That system had the potential for vast growth, a growth that took place in the late 1930s and during World War II, when several hundred vessels flying the Panamanian merchant flag aided the Allied war effort. What factors set the growth of the system in motion in the 1920s? What combination of attractions brought those first few vessels to Panamanian registry?

To an extent, the first transfers to the flag of Panama in the years after World War I were facilitated by longstanding features of Panamanian law. Based on Colombian law, the Panamanian Fiscal Code allowed for registry of vessels through Panamanian consuls abroad. With no shipbuilding industry of its own, Panama could encourage the growth of a fleet by allowing Panamanian citizens to purchase ships abroad, empowering consuls in the United States or Europe to issue provisional registries, and providing for permanent registry on the arrival of the vessels in Panama. However, the purpose and use of this feature of the law in the early years of the republic were limited to Panamanian citizens and companies. Most of the twenty-six locally owned vessels registered in Panama between 1903 and 1913 were small fishing and coastal boats under 30 tons. The largest vessel was the 451-ton *Panama*, a steamer used in coastal transport. Originally, this feature of Panamanian law had not been intended to attract foreign shipowners. Like similar features of law in Guatemala, Honduras, and Nicaragua, the provision was designed to stimulate and permit the assembly of a local fleet. Since overland travel in Central America was tortuous, ocean travel was essential even for rudimentary commercial and governmental service to isolated coastal regions.[1]

In 1916, Panama opened its registry to ships owned by Panamanian corporations that, in turn, were owned by foreigners. The provision of law opening domestic corporations to foreign control was not unique to Panama. Again, the mere existence of a feature of law held in common with other countries sheds little light on why American shipowners chose to take advantage of such a law in Panama in particular.[2]

The Attractions of Panamanian Registry

Panama possessed several specific attractions for American shipowners not found in other nations, and that, taken together, made it easy and convenient for Americans to do ship-registry business in Panama. Panama Agencies Company, a subsidiary of Grace Lines, maintained offices in Panama and provided services to a number of shipping lines in handling ticket sales, payments of harbor fees, lighthouse fees, canal fees, and other paperwork. Business thus could be conducted through an existing American service agency. In addition, transactions regularly were conducted in English; a law enacted in 1916 required contracts written in English to be accepted as legal. Further, the balboa, the Panamanian unit of currency, was linked to and exactly equivalent in value to the dollar. Panama's geographic location also could prove useful; since it lay astride shipping lanes through the canal from the Atlantic to the Pacific, ships acquiring a provisional registry could stop in Panama to make their registry permanent without deviating from a direct canal route from ocean to ocean.[3]

Other, more deep-seated reasons also contributed to the attractions that Panama in particular held for American shipowners. Americans generally believed that Panama had a special relationship with the United States. While officially sovereign, the Panamanian state had been created, according to well-established belief, by American intervention. Although Americans believed that Panama was, in some respects, a colony of the United States, that feeling was not widely shared nor sympathetically viewed by Panamanians. Walter LaFeber, in his study *The Panama Canal*, has demonstrated that, although Panama had a long history of regional autonomy and aspiration toward independence while under Colombian rule, Americans tended to overlook that background and to regard Panama as little more than an artificial sovereignty created by and for American use to allow for the construction and operation of the canal.[4]

There was much truth to the assertion that America had control over Panama. The continued sovereignty of the republic was guaranteed by the United States; its elections could be supervised by American military intervention; civil disorders were quelled four times prior to 1920 by incursions of American troops from the Canal Zone into the territory of the republic; American forces stationed in the Canal Zone could act on a moment's notice. Of all the sovereign entities in the world in the 1920s that had the power to issue a merchant flag for vessels, Panama, although not actually occupied by U.S. troops, was believed to be, and in fact was, the one whose sovereignty was most at the disposal of the United States. More to the point, in the event of war, any ship registered in Panama would be subject to the military protection of the United States, since Panama maintained neither an army nor a navy and constitutionally and by treaty was dependent upon the United States for military protection.[5]

Such factors made Panama attractive to American shipowners seeking to find a foreign flag for their ships. But why would American shipowners want to leave their own registry for foreign registry in the first place? For some shipowners, Panamanian registry could provide a mechanism for evading the restrictions of American maritime law, which many found difficult to live with. That law had undergone a series of modifications through the period from 1915 to 1920, partially as a result of the social reform drive of the Progressive era and partially as a result of the preparedness and war drive to build a strong American merchant marine as an explicit adjunct to American naval power.

Changes in American Maritime Law

The absence of a strong merchant fleet under an American flag had proven an embarrassment during the Spanish-American War, when the navy had purchased a "mongrel fleet" of merchant vessels previously owned and registered under foreign flags. Concern over the availability of colliers, tankers, and other auxiliaries lay behind legislation in 1915, 1916, and 1920, which established and strengthened the United States Shipping Board. The board was empowered specifically to build up a strong merchant fleet as a necessary supply and backup force to the military.[6]

A strong merchant marine would serve the country in time of peace as well, by helping the United States to play a part in world affairs and world trade. If the peacetime commercial shipping of the world fell into the hands of the British, the Germans, or the Japanese, America's sea power in both peace and war would be in danger. Such national and military justifications for strength lay behind the policy generally prohibiting the transfer of valuable American ships from the American flag to other registries.[7]

The Jones Act of 1920 had increased the enforcement powers of the United States Shipping Board, and had strengthened an inspection agency, the American Bureau of Shipping. American steamships were subject to periodic boiler inspection by the bureau. To assist in building up American shipyards, a longstanding tariff provision fixing a 50 percent ad valorum duty on repairs to ships conducted in foreign yards was strengthened and incorporated in the 1922 Fordney-McCumber tariff.[8]

Such means of protecting the national interest were natural outgrowths of one whole thrust of Progressive thinking, regarded by Herbert Croly and Theodore Roosevelt as "Hamiltonian." Alfred Thayer Mahan's arguments for strengthened sea power could be viewed as the maritime and naval side of this same philosophy. William Gibbs McAdoo, Edward Hurley, Admiral William S. Benson, and others worked to implement Mahan's vision of a vital maritime arm and argued for a national effort to direct maritime affairs in the interests of the common American good. Their efforts were reflected in the laws establishing the Shipping Board and its policies.[9]

Working against such values, however, was the other side of Progressive era ideology, which held that social justice and nonexploitative labor conditions should be established and guaranteed by the power of government to protect the weak against the excesses of the strong. In this spirit, crucial shipping legislation passed in the same period was designed to protect the seaman. Section 2 of the La Follette Seamen's Act of 1915 established eight-hour shifts, a six-day week, and a schedule of holidays for merchant crews. Section 13 required that three-quarters of the crew speak English and that two-thirds hold American able-bodied seamen's papers. Section 6 increased the required square footage of crews' quarters and strengthened earlier provisions of federal statutes covering required crews' diet.[10]

The reforms were intended to strengthen the merchant marine and to extend to seamen some of the benefits of social justice. From the point of view of the shipowner, however, the cumulative effect was to raise the cost of doing business. As long as American ships competed only against each other, as in the American coastal trade, such costs presented no greater disadvantage to one shipowner than to another. But when American ships competed against those of other nations that were not subject to those laws and reforms, American shipowners operated at a competitive disadvantage.

In the years from 1921 to 1923, the world was glutted by a surplus of shipping; the vast fleet built to carry world trade during the war drove down shipping rates and an already cutthroat business became even more competitive. To shipowners, the social reforms and restrictions imposed by the Shipping Board became convenient explanations for a shrinking proportion of the world shipping revenue. It appeared that, ironically, the very laws intended to strengthen American shipping would weaken its competitive position and drive it from world trade. The classic conservative arguments against governmental regulation of business could be put to work; the "do-gooder" meddling of reformers once again had been proven wrong.

The question of how to reconcile the apparently incompatible goals of the Progressive era—nationalism and social justice—had plagued the Progressive movement itself and helped lead to its demise. In the 1920s, the conflict of these two ideological slants in maritime policy led to heated debates over several alternate solutions, of which the ship subsidy idea was one. If the government could subsidize shipping, American working conditions could be met, and ships might operate at rates competitive with foreign shipping. Several efforts to pass a comprehensive subsidy system failed since they appeared to be pure special-interest legislation. But in 1928, Congress enacted a mail subsidy plan that provided aid to regular cargo liners but not to tramp steamers, tankers, or so-called proprietary vessels owned by companies such as Standard Oil or United Fruit for the transport of their own products. Another partial remedy was the continued exclusion of alien flags from American coastal routes—the traditional enforcement of "cabotage" first established in the United States in 1789. Still another solution could be found in the retention of ships directly owned by the government through the Emergency Fleet Corporation established during the war and operated by the Shipping Board. Such ships could operate at a loss, supported from general revenues, if necessary. This system, however, resembled state socialism, and Congress instructed the board to sell off those ships as soon as possible. To allow the government to operate in competition with private enterprise was unthinkable as a long-range solution.[11]

The disadvantages imposed by American maritime law were understood by everyone in the shipping business. Admiral William S. Benson, chairman of the Shipping Board in 1920–21, explicitly recognized the problem and saw that American shipowners might try to evade the effect of the laws by registering ships under flags with little or no restrictive legislation. Yet, foreign flag registry, he believed, also would undermine the American merchant marine, for the ships would be lost to American registry and American sea power. Benson preferred the plan advocated by President Harding, an extensive system of ship subsidies. He believed that government aid was a "necessity" that arose from the higher standards for workmen imposed by law and custom. If subsidies could not be passed, Benson believed that some system of governmental aid would be needed—perhaps preferential tariffs for goods carried in American ships.[12]

While the administrations of Harding and Coolidge struggled to find a formula that would provide an escape from the maritime dilemma inherited from the Progressive era, the Shipping Board continued to operate under its mandate; it wound down its schedule of manufacturing, sold off the ships of the Emergency Fleet Corporation, disposed of confiscated Central Power vessels, and attempted to regulate shipping policy in the national interest by prohibiting the transfer of valuable ships to foreign flags. Yet, the dilemma remained.

Although the Shipping Board generally refused to permit the transfer of registry of profitable ships, a policy set down in the Jones Act of 1920, loopholes in the administration of the policy allowed for the transfer of several major vessels to the flags of other states.[13] A few such vessels entered

Panamanian registry, attracted by the features already mentioned. But even before the first few vessels from the United States explored the advantages and attractions of Panamanian registry, the case of an individual ship transferred from Canada to Panama revealed some potential hazards and disadvantages in such registry. The *Belen Quezada* suffered the misfortune of confiscation as a prize of war in a brief conflict between Panama and Costa Rica. Yet the event, instead of discouraging American shipowners, offered a working example of the relationship between the nation of actual ownership and the nation of registry that helped clarify the advantage of such split or "dual" nationality for vessels.

The *Belen Quezada*

The *Belen Quezada* was owned by a group of Central American investors through a small corporation in Canada, and was transferred from Canadian to Panamanian registry 20 August 1919, through the Panamanian consul in Vancouver, British Columbia, Maximo Patricio Morris. While the evidence is inconclusive, the owners of the ship may have intended to use her for running liquor into the United States in violation of the Volstead Act when it came into effect in January 1920, a few months after their transfer of registry. The owners of the vessel, Enrique Clare and Browne Willis, were reported to the State Department as shady characters, deeply involved in smuggling. Clare, who had been born in Cuba, was a citizen of Panama. He had married into the family of Federico Tinoco of Costa Rica, a man notorious for having used the presidency of that country to loot the treasury. Clare later was arrested on suspicion of both drug and liquor smuggling. Willis purchased large stocks of liquor in Cuba, apparently for the purpose of smuggling into the United States.[14]

But the ship, if indeed intended by Clare and Willis as part of a proposed smuggling operation, never was caught in such activities. The first cargo of the 1,141-ton *Belen Quezada* under the Panamanian flag was lumber bound for Cuba. Under instructions issued in 1916, American consular officers were charged with representing the interests of Panama in ports where no Panamanian consuls were assigned directly. When the *Belen Quezada* anchored off Salina Cruz, Mexico, with severe labor problems aboard, the American consul sought instructions. The ship, he noted, "is believed to be the first vessel to fly the flag of Panama." He was correct, since the earlier local coasters of low tonnage registered in Panama all might be regarded as boats. The crew complained that the master, Browne Willis, refused to pay wages within a reasonable time or to conform to the rules of the American merchant marine. The crew feared Willis would simply refuse to pay them at all. Willis would not deposit his papers at the consular office, nor would he even communicate with the consul. The American consul did not feel "justified in exerting much influence upon the master," because of the Panamanian registry of the vessel, so the crew's complaints went unresolved, and the ship steamed on.[15]

In February 1921, a longstanding border dispute between Costa Rica and Panama flared into a short war. The Costa Rican authorities ordered the confiscation of the *Belen Quezada*, which was in the harbor of Puntarenas with a cargo of coal. The crew was ordered ashore, put up at a hotel, and then repatriated to the United States at American expense. The ship, meanwhile, was loaded with 500 Costa Rican troops prepared for an invasion of Panama. Concerted efforts by American representatives in Panama and Costa Rica, and the threat of American force against Panama, brought a quick end to the conflict, and the border was adjusted to Costa Rican satisfaction, leaving Panama smarting from the American insult. The ship was held by the Costa Rican government as spoils of war. (See Map 1.)

Three nations engaged in the legal debate over the status of the ship. The Panamanian position was that despite the various nationalities of the owners, the ship essentially was owned by Americans and that the American government was obliged to look after the interests of its citizens. The Costa Ricans took the stand that the ship was a legitimate prize of war, and

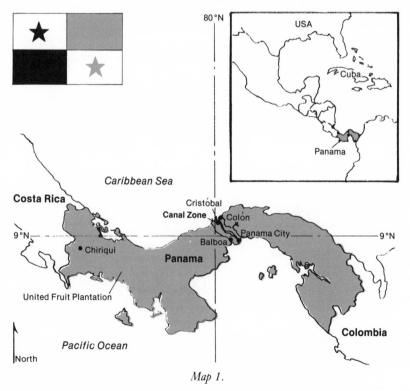

Map 1.

amended their constitution to allow the Supreme Court of Costa Rica to serve as a prize court for captured vessels. The Costa Rican court then dutifully awarded the ship to the Costa Rican government and rejected all private claims to her ownership. The *Belen Quezada* became the *Costa Rica*. She was sent on a trading voyage to Guayaquil, Ecuador, where she went out of commission and was laid up to rust by 1925.[16]

The State Department made inquiries into the Panamanian claim that the ship was American-owned, and found that American citizens held only about one-third of the stock in the vessel, which was shared among ten individuals of American, British, French, and Panamanian citizenships. A further complexity arose when John R. Gordon, an American citizen, claimed that he had been assigned all rights by the various owners. As an American, he sought the assistance of the State Department in the pursuit of his claim against the Costa Rican government, hoping to make the issue an intergovernmental one open to diplomatic solution, rather than simply a private claim. As the State Department investigated Gordon's request, some of the original owners sued Gordon for misrepresenting their arrangement with him. The New York District Court awarded the claim, for what it was worth, to Gordon. However, the protracted case outlived the ship herself.[17]

The *Belen Quezada* incident illustrated some of the advantages as well as some of the risks inherent in transfer to the Panamanian flag. Browne Willis had taken full advantage of the lack of Panamanian regulation of crew conditions to refuse payment to his seamen.

The Zafiro, *once a supply and dispatch vessel in Admiral Dewey's fleet in the Philippines. The ship was sold and resold, to be named the* Belen Quezada *in 1919. Registered in Panama by her owners for the apparent purpose of rumrunning, the ship was confiscated in a border war between Costa Rica and Panama in 1922, and then became the subject of a multi-sided legal battle. (Naval Institute Collection)*

The unlikely event of the war between Panama and Costa Rica exposed one distinction between the nation of ownership and the nation of registry. With no army of its own, Panama fought its own "war" with armed civilians and police. By constitution and treaty, Panama was required to rely on the United States for national defense. But when the United States chose not to endorse the Panamanian position, no defense was forthcoming.[18]

When the owners sought redress for a claim from the flag state, they were referred to the nation of ownership; the American courts and State Department displayed little eagerness to resolve the problem and their delays rendered the whole problem moot within four years. Yet, the State Department did regard the interests of American owners as worthy of investigation.[19]

The State Department position, that the interests of American owners of a Panamanian-registered ship legitimately were protected by the United States, resulted in a fruitless deadlock in this case, but it was based on a sound tradition of maritime law and would serve as a precedent to be cited later. To penetrate behind the flag of registry to the nation of the owner in a search for responsibility and the claim to diplomatic protection was to become an essential ingredient in the later fully evolved flag of convenience. If the United States would protect a ship like the *Belen Quezada*, whose operators were suspected of smuggling intentions and whose American owner established his claim only after an involved legal battle, then the State Department should be prepared to defend more legitimate shipowners who gave up the American flag for the Panamanian in the interests of lawful profit.[20]

The First Transfers from the United States

Among its other duties in the early 1920s, the United States Shipping Board had responsibility for confiscated Central Power merchant vessels and for merchant vessels turned over to the United States as part of the reparations agreements worked out at Versailles (41 Stat. 988, Section 4). The Shipping Board, as receiver, operated these vessels in 1921 and 1922 under charter-purchase arrangements with private firms. Under the private charters, a host of legal and financial problems arose to plague the board. A chartered vessel that lost money on a voyage accumulated debts; if the company operating the charter dissolved or went bankrupt, the debt would attach to the vessel itself and could be paid only by an auction sale of the ship. In coming to the decision to sell debt-laden ships, the board faced a conflict among several principles and policies that guided its actions. Considering the glutted condition of the world shipping market in 1922, ship sales, even of good-sized, modern freighters in reasonable repair, would have to be at very low prices. The price, on the other hand, would have to be high enough to pay off the debts for each ship. The alternative of paying the debts directly from other governmental revenues was not a legal possibility because of the board's status as receiver in relation to the ship. Six ships in such positions had an estimated combined value of $2 million; yet, market conditions in 1922 would dictate a price under $400,000 for all six vessels. That amount would more than cover the debts, but it would place the buyer of the ships in an unfair competitive position over other owners of American vessels. The low capital cost of the vessels would amount to direct government aid to the company or companies buying the vessels.[21]

The board decided that the way through these conflicting principles was to sell the ships at auction to an American corporation, with the stipulation that the ships must be transferred to a foreign flag to work in a trade in which other American ships would not compete. This restriction would violate the usual practice of prohibiting flight from the flag for profitable ships, but it would provide funds to cover the ships' debts and would prevent favoring the purchasing companies over others in competitive trade. Accordingly, six major freighters, ranging in tonnage from 3,900 to 5,600 tons, were offered at auction and sold in August 1922. Debts against the *Casco*, the *Isonomia*, the *Arcadia*, the *Pawnee*, the *Ida*, and the *Pequot* totalled $148,168.38, and the auction price finally accepted ($325,000.00) more than paid off the debts. The purchaser of the six vessels was Pacific Freighters, a company established in San Francisco specifically for the purpose of this purchase by Admiral-Orient Lines, which provided the necessary capital. The company planned to enter the ships into transpacific trade from Seattle to Shanghai, competing against the strong Japanese position in the trade. A seventh vessel, the *Tunica*, was sold under the same principles, to a New York firm, American Merchant and Forwarding Company, which planned to resell the ship in Europe.[22]

The decision regarding the nation to which the ships should be transferred was left to the purchasers. The Shipping Board simply required that the vessels be removed from American registry in order to take them out of potential competition with other American ships. The managers of Pacific Freighters chose Panamanian registry. Since very few American shipowners of this period were allowed to transfer abroad, and since this transfer was the first allowed for large, valuable, and potentially profitable freighters, the precedent-setting choice by Pacific Freighters to transfer to Panama bears close scrutiny. Because a transfer abroad was required and approved by the Shipping Board, the officers of the company felt no need to cloak their honest business motives for the choice of flag in more elegant appeals to national interest, ideals, or matters of high policy. In an interview with the *New York Herald*, W. L. Comyn, an officer of Pacific Freighters, explicitly stated the business attractions of Panamanian registry. "The chief advantage of Panamanian registry is that the owner is relieved of the continual but irregular boiler and hull inspections and the regulations as to crew's quarters and subsistence. We are under absolutely no restrictions, so long as we pay the $1 a net ton registry fee and 10 cents yearly a net ton tax."[23]

The officers hired to operate the ships were the former German merchant officers who had commanded the vessels before the war. They were to be paid on a Japanese pay scale, and the crews, it was planned, would be Japanese and Chinese. Comyn justified this proposed arrangement without apology for its open affront to American ethnic prejudices, to anti-German feelings, or to the flag. He kept his rationale in strictly business terms: "We are paying officers and crew according to the Japanese scale. This is our main competition on the Pacific and we cannot meet it under the American flag." Even if American-registered ships were to receive the subsidy of $10,000 per year then under discussion in Congress, they would not be able to compete with the Japanese, since the savings on manning costs alone for a Japanese ship of 8,800 tons would amount to $50,000 per year. As far as marine insurance was concerned, Comyn claimed that his company received equal rates with American flag ships. He considered unimportant the lack of military protection offered by Panama and half-jokingly declared that he had nothing to fear but a war between the United States and Panama. Comyn indicated that his company was not the first to discover such advantages, and he reported that many ship operators were discussing the possibility of Panamanian registry. By stressing the attractions of Panamanian freedom, of course, Admiral-Orient Lines also could make a backhanded protest against the very regulations they could now legally avoid with these ships. Comyn predicted that many other shipowners would follow his lead, but his prophetic and economically sound expectation was premature. The policy of the Shipping Board, which had provided a loophole for the Pacific Freighters fleet, continued to stand in the way of widespread emulation of the example.[24]

For the most part, the Pacific Freighters fleet drew little public attention. When the *Ida* arrived at Cristobal to transit the canal, the English language paper of Panama, the *Star and Herald*, noted dryly, "The vessel has the unique distinction of arriving at one end of the Canal under the American flag and leaving the other end under the Panamanian flag." Panama Agencies Company handled the paperwork of converting the provisional registry, issued through the Panamanian consular office in New York, into a permanent registry. When the *Isonomia* later called at Newcastle, Australia, the American consul there found it quite odd that a Panamanian ship was captained by a German officer with documents in German and "printed in the script of that country." He remarked laconically that the observation might be of interest at the State Department.[25]

Labor resistance to the new system began to flare up. At Shanghai, the first American crew of the *Ida* refused to sail further, until they were paid and guaranteed return passage to the United States. Cases of maritime disputes in China at that time were taken before mixed courts composed of European and American consuls and Chinese officials. The Shanghai Mixed Court investigated the seamen's complaints. The major issue was that Master F.E.W. Pennrich, one of the German officers recruited by Pacific Freighters, had hired and paid off seamen without any official supervision or properly executed ship's articles.

The use of a standard employment contract to enforce congressionally approved standards upon American shipping went back to 1884. Similar systems existed in the other major maritime nations. Additions to the required contract form in the 1880s and the 1890s had included provisions for hazardous duty, prohibition of flogging, and detailed specifications for each seaman's required diet. The eight-hour shift, holiday schedule, and improved diet in the La Follette Act were implemented through the required contract.[26]

In order to insure that seamen understood and agreed to the terms of the articles or contracts they signed, consuls abroad or shipping commissioners in American ports would witness and notarize the signing of articles. The articles would specify hours, duties, rates of pay, and the length of the voyage. Among other protections, American crews could expect a return voyage to the United States or passage to an American port. While Panama had no law requiring a standardized set of articles, seamen signing aboard expected some system of regular guarantees or, they believed, they would face exploitation.

Captain Pennrich, complained the crew of the *Ida*, avoided the usual system of swearing seamen to articles in the presence of officials. Pennrich said that, "in order to save money," he simply had proceeded to sign on seamen to his own draft articles at various ports, including Baltimore, Port Arthur, and Honolulu, without obtaining any official sanction. As a result, the men claimed, clauses had been added and deleted irregularly from the articles they had signed. They protested the captain's intention of setting them ashore in Shanghai without return passage. The mixed court ruled that the master should pay off the seamen with passage back to Honolulu. Pennrich agreed, and then signed aboard a crew of thirty-five Chinese seamen, this time following an official set of American ship's articles under consular approval, and sailed for the Philippines in February 1923.[27]

When the *Paul Regandanz* arrived at Port Said, Egypt, in October 1923, with a near mutiny aboard, the issues bore marked similarity to those that had troubled the *Ida* seven months before at Shanghai. The *Paul Regandanz* was the former *Tunica*, sold by the Shipping Board to a New York firm, which registered the ship in Panama and sold her in Holland. There the ship was renamed the *Stuyvesant* and sold to a company in Hamburg, where she once again was renamed, the *Paul Regandanz*, still under the Panamanian flag. At Port Said, the crew complained that Captain C. Tepsdorf had signed them aboard at Hamburg without obtaining official sanction of a set of articles at a Panamanian consular office. They claimed he simply took their names on a muster role, and later appended that signed list to a set of German ship's articles that stipulated pay in German currency. In 1923, the mark depreciated rapidly. The crew believed they should sign under Panamanian articles and receive pay in Panamanian currency or its equivalent. The crew knew little of Panamá or its maritime laws; they simply believed, correctly, that Panamanian currency was more sound than the German mark.[28]

The American consul at Port Said, Raymond Geist, representing the interests of Panama, heard the case. While he had few powers and no copy of any Panamanian maritime laws, he sympathized with the position of the men. He examined the documents and agreed that the articles had been added after the signatures had been obtained. Geist convinced Captain Tepsdorf to modify the existing articles to include a provision for pay in Panamanian currency, subject to a court decision on return to Hamburg. Geist reported to the State Department, drawing attention to what he called "a recent scheme adopted by unscrupulous operators, who purposely design in this way to take advantage of the alleged absence of Panamanian navigation laws for the protection of seamen shipped on such vessels." Captain Tepsdorf's view of the matter, on the other hand, was that the men clearly understood that they were signing under German wages, and that their protest amounted to a mutiny designed to win an increase in pay.[29]

The State Department checked with the American consul in Hamburg, Theodore Jaeckel, to determine the extent of the "scheme" alleged by Geist. Jaeckel reported no scheme, but simply one ship, which, despite its several name and ownership changes since the sale by the Shipping Board over a year before, had kept Panamanian registry. Mr. Bensel, managing director of the owning company in Germany, claimed that the motive for keeping the ship under the Panamanian flag was to avoid German navigation law, which would entail a boiler inspection and a delay before departure. Jaeckel's investigation in Hamburg did not reveal that the men had reason to believe they would be paid anything but German wages. Company officials claimed they might have the men arrested for mutiny on their return.[30]

While Geist in Port Said saw the issue as a labor-management struggle over the terms of the ship's articles and treated the case very much like the *Ida* case in Shanghai, the comments of the management in Hamburg revealed close similarities between the attractions of Panamanian registry for German and for American shipowners. Once a ship found its way to the relatively unregulated Panamanian system, a company took advantage of that registry to avoid the "harassment" of government safety and boiler inspectors. The company's own reasons for Panamanian registry were hardly as dramatic as a "scheme" but their explanation need not be dismissed as a polite rationalization for a system of exploitation.

Labor exploitation could go only to a certain point before business risks outweighed business advantages. While maritime unions in both Germany and the United States were weak and ineffectual in the 1920s, seamen were aware of and sensitive to rights that had been recognized by law. When masters and owners of these first Panamanian ships used the absence of a system of ship's articles to exploit the crew, a rudimentary strike or near "mutiny" could bring the voyage to a halt. When the crew protested to responsible consular officials or local port authorities, the resulting delay was simply bad business. The cases of the *Belen Quezada* at Salina Cruz, the *Ida* at Shanghai, and the *Paul Regandanz* at Port Said all showed that crews accustomed to contracts and decent conditions would not allow exploitation to go unchecked. An extreme form of resolution of such a labor crisis was demonstrated with the case of the *Nohab* in May 1926. This small Panamanian-registered steam yacht anchored in Miami with a destitute crew of fifteen aboard. The crew members protested their lack of pay, and the assistant director of the city welfare department contacted the State Department for suggestions. Before the State Department could reply, however, the local courts resolved the question through seizure and sale of the yacht to cover harbor fees and the men's wages.[31]

The *Reliance* and the *Resolute*

While the cases discussed so far illustrate some shadings of motivation in Panamanian registry, they drew little public attention among contemporaries. Beyond the scattered articles in shipping pages of New York newspapers, local news of crew disputes, and confidential consular reports, little record developed of the freighters whose transfer to Panama had been approved by the Shipping Board. Such merchant vessels, with their stubby, low silhouettes, their mundane cruises and cargoes, their underpaid and socially outcast crews, rarely attracted public notice or attention. By contrast, the great passenger liners were well-known and newsworthy. Everything about them made for good news copy—their elegance, their high speed, and their glittering social company at the peak of a neatly designated social microcosm represented by the distinctions between deck and steerage class passenger accommodations. The rivalry for the fastest Atlantic crossing, customarily entitling the record-holding ship to fly the "blue riband," and the questions of national honor implicit in the ownership and registry of such vessels attracted regular, intense news coverage. The daily press featured stories of the arrival of prominent or notorious passengers as well as the details of passenger liner speed, style, competition, and ownership changes.[32]

Thus, the transfer of two major passenger liners in October 1922, from American to Panamanian registry, evoked national and international attention, overshadowing the earlier transfer of the seven freighters. Indeed, so remarkable was the liner transfer to contemporary newsmen, that it left a permanent impression, reflected in the legal treatises touching on the origins of the modern flag of convenience. Most such treatments use as their starting point this relatively unique liner-transfer case.[33]

The background of the *Resolute* and the *Reliance* was in one respect like that of the *Arcadia*, the *Ida*, the *Isonomia*, the *Casco*, the *Pawnee*, the *Pequot*, and the *Tunica*. The two liners had been built in Germany. They were transferred in their construction ways to Dutch ownership by the Germans themselves in partial compensation for German submarining of neutral Dutch shipping and to avoid Allied confiscation. Thus, they were placed in Dutch hands at their launching in 1920, and steamed several voyages as the *Limburgia* and the *Brabantia* in the passenger route to Buenos Aires. The Allies, however, refused to accept the transaction, and forced the Dutch to sell the vessels. They were bought in January 1922 by a company owned by W. Averell Harriman, the American Ship and Commerce Corporation; he operated the ships with several other liners as United American Lines. Harriman renamed the two ex-German ships the *Reliance* and the *Resolute*, in honor of America's Cup racing yachts.[34]

On the transfer of these two vessels to the American flag, the Shipping Board agreed to a stipulation that if insufficient subsidy were to be passed to allow for a profitable enterprise with the liners, the board would not object to a retransfer to a suitable foreign registry, at any time within three years from the date of arrival under the American flag.[35]

On 31 October 1922, the company applied to transfer the two ships to Panama. The motive that received the most public attention was the concern of the operators with the effect of Prohibition on American ships. Ever since the Volstead Act enforcing the Prohibition Amendment had gone into effect on 17 January 1920, American ships had been in a dubious position. While it was clear that no ship of any registry in American waters legally could sell liquor aboard, it was possible to drink in a liner headed for American shores until the ship entered the 3-mile limit. But what of American ships on the high seas? The Eighteenth Amendment and the Volstead Act explicitly prohibited sale and consumption of liquor not only in the United States but also in "all territory subject to its jurisdiction." Since ships on the high seas were technically "territory" of the nation whose flag they flew, Attorney General Harry Daugherty issued a ruling prohibiting sale of alcohol on American flag ships anywhere in the world. In the storm of protest from American shipowners that followed the Daugherty decision, Harriman's company announced its intention to transfer the *Reliance* and the *Resolute* to Panama, and specifically linked the transfer request to the Daugherty ruling. Harriman's firm also joined several others in bringing suit against the ruling through the courts.[36]

When the Shipping Board approved the transfer of these two liners to Panama, it made clear through public announcement that the *Reliance* and the *Resolute* were special cases. United American Lines's original agreement with the board allowed for a transfer to a foreign flag; no such provision affected other ships under American registry, and therefore this case, warned the board, was not to serve as a precedent for further transfers.[37]

Nevertheless, the transfer of the two large liners attracted wide public notice and discussion. In justifying its decision to transfer, the company issued a statement that mixed a hint of practical business concerns such as those expressed earlier by W. L. Comyn of Pacific Freighters with explicit criticism of the Daugherty ruling. One purpose of the company announcement was to discredit the ruling by showing its adverse effect on business; as a statement of motives, Harriman's public position was therefore less straightforward than Comyn's clear exposition of shipping economics. Richard H. M. Robinson, president of United American Lines, gave the company's statement to the press: "Because of the keen competition of cruises arranged for foreign steamers, we believe that the cruises of the *Resolute* and the *Reliance* cannot be carried out successfully unless the passengers can be offered the same service and privileges as is [sic] offered of foreign ships."[38] Almost as an afterthought, Robinson noted in his public statement a concern with the national interest: "We have selected the Panamanian flag because we believe it to be the most acceptable to the interests of the United States."[39]

The private letter of application from Harriman's firm to the Shipping Board gave further insight into the motive for transfer, noting that "We have made a study of the laws of various countries which have no national aspirations to compete with the United States in the development of its merchant marine and its naval power." The corporation concluded that "The Panama flag will probably be the one most suited to our own necessities, and, we believe, most acceptable to the interests of the United States both in the development of its trade and as regards availability in time of military necessity." This remarkable assertion of private decision-making power over questions of foreign policy suggested that the study had been conducted at the State or War Department, or at least in consultation with those departments. As far as can be determined, no record of such a study or consultation exists.[40]

Harriman's attorneys for matters of international affairs were the firm of Sullivan and Cromwell. William Nelson Cromwell had been instrumental in arranging the legal details of early Panamanian independence, and the firm continued to serve as Panama's legal counsel in the United States. John Foster Dulles, who had visited Panama in 1917 to insure that Panama

would follow the United States in declaring war on Germany, had succeeded Cromwell in the firm as counsel for Panama. In this period, Harriman sought advice from Dulles on international legal matters. The rather
pompous assertion of knowing best the interests of the United States bore
all the earmarks of the Dulles approach noted by his biographers as present
even in his work as a private attorney. While diplomatic and military
considerations making Panama attractive were under general discussion in
the shipping community in 1922, the particular advice to Harriman outlin-
ing the acceptability of Panama to the interests of the United States may
have come from Dulles.[41]

For public consumption, the imposition of the Daugherty ruling was the
major reason for transfer away from the American flag. The gesture of the
transfer was intended as much as a protest against the ruling as a way
around it. Yet, independent observers detected other motives. A *New York
Times* reporter noted, "In addition to making a good deal of money for the
company by changing to the Panama flag, the operating expenses of the
Resolute and *Reliance* will be considerably reduced, as they can now carry
German stewards, Cuban firemen, and West Indian sailors, or crews of any
nationality the management may wish so long as they are not landed in this
country."[42]

In fact, the United American Lines did save operating costs without
going to such extremes. The American consul in Hamburg, on orders from
the State Department, discreetly inquired into the details. After noting the
advantage in serving wines and liquor for the cruises, Theodore Jaeckel
commented on several other advantages that the Harriman firm obtained by
operating under the flag of Panama. The 1922 tariff providing a 50 percent
customs duty on repairs conducted in foreign yards would no longer apply,
and since repairs could be conducted more cheaply in Hamburg than in the
United States, this represented a considerable savings to the United American Lines. The particular ship's articles employed gave the master more
discipline and authority over his crew than did standard American articles,
imposing severe fines against wages for leaving a ship without permission or
for disobedience or insolence to officers. However, Jaeckel reported that the
critical advantages were savings in the crew's wages and food budget. The
savings in wages would amount to between $17,000 and $18,000 per month
on each vessel, while the savings on food would amount to two cents per
crew member per day. The nature and detail of information obtained by
Jaeckel appeared to derive from an inside source, perhaps a purser.[43]

The Shipping Board disagreed with the Daugherty ruling, believing
American shipping had sufficient problems competing without the added
disability of "dry" voyages. Therefore, the board allowed the company to
evade the law by transfer, and to publicize the attractions of Panamanian
registry as a means of protesting and drawing attention to the ruling.

However, the Daugherty ruling was overturned within seven months by the Supreme Court, in *Cunard et al.* v. *Mellon et al.* 262 U.S. 100. The court held that while ships were under the jurisdiction of the nation whose flag they flew, they were not "territory" except metaphorically, and that, therefore, the Treasury Department had no authority to extend Prohibition on American ships beyond the 3-mile limit. Thus, the pressing reason given out publicly for the transfer to Panama was no longer operative after 30 April 1923. By 1926, the German firm, Hamburg-America Lines (Hapag) was reestablished, and Harriman sold the ships of the United American Lines to the German company, which transferred the whole fleet, including the *Reliance* and the *Resolute*, to German registry. However, from 1923 through the sale in 1926, the *Reliance* and the *Resolute* were kept under the Panamanian flag.

From a business perspective, the cost factors outlined by Consul Jaeckel in his confidential report continued to make Panamanian registry attractive even after the *Cunard* decision rendered the motive of Volstead-law evasion irrelevant. While the transfer had been permitted and publicized as a form of protest against the Treasury and Justice Departments by the Shipping Board, the company quietly could continue to benefit from the decreased costs of Panamanian operation until the German sale could be arranged.

The twin attractions of Panama to American shipowners were its laws and its national situation. Prior to 1925, the factors attracting Admiral-Orient Lines, United American Lines, and lesser firms were a mix of both factors. The special status of Panama was obvious not only to men like Dulles at Sullivan and Cromwell, who had been instrumental in shaping Panama's dependency on the United States, but it was clear also to the maritime community in general that Panama's was the "independent" flag that was the most "dependent" and, therefore, most in line with the nationalistic aspiration of the Shipping Board. In addition, Panama's shipping laws, the other attraction, offered opportunities for more effective international competition than did American maritime law. The Panamanian Maritime Code itself already had features that attracted the interest of shipowners.

2

The System Refined

In the mid-1920s, the Panamanian Assembly improved and modified the system of ship registry in an open effort to attract registries. The system quickly changed from an accidentally discovered haven for the debtor ships of the Shipping Board and for the protest registry of the Harriman ships into a more formal system, specifically and consciously designed to attract shipping. As the ease of registry began to draw smugglers, Panama quickly moved to protect the flag of Panama both from such illegitimate uses and then from zealous official American interference with the ships under the flag. The pressures exerted by the United States to control both the ships and Panama's national legislative process evoked strong resistance in Panama, showing that the extension of the fleet, while primarily undertaken for revenue purposes, was a question closely wrapped up in one of the central issues of Panamanian politics—defense of the country's sovereignty from affronts and incursions by the United States.

Panama's Maritime Code

The legislation allowing the registry of foreign-owned ships in Panama had grown in a somewhat accidental fashion prior to 1922. After the public notoriety that the transfer of the *Reliance* and the *Resolute* attracted, the Departments of Commerce and State in the United States received many requests from shipowners for a set or copy of the laws governing ship registry in Panama. The director of the American consular service requested that the American consul in Panama, George Orr, draft a report explaining the status of the law. In his report, Orr noted that "no special compilation has ever been made." He pointed out that, "Up to the present time, comparatively little attention has been given by the Panama Government to specific laws relating to registry and inspection of merchant vessels, doubtless because the merchant marine of the Republic consisted only of a few small steamboats and a number of motor and sailing craft engaged in the coasting trade." He noted, however, that with the "recent transfer of transatlantic steamers" the registry system "assumed important proportions."[1]

Orr carefully reviewed the law and found a scattering of passages relevant to ship registration. In addition to articles in the Commercial Code that allowed foreign corporations to register vessels, Orr found three articles in the Fiscal Code that specified the fees for registry and that allowed consuls abroad to issue temporary or provisional registry. Provisions allowing foreign corporations to register and own ships had been added in a 1917 law, but there still was no "maritime code" per se.[2]

The success and publicity surrounding the *Reliance* and the *Resolute* transfers, the resultant flurry of interest among American shipowners, and the State Department's inquiries encouraged the Panamanian Assembly to compile the scattered provisions and draft a single law incorporating them. A bill was presented for its first reading early in 1923, and was enacted 12 January 1925.

The new law brought together the specific existing attractions of the Panamanian codes. The system of registry through consuls abroad, previously covered by Article 589 of the Fiscal Code, became Article 18 of the new law. The 1925 law made the procedures and steps for ship registry clearer and more concise, producing the neat, packaged code requested by shipowners.

Yet, several features of the law were written to provide Panama, at least on paper, with new benefits. Article 16 revived an old Colombian requirement regarding the nationality of the crew, and stated that at least 10 percent of any crew on a Panamanian-registered vessel be citizens of Panama, "provided those applying for employment are up to the physical and moral standards required for the post." The proviso made it clear that the 10 percent was what a later era would call an employment guideline; no recruitment goals or special training were specified to bring employment up to a minimum quota. If insufficient numbers of qualified Panamanians applied for crew jobs, Article 16 did not apply. Article 17 empowered the Panamanian president to establish a maritime academy and to require that Panamanian-registered vessels employ its graduates. Although this provision received attention in the local press, it remained a dead letter in that no such academy was established, and the article itself was dropped in later reprintings of the code. Another advantage, and perhaps the only concrete one, was revenue. The press in Panama noted increased rates charged under the law for some of the registry services. Revenue problems plagued Panama through the mid-1920s. The Panamanian Foreign Ministry took the position that the law was made more liberal in order to attract more transfers. With slightly higher rates, and more vessels, the system held the promise of easing the revenue crisis.[3]

There is no evidence that the ship registry system was designed or that the revised law actually was drafted by American advisers or by an American interest group. Rather, the new statute was compiled, organized, and presented to the Panamanian Assembly and public as essentially a law to benefit Panama. While the provisions for hiring Panamanian seamen and for the establishment of a maritime academy remained ineffective, the predictions of revenue were somewhat more realistic. By compiling laws and making the registry system more organized, more foreign shipping would be attracted. Even though the 1925 law was a local product, it was the first attempt to devise a system of ship registration specifically written as a "flag of convenience" law. By facilitating foreign registry and offering no system of regularized crew conditions, Panamanian legislators put together the convenient features of Panamanian law that already had attracted Admiral-Orient and United American Lines. In this indirect way, the law reflected the concerns of American shipowners. The preferences, interests, and inclinations of the shipowners were written into the law almost as well as if the shipowners had written the law themselves.

Rumrunning

The possibility that the flag of Panama would be used for less legitimate purposes, specifically to protect liquor smuggling activities, had existed ever since the implementation of the Volstead Act in January 1920. The actions of Browne Willis and his associates in acquiring the *Belen Quezada* had suggested that they planned such a use. An early case of a Panamanian vessel engaged in liquor smuggling came up in 1923, when the steamship *Taboga* discharged Chinese seamen in Halifax, Nova Scotia. As in the other labor-dispute cases, the seamen approached the American consul, seeking repatriation. However, the seamen could offer no proof of American citizenship, and some could not speak English. The consul, more concerned with the national status of the crew than the business engagements of the ship, commented in his dispatches that the *Taboga* and her captain were "known to be involved in liquor smuggling." The ship was confiscated and the seamen carefully screened for repatriation.[4]

As a control on the rapidly expanding liquor smuggling business, the United States entered into treaties or conventions with eighteen nations between 1924 and 1930, which would allow American Coast Guard vessels to search on the high seas, suspected rumrunners registered under the flags of these states. Discussions between the State Department and Ricardo J. Alfaro, Panamanian minister to Washington, resulted in a convention signed June 1924 and fully ratified by January 1925. The convention, almost identical with those signed between the United States and the seventeen other nations, gave the United States the right to board vessels carrying the Panamanian flag on the high seas when the vessel was under suspicion of violating the Prohibition laws. The right to such boarding was limited in all the treaties to one hour's steaming time from United States territorial waters, which, at that time, was agreed to be 3 miles from shore. In effect, the conventions extended the right of search from the 3-mile territorial limit to 14 to 21 nautical miles, depending on the speed of the Coast Guard vessel engaged in any particular chase.[5]

On the Pacific Coast of the United States, the Coast Guard encountered far less rumrunning than on the East Coast, partly because the lack of small harbors on the Pacific made the Coast Guard's task of enforcement easier. Nevertheless, several vessels from Vancouver were noted discharging liquor cargoes off the American coast. Under the Canadian Customs Act, it was illegal to designate a false destination for cargo on a ship's manifest. Thus, if a Canadian ship left Vancouver with false papers indicating a Central or South American destination for a cargo of liquor, and the vessel was apprehended making a transfer to a small launch off the American coast, based on Coast Guard-supplied evidence, Canadian authorities would proceed against the owners of the vessel with charges of filing a false manifest. However, Canadian authorities would not use this provision to take action against ships under the registry of a third nation. For this reason, the office of the Panamanian consul in Vancouver, Maximo Morris, became relatively busy with ship transfer business.[6]

The *Gertrude*, an old German-built "iron steamer" of Belgian registry, anchored in Vancouver in 1925. She had made a difficult voyage from Europe that brought near-starvation to the crew off the west coast of Mexico, where they survived on dried seal meat. In January 1926, J. Ward, representing a rumrunning firm, Consolidated Exporters, submitted papers changing the name of the *Gertrude* to the *Federalship*, and secured a provisional Panamanian registry from Consul Maximo Morris.[7]

American Coast Guard officers soon reported the ship engaged in smuggling, but did not catch the *Federalship* in or near United States territorial waters. The Treasury Department complained to the State Department, which, in turn, pressured Panama to do something about the illegal and improper uses of its flag. The Panamanian response was careful. The foreign minister commented to the American minister in Panama that there already had been "several embarrassing cases," and that, therefore, a law was already pending in the Panamanian Assembly authorizing the "cancellation of Panama registry of vessels habitually engaged in smuggling, illicit commerce, or piracy." This act was passed and duly signed into law on 11 December 1926.[8]

American officials were pleased to learn of the new act. If Panama were to cancel the registry of a smuggler, then the ship might be caught with no legal flag at all. If a smuggling vessel operated with no registry, it could be confiscated on the high seas as a "ship without nationality" and, in effect, under pirate status.

At the State Department, Under Secretary Joseph C. Grew took the attitude that Panama had passed the antismuggling law as a result of the information provided to Panama by the State Department regarding the *Federalship*, despite the fact that the law was already under consideration prior to the State Department pressure. He and others at the State Department preferred to believe that Panama's Assembly wrote Law 54 of 1926 in response to American pressure, and that the law was designed primarily to facilitate seizure of Panamanian ships on the open ocean by nullifying the registry of well-known smugglers.

Joseph C. Grew, shown on appointment as under secretary of state in 1924. Grew sought to pressure Panama into cancellation of registry of accused rumrunning vessels. (Library of Congress)

The *Federalship* steamed from Vancouver on 22 February 1927 with a crew of twenty and a cargo of 12,500 cases of Scotch worth at least $1 million. The next day, the *Federalship* was spotted by the Coast Guard cutter *Algonquin* 75 miles off the Oregon coast. The cutter followed and noted that the *Federalship* raised a Panamanian flag. In radio contact with Coast Guard Division Headquarters in San Francisco, the commander of the *Algonquin* asked for instructions. Checking with Washington, the San Francisco command ordered the ship seized, on the assumption that the registry was void under Law 54. A second cutter, the *Cahokia*, joined the chase and on 1 March 1927, 270 miles south-southwest of San Francisco, the *Algonquin* fired on the *Federalship*, inflicting slight damage to a rail. The *Federalship* stopped, was captured, and taken in tow to San Francisco with its cargo intact.[9]

The storm of controversy that emerged over the taking of the *Federalship* twenty hours' steaming time from the coast revealed the discrepancy between the American and the Panamanian views of Law 54. Alfaro issued a sharply worded protest over the seizure, which Washington took as an effort to embarrass the United States. In essence, Alfaro claimed the seizure was a direct violation of the 1924 treaty that limited the right of seizure to a one-hour steaming distance from United States territorial waters.[10]

Grew instructed John Glover South, American minister in Panama, to point out to the Panamanian Foreign Ministry the error in Alfaro's thinking. Since the ship was a smuggler, its registration was false, and the ship was, therefore, not entitled, under Panama's own new law, to the protection of the Panamanian government. "You should refer," Grew pointed out didactically, "to the fact that it appears Law No. 54 of 1926 was enacted as a result of the information concerning the operation of the *Federalship*. . . ." Grew continued, "You should add since this legislation was enacted so that the Government of Panama would not be called upon to intervene in behalf of aliens engaged in violating the laws of a friendly power, the interested authorities of this government believed that . . . the Government of Panama would not feel called upon to raise any objection to the seizure. . . ."[11]

However, Panama did not regard American claims that a ship was a "notorious" smuggler as sufficient proof to cancel the registry and deny the ship the protection of the flag. The strongly asserted Panamanian view was that evidence of suspected smuggling should be presented to the Panamanian authorities. The charges then would be submitted to the registered owners of the vessel for a reply. After receiving the reply, the Panamanian treasury officials would determine whether to order a cancellation, with due notice to the owners. If the ship could not reregister with another state, then the ship would be "without a flag," and only then would the ship be subject to high-seas seizure. In the meantime, while various ships still flew the flag of Panama legally, Panama would expect the United States to adhere to the terms of the convention, and not board any Panamanian flag vessel beyond the hour's steaming time of the pursuing vessel from an American territorial water line.[12]

Grew and others at the State Department were astounded by this position. They believed that Panama would welcome the chance to avoid being called upon to protect notorious criminals, especially since those criminals were not Panamanian. Grew, several times, pointed out to Alfaro that there was no obligation on the part of Panama toward the responsible owners, since they were nationals of the United States, Canada, or Italy. Even the officers and crew of the ship were not Panamanian. To make matters worse, Panama refused to consider evidence against the *Federalship* as long as the United States continued to hold the ship.[13]

The American courts broke the deadlock. In response to the indictments against them as officers of the *Federalship*, Joe Ferris and Stuart Stone brought a plea of lack of jurisdiction before the Federal District Court in San Francisco. They contended that the seizure was illegal under the international convention between the United States and Panama. In his ruling, Judge George M. Bourquin noted that such treaties, as international law, were "the supreme law of the land." In the treaty, Panama conceded the right to seizure on the high seas, but only within one hour's steaming time; by entering into the convention, the United States had abandoned all claim of right to seizure exceeding the agreed limit. Judge Bourquin pointed out that the vessel *Quadra*, also owned by Consolidated Exporters of Vancouver, but under Canadian registry, had been seized within one hour of the Farallone Islands; under the convention with Britain, that seizure fell within American jurisdiction. The *Federalship*, in effect, demonstrated the converse of the same principle. The court could not hear charges against individuals apprehended in an illegal seizure and the judge sustained the plea of lack of jurisdiction.[14]

The 12,500 cases of liquor aboard the *Federalship* had been confiscated and placed in a storehouse for safekeeping during the investigation and trial. Before the release of Stone and Ferris, the liquor was stolen from the federal warehouse. On their release, Stone and Ferris steamed the *Federalship* out of San Francisco harbor, free, but $1 million poorer for the experience.[15]

The Panamanian Foreign Ministry believed the Bourquin decision in the *Federalship* case fully justified its position. While the *Federalship* awaited her hearing, the Coast Guard seized another Panamanian-registered rumrunner, the *Hakadata*, off the Mexican coast. Although the *Hakadata* was taken more than a mile outside Mexican territorial waters, she was 64 miles beyond American jurisdiction, thereby well beyond the one-hour extension allowed under the treaty. Again, State Department attempts to cancel the ship's registry in Panama only resulted in a further enunciation of the "no cancellation until release" policy. The United States District Court in Los Angeles ordered the release of the smugglers on grounds identical to those in the *Federalship* case.[16]

Alfaro attempted to clarify the position of the Panamanian government in an extensive note to the United States State Department on the *Hakadata* case, prior to the court decision that released the smugglers:

> Panama asked for the release of the vessel because its capture was against the treaty of June 6, 1924, and because it is necessary to return the vessel to the jurisdiction of Panama for the purpose of applying the sanctions provided by the law of Panama against vessels engaged in unlawful traffic like that which is charged against the *Hakadata*. But Panama took no action whatsoever in behalf of the Captain and members of the crew who are not Panamans and will not ask for indemnity for the damage that may have been caused to the American owners of the vessel. Panama has nothing to do with the rights or interests of American citizens in the *Hakadata* just the same as it had nothing whatsoever to do with the rights and interests of British subjects in the *Federalship*.[17]

Panama, Alfaro made clear, simply sought to protect the sovereignty that went with the flag, but not to engage in the protection of individual smugglers or their actions.

Two other vessels, the *Chasina* and the *Helori*, were known liquor smugglers flying the Panamanian flag, and the State Department undertook negotiations for the cancellations of their registries. Through the summer of 1927, the Foreign Ministry and the Treasury Department in Panama worked slowly in response to repeated requests for cancellations of the registries of the *Federalship*, the *Hakadata*, the *Chasina*, and the *Helori*. While under constant pressure from the American State Department, the Panamanians proceeded carefully and correctly in each case.[18]

The *Chasina* first had come to the attention of Panama as an illicit ship earlier than the other cases, in November 1925. At that time, the State Department simply sought cooperation of the Panamanian government in cancelling the registry. Alfaro had agreed on cancellation, if evidence of smuggling would be submitted. When no seizure produced evidence, Grew attempted to use other arguments. In October 1926, he unsuccessfully tried to secure cancellation of the *Chasina* on technical grounds; he claimed the ship never had called at a Panamanian port to convert its provisional registry into a permanent one.[19]

While this case was being considered, the other cases developed. In May 1927, Panama gave the owners of the *Hakadata* a chance to repond to charges formally lodged by the United States. After an appropriate wait, the secretary of finance and treasury in Panama, Dr. Eusebio A. Morales, drafted an executive resolution canceling the registries of both the *Hakadata* and the *Chasina* effective 31 August 1927.[20]

Panama's ambassador to the United States, R. J. Alfaro. Between 1925 and 1928, Alfaro protested U.S. seizures on the high seas of Canadian- and American-owned rumrunners registered in Panama. (Organization of American States)

Similarly, reacting to the lack of support in Panama for their damage claims and to repeated inquiries regarding their activities, Consolidated Exporters finally canceled the registry of the *Federalship*, leaving unpaid $115.32 in fees and taxes due Panama. The ship was sold and went into local service off British Columbia under a new name and Canadian registry.[21]

Thus, by the end of the summer of 1927, these four smuggling vessels had been forced from Panamanian registry by the application of Panama's method: examination of evidence, request for response, fair warning, and either cancellation or voluntary withdrawal. The American method— retroactive cancellation under Law 54 of 1926 on suspicion of smuggling in order to strip the vessel of a flag and to open it to seizure as a pirate vessel—collapsed as a maritime fantasy.

Internal Panamanian Politics

The American minister in Panama, John G. South, had the difficult task of urging a faster pace for the cancellation of the registries of all the smuggling

vessels and attempting to represent the American position to the Panamanians as best he could. More clearly than Grew and others at the State
Department, South understood the Panamanian position that her
sovereignty over the vessels could not be disregarded. The cancellations
went forward according to the Panamanian pace and approach. South,
either to impress his superiors or because he believed in his own importance, preferred to report that the cancellations were achieved because of
his detailed knowledge of the complex balance of internal Panamanian
political factors and because of his experienced use of the special relationship that Panama had with the United States.[22]

Under Article 18 of Panama's constitution, the United States could be
called in to supervise elections. American intervention in the election
process was to occur only on invitation from the ruling administration. If
some individual officials within the government, together with responsible
private citizens in opposition to the ruling regime, would request American
intervention, it was not clear how the American authorities would react.
While such a semiofficially invited intervention would seem unlikely, the
possibility that it might occur loomed large and itself became an issue in
Panamanian politics in 1927.

Belisario Porras, a former president of the republic, hoped to be able to
force American intervention in the election of 1928 on the grounds that the
incumbent administration denied cedulas or voting-authority cards on a
large scale to his followers. While the State Department hesitated to
respond to petitions for intervention, Minister South arranged that massive
lists of depositions and complaints sent to the embassy in Panama would be
forwarded for review, consideration, and filing in Washington.

By 1927, United States-Panamanian relations had reached a low point on
a wide range of issues. In addition to the rebuff Panama suffered over the
Costa Rica border question, an attempt to resolve longstanding issues over
Panamanian commercial enterprises in the Canal Zone had resulted in a
negotiated settlement in the Kellogg-Alfaro Treaty. Yet, that treaty would
entail a firm prior commitment of Panama to join with the United States in
any war involving the United States. This and other commitments on the
part of Panama in the draft treaty aroused a storm of protest and a fever
pitch of anti-American sentiment through early 1927, and the treaty never
was ratified. Panama had sought, through inter-American conferences and
through membership in the League of Nations, to offset *yanqui* power, with
little success through the mid-1920s.[23]

Against these developments, the administration of Arnulfo Chiari took
care not to offend local American authorities, either in the Canal Zone or at
the embassy. Minister South attributed some of his success in obtaining
ship-registry cancellations to Chiari's fear of American intervention in the
elections. In particular, he traced the cancellation of the *Chasina* and the

Helori to the "political consideration" of the "activities of Dr. Porras and his followers," and their campaign for intervention, which South, himself, had assisted by receiving and transmitting petitions.[24]

Despite his willingness to pressure the Chiari regime and to lay claim to proconsul powers, South recognized that the protection of the vessels registered under the Panamanian flag was a sensitive issue with far-reaching implications. A charge that a particular administration in Panama was too cooperative with the United States and that it was not sensitive to North American infringements on sovereignty made for good local political ammunition. Thus, for public consumption, the Chiari administration might have appeared overzealous in the protection of the vessels. In regard to the instructions from Grew, which suggested that Law 54 of 1926 ought to relieve the Panamanians of any responsibility, South commented, with delicate understatement, that such a position indicated "some misconceptions as to the Panamanian Government's point of view." He clarified that position for Grew: "Panama has no desire to permit the use of its flag to cover illegal activities, but it is not for this reason disposed to overlook what appears to it to be an illegal aggression against a vessel carrying its flag." Panama was particularly aware of questions of sovereignty, South pointed out. "The Government's sensitiveness regarding the seizure is intensified by the suggestion . . . that the *Federalship* would not have been seized had she been flying the flag of a larger and more important country."[25]

In dealing with the United States regarding the merchant flag, the Panamanian government was in an extremely difficult position. If the Panamanian regime allowed the Americans simply to seize Panamanian ships on the assertion of suspected smuggling, without regard to the 1924 treaty, the governing regime would provide local opposition leaders demanding an even stronger anti-American stand with clear proof that the administration neglected to defend the national sovereignty. Such symbolic actions took on added importance in the light of unresolved questions and tensions arising from canal jurisdiction, the abortive Kellogg-Alfaro Treaty, and frictions over the use of American troops in Panama. Yet, if the local regime took too strong a line against the United States, to the point of angering or losing the confidence of the American minister or Canal Zone governor, the possibility of American intervention in the election in support of the opposition might be enhanced. Even the threat of such intervention might lead to weakened support among local politicians, and a drift of influential party leaders to the opposition. Assertion of Panamanian sovereignty was essential for local political reasons, yet too great an assertion of that sovereignty was inadvisable, also for local political reasons.

The debate over these issues emerged in Panama's newspapers. Panama's chief of the Maritime Bureau publicly denied the charge that Panama hired out its flag to shelter and protect liquor smugglers. Instead, he claimed that low registry rates and no minimum wage scales for crews attracted foreign vessels. Some of the local press in Panama took a pro-Chiari stand, urging that Panama's flag should be protected from misuse by shady operators, and that foreign consuls abroad should exercise greater care in accepting registries. United States actions against the *Federalship* were aggressions against the flag, and the strong stand of Alfaro in Washington should be supported.[26]

Minister South analyzed the major political considerations as rooted in personal, not ideological factors. He felt that Dr. Morales, the secretary of the treasury responsible for registry cancellations, angled for American favor. Morales, speculated South, hoped to embarrass President Chiari by issuing instructions to cancel the *Hakadata* registry, and hoped either to emerge as the compromise candidate for the presidency between the Chiari and Porras groups, or to join with Porras in the event of an American intervention in favor of Porras. Whether his motive was so personally ambitious or so devious, Morales did rather cautiously cooperate with the American ministry through the summer of 1927, canceling ships after appropriate notification of owners. Yet, Morales was no American "lackey," for immediately after ordering cancellations, he went to Geneva to argue for a League of Nations recommendation that sovereignty over the Canal Zone itself be submitted to arbitration.[27]

The decisions of Chiari and Morales to postpone action until local concern over the *Federalship* seizure died down, and at the same time to placate the American minister with gradual actions on the other vessels had the desired effects. The maritime flag question did not become a major issue in the 1928 elections; and the Panamanian government earned a reputation with the State Department for cooperation on maritime issues. By falling back on technicalities and requiring presentation of evidence before coming to a conclusion, the Panamanian government scrupulously defended the form of sovereignty as represented by the merchant flag without ever accepting the American position, which had challenged the sovereignty of Panama head-on with the *Federalship* and *Hakadata* seizures.

Grew's efforts to employ legal arguments to subject Panamanian decisions to American power had not worked. Grew wrote to Alfaro suggesting that the *Belen Quezada* case set a clear precedent for the *Federalship*. In the *Belen Quezada* case, Grew pointed out, Panama had asked the American government, as representative of the owners of the ship, to pursue claims against Costa Rica, which the United States had done. Why not expect the American government, as the government of the owners in the smuggling cases, to exercise any required protection of the rights of owners? Grew met his match as the legally trained Alfaro reasoned out his reply. Alfaro saw the two cases as fully distinct. In the case of the *Belen Quezada*, the United States had indeed had a role to play. The damages arising came from an act of war; the property of American neutrals was the responsibility of the United States, and the American government was obliged to represent its citizens. In the case of the *Federalship* and the *Hakadata*, however, the United States had authorized its agents to violate a treaty with Panama; the Panamanian government did not try to protect the interests of individual shipowners, but only to protect its treaty rights. By such an argument, Alfaro put the dual nationality of the vessels in sharper focus than did Grew.[28]

Alfaro's reasoning was backed by Panama's actions. The Panamanian minister of foreign relations considered, but rejected, an explicit request by the owners of the *Federalship* to submit a diplomatic claim for damages in their behalf. Not only would the owners have to repair the gunshot damage to the ship's rail at their own expense, but they would have to absorb the $1 million loss of the 12,500 cases of Scotch.[29]

The Panamanian argument on grounds of principle reveals that the procrastination through bureaucratic detail was more than a political expedient on the part of Panama to find a way through the local dangers inherent in dealing with American power while protecting the form of sovereignty for local political consumption. Panamanian officials did not, on principle, accept the idea that they had sold their sovereignty or hired out the flag; some American officials preferred to see Panamanian ship registry in that light. Grew and South, as well as others in the American bureaucracy, were quick to conclude that Panamanian decisions were made either under American pressure and threats of power, or for venal motives of personal ambition and greed. Such factors, rather than protection of sovereignty and national revenue, they presumed, shaped and modified Panamanian practice.

The System in Operation

As a result of the tensions over the registry of smugglers, and the eventual quiet resolution of the problem, American officials at the State Department expressed satisfaction with the Panamanian system of ship registration. Panama, it was believed, had cooperated because the local regime feared American pressure; a good system had emerged and should be kept alive. Panama's flag was, in fact, less attractive to smugglers as a cover than many other flags. The United States Treasury Department reported that by July 1927, of 143 known smuggling vessels, only 3 were registered in Panama, while 112 flew the British flag and 18 flew the flag of Honduras. In September 1928, out of 113 smuggling vessels, 89 were British, 8 Honduran, 7 French, and only 2 were Panamanian.[30]

One feature of Panamanian registration that continued to involve the United States was the consular arrangement that had been worked out in

January 1916, setting up rules for American consuls to provide service in those ports where Panama itself maintained no consul. In this simple fashion, Panamanian ship registration became an adjunct of American officialdom. American consuls had been involved in Salina Cruz, Port Said, Halifax, and Shanghai simply to adjudicate labor problems on ships registered through the Morris office in Vancouver, or through the Panamanian consular office in New York. But, early in 1928, the State Department faced another unpleasant aspect of the system in China. The American consul in Shanghai reported that a local company of doubtful reputation wished to register a ship in Panama and had come to him as the representative of Panama. Remembering the case of the *Ida*, he pointed out with a sense of moral distaste that the ships under Panamanian registry had caused "considerable difficulty." Would it be appropriate for the United States to add its prestige by sanctioning such operations, and allowing the ships to register through American consular officers?[31]

The department's response forestalled a full resolution of the question, by instructing the American consul to recommend that the shipowners deal directly with the Panamanian consul in Hong Kong; future requests were to be referred there as well. However, where no local Panamanian consul was directly available, the department would have no choice but to cooperate, because Panama had helped on the smuggling issue. The department's legal adviser commented that if American consuls refused to register vessels for Panama, "some resentment would be felt by Panama which might have repercussion with respect to future cooperation." Henceforth, when requested, American consuls were advised to assist in registering ships with Panama where no conveniently located Panamanian consul was available.[32]

In still other ways, the system was refined. As early as 1923, the managers of Pacific Freighters inquired as to the appropriate call letters to use on shipboard radios. In a four-way correspondence among the Grace-owned Panama Agencies Company, the governor of the Canal Zone, the commandant of the United States Naval District in Panama, and the State Department, it was agreed that Panama should issue its own radio call numbers from a block to be assigned from the International Bureau of Radiotelegraphy. While members of each agency recognized that they were dealing in a sensitive area of potential interbureaucratic jurisdiction, and politely deferred to each other, all the agencies involved, including the private company, acted on the premise that the issue should be resolved by cooperation among American offices. The agencies solved the problem and presented the solution to Panama.[33]

The registration of smuggling vessels through Maximo Morris had revealed a recurrent problem with the system, that of corrupt or corruptible consuls. After the cancellation of the smugglers' registries in 1927, the Panamanian government dismissed Morris and sought a replacement. The

Panamanian Foreign Ministry invited the American State Department to supply nominees for the Vancouver post, and, although John G. South urged the department to comply, Washington hesitated to play such an openly colonial role. No official list of nominees was transmitted, nor was the suggestion accepted that the American consul in Vancouver supply names.[34]

By 1928, the system operated fairly well. The original hodgepodge of fiscal and commercial provisions had been consolidated into Law 8 of 1925 and Law 54 of 1926, which organized the registry, provided low rates, did not include mention of a set of ship's articles, and which allowed Panamanians to cancel undesirable ships. The organized system could be administered around the world. Panama paid and maintained consuls-general in Liverpool, Hamburg, Genoa, New York, New Orleans, Havana, Kingston, Barcelona, and Bordeaux. Paid consuls were assigned to London, Southampton, Le Havre, San Francisco, Hong Kong, Yokohama, Antwerp, and Boston. Three vice-consuls were maintained, in New York, Chicago, and Mobile. In many lesser ports, honorary consuls such as Morris, usually nationals of the host country, were appointed. The main source of revenue for honorary consuls derived from fee collection. They were entitled to retain half of collected fees to a maximum of $200 per month, which may have encouraged registry of ships with questionable reputations.[35]

Where no official Panamanian consul or honorary consul represented Panama, American consular offices would provide service. On request, they were provided with copies of the appropriate sections of the Panamanian legal code; after the mid-1920s, the separate maritime law could be printed as a pamphlet in an English version, and sent for the use of the American consuls. With the addition of the services of American consuls, the system of ship registry could operate in all the major and most of the minor seaports of the world.

But, as we have seen, the policy of the United States Shipping Board stood in the way of massive transfers to Panama. The board approved transfer only for those vessels that, in its judgment, would not compete with American shipping, that were not a loss to the strength of the American merchant marine, and that had a legitimate reason for transfer to Panama such as the conduct of local business. The board authorized about thirty transfers from American to Panamanian registry altogether through the 1920s, and by 1927 had reduced the approval of such transfer requests to a standard procedure, which set several obstacles. The applicant filed with the Shipping Board a request form that included a statement or rationale for the transfer. Such statements, when approved, included assertions that the owner did not intend to operate in competition with American ships, and that his ship could not be operated at a profit under the

American flag. In cases of small or fast vessels, the board automatically would refer the case to the Treasury Department for a check against lists of suspected smuggling vessels and owners. Only after the ship passed those requirements would the board issue an order of transfer. Using this document, the owner then could secure a provisional Panamanian certificate of registry through a consular office and remove his ship to Panama for local use and permanent registry.[36]

Through the 1920s, the clear majority of the ships transferred to Panama from the United States through this procedure were not true "flag of convenience" registries. While the owners took advantage of the lower registry rates and other advantages of evading American maritime law, for the most part, their vessels did not compete in international trade and genuinely were moved to Panama for the purpose of operating in Central American waters. Some of the owners planned to use the ships in Panama or along the Mexican coast, as in the cases of the *Maspeth*, the *Centralia*, the *Lincoln Land*, the *Viking*, and the *Buckhannon*. Such vessels were employed by companies doing business in Central America in connection with their local enterprises. On a larger scale, the Pacific Mail Steamship Line, an American-owned firm that registered most of its passenger liners in the United States for trade to and from American ports, transferred the *City of Para* to Panamanian registry for local use in Central America, as a feeder service to its longer-distance lines. Similarly, Panama Mail Line registered two local steamers, the *City of San Francisco* and the *City of Panama* under the Panamanian flag in 1925.[37]

In other cases, the sale of an uneconomical ship to a foreign owner, or to a partnership controlled by its foreign members, would require transfer to foreign registry, since American registry required majority American ownership. Such a motive lay behind the approved transfers of the *Lebanon*, the *Oronite*, and the *Binghamton*.[38]

This small number of transfers to Panama was processed by the board very much like hundreds of transfers to other nations for local use or foreign ownership; Italy, Mexico, and Canada each received far more vessels than Panama. The Panamanian transfers were not significant in number or tonnage and formed a very small proportion of the total number of ships permitted by the board to abandon the American flag. Because of the careful scrutiny exercised by the Shipping Board, the Panamanian law, despite its improvements through the 1920s, and despite its world-wide availability, could not attract a major fleet of vessels away from the American merchant marine.

However, American owners who already had their ships registered under another flag, such as that of Great Britain, could transfer them to take advantage of Panamanian registry without clearing the transaction through the United States Shipping Board. The American company to lead the way in this regard was United Fruit Company, which transferred six of its large and efficient banana transport vessels from Britain to Panama in 1928, and followed with seven more in 1930 and 1931. Claude D. Doswell, vice-president of the company, recalled the decision for a congressional investigation a few years later. An official of Panama had invited the company to make the transfer as a gesture of goodwill, and United Fruit decided to comply, as it sought government approval for plantation expansion. Doswell recalled, with some confusion of chronology, that the Panamanian government improved the law, "even amended it some," in order to make it more appropriate for United Fruit. Doswell, like some members of the State Department, was quick to believe that Panama would cooperate with Americans by altering law under pressure. While the 1925 codification of law did ease the registry process, Doswell took too much credit by asserting that the 1925 law had been designed for his company alone to facilitate transfers made in 1928, 1930, and 1931. Nevertheless, the low rates and labor costs, combined with a clear-cut set of regulations, no doubt attracted United Fruit, as did the possibility of doing a political favor for the local regime. With similar motives—made explicit for the Shipping Board—a competing company, Coyumel Fruit, received board approval to transfer one vessel to Honduras. Cheaper operating costs and good local politics attracted the banana fleets to Central American registry.[39]

By the end of the 1920s, the Panamanian merchant fleet had grown slightly from a collection of locally owned coastal and fishing craft to a mix of international freighters and merchant vessels, owned by a small but growing variety of corporations. The stage was set for further growth and expansion, if other American or European owners of foreign-registered ships grew dissatisfied with their flag states.

While the proposal was not developed fully at the time, the considerations that lay behind the development of the small-scale Panamanian fleet could lead to an informal kind of solution to the basic dilemma facing American shipping policy. The conflict between national interest and social justice remained to plague American shipping over the next decades, and the conversion of the Panamanian system into one of the ways out of that dilemma was foreseen in the 1920s by only a few hard-nosed cynics. The end of American innocence had only begun to set in, and a few men regarding themselves as realists could find in the Panamanian flag a scheme that might work. One such prophetic and amoral view of Panamanian registry as a "demonstration" of a solution was articulated by Congressman Robert Bacon in a letter to the *New York Times* shortly after the spectacular *Reliance* and *Resolute* transfer. His analysis is worth examining at length for its explicit recognition of the possible role that Panama might play:

The real difficulty in starting an American merchant marine, is, first, the La Follette bill, which insists upon one-half to two-thirds of the deck and engine departments being composed of American citizens; second, all sorts of interference by government and labor unions, the eight-hour law, etc., and third, the Captain should be in absolute control of his ship three miles from shore. It would take so long to convince any collection of politicians of these facts that a simple demonstration would be to sell a number of our ships with the privilege of allowing the owners to sail them under the Panama flag. The ships could then be run on the same plan as our old merchant marine, unhampered by labor unions and "sea lawyers" and when the Captain called any or all hands on deck there would be no question of overtime.[40]

Few businessmen in 1922 publicly expressed their hostility to the social reform efforts of the government or to the ill-organized attempts at seamen's unions in quite the authoritarian tone chosen by Bacon. Yet, his perception of the registry of an American merchant marine under the Panamanian flag as a solution to the difficulties of establishing a competitive fleet had within it a policy twenty years ahead of his time.

If American sea power could rely not only on those ships directly under the American flag but also on those receiving American protection while under another sovereign flag, then the dilemma would be resolved. Americans could have their social justice legislation for American flag ships; but Americans could also compete internationally with cheaply operated vessels under foreign registry; ships registered through such a system might not be lost to American sea power in the long run.

The control exercised by the United States over Panama as a result of the canal, the presence of troops, and the demilitarization of the Republic of Panama itself made the choice of Panama for such a role quite natural. Although the Kellogg-Alfaro Treaty, which would have cemented Panamanian dependency even further by requiring Panama to declare war on enemies of the United States, was never ratified, such a treaty would not be needed in the long run, since the United States had sufficient power and legal grounds to impose its will. Since the canal would make Panama a hostage to American policies, shipowners could feel secure that their ships ultimately would receive American protection. The U.S. Navy could regard American-owned, Panamanian-registered ships as a branch of American sea power.

The advocacy of such a way out of the dilemma could not be made by businessmen or politicians in the 1920s who chose to show respect either for the ideals of social justice or for the national sovereignty of small nations. Only when respect for those ideals had withered to mere lip service and then could be abandoned altogether under the pressure of the events of World War II, would the policy be advocated openly and widely. The Progressive values out of which the maritime dilemma originated also imposed constraints on the possible policies that might be offered as solutions to that dilemma. While direct subsidy seemed special-interest legislation, government ownership seemed socialistic. To evade American restrictions while retaining American control under a pseudosovereignty violated both social justice and the fiction of the equality of states.

The fact that Panamanian ship registry in the 1940s would provide a solution to the dilemmas of American shipping might lead one to conclude that its design in the 1920s was based on some long-range plan, and to believe that American policy makers shaped the system with the eventual solution in mind. Evidence does not support such a conspiracy theory of the development of the Panamanian system for American purposes.

Rather, American shipowners in 1922 perceived the dilemma in concrete, short-range, business terms: how to compete and to make a profit in the glutted world market when "hampered" by reforms. Seeking to escape those reforms was not allowed by the Shipping Board, except in rare cases that could be justified on technical grounds. Those cases, examined closely, show that shipowners understood the business advantages of Panamanian registry and saw transfer to a dependent state as compatible with American interests.

The Panamanian Assembly realized the potential for revenue if even more ships could be attracted, and therefore codified and improved the law. When smugglers took advantage of the improved law to evade Canadian and American controls, Panama's Foreign Ministry defended the flag against American assumptions of full control. Defense of the rights represented by the maritime flag, while crucial to Panama and part of a larger resistance by Panama to American encroachment on its sovereignty, did not in the end protect the smugglers. American belief that Panamanian authorities cooperated to suppress the smugglers led to continued American consular support of the Panamanian ship registry system. By 1928, that system could work efficiently on a world-wide scale.

The system did respond to the pressures of shipowners, and to their desires for an unregulated business environment. But Panama fought the American business and official view that Panama's sovereignty was a sham and its flag a symbol of sovereignty for sale. As the system adjusted to such pressures and assumptions, it took on some of the qualities that American businessmen sought—a cheap, convenient, efficient system that left each shipowner free to make his own labor policy and to maintain his ship as he saw fit. Convenience had evolved.

3

Oil and Fruit

A NUMBER OF AUTHORS, writing after World War II, attributed the growth of the Panamanian fleet and particularly the transfer of vessels from the United States to Panama primarily to evasion of the American neutrality laws of the 1930s. That explanation results from the confusions of hindsight; while attempts to avoid the effects of the Neutrality Acts in the period from September 1939 to December 1941 did account for many transfers from American to Panamanian registry, that factor does not explain the growth of the fleet before September 1939.[1]

In the early years of the decade of the 1930s, the maritime policy of the United States, as shaped by Herbert Hoover, was an attempt to resolve the maritime dilemma inherited from the Progressive and World War I eras, and to build a strong peacetime merchant marine to assist in U.S. foreign trade. The Roosevelt administration reshaped that policy, shifting the emphasis from peacetime commerce to considerations of defense. However, the policies of both Hoover and Roosevelt discouraged direct American vessel transfer to Panama or to other nations in the interest of building the American-flag fleet. Therefore, very few ships of American registry were transferred to the Panamanian flag in the period from 1928 to 1939. Those that did transfer, were not engaged in evading the Neutrality Acts. But, in the same period, over one hundred vessels transferred from European, not American, registry for reasons that differed from situation to situation. About one-third of the ships of European registry that transferred to Panamanian registry were owned by American corporations. Such proprietary-line vessels were joined by European-owned ships formerly registered in Spain, Greece, Britain, and Norway. The nature and versatility of Panama's registry system and its potential for the evasion of a variety of tax, labor, and diplomatic considerations were demonstrated by such transfers from European flags. These transfers prepared the way for more widespread use of this option, after September 1939, by vessels from all over the world.

Hoover and Roosevelt—Presidential Perceptions

As the decade of the thirties began in the United States, maritime industry spokesmen and policy makers in Washington continued attempts to solve the lingering maritime problems of the earlier decade. Herbert Hoover had demonstrated his concern with maritime questions since early in the 1920s, when he served as secretary of commerce under Presidents Harding and Coolidge. Hoover's solution to the maritime dilemma consisted of several points that he developed over the period from 1921 through 1925. He believed policy should be developed after receiving input from a wide variety of sources, but often his communication with such groups, committees, and experts, seemed structured to develop a groundswell for ideas that he already had developed in consultation with his closest advisers. Hoover worked to acquire backing for his ideas by other members of the Coolidge cabinet and by the business community, as represented through shipping organizations and the Chamber of Commerce.[2]

Hoover favored government assistance to overcome the differential between American and foreign shipping costs, and predicated his maritime policy on the transfer of government-owned shipping to private hands to operate under the American flag. Hoover believed that the La Follette Seamen's Act and American living standards imposed a set of labor costs on shipping that could not be rolled back. He believed that those standards should be supported by the enlightened business community, and argued that subsidies should be structured to support cargo lines and cargo vessels, not fast passenger ships. In this regard, he differed from members of the Shipping Board and navy advisers who desired subsidies to support fast ocean liners, which could be converted to troop ships in an emergency.[3]

Hoover argued that the Shipping Board was an inefficient structure that was unresponsive to presidential direction and that improperly combined regulatory functions, ship operation, and general services to the maritime community. He advocated the separation of these functions, leaving only the job of regulation with the Shipping Board, so that it would be similar to the Interstate Commerce Commission. This concern with administrative efficiency dominated Hoover's statements, reports, speeches, and positions on the maritime question through his period as secretary of commerce. He would place the operation of government-owned vessels entirely under a separate Fleet Corporation, which would be managed like a business with a director responsible to a corporate board. Maritime services would be administered separately by appropriate regular departments, such as commerce or treasury.[4]

Shipping Board member Edward C. Plummer tried to point out to Hoover that the regulatory function theoretically performed by the board remained vestigial at best in that the board made no significant attempt to interfere in shipping rates. Those rates, Plummer argued, fluctuated with minute market conditions such as the availability of vessel space, departure dates, and specific available competition. A vessel with empty cargo space would charge less for that space as the sailing date neared, and would vary the rate of decline dependent on competitive sailings. Plummer believed that cargo rate regulation was therefore an impossible task, and that Hoover's repeated assertions that the regulatory function should be separated from the operating and service functions was simply administrative jargon with little bearing on the actual functions of the Shipping Board.[5]

Hoover maintained that ship operation by the government should be handled in an agency structured along businesslike lines, with a responsible managing director making crucial decisions and consulting with a board only for policy purposes. Hoover secured support for this position from other cabinet members in an interdepartmental report drafted and delivered to President Coolidge in 1924. To muster community backing for the position, Hoover arranged that the ideas would be discussed at a series of regional meetings of the Chamber of Commerce through the fall of 1925. The Chamber of Commerce report closely followed Hoover's suggestions as to dividing the functions of the Shipping Board.[6]

While Hoover continued to emphasize administrative realignment as crucial to the shipping health of the nation, he endorsed other maritime reforms supported widely throughout the business community. Hoover believed that government ownership of vessels should be terminated as quickly and smoothly as possible. The plan he favored was the temporary operation of shipping lines by the government and the sale of those lines to separate private concerns headquartered in different ports. Vessels would be sold, not simply as separate ships, but as parts of ongoing, government-established lines, with customers, contacts, port and docking arrangements, and American exporter support. The lines would be sold, under the American flag, to local concerns based not only in New York but also in other Atlantic, Gulf, and Pacific port cities, and would be supported by capital acquired in the regions served by each particular port. Individual vessels that did not fit into such lines would be sold as scrap or as working ships to foreign operations under the condition that they would not work in trades competitive with American-based lines. Hoover also supported the concept of construction loans from the government to private companies, but only for cargo, not for passenger vessels. He supported the plan of postal contracts, which would provide the lines purchased from the government with needed assistance in maintaining American standards of labor while competing with foreign lines.[7]

The policy Hoover developed while he was secretary of commerce was implemented through a series of legislative acts and administrative decisions over the period from 1928 through 1933. The Merchant Marine Act of 1928 established a Construction Loan Fund of $125 million and authorized additional appropriations to bring the fund up to $250 million from which twenty-year loans for up to three-quarters of the cost of ship construction would be made to shipowners. The act also set up an ocean mail contract system, operated on routes as certified by the postmaster general. The contracts allowed for a graduated scale of rates per mile, depending on the speed and size of the vessel. Ships over 20,000 tons capable of 24 knots received $12.00 per nautical mile, while slower and smaller vessels received lower rates, down to $1.50 per nautical mile. The rates were to be paid regardless of the amount of mail carried, and were based on approved rates and vessel types.[8]

As with many of Hoover's administrative reforms, the world-wide depression made full realization of the maritime plan difficult, if not impossible. Nevertheless, by the end of his administration, the surplus fleet had been reduced, over fifteen private lines had been established, the number of government-operated lines had been cut back, an annual $25 million postal contract fund had been approved, and his plan for separation of the operating and regulatory functions of the Shipping Board had been achieved. The Fleet Corporation handled operating affairs, the postmaster certified routes and awarded forty-four mail contracts, and the Shipping Board, now called the Shipping Board Bureau, was reduced in size and function.

Despite the partial implementation of Hoover's carefully thought out plan, and despite the work that had gone into achieving business and shipping company support for that plan, several aspects of the system were open to severe criticism. Only through the ocean mail contracts could the cargo lines established under the government program continue to operate as private businesses. Those ocean mail contracts provided an opportunity for political criticism—to the public it seemed outrageously corrupt to use government resources to pay several thousand dollars per ounce for the delivery of mail to Europe or South America. Government financing of money-losing, government-owned ships had been supplanted by government guarantees of profits to money-losing, privately owned ships. While cast in the guise of supporting regular mail runs on specified routes, the mail contracts amounted to indirect operating subsidies to offset losses incurred by companies as they sought to pay American operating costs out of revenues set by the international market.[9]

That international market developed low rates not simply because of lower standards of pay and conditions for foreign seamen, but because

Britain, Italy, Germany, France, Holland, and Japan each had extensive governmental programs of direct financial support for shipping, based on explicit concern with the military potential of merchant shipping. Hoover carefully had avoided any sea power implications in his shipping program.[10]

Hoover was regarded by the military establishment as a pacifist and as hostile to naval expenditure. His emphasis on the commercial function of a healthy maritime industry and its benefits to American industry and commerce overlooked the defense side of the policy problem that had haunted President Harding in 1921, Admiral Benson in 1922, and other naval writers through the mid- and late 1920s. Naval publications during the period reflected the frustration and concern over the strictly commercial direction of maritime policy. As a case in point, the *United States Naval Institute Proceedings* devoted its October 1927 issue to sea power aspects of the merchant marine, with such articles as "The Merchant Marine—its value in Peace and War," "A National Merchant Marine is Vital to Our National Security," "Sea Power and American Destiny," and "The Lack of Modern Tonnage a Severe Handicap in the Expansion of Our Foreign Trade and National Defense." These and other articles viewed with alarm the decline of the merchant marine since the Great War. The articles suggested few specific remedies, but navy writers clearly hoped to arouse opinion to support pending subsidy legislation, which would favor faster vessels as potential naval auxiliaries and link sea power considerations to the discussion of maritime policy preceding the passage of the 1928 Merchant Marine Act. In the light of Washington Naval Conference agreements to limit warship construction, the voluntary or unilateral American restriction on new commercial vessel construction seemed unwise as Britain, Japan, and Germany all vigorously engaged in shipbuilding that far outstripped American shipyard production. The drastic decline in the percentage of American foreign trade carried in American-flag ships appeared ominous from the perspective of sea power advocates.[11]

Franklin Roosevelt brought an entirely different style of operation to the White House, as well as a different set of emphases on maritime issues. More of a politician and less of a technocrat than Hoover, Roosevelt did not personally work out a comprehensive long-range maritime plan, but he indicated his preference for a clear-cut and explicit system of subsidies. As a former assistant secretary of the navy, he favored naval expansion. Roosevelt turned to Congress for a comprehensive new maritime law that would recodify America's shipping law and policy, incorporate reformed administrative procedures, restructure subsidies, and place more emphasis on defense.[12]

The Merchant Marine Act of 1936 set up a "New Deal" for the maritime industries of the United States. The Shipping Board was abolished and replaced with a Maritime Commission of five members appointed by the president. Operating as a board of directors, the commission took over the management of Shipping Board and Fleet Corporation properties. The act empowered the president to designate the chairman of the commission, as well as to appoint its members; the earlier Shipping Board had elected its own chairman and always had acted somewhat independently of the president and cabinet, to Hoover's dismay. As an executive agency responsible to the president, the new commission represented some of the improvements for which Hoover had long argued. However, the commission combined regulatory, service, and management functions in a way that Hoover always had disapproved, and thus went much further in centralizing power than he had desired.[13]

The commission set up under the 1936 law was headed first by Joseph Kennedy; it was given a navy orientation by the appointment of Rear Admiral Emory Land. Land, a 1902 U.S. Naval Academy graduate with a quick wit, salty vocabulary, a love of academy football, and a solid service career in which his last post had been naval constructor, brought apparently boundless energy to the commission. On the departure of Kennedy to represent the United States in Great Britain in 1938, Roosevelt, as part of his concern with the defense side of maritime policy, designated Land as chairman of the commission. Land soon established the commission as an aggressive agency devoted to building up a strong merchant fleet that would serve as an arm of defense. Land had little patience with arms limitation, neutrality, or organized labor, and his outspoken opinions on all of these questions soon earned him a reputation for newsworthiness. The 1936 act provided Land with a powerful instrument to implement his and Roosevelt's ideas.[14]

The 1936 act abolished the ocean mail contract system and established two direct systems of subsidy. The construction differential subsidy assisted in the construction of merchant vessels, provided they conformed to "defense features" approved in the planning stage by the navy. Under this system, ships would be built under contract to the Maritime Commission in response to a call for bids; on delivery, the commission would sell the vessel to the operating company at a price equivalent to the cost of construction in a foreign shipyard. Thus, the commission would take a loss and absorb the differential, not to exceed one-third to one-half the cost of the vessel.[15]

The second system of aids, the operating differential subsidy, provided for direct subsidies for vessels operating in foreign trade as public carriers on approved routes in competition with foreign-registered ships, in order to make up losses incurred in charging competitive rates. The 1936 act, through selective repeal of earlier acts, retained for the Maritime Commission many of the powers of the earlier Shipping Board and Fleet Corporation, particularly the power to approve or disapprove transfers from American to foreign registry. Section 902 of the act specifically reaffirmed the right of the government, through the commission, to requisition any vessel under American flag in time of emergency. The commission under Kennedy and Land could own, charter, and regulate vessels, as well as fund the construction and operation of privately owned vessels.[16]

The shipping dilemma of the 1920s at last had been resolved directly through an explicit acceptance of subsidy. American ships now could compete with foreign ships for world trade; the U.S. government would provide direct financial assistance with an emphasis on military considerations. American seamen would be guaranteed minimum wage scales and working conditions. American-owned vessels eligible for operating subsidies by virtue of steaming on approved cargo line routes now would be able to carry the flag and function successfully in foreign competition and, at the same time, meet the working conditions of the La Follette Seamen's Act and more recent labor standards. However, vessels owned by proprietary lines, such as company-owned oil tankers and refrigerated fruit ships, were not eligible for these aids, since the subsidies applied only to vessels operating as public carriers on certified routes. In the case of proprietary vessels, the incentive to escape American registry remained, since without subsidies they could not compete with foreign-registered lines in order to achieve the best cargo rates for their owners.

The oil tankers and fruit carriers that transported only cargoes owned by the ship-owning corporation faced the same dilemma originally faced by the whole fleet: how to maintain American ownership, yet bring cargo rates to the level of foreign competition. During the 1930s, those American corporations that already owned foreign-registered proprietary lines, particularly United Fruit Company and Standard Oil of New Jersey (ESSO), were attracted to the flag of Panama. For these vessels, already registered under a European flag, transfer to Panama would not entail securing approval of the Shipping Board or the Maritime Commission. Furthermore, when such proprietary lines purchased a vessel constructed abroad, no approval was required for its direct registry under the Panamanian or other flag. As the absence of manning regulations, social legislation, and taxation of the Panamanian system became known more widely, the American-owned, foreign-registered proprietary lines became attracted, as did a number of European-owned fleets. With the transfer of these fleets to Panama in refuge from legal and diplomatic complications, the flag took on a markedly international character.

United Fruit Company

In 1929, officials of United Fruit Company, including Vice-President Claude D. Doswell and the company's attorney, Elisha Hanson, conferred with the postmaster general and with Hoover's staff. They hoped to obtain a commitment that the government would certify some of the routes operated by American-registered United Fruit Company vessels between ports on the Gulf of Mexico and Central America as official mail routes upon which contracts would be granted later. In exchange for that commitment, Hanson suggested, United Fruit would plan to build ten vessels in the United States at an estimated cost of $29 to $30 million. Although a route was certified and United Fruit obtained a three-year contract for mail early in 1930 for one of its American-registered lines, Hoover's staff was angered to discover that the company did not initiate the proposed construction program immediately. Furthermore, United Fruit made no move to withdraw its other vessels from Panamanian, Honduran, or British registry. Grace Lines, which owned two Panamanian-registered liners of the Panama Mail Line in regular West Coast service, the *City of San Francisco* and the *City of Panama*, entered a similar agreement, and in 1930 that company transferred both ships to American registry.[17]

In 1930 and again in 1933, Congress considered bills that would deny ocean mail contracts to companies such as United Fruit, Munson Lines, or International Mercantile Marine (IMM), which owned foreign-flag subsidiaries. Doswell testified at the hearings of the House Committee on Merchant Marine and Fisheries regarding the first of these bills, explaining the rationale of United Fruit in acquiring, holding, and expanding its Panamanian-flag fleet.[18]

Registry under the Panamanian flag, he pointed out, "can not be considered as a disadvantage to the American merchant marine or the violation of the real aim sought to be established by the proposed law." Doswell argued that the company's decision was also in line with Hoover's policy of "cementing our relations with Latin America." If Panama or Honduras were to pass restrictive legislation against foreign-flag vessels, United Fruit would be in a protected position, and would not be handicapped. United Fruit originally planned to place some ships under the flag of each of the countries where the company had producing facilities, he said. Although some of the countries did not allow for the practice, Panama's registry welcomed foreign-owned vessels and the company believed local registry to be politically advantageous. Having accepted the local flag, the company would create ill will through cancellation or withdrawal from either Honduran or Panamanian registry, Doswell argued.[19]

The company, however, earned ill will for itself in the United States as it continued to operate the mail contract with American-registered vessels, and transferred two new ships and five older ships from its Glasgow-headquartered office to Panama in 1930 and 1931. (See table 1.) This growing foreign flag operation by a company with a mail contract that amounted to a subsidy brought complaints from other shipowners. J.

The steamship Platano, *shown in San Francisco harbor. The 6,012-ton banana "reefer" was one of thirteen ships transferred from Britain to Panama by United Fruit Company over the period 1928–31. (Naval Photographic Center)*

Caldwell Jenkins, vice president of Black Diamond Steamship Company, among others, protested and offered support for the Senate bill that would outlaw the practice. The publication by Charles Kepner and Jay Soothill of an exposé of United Fruit, *The Banana Empire* (Vanguard, 1935), contributed to the storm of public indignation. Kepner noted that it was ironic that a "law designed to develop and encourage the maintenance of a merchant marine should become an instrument to favor a company which has always had a large proportion of ships under foreign registry."[20]

United Fruit Company officials, however, countered such attacks with the argument that if their American-registered vessels were not subsidized through a mail contract, the company would continue to turn abroad for cheaper ship construction; on the other hand, if the mail contract continued and expanded, the company would undertake to build vessels for the lines in American shipyards and to register those vessels in the United States. But Kepner calculated that a ten-year contract for mail would yield United Fruit $21 million; government construction loans at low interest would account for about $7 million; thus, he felt, the line almost would obtain the $29 million vessel order entirely at the taxpayers' expense. The debate became moot in 1936, with the abolition of the ocean mail contract system.[21]

The Panamanian and Honduran operations of United Fruit were not true "flag of convenience" registries in the sense in which the term came to be used after 1950. In the case of both flags, United Fruit had specific, local business reasons for registry of its vessels with those nations. Whether or not the registry revenue earned by Panama helped smooth the way politically for United Fruit to establish large new plantations in the Chiriqui

Table 1.
United Fruit Company Vessels Transferred to
Balboa Shipping Company, Panama

Ship	Year Built	Year Transferred	Tonnage
Macabi	1921	1928	2,802
Manaqui	1921	1928	2,802
Mayari	1921	1928	2,802
Marani	1921	1928	2,802
Darien (La Marea)	1924	1928	3,689
La Playa	1923	1928	3,682
Musa	1930	1930	5,833
Platano	1930	1930	6,012
San Benito	1921	1931	3,724
San Blas	1920	1931	3,628
San Bruno	1920	1931	3,627
San Gil	1920	1931	3,627
San Pablo	1915	1931	3,305

Source: Lloyd's of London, *Lloyd's Register of Shipping*, 1932.

province of Panama, as claimed by Doswell, the fact remained that the company had some carrying trade with Panama and had reasonable expectations of local political benefits from registering vessels in that republic.[22]

Standard Oil and Danzig

In 1935, the flag of Panama received the single largest addition to its numbers up to that time, as Standard Oil of New Jersey (ESSO) transferred all the ships of its Baltic subsidiary, Bapico, from the Free City of Danzig to Panama. The merchant flag of Danzig, while referred to by some authors as an early flag of convenience, had few of the characteristics of the convenience pattern established by Panama, and was as much a maritime anomaly as the city-state itself was an anomaly in international relations. Although the origins of the Danzig merchant flag are relatively obscure, a look at this development is essential to an understanding of the evolution of Panama's fleet, since a few precedents and patterns established by ESSO in Danzig were carried over to the Panamanian registry.

In 1919, as the peace talks proceeded at Versailles, the Allies requisitioned ships held by German individuals and corporations as an installment on reparations demanded by France, Britain, Belgium, and Italy. Eight operable vessels of the German subsidiary of ESSO, Deutsch-Amerikanische Petroleum-Gesellschaft (DAPG), were taken and transferred to Britain in August and September of 1919.[23]

The company's astute German manager, Heinrich Reidemann, who had pioneered the development of tankers, fought the DAPG transfer to no avail, as did ESSO's attorneys in the United States. Meanwhile, however, a loophole appeared for the retention of four vessels belonging to ESSO that were under construction in German shipyards. While the negotiations at Versailles went forward, the Reparations Commission concluded that German-owned vessels owned by citizens who lost their German citizenship through residence in areas severed from German sovereignty—areas such as Schleswig-Holstein, Memel, and Danzig—should not be subject to requisition. The Versailles treaty established Danzig as a unique entity, setting up the city as a quasi-independent state in a customs union with Poland, through which Poland would have access to the sea. Although Danzig would be obliged to provide port facilities and transit for Polish imports and exports, and to accept Polish direction of its foreign affairs, the city was to have many of the attributes of sovereignty. Article 8 of the treaty between Danzig and Poland and the constitution of the Free City of Danzig, both affirmed Danzig's right to issue a merchant flag.[24]

Under Article 105 of the Versailles treaty, Heinrich Reidemann's brother, Dr. William Reidemann, as a resident of Danzig, would become a citizen of the Free City of Danzig when the treaty came into force on 10 January 1920. Prior to that date, he remained a German citizen. Nothing in the armistice or Versailles agreement prevented one German from selling uncompleted ships to another. Thus, the Reidemanns moved quickly to sell the four vessels in the shipyards to a new company set up and wholly owned by William, the Baltisch-Amerikanische Petroleum-Import-Gesellschaft, mbH (Bapico). The four tankers of the "Reidemann Line," the *Niobe*, the *Gedania*, the *Vistula*, and the *Baltic*, were removed from German ownership when Dr. Reidemann became a Danzig citizen and registered the ships under Danzig's flag in 1920. Despite an initial move by the Reparations Commission to ignore the legal niceties and confiscate the vessels, the commission finally decided, in several cases from August 1920 through May 1921, that all Danzig-registered vessels, including the Bapico fleet, were immune from seizure.[25]

ESSO then formally acquired Bapico and operated the line as a subsidiary for German and other Baltic ports through the continued device of Danzig registry. Revenues from the company and loans from the parent corporation were used to purchase German-constructed vessels, which, in turn, were registered in Danzig. ESSO thus was able to plow its Baltic earnings back into expansion of the fleet without subjecting those earnings to American taxation or attempting to exchange German earnings for more stable currencies. ESSO transferred one vessel, the *Josiah Macy*, to Danzig from the United States in 1923. Robert Hague, manager of ESSO's Marine Department, justified the request to the Shipping Board to transfer the

Josiah Macy to Danzig and the *S.V. Harkness* to Denmark, on the grounds that the company wished to experiment with the installation of diesel engines in the two tankers. Hague frankly requested the transfers on the grounds that the work, if done in United States yards, would be too expensive. If ESSO installed the engines in European yards while the ships remained under American registry, the work would be subject to an import duty of 50 percent.

Hague regarded the transfer as in American interest, since it would encourage experimentation with the modern technology of diesel engines. Despite Admiral Benson's announced policy of not accepting requests for transfers that sought to evade American law, the board accepted the logic of the company. ESSO later arranged to transfer the Danish-registered *S. V. Harkness* to Danzig, and changed her name to the *Svithoid*. Most of the rest of the Bapico fleet that developed under Danzig's flag, however, was constructed in German yards at Kiel and Emden, and therefore did not require Shipping Board approval for transfer. The ESSO fleet in Danzig grew steadily until by the mid-1930s it included twenty-five tankers, many of them modern, state-of-the-art vessels exceeding 10,000 tons.[26]

Danzig developed no true flag of convenience fleet, with multiple owners transferring their vessels from other registries. While some local vessels registered in Danzig, no other American or foreign company was in a position to duplicate the procedure that ESSO had employed. Heinrich Reidemann legally had sold the DAPG vessels to his brother, who had a legitimate claim to Danzig citizenship. The action was taken in the months after the Versailles treaty terms were known, but before the treaty went into force. The procedure followed in setting up Bapico was legally unassailable, but could not be imitated after 10 January 1920. The rest of the Danzig fleet, as reflected in the maritime records of the interwar period, was made up of smaller coastal and fishing vessels, genuinely operating out of Danzig as a home port. The Bapico vessels rarely, if ever, called at Danzig.[27]

In 1935, Bapico was only one of eighteen shipowning subsidiaries that ESSO controlled around the world, encompassing a total fleet of 190 vessels. The Bapico fleet was the second largest of those fleets, and the largest foreign-registered fleet owned by ESSO. (See table 2.) Bapico alone accounted for more than half of ESSO's European carrying capacity. In 1935, after examining the maritime laws of a number of states, ESSO decided to transfer the whole Bapico fleet of twenty-five ships to Panamanian registry, under a new firm there, Panama Transport Company. The design of Panama's law in the mid-1920s to attract American owners and tonnage revenues at last had brought results.

ESSO's authorized history, written after World War II, reviewed the motives for the 1935 transaction, placing emphasis on the concern of ESSO

Table 2.
Tanker Fleets Owned by ESSO, 1935

Flag	Company Name	Number of Ships
United States	Standard Oil Company of New Jersey	63
Danzig (to Panama)	Bapico (Panama Transport Company)	25
Canada	Imperial Oil, Ltd.	21
Britain	Anglo-American Oil Co., Ltd.	21
Britain	Lago Shipping Co., Ltd.	19
Italy	La Columbia—Societa Marittima	6
France	Standard Française des Petroles	5
Venezuela	Creole Petroleum Company	4
Argentina	Cia. Transportadora de Petroleos, S. A.	4
Holland	N. V. Nederlansche Koloniale	4
Holland	N. V. Petroleum Industrie	3
Germany	DAPG & Waried Tankschiff Rhederi	2
Miscellaneous	(Six Companies)	13
Total		190

Source: Henrietta M. Larson, E. H. Knowlton, and C. S. Popple, *History of Standard Oil Company (New Jersey), 1927–1950*, p. 297.

officials about the takeover of Danzig by the Nazi party. In 1935, stated the company history, ESSO's "leaders saw in Hitler and his Nazi program a growing threat to Danzig—which could easily lose its neutral status and be taken over by Germany—and indeed a threat to the peace of Europe."[28]

However, there are several problems with the anti-Nazi emphasis in the explanation offered by the company's official history. The Nazi party already had won the local elections in Danzig two years before the transfer; further, the local Nazi administration in Danzig was more conciliatory toward Poland than the prior city-state administration had been. ESSO retained German officers and crews aboard the vessels even after they were under Panamanian registry, from 1935 through 1939, removing them only on the outbreak of war in Europe, suggesting that company suspicion of Germany was not too severe in the mid-1930s. Vessels owned by ESSO in two *German* corporations, DAPG and Waried Tankschiff Rhederi, were not removed from German registry. Instead, the ESSO fleet under the flag of the Third Reich was increased from two to four, and ESSO raised its total tonnage in Germany from 31,000 tons to 61,000 tons in the period between 1935 and 1939.[29]

A number of pressing business factors and diplomatic considerations were at work in 1935 that held more importance than the long-range political objection to Naziism suggested in retrospect by the authors of the company history. In early 1935, Poland agreed to a Hague Convention of

1907, which allowed for the impounding of vessels by an enemy on the outbreak of hostilities and extended the effect of the convention to Danzig. In effect, Polish adherence to the convention would allow ships registered under Danzig's flag to be seized in ports of states with which Poland went to war. ESSO's vessels could be exposed to this risk in the Bapico fleet; of course registry in Panama would avoid such dangers. Immediately prior to the transfer to Panama, ESSO and other American oil companies entered protests with the Polish government regarding a system of tariff surcharges amounting to 26.5 percent of value on lubricating oils. Coupled with a series of administrative delays, the surcharge destroyed the ESSO market for lubricating oils in both Danzig and Poland. The local manager of Bapico, Mr. Sentfleben, told American representatives that he was "inclined to believe that the Polish authorities are trying to ban or at least greatly diminish the importation of American oil products and to force customers to use inferior Polish oils."[30]

For such reasons, none of which were brought forward in the company history, ESSO indeed had reason to doubt both Danzig's security as a merchant flag and the health of the business climate under Polish rule by 1935. While the company history is smoothly written and impressively documented from closed company archives, it does reflect a tone of self-congratulation on early anti-Naziism, a tone more in keeping with the authors' postwar recognition of the dangers of Naziism, than with the style of operation of the company in the prewar years. There is little available contemporary record to indicate that ESSO, or indeed, other American-based international firms, found it impolitic to deal with Nazi officials in 1935. The manager of the Marine Transport Division of ESSO was Bushrod B. Howard, a 1911 U.S. Naval Academy graduate who had retired from the navy in 1920 to work for ESSO. Recently transferred from Europe, Howard may have been sensitive to the risks involved in continued Danzig registry. Although ESSO's Marine Division, under Howard's leadership, evidenced some foresight in removing the vessels to Panama, that foresight apparently was based on evidence of Polish, not Nazi, difficulties.[31]

The establishment of the Panama Transport Company fleet was a crucial step in the growth of Panamanian registry. These vessels, under American ownership and control, served in later years in the American war effort. The delicate task of removing the German officers and crews would provide one test of whether the vessels of such a multinational corporation would be turned to the purposes of the owning nation, the nation of registry, or the nation of the officers and crew. More immediately, the large-scale transfer doubled the tonnage under Panamanian registry, since the twenty-five vessels collectively accounted for more than 230,000 tons of registry. Because the ESSO Bapico fleet was the largest foreign proprietary fleet under American ownership, the decision impressed other individual and corporate shipowners. The ESSO move added prestige as well as tonnage to the Panamanian fleet.

Having acquired the Bapico fleet, Panamanian administrations worked to service that fleet and solve its problems. The explicit exemption of shipping company profits from taxation by Panama in 1936 may have been implemented at ESSO urging. Direct evidence shows that when ESSO discovered its Panamanian-registered vessels to be subject to high fees for remeasurement in Finland and Sweden, Panama cooperated by establishing reciprocity with U.S. measurement scales and by opening negotiations for a navigation treaty with Finland.[32]

Other tankers soon registered in Panama, following the lead of ESSO. In December 1935 Standard Oil of California placed two tankers, the *Bahrein* and the *California Standard*, under Panama's flag in a different and independent subsidiary, the Foreign Tankship Corporation. ESSO transferred four more vessels to Panama in 1938 and early 1939. Through the mid-1930s, several Norwegian oil tankers and whaling vessels were transferred to Panama, in part because of the example of the successful ESSO operation there.[33]

Record Keeping and Reforms

Ships entered and left Panamanian registry until the mid-1930s under very casual record keeping, which was not improved until the 1935 reforms of the Harmodio Arias administration. Hoping to determine exactly which American ships had registered under the Panamanian flag, the United States Department of Commerce in 1931 attempted to work through American shipowner associations, the State Department, and Panamanian agencies. Due to the "administrative demoralization" found in Panama, the investigators resorted to independent studies of assorted listings. Lists that were provided to the American investigators by the Panamanian Department of Telegraph, which presumably would issue radio call numbers, and the Department of *Hacienda y Tesoro* (Treasury), which was to collect the revenues, included ships previously transferred to other flags, such as the *Reliance* and the *Resolute*; those forced out of the registry, such as the *Federalship*; and those that had changed their names, such as the *Stuyvesant*, which had become the *Paul Regandanz*. The Department of the Treasury even recorded the continued registry of the *Belen Quezada* long after it had sunk in the Guayaquil harbor. The American investigator in charge of the study regarded the lists as "not over 50 percent accurate," a slightly harsh judgment. Table 3 is a tentative presentation of the sources of vessels that had entered the registry of Panama by 1931, and includes those that stayed only temporarily under the Panamanian flag.[34]

Table 3.
Ships Listed by Panama Departments of Treasury and Telegraph, 1931

Nation of Ownership	Number of Ships
Canada	4
Spain	6
United States	
Pacific Freighters & *Paul Regandanz*	7
Harriman Lines	2
United Fruit Company (from Britain)	8
Other American Owners	14
Panama	7
Total, excluding duplication	48

Source: RG 151, USNA, Foreign and Domestic Commerce, 518 Panama, Peck to Department of Commerce, 15 January 1931.
Note: Data from these two departments included ships known to be removed from registry.

It should be noted that the total number of vessels under the Panamanian flag in any one year fluctuated, not only from increases by transfer, but also from decreases through transfer to other registries, scrapping, and wrecks. *Lloyd's Register of Shipping* showed the totals given in table 4. While Lloyd's records tended to be more accurate than those maintained in Panama, even the *Register* sometimes contained ships attributed to Panamanian registry in this period after independent sources confirmed their transfer or destruction. The decline in registries in the period from 1934 through 1935 may be attributed to the worsening world depression.

In the period from 1935 through 1941, the Panamanian government made several efforts to reform and strengthen the administration of ship registry and to improve record keeping. Defalcation and charges of bribery at certain Panamanian consulates in Europe were investigated in 1935. Through 1936, the tonnage measurement system employed in Panama was brought into conformity with the American system. In 1936, a Panamanian executive resolution exempted shipping company revenues from Panama's 1934 income tax law. In 1937, the United States and Panama exchanged diplomatic notes exempting each others' vessels from remeasurement for port duties. In justifying the improved measurement system, the law stated, in translation, that, "The Executive Power considers that it is convenient to the Republic to facilitate, as far as possible, the situation of the ships which adopt our flag by which there is stimulated the registration of ships." The concerted effort to attract and hold registry for the revenue it would produce, and to reform the system's operation through cooperation with shipowners and through explicit exemption from taxation was reflected in the total tonnage figures during the late 1930s.[35]

Table 4.
Total Ships and Tonnage under Panamanian Registry, 1924–39

Year[a]	Number of Ships	Gross Tonnage
1924	14	83,776
1925	18	97,566
1926	20	100,914
1927	21	47,291
1928	29	71,492
1929	27	61,634
1930	28	74,697
1931	41	130,600
1932	43	137,741
1933	83	237,033
1934	71	271,380
1935	42	136,859
1936	81	429,350
1937	103	512,358
1938	134	611,207
1939	159	717,525

Source: Lloyd's of London, *Lloyd's Register of Shipping*, 1924–39.
[a]Tally taken as of June of the year indicated.

American Uses of the Panama Flag in the 1930s

While most American shipowners who engaged in international trade in the 1920s and the 1930s recognized the attractions of Panama's law, few were in a position to register their vessels under her flag. In the light of Hoover's policies, which emphasized the building of American commerce with American ships, an efficient, profitable vessel simply would not be allowed to transfer. Hoover's administration of the ocean mail contract system was intended to provide subsidies to American-flag vessels and to keep them profitably employed. With the incentive of that system, Grace Lines had brought two vessels back from Panama to the United States, but the United Fruit Company continued its policy of building a Panamanian fleet similar to its Honduran fleet. United Fruit, since it had purchased British-constructed ships and registered them in Britain, could not be prevented by American maritime authorities from transferring its ships where it pleased.

ESSO was in an advantageous position for different reasons. Through the quick thinking of the company's German manager, Heinrich Reidemann, the company had preserved ownership of four tankers that otherwise would have been seized by the Allied Reparations Commission. Those ships formed the core of the Bapico fleet that grew up in Danzig. Despite Shipping Board policies, two American tankers were transferred by ESSO to Danzig, one directly, and one through Denmark, on grounds of experimentation with diesel engines. As the line produced earnings in Germany, ESSO plowed the earnings into newly constructed tank vessels from German shipyards. Despite the rise of Naziism in Germany and a local Nazi party takeover in Danzig, ESSO remained content to operate its fleet under the Danzig flag with German crews and officers.

By 1935, however, Polish-German tensions and Polish controls over Danzig's economy resulted in discriminatory tariffs on oil products against which ESSO and other American oil firms loudly protested. ESSO decided to transfer the whole Danzig fleet of twenty-five vessels to Panama. At the same time, ESSO both directly and indirectly pressured the government of Panama to improve its administration of the law and to arrange treaties and tax exemptions that would allow the company even more freedom. Panama's compliance is understandable in view of the massive registry fee brought by the ESSO transfer. Despite the company's later assertion that the flight from Danzig was evidence of political foresight, the contemporary record shows a set of business motives behind the transfer.

The evolution of multinational corporations, with their lack of national identification, their patterns of tax evasion, and their sophisticated manipulation of currencies, government policies, and national legislation, had not reached the stage of complexity that emerged in the postwar years. Nevertheless, United Fruit and ESSO displayed, in the 1930s, some of the practices that would come to characterize multinational corporation behavior in the 1960s and 1970s. Both of these enterprises benefited from the lack of corporate income tax on shipping companies registered in Panama. Balboa Shipping and Panama Transport Company were able to put earnings into corporate activities without subjecting those gains to taxation. From the perspective of such operations, the concept of seeking the most convenient maritime registration was only one relatively minor technique in an emerging pattern of taking advantage of the variations in the laws of different nations.

As Roosevelt administered the 1936 Merchant Marine Act prior to the outbreak of World War II, there were very few opportunities for American-flag vessels to transfer to Panama. Although Roosevelt's system was based on a different, more defense-oriented set of premises than Hoover's maritime approach, the merchant marine policy of the United States under both presidents specifically directed the strengthening of the U.S.-flag fleet and the retention of valuable shipping. But, the modification and improvement of Panama's law under the Harmodio Arias administration in the mid-1930s as a result of ESSO demands, together with the prestige added to the fleet by both the United Fruit and the ESSO transfers, attracted the interest of shipowners in Europe.

4

Flag of Refuge

THROUGHOUT THE 1930S, the disruptions and crises of European politics created a generation of political refugees. For shipowners, the possibility of changing the nationality of a ship appealed for a variety of reasons, and ships, like people, found refuge under foreign flags from the ominous developments of the decade. For some, improvements in social legislation increased the cost of operation, in a time when profits were very slim or nonexistent. Some owners claimed that payment of social security taxes or manning a ship to the required level simply would break the business. Escape from such costs increased the interest of Greek, Spanish, German, and other shipowners in Panamanian registry, as similar considerations for a decade had attracted American owners. For others, the possibility of double or triple taxation because of operation and funding in two or three nations made the income-tax-free environment of Panamanian registry attractive, as it had been for ESSO. The 1936-39 civil war in Spain, and the growing persecution of Jews in Central and Eastern Europe generated a host of clandestine traders, some of whom found in Panamanian registry an excellent cloak and refuge for their operations in the name of liberation. All such uses, whether fully legal or falling in the gray area between national law and international politics, between smuggling and free trade, created in Europe a lasting impression of the Panamanian merchant flag as a cover for shady operations. To Europeans, the concept of a "convenient flag" earned distinctly unethical connotations over the decade.

Basque Transfers

Several local companies in Bilbao on the Basque coast of northern Spain supplied the first European-owned vessels to transfer from European registry to Panama. Between 1926 and 1933, at least nine medium-sized freighters transferred from Bilbao and nearby Santander, as indicated in table 5. The available record suggests that the Basque transfers prior to the Spanish Civil War were facilitated by a corrupt consul and motivated by a variety of economic factors; later a few more ships escaped a requisition order during that war. With the exception of the *Bolivar*, which was built in 1920, each of these vessels was quite old, built before 1907.

Commentators on Basque economic conditions before the civil war noted that several shipping companies in Bilbao underwent severe economic retraction in the period, despite earlier successes during the Great War. These conditions led to a 46 to 84 percent depreciation of their stocks on local exchanges over the period between 1929 and 1934, and coincided with the cluster of ship transfers to Panama. Of course, such declines in stock value were common to many major enterprises and to shipping all over the world at this time. The American consul in Bilbao attributed the "indefinite" situation of the Spanish Merchant Marine in 1931 to such factors as the change in regime from the dictatorship of Primo Rivera to the republic, the world economic crisis, and the falling gold value of the peseta.[1]

While factors such as high operating costs, social reforms, and discrimination by Spanish officials against Basque owners may have entered into the decision of the shipowners to transfer, their choice was aided at first by the work of the Panamanian consul in Bilbao. The consul was accused of illegally retaining over $4,000 in fees due Panama in 1935, when he was investigated as part of the Panamanian drive to regularize and reform the ship registry system operating through Panamanian consuls in Europe. The Harmodio Arias administration investigated several charges of defalcation and embezzlement by consuls, including a $20,000 shortage in the London consulate. The American ambassador to Panama noted of the investigation: "It has been known for some time that the Government has

Table 5.
Basque Transfers to Panama, 1926–33

Ship	Owner	Tonnage
Adriatico	M. Y. Fernandez	3,024
Anton	A. Menchaca	3,553
Bolivar	N. Gauna Corral	5,112
Ereno	C. M. Elanchove	3,599
Ignacia Aguado	F. Fernandez Aguado	2,846
Pilar	F. Fernandez Aguado	3,434
Ripa	Compania de Nv. Vizcaya	2,747
Santa Marta	F. Fernandez Aguado	3,486
Vat	Tomas Pero-Sanz	3,301

Source: Lloyd's of London, *Lloyd's Register of Shipping*, 1926–33.

been systematically defrauded by its consular representatives, most of whom have been making no accounting whatever of official fees collected." In the light of these charges, the cluster of Bilbao registries in the period between 1926 and 1933 appears to have been stimulated partially by the transitory cause of a willing and corrupt consul, a situation similar to the earlier group of rumrunner registries at Vancouver.[2]

Another motive became apparent later when the largest Basque company, Sota y Aznar, transferred three of its vessels to Panama during the Spanish Civil War, thereby removing the ships from the effect of a Republican war decree requisitioning all ships registered at Bilbao. Although the total number and tonnage of the vessels transferred from Bilbao to Panama from 1926 onward is small, the Basque ships were significant because they were the first European-owned ships to transfer and began a widespread pattern of international use of the Panamanian flag through consular registry.[3]

Greek Owners

Throughout the 1930s, several Greek shipowners transferred their vessels to Panama. A range of social legislation in Greece, designed to insure the employment and the wages of Greek seamen, had caused a number of Greek shipowners to move to British registration and to London headquarters in the early 1930s. In 1932, N. Kyriakides, vice president of the Union of Greek Shipowners, warned that Greek owners were considering foreign flags because of rules requiring large numbers of hands and high wages, as well as the lack of discipline on ships and the required contributions to the seamen's pension fund. "A mere instinct for self-preservation," he claimed, would drive shipowners away from their own flag.[4]

Under the Metaxas government in Greece, 1936–41, social security contributions were increased and the manning laws were enforced rigidly. By 1938, the charges for seamen's social security totalled 41 percent of the basic wage rates, with 33.5 percent contributed by the employer and 7.5 percent by the crew members. Crew wages for a twenty-nine-man vessel under the Greek flag were £290 per month, while Italian owners paid £227 for an equivalent twenty-eight-man vessel, and Yugoslavs paid £230. One Greek shipowner claimed that under the Panamanian flag he could reduce his crew from the sixty-two required under Greek law to twenty-two.[5]

An expert on Greek maritime law estimated that by 1941, over 90 percent of Greek-owned vessels operated in Latin American trades out of London. While the London headquarters of the firms allowed Greek shipowners to avoid the Greek social security system, transfers from Greek to British registry also evaded manning requirements enforced by Greek consuls in the ports of call. Among other restrictions, the law required that all officers and 75 percent of the crew of Greek-flag vessels be Greek citizens, and specified the numbers of men required for each rank of tonnage capacity. This law imposed special difficulties upon owners of ships that rarely called on Greece, such as those plying between Western Europe and Latin America, for Greek-citizen replacements might not always be found.[6]

Aristotle Onassis later claimed to be the first Greek shipowner to discover the advantages of Panamanian registry. While his claim to being first is incorrect, his memory of the incident that spurred his decision to transfer to Panama coincided with the legal and economic problems that prompted the flight of Greek owners to the Panamanian refuge. As a well-known raconteur, Onassis enjoyed recounting the story of his initial decision. According to his version, his vessel, the *Onassi Penelope*, was immobilized in Rotterdam because the local Greek consul would not issue clearance papers until Onassis replaced an assistant cook, who had fallen ill, with another Greek cook. There were simply no Greek cooks to be had in Holland. After telephoning and telegraphing all night, Onassis claimed, the next day he switched registry to Panama. Under the Panamanian flag, Onassis could hire and replace crew members without regard to their citizenship. When the Greek consul came aboard, Onassis ordered him off the "Panamanian" ship, thus beginning the exodus of millions of tons of Greek shipping to Panama.[7]

Manuel Kulukundis, another Greek shipowner, also claimed that his registry in Panama was the first of the Greek transfers to that flag, and he told a similar story, involving a radio operator. The records of the registries indicate that Kulukundis preceded Onassis by several years in "discovering" the freedoms of Panamanian registry. Kulukundis, however, already had escaped the manning requirements of Greek registry by transfer to Britain. Kulukundis took his vessels back to Greek registry after 1935. While Kulukundis preceded Onassis in experimenting with Panamanian registry, it was Onassis who obtained the benefit of refuge from Greek manning requirements.[8] Table 6 shows the timing of the Greek registries in the 1930s.

Norwegian Ships

Transfer of vessels from Norway to Panama began as a reaction to the double taxation to which multinational concerns could become exposed. In 1928, Erling Naess helped promote a corporation, Vikingen, Ltd., with support from a Norwegian whaling company, Johan Rasmussen, and with the financial backing of the British banking house of Guiness, Mohan and Company. Naess used his contacts to bring together Norwegian whaling expertise and British capital in a firm headquartered in London. The

Table 6.
Greek-Owned Vessels Registered in Panama, 1932–40

Years Registered in Panama	Previous Registry	Ship Name	Owner	Home Port
1932–35	Britain	Mount Athos	M. Kulukundis	London
1932–35	Britain	Mount Dirfys	M. Kulukundis	London
1933–35	Holland	Virginia Nicolaou	N. Nicolaou	Athens
1933–35	Britain	Ekaterini Nicolaou	N. Nicolaou	Athens
1933–35	Britain	(15 vessels of "Mount" series)	M. Kulukundis	London
1933–35	France	Mount Pelion	Kulukundis & Costomen	Athens
1933–35	Britain	Mount Pentilis	Kulukundis & Costomen	Athens
1934–35	Britain	New Georgia	Paramithiotis	Athens
1938–40	Greece	Onassi Penelope	A. Onassis	Buenos Aires
1938–40	Greece	Onassi Socrates	A. Onassis	Buenos Aires
1938–41	(Various)	(12 to 15 vessels in clandestine trades)[a]		

Source: Lloyd's of London, *Lloyd's Register of Shipping*, 1932–41.
[a]See Table 8.

company operated the whaling factory ship, the *Vikingen*, under British registry for two years, but discovered that the Norwegian partners had to pay both British taxes on the corporate profits of the firm and personal Norwegian income tax on dividends they received in Norway. Naess, hearing of the Panamanian registry system and the formation of ESSO's Panama Transport Company, went to the United States to consult with maritime lawyers as to the system's operation. He then moved the head-quarters of the company to Paris, because under British law inland revenue was collected only from British corporations with their center and main operation in Britain. He registered the corporation's ships in Panama, which charged only registry fees and no taxes. Both British and Norwegian participants in the company then paid income tax only on dividends; France charged no taxes on corporations with entirely foreign operations.[9]

The Vikingen system was so successful that the whaling company expanded, adding a tanker company, a second whale factory ship, two fleets of Panamanian-registered whalers averaging over 300 tons each, and two dry cargo ships. By 1940, Naess had fully established the tax-refuge aspects of Panamanian registry, with over twenty vessels employed in the Vikingen Corporation, the Vestfold Corporation, and the Tanker Corporation of Sandefjord, Norway. Smaller Norwegian enterprises emulated the Naess group.[10] (See table 7.)

Clandestine Trades

The registry of the Panama Transport Company fleet by ESSO and of the Balboa Shipping fleet by United Fruit, coupled with the burgeoning growth of Norwegian and Greek registries, publicized the attractions of the Panamanian flag to the businessmen and shipowners of Europe. In addition, the flag continued to attract users for clandestine purposes, as it had when the *Belen Quezada*, the *Helori*, the *Federalship*, and others made headlines in the previous decade. In the spring of 1933, an ingenious promoter made what for its time was a unique use of Panamanian registry. Cruising the *Playa* (or the *Playa Ensenada*) in international waters off Los Angeles, he established a "pirate" radio station that played music, sold commercials, and evaded requirements of the newly established Federal Radio Commission, which was the forerunner of the Federal Communications Commission. Protests from American stations and officials were routed to the State Department, which relayed the protest to Panama; after several months of operation, Panama agreed to threaten cancellation of registry. The *Playa* went off the air.[11] More significant clandestine operations emerged in the Mediterranean.

Table 7.
Norwegian-Owned Vessels Registered in Panama, 1930–39

Ship	Owner	Tonnage
Anglo	Anglo SS Company	2,978
Astriana	Hamre	522
Essi	Essi Corporation	1,192
Granville	Pacific Asiatic Shipping	5,745
Matros	Yngvar Huistendahl	4,358
Norbris[a]	Tanker Corporation	7,619
Nore[a]	Tanker Corporation	7,619
Norlys[a]	Tanker Corporation	9,892
Norseman	Norseman SS Company	4,950
Norvinn[a]	Tanker Corporation	6,322
Tai Ping Yang	Wilhelm Wilhelmson	7,044
Tai Shan	Wilhelm Wilhelmson	6,604
Vestfold[a]	Vestfold Corporation	14,547
Vikingen[a]	Vikingen Corporation	14,526

Source: Lloyd's of London, *Lloyd's Register of Shipping*, 1930–39.
[a]Ships of the Naess group. In addition, fifteen whale catchers ranging in size from 250 to 355 tons worked with the *Vestfold* and the *Vikingen*.

Shortly after the rebellion of the army and rightist groups under Francisco Franco against the Republican government in Spain in 1936, twenty-
eight European powers signed a nonintervention agreement in which they
pledged not to send weapons to either the Rebels or the established government—the Loyalists. While the United States did not join that agreement,
the State Department pressured American firms to abide by the agreement.
The American Neutrality Act was amended in January 1937 to apply to
civil wars, and American ships then legally were barred from transporting
weapons or aircraft to either side.

Several major routes of arms supply developed for the Loyalists. In
addition to direct supply overland from France, French companies purchased American aircraft and arranged to fly them to Spain with volunteer
French pilots. A more risky route consisted in smuggling by sea past the
nonintervention patrols maintained by the British, French, German, and
Italian navies. By June 1937, the Germans and Italians withdrew from the
patrols, leaving the enforcement of the nonintervention agreement largely
in British hands. A number of Italian submarines, operating without
identifying themselves, as well as Italian aircraft openly based in Spain,
cooperated with Rebel forces in attacking shipe supplying the Loyalists.[12]

Greece was among the states signing the nonintervention agreement.
Any Greek-registered vessel, or any Greek-owned and British-registered
ship, apprehended by the nonintervention enforcement fleet, would be
subject to the penalties of law of the nation of registry. However, Greek
ships transferred to Panama could operate without interference from the
British naval vessels off Spain, as long as officially they had not sailed from a
European port, since Panama did not join the nonintervention agreement
nor did it impose an embargo on shipments to Spain. Of course, ships of all
registries ran the risk of encountering Rebel naval or air patrols, or so-called
pirate Italian submarines.[13]

A fleet of over 200 small craft of French, British, and Panamanian
registry operated out of Marseilles and Sête in France and Oran in Algeria
to supply the beleaguered Loyalist forces. The U.S. Office of Naval
Intelligence (ONI) reported that in August 1938, 161 vessels reached
Loyalist ports. Of these, 103 were British, 17 were French, 14 were Greek,
and 11 were Panamanian-registered. The Panamanian ships, the ONI
reported, carried mostly airplanes and airplane parts from Marseilles to
Barcelona. Those vessels sailing from France would file their destinations as
Hong Kong or Buenos Aires, only to return in a few days for another cargo.
To confuse Rebel espionage, shipowners frequently changed the vessels'
names. The crewmen, mostly Greeks, earned the high rate of about £75 per
month. In Marseilles, longshoremen joked that, "The Greeks will win the
Spanish Civil War."[14]

A group of related firms, including Socdeco in Antwerp, Rudolf Wolf and H. V. Hunzedal in Holland, and Eduoard Godillot in Paris, cooperated in this clandestine trade. Godillot operated two ships, the *Alice* (also called the *Margit of Colon*) and the *Ilona*, both under the Panamanian flag, as part of the supply system of the Loyalists. Rebel forces captured and held two Dutch-owned, Panamanian-registered vessels, the *Andra* and the *Hordena*. The *Hordena*, reputedly backed by "Russian capital," carried a cargo of 22 airplanes and 30,000 army uniforms on its capture. Dutch Foreign Office negotiation secured the release of both crews only after the crews had been incarcerated for several weeks.[15]

In a frank conversation, taken down verbatim, American Consul-General Harold Shantz, who temporarily was charged with handling Panamanian affairs in Athens, questioned Alexander Davaris, a Greek shipowner, about his fleet of six Panamanian-registered freighters that supplied ammunition to Loyalist forces. With a fine sense of irony, Davaris explained that he purchased German and Italian ammunition, secured export licenses to take it to Mexico, and then sailed for Barcelona to sell it to the enemies of Germany and Italy. His men received "war-risk" bonus pay, and he had no trouble recruiting seamen.[16]

"How long does the trip take?" asked Consul Shantz.

"This ship will be back in about twelve days," said Davaris. "It does eighteen knots."

"I see the *Ilona* has been rechristened seven times. What's the idea?"

"I change the name of the ship after every trip," replied Davaris.

"Do you carry anything besides munitions?"

"Some food. They're short there."

"Do you ever lose any ships?"

Davaris knocked wood. "Not yet. The Italians got two of my men once, though."

"Airplane fire?"

"Yes," said Davaris. "The Italians are the only ones I'm afraid of."

"Why do you always want Panama registry?"

"It's cheaper. Too many Greek taxes."

Davaris claimed to be the only supplier of ammunition to the Loyalists who was operating directly out of Greece.[17]

The British "Passport Control Office" (an intelligence office) informed Consul Shantz that "Davaris was going after Palestine trade, seeking to sell arms to the Arabs, and at the same time to supply them with plenty of targets in the persons of illegal Jewish immigrants." Shantz asked to be relieved of charge of the interests of Panama, arguing that representation of such enterprises by American consular offices damaged American prestige in the eastern Mediterranean. State Department officials reluctantly agreed that Panamanian registry "might in some instances facilitate nefarious activities." After review of Shantz's request, the State Department reaffirmed the right to deny service to ships engaged in illegal or questionable activities, and put Panama on notice, 10 December 1938, that no further services for such vessels would be performed in Athens by the American consular office.[18]

By mid-1939, several other Greek shipowners who had supplied weapons, ammunition, airplanes, and spare parts to Spain became involved in the growing operation of transporting Jewish refugees to Palestine. Mossad, the underground branch of the Haganah, the armed wing of the Jewish Agency, worked with several Panamanian-registered Greek vessels to transport refugees from Black Sea and Adriatic ports. Mossad contracted to use vessels owned by the Vernikos family, which had been involved in several earlier clandestine ventures. In 1933, one of their ships had smuggled the liberal Greek leader, Eleutherios Venizelos, out of Greece to Rhodes as he fled the coup that deposed him. Vernikos ships also had worked in weapons supply to Spain. Mossad recruited the Vernikos ship, the *Atrato*, to bring Polish Jews from Susak, Yugoslavia, to Palestine. Working with another Panamanian-registered Vernikos ship, the *Colorado*, which could pass Yugoslav port inspections as capable of carrying passengers to the supposed destination of Mexico, the *Atrato* set up a transport service operating on the edges of legality. British authorities in Palestine planned to stem the tide of immigrants there by establishing an immigration quota of 15,000 per year and denying landing permits for numbers in excess of the quota. Thus, Polish, Hungarian, Rumanian, and German Jews escaping the varieties of persecution facing them through 1938 and 1939 had to slip into Palestine without port clearances or British-issued immigration visas.[19]

Although he found the whole operation distressing, the American consul in Palestine charged with responsibility for handling Panamanian consular business kept a close record of the movements of Panamanian-registered Greek vessels engaged in refugee transport. While the American State Department worked to get Panama to take over its own representation in Palestine, the American consul reported the arrivals of the Vernikos-owned *Colorado* and the *Atrato*, as well as other Panamanian vessels.[20] A partial list, derived from the consul's reports and other sources, is shown in table 8.

Not all the refugee vessels succeeded in slipping past the authorities. The British detained the *Noemi Julia*, the *Liesel*, the *Colorado*, and the *Atrato*; forced the beaching of the *Parita*; and burned the *Rim* off Rhodes. One of the greatest tragedies of the refugee work occurred on the *Struma*, which, under the Panamanian flag, was denied passage through the Bosporus by Turkish authorities in World War II. Turned back to the Black Sea without sufficient fuel to make a port, the vessel exploded, apparently from hitting a

Table 8.
Panamanian-Registered Refugee Transports, 1938–39

Ship	Owner	Home Port	Tonnage
Aghios Nicolaous	Katsourakis	Piraeus	856
Artemisia	Davaris	Piraeus	n.d.[a]
Atrato	Vernikos	Piraeus	663
Colorado	Vernikos	Piraeus	591
Draga	Davaris	Piraeus	643
Fossoula	Cie. Nouvelle	Marseilles	1,282
Liesel	n.d.	(Rumania)	n.d.
Noemi Julia	Cia. Maritima	London	1,300
Parita	Minacoulis	Marseilles	800
Rim	G. Shembri	Istanbul	552
Tiger Hill	Hellenic Coast	Piraeus	1,499
Varko	Mediterranean SS Co.	London	1,437

Sources: Ehud Avriel, *Open the Gates*; Steger to State, 21 September 1939, Decimal 867n.55/196, RG 59, USNA; Shantz to State, 14 November 1938, Decimal 819.851/34, RG 59, USNA; Lloyd's of London, *Lloyd's Register of Shipping*, 1939.
[a]n.d.—no data available.

mine, and sank on 24 February 1942, drowning 768 refugees and the entire crew.[21]

The Flag of Refuge

In addition to the Basque, Greek, Norwegian, Danzig, and British fleets that entered Panamanian registry, individual vessels whose owners were from a wide variety of nations were registered under the Panamanian flag. Documented references to Panamanian registry by owners in Sweden, Germany, Denmark, Holland, France, Algeria, Egypt, Turkey, Rumania, Bulgaria, China, and Japan can be found in the period from 1935 through 1939. Primary evidence and secondary treatments of most of these situations are too widely scattered and shallow to allow for detailed analysis of motives, but the variety of registries does demonstrate that the efforts of the Panamanian government to develop a tax haven and a no-questions-asked system won quiet recognition all over the globe. The U.S. Office of Naval Intelligence continued to suspect that Japanese fishing boats registered under the Panamanian flag and operating off the Canal Zone were engaged in espionage in 1934. After the Japanese invasion of China in July 1937, numerous Chinese shipowners sought the protection of other flags, including both the American and the Panamanian. Japanese-owned ships previously registered in China transferred to Panama, apparently to seek a neutral flag, while the American consul in Shanghai noted increased requests for service from Panamanian ships. A German shipowner, Herman

The Amano, *a Japanese-owned fishing boat registered in Panama, shown here in 1937. The Office of Naval Intelligence suspected such vessels served to spy on the approaches to the Panama Canal through the 1930s. (Naval Photographic Center)*

Vogemann, suffered criticism in the press of Hamburg for evading social insurance and German salary levels through the Panamanian registry of the *Vogtland*. Vessels owned by Dutch, Bulgarian, Rumanian, and Turkish firms all helped transport refugees to Palestine under the Panamanian flag.[22]

American consuls found themselves obliged to operate a system that served as a refuge for vessels from the political, economic, and social upheavals and the governmental restrictions of the turbulent decade. That responsibility often caused the American officials embarrassment, and several besides Shantz in Athens sought assistance or special instructions from the State Department, hoping to deny registry or other services to vessels whose purposes and motives they found contrary to American policy or best interests. Some expressed dismay at the system. H. Earle Russell reported from Egypt in 1934:

> The port of Alexandria is visited quite frequently by vessels of Panama registry, but these vessels are Panaman in name only, as they have never been in a Panama port and the entire personnel of officers and crew does not include a single Panama citizen. . . . The status of these vessels is extremely peculiar. It is apparent from remarks let drop by one or two of the masters at this office that the owners have found it much more profitable to fly the Panama flag, and even to pay the fines assessed by the Panama government through its Consuls abroad upon vessels not resorting to Panaman ports within a period of six months, rather than to pay certain other taxes and duties evidently assessed by European governments.[23]

Consul O. Taft in Algiers adopted an even more critical note of disdain; he found both sides in a labor dispute aboard the *Dora* contemptible: "My impression of the whole affair was that the Captain was undoubtedly engaged in clandestine trade of all sorts, and that the crew was made up of entirely untrustworthy persons." Despite such objections, however, the State Department reminded its consuls to render services to Panamanian vessels where charged with representing Panama, and to do it within Panamanian, not American, rules and parameters. However, when the consuls continued to complain, the State Department decided to deny service to particular vessels or shipowners, as in the case of Davaris at Athens.

The American embassy in Ankara, Turkey, complained that the Istanbul consular office was being asked to provide services to the *Beme*, which had been involved in a ship collision in the Bosporus. The ship, reported the embassy, was involved in "contraband" oil trade from the Black Sea to Spain. The State Department first demanded to know why the ambassador referred to the trade as "contraband" since even the powers signing the nonintervention agreement had not embargoed petroleum. State also enquired whether the representation of the *Beme* adversely affected American prestige. After learning details of the ship's operation, Secretary of State Cordell Hull informed Panama that no further services would be performed for that particular ship.[24]

Panama's flag attracted operators in the clandestine trades not simply because of its ease of use, but also because Panama was a "traditional" neutral in such conflicts as the Chinese-Japanese war and the Spanish Civil War, in the sense that it passed no laws and joined no international agreements preventing its vessels from trading with either side. While some American officials regarded the legal petroleum sale to Spain as a "contraband" trade, in fact even the sale of weapons fell within the traditional rights of neutrals to freedom of the seas as advocated by Woodrow Wilson in the First World War. Similarly, Panama entered into no agreements with the British that would make it a violation of Panamanian law to load immigrants destined for Palestinian ports. Despite such considerations of international law, by December 1938, the State Department decided that the representation of Panamanian ships engaged in clandestine traffic would only embarrass and discredit the United States, and on a case-by-case basis, the department denied representation to particular vessels.

Many of the shipowners who sought out Panamanian registry understood that Panama's failure to defend its vessels against seizure or to insist on freedom of the seas in the Wilsonian sense was the price of refuge, and such shipowners sought diplomatic help from their own governments. The owners of the *Hordena*, despite their procommunist position, sought the assistance of Dutch, not Panamanian, diplomats in securing the release of the crew. Off Palma, Franco's forces seized and condemned as a "prize of war" the Norwegian-owned *Norseman*, registered in Panama. The vessel had been en route with a cargo of grain from the Black Sea to Oslo. The Norwegian, not the Panamanian, government issued a sharp protest. Rebel vessels stopped and detained the ESSO-owned, Panamanian-registered *Josiah Macy* off the Balearic Islands, 6 December 1936, en route to Italy. Attempts by ESSO's attorney, Henry Dodge, to secure a diplomatic protest from Panama over treatment of the tanker produced no results, and the company complained to the State Department. The seizure of the *Josiah Macy* can be regarded only as an ironic error, rather than as evidence of American use of the Panamanian flag for evasion of American neutrality law. The vessel's cargo was intended for the Italian allies of the Rebels seizing the vessel.[25]

American-owned vessels did not register under the Panamanian flag to supply either side in Spain. Since petroleum was not embargoed under the 1936–37 neutrality regulations, Texaco continued to supply Franco's forces openly and legally using American-flag tankers. Several American-owned and -registered ships supplying the Loyalists earned notoriety, and the American-flag tanker *Nantucket Chief*, which was seized by Rebels on 22 January 1938, earned a State Department protest. Two American-flag vessels, the *Wisconsin* and the *Oregon*, operated to supply the Loyalists at Barcelona without being attacked. However, Arcon Steamship Company, a London corporation, purchased the two ships from National Bulk Carriers for £25,000 each, prior to their Spanish voyages. American officials hastened to arrange the transfer of the vessels to British registry. In the meantime, it appeared that the American flag even offered a degree of protection against Rebel confiscation or attack, out of fear of angering the United States. A Loyalist plan to follow up on the apparent protection by chartering a number of American-registered ships to supply noncontraband goods did not materialize before the collapse of the regime.[26]

The bitter controversies that emerged between organized labor and shipowners choosing Panamanian registry in the post-World War II period led some later authors to read back into the growing Panamanian registry of the 1930s a pattern of escape from labor unions. Although several labor protests against exploitation had marked the beginnings of Panamanian registry in the early 1920s, only a few such struggles aboard Panamanian vessels surfaced in the 1930s. Most of the shipowners who transferred their ships to Panama in the 1930s did not do so to obtain lower wages. Labor peace prevailed aboard the large modern fleets of United Fruit and ESSO, which continued the wage scales and labor conditions established under previous registries. The owners of older, smaller, and less reputable vessels engaged in clandestine trades paid high hazard rates to their crews, thus avoiding many complaints, although one dispute over delayed payment aboard the *Dora* emerged during its gunrunning to Spain. Naess and other Norwegian owners worked out agreements with Norwegian sailors' unions in which the Norwegian scale would be supplemented with extra pay to cover social security payments lost by transfer out of Norwegian registry. Greek transfers both to Britain and to Panama evaded the social security and manning requirements imposed by law, not by collective bargaining.[27]

Panamanian ships had a reputation for dismal accommodations by the standards of the major maritime nations, and resultant savings in capital costs might be regarded as an indirect form of labor-cost savings. However, many of these conditions derived from the fact that the smaller steamers registered with Panama were often more than forty years old; crew quarters and plumbing on coal-burning freighters built in the 1880s were primitive by 1939 standards. Such criticisms, however, could not be applied to the modern United Fruit "white fleet" and the other proprietary lines.

By 1939, Panama established its maritime flag as "convenient." Although the term *flag of convenience* was not employed regularly until the early 1950s, the concept that registry in Panama was convenient for a variety of reasons became increasingly understood in maritime circles in the late 1930s. When the American chargé d'affaires in Panama forwarded information that the Panamanian minister of labor, commerce, and industries proposed to negotiate a system of preferential employment of Panamanian seamen aboard Panamanian vessels, he enclosed a report noting that, "Inasmuch as foreign shipping interests have registered vessels under the Panamanian flag for reasons of convenience and economy which are well known," he believed such negotiations to be impracticable. He noted that the provision, if put into effect, might drive shipowners to "other convenient flags." At the State Department, the idea that the Panamanians really would attempt to force employment of Panamanian nationals was discounted; one official noted "the proposal . . . is so manifestly ridiculous as to make it appear that the said proposal is 'eye wash' for local consumption."[28]

While the idea of preferential Panamanian employment had been incorporated in the 1925 law establishing Panama's maritime system, no effort had been made to enforce it. Instead, Panama regularized and expanded the system for the revenue it earned for consuls and for the central treasury, but not for Panamanian seamen. As most official American observers assumed, Panama's main purpose in maintaining the system was monetary. When Panama issued new regulations regarding the measurement of vessels, the American ambassador in Panama noted that the language of the regulation makes "no attempt to conceal the fact that it is hoped thereunder to attract further registrations to Panama, to the consequent benefit of the national treasury." A U.S. Army G-2 officer in Costa Rica made a similar comment on Panama's developing registry. "It is believed," noted Colonel Nicolas Campanole in 1936, "that the aim of this high registration of foreign tonnage under the Panamanian flag is the production of revenue for the Republic of Panama and the escape from taxation and control of their own countries, the control and supervision of the Panama government being negligible."[29]

The Panamanian fleet grew through the 1930s without attracting widespread attention. The modernizing multinationals in both Europe and the United States had reason to proceed quietly. In doing so they avoided the glare of publicity, since there was little public sympathy or understanding for clever devices that allowed the amassing of tax-free wealth, especially during the hard years of the Great Depression. Even the more newsworthy and dramatic clandestine trades of weapons supply to Spain and the transport of refugees to Palestine proceeded with little public notice, in the shadow of yet more dramatic world-shaking events, such as the Munich Pact and the fall of Madrid. Small announcements on the financial pages of the *New York Times* would indicate, from year to year, the total number of vessels and the total tonnage registered in Panama as recorded in *Lloyd's Register of Shipping*. No liners of the rank of the *Reliance* or the *Resolute* would put the developments on the front pages before the eyes of the world. Policy makers and opinion molders as well as the general public remained largely ignorant of the slow growth and increased flexibility of the Panamanian system, despite carefully filed reports of consuls, Commerce Department investigators, and intelligence officers. A small number of maritime lawyers, including Arias, Fabrega, and Fabrega in Panama and Herman Goldman in New York, could advise clients on the advantages of the law. The Panamanian consular network could quietly continue its service of the fleet.[30]

Thus, when war broke out in Europe on 1 September 1939, few people, beyond the shipowners already employing Panamanian registry, could have visualized the unique and important roles the flag of Panama was destined to play.

5

Neutrality, 1939–41

THE FUNCTION OF AMERICAN NEUTRALITY LEGISLATION in the period between 1935 and 1939 was to supplant traditional legislation with a new set
of laws embodying some of the ideas of isolationism. The Nye Committee,
which in 1934 investigated the causes of the First World War, together with
several popular books, such as Walter Millis's *The Road to War*, that brought
the views of "revisionist history" to the public, traced the American involvement in that war to shipping. Whereas Woodrow Wilson had insisted
on the right of American ships to carry goods, including weapons, to
belligerents during that period without suffering attack, the Neutrality
Acts of 1935 and 1937 would prevent such trade and avoid the kinds of
attacks on U.S. merchant shipping that early in 1917 had led to war. The
Neutrality Acts of 1935 and 1937 required the president to announce when
a state of war existed and to impose an embargo on weapons sales to either
side. The acts further required that American citizens be warned that they
traveled on belligerent vessels at their own risk.[1]

The German invasion of Poland on 1 September 1939 caused the administration to rethink the effects of the existing neutrality laws. Roosevelt
argued for modification of the Neutrality Acts to allow him to distinguish
between aggressors and victims, and to supply arms to the victims. Other
critics of the acts pointed out that the embargo on arms was itself not
"neutral" in the abstract, since in many respects Germany was better armed
than Britain or France. Thus, a continued embargo would work against
Allied interests and slightly favor Germany. After a national discussion and
a month of debate, Congress finally amended the law in November 1939.
The new bill, incorporating amendments introduced by Senator Key Pittman of Nevada, removed the embargo on weapons. American vessels were
to be prohibited from entering war zones, American citizens were prohib-

ited from traveling on belligerent ships, and American merchant ships could not be armed. But, either side could purchase goods and transport them aboard their own vessel or those of other neutrals. This so-called Cash-and-Carry Act of 1939 favored the British, with their control of sea surface transport.[2]

In the period from September 1939 through May 1940—the so-called phony war—little action took place on the western front since Britain and France could do little to aid Poland unless they were to launch an invasion or to bomb German targets. Both countries felt unprepared for either course of action. According to William Langer and S. Everett Gleason, the phony war in Europe was matched by a "phony neutrality" in the United States. Both the president and much of the American public were clearly pro-Allied, and the "cash-and-carry" system, with its cloak of neutrality but its tendency to favor the Allies and to allow British purchase of American weapons, suited the national mood.[3]

Even though the export of weapons no longer was embargoed, petroleum and food continued to be the main exports from the United States to the Allies, because Britain and France wished to build up their own armaments and aircraft industries. Yet, from the British point of view, the new law imposed some difficulties, since shipping was in great demand to supply British outposts throughout the empire. With American shipping suddenly banned from the eastern Atlantic, the "carry" part of the legislation imposed more difficulties than the "cash" part. On the American side, Latin American, Asian, and Mediterranean trade could not absorb the tanker and dry cargo tonnage idled by the closing of the North Atlantic routes. Shipowners believed the prohibition of American vessels from the trade had singled out one particular economic segment, the shipping industry, as the scapegoat for American neutrality policy.[4]

Several solutions to the shipping problems generated by the Neutrality Act of 1939 were obvious immediately and were employed over the next few months. One answer was the extensive sale and transfer of ships to British companies. This procedure would involve no violation of the neutrality law, even though it was clearly a pro-Allied act, since the British would pay cash, and by owning the ship would secure its transfer to the British flag. When the ship left an American port, it no longer would be American. A second method, which received less public notice, was the quiet rerouting of British- or Canadian-flag vessels to take up the reduction in American service. Thus, for example, ESSO directed its Canadian subsidiary to carry a heavier transatlantic trade to substitute for American-flag tankers removed from the route. A third method was to sell and transfer American ships to foreign companies registered under another neutral flag, such as Brazil. The vessels then could operate under the flag of the neutral, carrying goods to Britain. If such a recently sold and transferred vessel were torpedoed and sunk, the United States would not be involved in any way.[5]

Panamanian Registry and Shipments to the Allies

The most controversial way around the shipping problems caused by the Pittman amendment was the transfer of registry to Panama, with ownership retained in American hands. Such action had been predicted as early as 1937, when a cash-and-carry amendment to neutrality had been considered. In the State Department, the legal adviser had pointed out that transfer of ships to other neutrals posed no danger to neutrality, since the Maritime Commission, under powers retained in the 1936 Merchant Marine Act, could approve or disapprove all transfers. In 1937, the State Department's legal adviser assumed that companies might attempt the device of transfer, but that the Maritime Commission could enforce neutrality by preventing any such transfers. By 1939, however, the commission, Roosevelt, and some of his closest advisers sought means around the neutrality legislation, in order to keep Britain supplied. Instead of placing impediments in the way of the transfer process, the commission, under Admiral Land's direction, developed means of facilitating it.[6]

At the emergency meeting of the Pan-American states held in September and October 1939, in Panama, the major decision was to declare a "Quarantine Zone" which, in violation of maritime practice and traditional international law, effectively extended territorial waters 300 miles into the Atlantic, barred belligerent activity in the zone south of the Canadian border, and proposed naval patrols of the area by the Pan-American states. This extended zone at first was disapproved by Secretary of State Cordell Hull and by naval officers. The State Department viewed the zone as illegal, and the navy saw it as unenforceable. At the State Department, wags called the zone the "chastity belt" and predicted it would not deter German or British actions.[7]

A minor agreement reached at the Panama conference received far less notice; it recognized as legal all transfers of ships to an American republic. The purpose of this agreement was not to facilitate transfers of ships to Panama in order to aid in the sale of goods to Britain. On the contrary, it was an assertion of the right to regard some eighty or ninety German ships that might be seized in Latin American harbors as fully transferred to the requisitioning neutral power. Belligerent states long had exercised the power of requisition over neutral ships, a practice called angary in international law; yet the reverse practice, that of neutrals seizing belligerent ships, had been employed with a few precedents in the First World War but never had received legal recognition by the British. Both Britain and France announced that they would regard Latin American neutral seizures of

German vessels as illegal and would reserve the right to regard the ships as enemy vessels and to seize them as prizes in international waters. Although the Latin American intent was to acquire the ships as security for German debts to Latin American creditors, Britain suspected that the procedure would be employed to generate new German credits for purchases in Latin America. In the light of later extensive transfers to Panama from the United States, this provision, which originally was intended for essentially neutral purposes as the assertion of a power not recognized by Britain, seemed to be the redundant assertion of a practice (transfer of neutral vessels from one neutral state to another) that Britain and other nations long had recognized. The assertion of the right of "reverse angary" was accepted by neither Britain nor France, and only two or three Axis ships were seized in Latin America under this provision. It was ironic that scholars like Samuel Flagg Bemis later would claim that this provision, designed to thwart British power, was *intended* as a means of implementing American ship transfers to Panama to aid Britain, especially since the American representative who negotiated the agreement in Panama, Undersecretary of State Sumner Welles, was adamantly opposed to American transfers to Panama at this point.[8]

Even though intended to provide for the recognition of the seizure of German vessels, the reverse angary provision was phrased in such a way that it affirmed the legality of the transfer of ships to Latin American republics in general, and it therefore could be referred to in later correspondence as providing a justification for American transfers to Panama. While such affirmation of an existing practice was not required from a legal point of view, it could be useful to members of the Maritime Commission. The inclusion of the affirmation in the Declaration of Panama gave a kind of international political sanction to a practice that had legal precedents extending back to 1920 in the case of Panama and an even longer tradition of precedents in the case of European powers.[9]

ESSO was the leader in the procedure of transferring vessels from the United States to Panama. Even prior to the outbreak of the war in Europe, ESSO applied for and received permission to transfer four tankers from its New Jersey company to the Panama Transport Company. Between September 1939 and February 1940 the company transferred fifteen more tankers to Panama. Through such transfers, ESSO maintained its ability to supply nations in the war zone. Between September and November 1939, oil was not on the embargoed list and could be sent freely to belligerents on ships of American or foreign registry, if the shipowners would risk submarine attack. Most American firms delayed sailings in this period, recognizing the potential submarine threat. After the act was passed, ESSO was not enjoined from using Panamanian ships to trade in the war zone, since American neutrality legislation, of course, did not apply to Panamanian ships. If such ships were sunk by German submarines, the United States would face no violation of its Neutrality Acts nor any violation of its neutrality in the abstract sense, and no chain of events leading from torpedoing to a declaration of war, similar to the pattern of February and March 1917, would ensue.[10]

Before employing the ships in the war zone, ESSO faced a difficult problem. The twenty-five vessels that formed the core of the Panama Transport Company fleet, which had been transferred from Danzig, still had German crews on 1 August 1939. In August, the company ordered sixteen of the crews paid off and dismissed; it replaced twelve of them with American crews and four with British crews. In September, German crews on the remaining nine vessels were replaced. Once the war zones were declared, the crews on vessels sailing to Europe once again were changed, with the American seamen replaced by groups of Danish, Norwegian, and Canadian men.[11]

The act of paying off and dismissing the German crews in late August and in September 1939 later was regarded as a clear and relatively successful test of the principle that came to be called "effective control." But the process was not as smooth as the advocates of that system asserted. When the crew of the *Calliope*, anchored at Rio, refused to leave the ship and in effect conducted a sit-down strike in August, ESSO anticipated a series of difficulties including resistance and sabotage. Vice President Sadler of ESSO called Admiral Harold Stark, chief of naval operations, and asked for naval or Coast Guard assistance in arranging the changeover in crews on the company's ships as they came into the New York harbor. Sumner Welles noted that, "The company now runs to us for help. . . . This is

The Calliope, *one of twenty-five ESSO ships transferred from Danzig to Panama in 1935. This 8,426-ton tanker was immobilized in the harbor of Rio de Janiero in 1939 by a sit-down strike when the German crew refused company dismissal orders at the outbreak of World War II. (Exxon Corporation)*

obviously a clear-cut case of where the Standard Oil Company of New Jersey has deliberately evaded our shipping laws in order to obtain easier labor conditions and is now caught in a jam." Despite Welles's distaste for the operation, harbor authorities and local police in New York and New Jersey were alerted for possible trouble.[12]

Several factors made widespread resistance to the changeover a dangerous possibility that had to be handled carefully. Even for those changeovers that were accomplished after the war had broken out, there would be little legal justification for crew resistance. Yet, in war, legal niceties counted less than power. The orders for paying off the crews arrived while the vessels were in port; any resistance would have to take place under the noses of port authorities. The tolerance of the authorities for the sit-down strike by the German crew aboard the *Calliope* in Rio delayed that vessel for two weeks. But the crew changeovers proceeded in the American harbors without difficulty. If a vessel had attempted to leave after an act of mutiny or piracy, it could have been stopped by the navy. Closer to Germany, ESSO arranged that the *Svithoid* stay out of the Baltic, and dismissed the German crew in Norway, placing a Norwegian crew aboard.[13]

ESSO, however, lost control of twenty-five tankers to Axis powers through confiscation in Axis ports. The Allies were able to sink eleven of the ships and to capture three others, leaving eleven ESSO-owned ships serving the Axis on 1 December 1941. (See table 9 for these and other ESSO losses and gaines, 1939–41.)

An even more adventurous exercise of control by a corporation facing the dangers of war was demonstrated by "Cap" Rieber, general manager of Texaco. On the outbreak of the war, he sailed to Italy and flew from there to Germany to negotiate for the release of a German-constructed tanker interned in Hamburg. Negotiating directly with Admiral Erich Raeder, commander-in-chief of the German Navy, Rieber later claimed to have told the German admiral that the tanker never would take oil to the Allies. If it did, Raeder had Rieber's personal permission to torpedo it. The Germans allowed Rieber to take the *Skandinavia* past their blockades, as did the British. Then Rieber placed the ship in neutral trade in Latin America, under Norwegian registry.[14]

While it was a difficult position to advocate in the growing atmosphere of pro-Allied sympathy and legally maintained neutrality, American companies hoped to retain the markets that they had built up over decades, even when those markets were in the Nazi sphere. ESSO transferred its tankers for reasons that had motivated its earlier transfers, as the company sought to find the best way to preserve its properties and its markets through variations in national laws. The company history, with a quiet assertion of the power of the corporation to set its own policy, stated:

Table 9.
Inter-Flag Transfers of ESSO-Owned Ships, 1939–41

Flags	August 1939	Bought	Trans- ferred	Sold	Lost at Sea	December 1941
Neutral						
United States	71	+12	−18	−6	None	=59
Panama[a]	29	+9	+18[b], −4[c]	None	−6	=46
Other	13	+2	+1, −1	None	None	=15
Total neutral	113	+23	−4	−6	−6	=120
Allied	82	None	+4[c]	None	−13	=73
Axis[d]	24	+1	None	None	−14[e]	=11

Source: Compiled from Henrietta M. Larson, E. H. Knowlton, and C. S. Popple, *History of Standard Oil Company (New Jersey), 1927–1950*, pp. 394–95.
[a]Includes ships of Panama Shipping Company and Panama Transport Company. Panama Shipping was a joint venture of ESSO and Socony.
[b]ESSO to Panama Transport Company.
[c]Panama Transport Company to Anglo-American Oil Company, Ltd.
[d]Includes German, Italian, and Axis-controlled Dutch, Danish, Norwegian, and French lines.
[e]Includes three ships seized by Allies and chartered to Allied-controlled ESSO affiliates.

Because its affiliates had producing properties, refineries and ships in many countries in different parts of the world, Jersey [ESSO] had several product sources and shipping facilities with which to supply the Allies. Consequently, it was not so tightly restrained by American neutrality law as were some other companies. It had a special advantage in that its ships, which at the outbreak of the war constituted the world's largest tanker fleet owned by one concern, were registered in various countries.[15]

Evidence for this concern with company markets over matters of national policy can be found in the continued sales by ESSO to refineries and transshipment docks at Tenerife in the Canary Islands as late as 1941. Ostensibly, this petroleum was sold to the Spanish state monopoly, but the orders contained high percentages of naval grade fuel. British and American intelligence agents suspected that Tenerife deliveries often found their way from Spain to Germany. On 7 March 1941, Panama Transport Company's *W. H. Libby* was observed transferring cargo directly to German and Italian tankers. Sales, from ESSO fields in Rumania and Iraq, continued more openly to Italy, which remained officially neutral through early 1941.[16]

While many Americans had doubts about the legitimacy of aiding the Allies through petroleum sales under the Panamanian flag, those who would publicly endorse such actions did so because they were pro-Allied. Few public figures in 1939–40 would have cared to defend the use of Panama's flag by American companies to sell oil, even indirectly, to Hitler's forces. The company history, of course, emphasized only the pro-Allied circumvention of neutrality.

The Panama Flag in the Neutrality Debate

Immediately after the passage of the Neutrality Act as revised in November 1939, the Maritime Commission announced that it was considering the transfer to Panama of nine ships of the United States Lines. These vessels then would continue to carry passengers and cargo to Britain. Protests over this proposal focused American public attention on the issue of Panamanian registry and crystallized opinions. The several positions that emerged during this brief debate laid the basis for future controversies; the issues discussed in 1939 and the terms introduced at that time shaped arguments over flags of convenience for the next forty years. Four positions on the purpose of the intended transfer to Panama can be summarized as follows:

1. Commercial convenience to maintain business as usual
2. Strategic convenience to maintain aid to the Allies
3. Diplomatic subterfuge to avoid the strict meaning of neutrality
4. Business subterfuge in the form of "runaway ships" that avoided American labor conditions

Shipowners and representatives of the shipping industry saw the transfer in much the same light as earlier transfers for commercial purposes, designed to maintain business as usual. Robert C. Lee, an executive with Moore-McCormack Lines, noted, "We should not allow war hysteria to destroy our business sense. The only question about American ships operating is whether they can involve us in war. These ships, under the Panama flag, will not involve us. . . ." At the height of the controversy, the editors of the industry trade magazine, *Marine Journal*, commented: "The transfer is entirely legal and from every practical point of view highly desireable.. Moreover, there have been several transfers of oil tankers over which not a word of protest was heard." The editors believed opposition to the transfer was based on "a strange incapacity to arrive at realistic solutions." The editors noted that Cordell Hull "thought more of consistency than of practical considerations affecting the merchant marine and enthusiastically supported the contentions of the professional pacifist and goozlefixers that the transfer would be a subterfuge to get around the strict letter of the neutrality act." Frank Taylor, president of the American Merchant Marine Institute, also emphasized the practical and realistic business view of the matter. "We must insist," he said, "upon the free privilege of sending American products to the nations which normally are our best customers. Facing this situation in a realistic manner, as the American Atlantic Lines have done, permission has been sought to transfer the registry of old vessels to a foreign flag."[17]

When Maritime Commission members explained their own rationale for the proposed transfers, they demonstrated a slightly different line of thought. The United States, argued Emory Land, would not violate neutrality in any way by allowing the transfers. Land testified at the Senate Foreign Relations Committee: "I do not understand neutrality; I do not know anybody that does." Land's sarcasm tended to get the better of him—he clearly understood neutrality to mean that the law should keep the United States from getting into shooting conflicts with the belligerents. Speaking to a receptive audience at the Society of Naval Architects and Marine Engineers, Land commented on the relationship of neutrality to the transfers:

> It is my understanding that the (Pittman) Act was passed for two purposes, (a) to protect the American flag, (b) protect the American citizens. In any transfer of registry or in any sale of ships these purposes are accomplished and no claims can be made against the Government in any way—no United States citizens will be on such ships and the ships themselves are no longer United States flag ships.[18]

The official release of the commission on the decision reflected the idea that the use of the flag would represent a diplomatic convenience: "The proposed transfer to a foreign flag would divorce the ships involved from any and all protection afforded by the United States flag."[19]

Max Orell Truitt, a member of the commission, took a hard-headed and pragmatic view:

> I don't see any element of a dodge at all; I think it is a completely sound, bona fide situation all around. Congress unquestionably intended to keep the United States flag from going down in the brine and to keep United States seamen from losing their lives. But nowhere in the act does it say an American citizen could not operate a foreign flag vessel with a foreign crew. . . . He is not risking the United States flag or the lives of United States Citizens.[20]

The commission acted on orders from Roosevelt, whose public position at first was nearly identical with that of the commission members. In response to reporters' questions, Roosevelt said that he did not believe the nation's neutral status altered the right of its citizens to sell property to another neutral national.

Roosevelt's pragmatic and pro-Allied position on this question was fairly typical of his approach to many other issues during the following months of "phony neutrality," and it is clear from other actions that Roosevelt hoped to provide as much assistance to the Allies as he could, within the technical letter of the law. The much more prominently discussed "Destroyer for Bases" deal of 1940, first advocated by the pro-Allied Century Group and the more widely based Committee to Defend America by Aiding the Allies, reflected a similar approach. The destroyer deal was a thinly disguised form of arms sale to Britain, without the "cash" required by the Neutrality Act of 1939; in a stretching of the law, the destroyers had to be declared surplus to avoid restrictions against the sale of warships. In a lesser-known, confidential procedure, Roosevelt ordered the Maritime Commission to place technical difficulties in the way of transfer of scrappable older merchant vessels to Japan, even though scrap and old merchant ships were not legally embargoed, because Japan was not recognized as a belligerent. Since Roosevelt had chosen not to designate the China-Japanese conflict as a war, official neutrality did not apply in that situation in order that the United States could aid China without restriction. Thus, in both his public and his confidential actions, bending the law to send warships to Britain and using red tape to deny scrapped freighters to Japan, Roosevelt followed a pattern of using technical features of law to aid the Allies and to hamper the Axis powers. The device of Panamanian registry of American-owned ships clearly reflected Roosevelt's personal style of using legal loopholes to favor the Allied cause, and was only one of a number of such devices.[21]

The proposal to register American-owned vessels in Panama struck German officials as a clearly unneutral action. The American embassy in Germany summarized the German press response to the American debate, showing that Berlin viewed Cordell Hull's opposition to the plan as a voice for true neutrality. The Berlin papers called the idea to transfer ships "a plan concocted by shipping firms and other interested circles to place at the disposal of the Allies through the back door of the flag of Panama large amounts of American tonnage for the transport of their war needs from America to Europe."[22]

But in the public debate of the United States Lines transfer, Admiral Land received little vocal support. One avowedly pro-British syndicated columnist and radio commentator, Boake Carter, spoke out in favor of the idea. Since Carter was a British national, his pro-Allied position won little following in 1939. Union leaders even claimed he was in the pay of the "shipping lobby." More solid support for Land came from Senator Tom Connally of Texas and Senator Josiah W. Bailey of North Carolina, who agreed with Land's idea that the transfer was fully legal, and would avoid insults to the flag or killing of American citizens. "However," Bailey noted, "as the Great Apostle said, 'some things are lawful that are not expedient' and perhaps for the present we have a case of bad timing."[23]

Assistant Secretary of State Adolf Berle had been forewarned by Admiral Land that Panamanian registry might be considered once the neutrality law was amended. "The Maritime Commission," Berle noted in his diary, "on the whole thinks its job is to run ships through hell and high water, which is good naval tradition, but the American people won't stand for it." When Land personally explained the logic of allowing Panamanian registry for American-owned ships, Berle thought the idea a "hypocritical business." Even so, he could understand the merits of the plan. "I suppose," he mused, "if somebody wants to go into the blockade-running business under the Panamanian or Costa Rican flag, there is no great reason why they shouldn't."[24]

Roosevelt had not consulted directly with Secretary of State Hull regarding the proposal to shift the United States Lines ships. Before announcing the proposed transfer, Land telephoned Hull and informed him that Roosevelt had given prior approval to the transfer. Hull indicated he had no objection to the transfer, since it involved no questions of foreign policy. Adolf Berle first agreed with Hull, that it was an appropriate, if disreputable, legal action. But Berle still had his reservations. Hull's statement that it had nothing to do with foreign policy, Berle noted, "saved our souls; and accomplishes nothing." Berle went on, "But I have a horrible feeling that it is just the way the American people feel about this. They don't want American ships to go abroad because they might get into trouble. Nevertheless, they do want the commerce and the trade there. So a dirty subterfuge like getting behind the flag of a defenseless neutral will probably fit them."[25] Berle and others at the State Department advised Hull of their objections, and he changed his mind. Hull called Land back to explain. "It was now clear to me," he later wrote in his memoirs, "that the transfer to Panamanian registry of ships . . . was a subterfuge to escape the provisions of the Neutrality Act." Hull then issued a public statement condemning the proposed transfer as a violation of the intent of the neutrality law.[26]

Support for Hull's view came from a wide variety of sources, including the editorial pages of the *New York Times*. After explaining how the transfers would allow for trade with belligerents in American-owned ships without technical violation of the neutrality law, the *Times* commented that the plan came as a surprise because it was "being said after the debate in Congress and not before it." The editorial concluded, "While the plan may remain within the letter of the Neutrality Act, it violates the spirit of that measure."[27]

A more cynically stated kind of support for Hull's position came from the president of Kimberly-Clark Corporation, Samuel Pillsbury. He believed that such a transfer in fact would endanger the neutrality of the United States, and could lead to war.

This unneutral act of giving over some of our ships to one of our "vassal states" would make all Germans furious with the United States. . . . And to be practical, would not German subs do all they could to sink these Panamanian ships loaded to the gunwhales [sic] with contraband? I think they would, and I also think that these "inhuman" sinkings would soon infuriate the short-minded American people to the extent that we would again become involved as in 1917.[28]

The most concerted and organized protest against the proposed transfer in November 1939, came from labor unions whose members saw the plan as a means of putting American seamen on the beach. American crews already had faced increased unemployment as a result of the termination of European routes by American lines. The Panamanian-registered United States Lines ships would operate with lower-cost foreign crews. Most vocal were the spokesmen of the CIO-affiliated National Maritime Union (NMU). The union's president, Joseph Curran, telegraphed Hull:

> On behalf of 65,000 members national maritime union, I wish to protest vigorously unamerican action of United States Lines and Maritime Commission in turning American vessels over to Panamanian flag decasualizing American seamen and endangering neutrality of the United States. This action bears out my contention that Maritime Commission is agency of ship operators and is stabbing American seamen in back.[29]

Letters and telegrams came from other maritime unions to the secretary of state, the commission, and the White House, including protests from the Marine Cooks and Stewards, the Maritime Federation of the Pacific, and the National Organization of Masters, Mates and Pilots. Once the labor protest over the United States Lines transfer proposal got underway, it developed a momentum of its own, as locals and international councils passed resolutions. Unlike the strict constructionists of the State Department, however, Curran and the other labor leaders also protested the earlier transfer of ESSO tankers. The various transfers, whether involving a sale or not, seemed to labor as means of removing ships from the American labor market and American labor conditions, as well as breaches of neutrality.[30]

While the debate proceeded in the United States, no one thought to ask what Panamanian officials thought. President Arosemena said he did not "propose, for the sake of a little additional revenue, that the Panamanian flag figure as an object in prize lists of captured vessels," and that he would personally oppose such transfers. However, before Arosemena's objection could be put to the test, the State Department presented Roosevelt with a way out of the apparent internal crisis over the issue in his own administration.[31]

Adolf Berle took credit, at least in his diary, for finding the formula that broke the impasse over the United States Lines.

I cruised into the Secretary's office and there we found the whole problem of the transfers of ships to the Panamanian flag fairly boiling. I had had a brain storm and drafted out a statement which I thought settled the matter. The Act permits the transfer of these ships, but the spirit of the Act would indicate a bona fide sale to independent interests. I looked in at the White House with the suggestion that this ought to be introduced in the matter. . . .[32]

A few hours later, Roosevelt called in Berle and told him he hoped the United States Lines would withdraw its application and get to work on a bona fide sale. Berle often interpreted such observations by Roosevelt as instructions, and accordingly, the next day, Berle "got to work" on United States Lines to withdraw its application for transfer. Berle put pressure on Basil Harris, a Treasury Department official and the holder of the largest bloc of United States Lines stock.[33]

Even though United States Lines withdrew the application for transfer in a few days, the Maritime Commission used the Berle formula and allowed more than 250 ship transfers, when accompanied by a sale, over the next eighteen months, to a variety of nations, including some directly to Britain. The totals transferred by July 1941 are shown in table 10.

After Roosevelt announced on 15 November 1939 that the United States Lines application had been withdrawn, Joseph Curran pointed out to the president that the continued transfer of tankers by ESSO and other trans-

Table 10.
Transfers from the United States to Foreign Flags,
September 1939 to 1 July 1941

Flag	Number of Ships over 1,000 g.t.	Total Tonnage
Belgium[a]	9	68,776
Brazil	20	94,584
Britain	126	705,407
France	11	46,199
Greece	11	48,753
Honduras	7	20,524
Panama[b]	63	358,460
Other[c]	20	101,505
Total	267	1,443,208

Source: Maritime Commission Press Release, July 1941.
[a]United States Lines transfer, 1940.
[b]Does not include ex-Danish ships under Public Law 101.
[c]Includes Peru, Thailand, Australia, Venezuela.

fers to Panamanian registry "still expose our country to the involvement in war." The NMU urged the return of such ships to American registry.[34]

However, Hull had no objection to the continued transfers to Allied or neutral powers, if the ships also were sold. Hull recommended that even old Maritime Commission ships first be sold to private firms, which in turn would sell the ships abroad. The State Department also insisted on assurances that the ships sold were not required for the American merchant marine and would be replaced by new ships.[35]

When Land was called upon to defend such sale-and-transfer decisions to a general audience, he carefully placed emphasis upon the benefits that accrued to the United States, such as the disposal of "junk ships"; the retrieval of funds to be put into new ship construction; and the aid to the United States trade by provision of cargo space for American goods. To the shipping industry, Land emphasized the sales to Britain as strengthening American defenses by providing Britain with shipping.[36]

For John Franklin, president of United States Lines, the reversal of position at the Maritime Commission was frustrating. After agreeing to withdraw the application, Franklin complained to Berle that his line effectively was being ruined by the Neutrality Act and by the State Department interpretation of the act. In response to the "bona fide sale" idea, Franklin established a company in Norway to which he might transfer some of the ships. Although Berle and others suspected that the Norwegian outfit was a false front set up just for the purpose, the commission was willing to accept the arrangement, which, after all, resembled the Panama Transport Company arrangement for ESSO. However, the Norwegian government refused to accept the transfer, because of German pressure, and in February 1940, United States Lines turned to Belgium for the transfer. On advice from Roosevelt, Land cleared the final Belgian arrangement with congressional leaders, and the transfer-and-sale came off without much fanfare or opposition.[37]

After the heated but short-lived controversy in November 1939, Roosevelt ordered a survey of related correspondence received both in the White House and at the State Department. Of 409 pieces of correspondence received by 11 December 1939, only 5 favored transfer; the other 404 opposed it. The survey of correspondence was quite an inaccurate way of sampling public opinion, but nevertheless, a 98.7 percent opposition was impressive, no matter how unscientific the sampling method. Perhaps the sample was skewed in the direction of opposition to the transfer since few correspondents with the White House or the State Department would care to argue the cynical line that Congress passed the Neutrality Act with the intent to save American lives and at the same time expected American business to make a maximum profit out of the increased trade that Allied war orders would bring. In November 1939, many Americans wanted to believe that the neutrality law really did embody neutrality in the abstract, and was not openly pro-Allied; many sincerely opposed efforts to aid the Allies through loopholes in the law. Adolf Berle at first believed American popular self-deception over neutrality would extend to acceptance of loopholes in the law and to devious means to earn money while aiding the Allies. "As far as I can see," he noted, "the American people does not quite have the courage of its own cowardice. It is really a scheme by which you have your cake, and eat it too—have the commerce out from under the American flag, but have the commerce with your left hand. It is not inspiring." Despite Berle's initial feeling that the plan was in accord with American popular attitudes, the Panamanian registry idea was too clearly a subterfuge, as he himself thought, and too obviously a use of a loophole to win much support in 1939; few defenders of Land's position could be mustered beyond shipping spokesmen and occasional pro-Allied writers. Later, after June 1940, the advocates of the use of such loopholes, and of aiding the Allies by all legal means, would organize into lobbying and pressure groups. But in November 1939, Roosevelt could not count on any broad-based or organized public support for the proposal.[38]

The distinction in views between Hull, the *Times*, and others who believed the proposal a subterfuge on the one hand, and the commission, Roosevelt, and the other advocates of strategic convenience on the other, came down to a distinction in views about neutrality itself, and about the nature of a ship's national identity. Those who saw the use of the Panamanian flag as a subterfuge believed in a strict construction of neutrality; they viewed the Neutrality Act as a means for keeping American *actions* neutral by preventing American behavior favoring any belligerent. The pragmatists like Land and Roosevelt viewed the law as a means of keeping America's *status* neutral by preventing possible grounds for belligerent acts against the United States. The two positions were quite close in 1939, and advocates of both views could believe the "cash-and-carry" idea represented their understanding of neutrality. However, with the public consideration of the ship-transfer idea in the week after the Neutrality Act was signed, the difference in emphasis at once became very clear.

For those believing in a strict construction of neutrality, the principle of neutrality itself was primary. The United States should not engage in activities or actions that were unneutral. By this line of reasoning, the 1939 law was designed to prevent unneutral acts, and the "spirit of the law" was to avoid American actions that would assist one side more than the other. The act of aiding the Allies through registry transfers of American-owned vessels would be seen as a clear violation of the intent of the legislation. Furthermore, this view held, the transfer of registry did not mean that the ship was not American—in the words of the *New York Times*, such registry was a "mere device." In this regard, the strict constructionists would not look to the flag for a ship's national identity, but to the nationality of the ultimate owner. Once a ship was *sold* abroad, the American interests would not be seen as aiding one side or the other with the ship.[39]

For the few defenders of the proposal to shift the ships to Panama, the neutrality law was simply a regulation to prevent the United States from getting into war while the nation proceeded to do what was right, to aid the victims of aggression. This pro-Allied form of neutrality implied that the "spirit" or the "intent" of the law was not to preserve some abstract form of neutrality—which Land claimed was impossible to fathom—rather, its intent was to prevent the American flag from flying over a ship that could become the target of belligerent attack. From such a perspective, the removal of a ship from American registry and registering her under the flag of another neutral power was a perfectly proper action within the intent of the law. For the purposes of international incidents involving the flag, the ship no longer would be American. A ship's nationality, by this view, was simply a function of registry and flag, not of ownership.

As the war went on, the two arguments defending the transfer procedure, the strategic convenience argument and the business-as-usual argument, began to merge. As shipping companies rerouted vessels, arranged for intergroup transfers, and then chartered their ships to the Maritime Commission, the companies came to accept governmental control and direction of their ships, and came to view their activities as participation in aid to the Allies, and later, as participation in the war effort. The United States Lines argument, that its business would be taken over by the British in a "nascent monopoly" if an effort were not made to keep ships operating, won some support at both the Maritime Commission and the State Department. But such considerations remained a minor note compared to strategic questions of neutrality and defense. Although the companies' view of the use of the Panamanian flag had a longer history than Admiral Land's view, in that it had evolved through the 1920s and 1930s, the characteristic multinational advocacy of the use of variations in national laws for the sake of profit and corporate growth was put aside temporarily. The argument that markets and foreign holdings took priority over national policy would not emerge again until peacetime once again would allow such sentiments to appear as simply good business, rather than as potentially treasonable ideas. The strategic convenience line of thought became more respectable with Dunkirk, the fall of France, and the Battle of Britain. As American popular opinion responded to the need to aid Britain, defenders of strict neutrality changed their minds and came to tolerate a more technical or legalistic view of neutrality, to accept means of aiding the Allies, and, eventually, to a willingness to modify the neutrality law itself to allow armed U.S.-registered merchant ships to sail directly to Britain.

In 1939, the two positions supporting the practice, both the corporate view and that of the commission, accepted the well-precedented legal fiction of a ship's dual nationality, following the concept that, legally speaking, registry bestowed nationality, while ownership did not. Neither of the two kinds of opponents of the practice, the strict constructionists of neutrality and the labor union officials, accepted that fiction. They regarded the act of registry as the establishment of artificial sovereignty purchased only for the purposes of subterfuge to avoid American legislation—neutrality law or labor law, or both. As the debates over the practice continued into the postwar decades, similar distinctions in perception would persist. A body of international law interpretation would grow in defense of the concept that nationality flowed from registry, not from ownership. Yet, that view, no matter how formally defended from tradition and precedent, would not overcome the political objections of those who saw in the practice a dubious adoption of a legal fiction for the purpose of evading laws.

American Efforts to Control Panama's Flag

Over the period from November 1939 through 7 December 1941, the Maritime Commission and the State Department encountered a series of minor problems in dealing with ship registry in Panama. Both offices attempted to obtain Panama's cooperation and to bring Panama's day-to-day practices into conformity with announced and unannounced policies of the United States. At the same time, U.S. policy moved from a pattern of covert aid to more and more open cooperation with Britain. The institution of the Lend-Lease Act in the spring of 1941 demonstrated how far the United States had come from adherence to abstract neutrality. As the policy of the United States moved from formal neutrality to active pro-Allied "nonbelligerency," both the Maritime Commission and the State Department expected Panama to follow along.

The flexibilities and conveniences built into the registry system of Panama for essentially commercial reasons over the 1920s and 1930s made some aspects of cooperation easy to obtain; however, those same flexibilities and conveniences opened the possibility that the flag of Panama might be used by the Axis or the Allies as well as by the United States. The law was "liberal to the extent of being lax," complained one officer at the State Department. In a series of minor policy issues and decisions, the United States took advantage of its special relationship with Panama to pressure the system to reflect only American policy. Thus, through 1940 and early 1941, American problems with Panama's merchant flag fell into two categories: how to utilize the flag for purposes of American-defined, pro-Allied support; and how to prevent use of the flag by Japan and Germany.[40]

The United States began to cooperate with the British by helping to prevent the continued use of the Panamanian flag by Greek-owned ships carrying Jewish refugees to Palestine. By 1940, Greece made it illegal for its citizens to register vessels in Panama, and the American refusal to represent such vessels in ports where there was no Panamanian consul added further to the British campaign to terminate the flow of refugees. The United States cooperated with British policy on this count by canceling the services extended to the *Parita* and by noting without objection the British seizure and diversion of the *Darien II* to take refugees to a British-approved detention camp on the island of Mauritius, rather than to Palestine.[41]

Admiral Land sought the assistance of the State Department in securing rules and regulations governing Panamanian-registered shipping. He asked that the State Department get Panama to outline the size and dimensions of Panama flags to be painted on the sides of recently transferred ships, and to establish a rule requiring nighttime illumination of the flag. The Maritime Commission then would work to enforce the Panamanian rule aboard American-owned ships. It was hoped that Germany would respect neutral Panamanian shipping, despite its routing to the Allies. Land preferred that the ruling have the status of official Panamanian policy rather than simply a Maritime Commission regulation.[42]

More vexing were the variety of direct and indirect uses of the flag of Panama by the Axis. The tanker *Janko* went into trade with Japan, and apparently remained under the control of a Norwegian citizen, Andres Jahre, who lived in Norway under German occupation. The British Ministry of War Transport did not believe the claim that the ship was managed by a Swedish firm, even after the charter of the ship to a British oil company. The British decision on the requisition of the *Janko* as an "enemy" ship was difficult. First, the British had to demonstrate to their own satisfaction that the ship was indeed under enemy control; then, the British had to sort out the claims of two governments in exile, the Dutch and Norwegian, each of which wished to confiscate the ship and turn it over to the British. The Dutch claimed jurisdiction because, by September 1941, the vessel was immobilized in the Dutch-controlled harbor of Aruba in the Caribbean. At the State Department, officials debated whether it was necessary to keep Panama posted on the details, and decided to inform Panama only on the final decision to allow for Norwegian requisition.[43]

Other individual cases of Axis use continued to involve the State Department and the Maritime Commission in setting Panamanian policies. The continued supply through 1940 and 1941 to Spanish refineries by Panamanian-registered vessels belonging to Texaco and ESSO, and the American corporate "business-as-usual" approach angered the British, who viewed Spain as a major source of German supplies. The *Daylite*, a former U.S.-registered ship, operated under Panamanian registry in trade out of Japanese-occupied China to the Portuguese enclave of Macao. American policy makers decided that the continued trade was useful and prevailed on Panama to keep the vessel registered, despite British objections. After Pearl

Harbor, the Japanese confiscated the ship. The covert and unannounced American embargo on transfers of scrappable ships to Japan could not be put in writing, but the State Department quietly discouraged Panama from transferring any scrap ships to Japan, through placing technical difficulties in the way of the transactions. In 1941 Finnish vessels in Latin American ports were regarded by Britain as enemy ships. The admission of Finnish ships to Panamanian registry would free them from possible British confiscation, if Britain would bend its rule denying recognition to ships transferred from enemies to neutrals. Therefore, Panama carefully secured prior American agreement to indemnify owners in case of British action against the ships. The United Fruit Company, through its German subsidiary, owned the *Wessermund*, registered in Panama. Careful negotiations with Britain preceded the American approval of the vessel's transfer from Panama to Honduras; the British agreed that she would not be subject to confiscation as a former German ship. Again, the British suspected that the assets of the company might be used to aid the Axis war effort.[44]

In the cases of the Danish, Finnish, and Italian ships, Panama's cooperation with the Maritime Commission greatly helped Roosevelt's policy of aid-short-of-war to Britain. The English remained suspicious about the use of Greek ships to smuggle refugees, about vessels in trade with Japan, about the use of Panama's flag over ships to earn credits for the Axis in Latin America, and about the supply of oil to the Axis under the protection of the Panamanian flag.

The incidents of the neutrality period established several patterns in the relationship of Panama's merchant flag to the war that continued after Pearl Harbor:

–The United States Maritime Commission attempted to utilize Panama's flag as an adjunct to American shipping.

–The State Department considered and transmitted Maritime Commission requests and recommendations to Panama in the issuance of decisions and regulations.

–The Maritime Commission and the State Department established a system of prior approval over cancellation of Panamanian registry.

–British requests for particular Panamanian actions were subjected to prior approval of the State Department.

–The State Department closely watched Panamanian ships dealing with Axis powers.[45]

Through the precedents and procedures worked out in this period, Admiral Land at the commission and a group of concerned officers at the State Department, including Breckinridge Long, Sumner Welles, and Jesse Saugstad, attempted to insure that the conveniences and the open registry of the Panamanian system primarily serve American policy purposes. Disagreements or differences in policy emphasis between the British and the Americans were worked out between the two major powers, and the United States, through the American minister in Panama, then instructed Panama on the course to follow. Since the United States undertook to guarantee that shipping claims in particular cases against Panama would be paid by the United States, Panama's financial risk was reduced, while its revenues from tonnage fees climbed. Although for the most part Panama cooperated with American policy leadership on such questions, the decisions and incidents were minor and they exposed Panama to little diplomatic or military risk until the summer of 1941.

Arming Panamanian Ships and the Arias Overthrow

Acting on direct orders issued by Roosevelt on 30 April 1941, Land worked to build up cargo and tanker tonnage to Britain, utilizing both ship rerouting and transfer of ships to Panama. Roosevelt's instruction to Land was an explicit order to aid Britain, and to use ship transfer for that purpose.

> As part of the defense effort to which this country is committed I wish you at the earliest possible moment to secure the service of at least two million tons of merchant shipping which now exists . . . and make their cargo space immediately effective in accomplishing our objective of all-out aid to the Democracies. This program falls naturally into two parts. First, to arrange for the utilization in routes to the combat zone of foreign ships or ships which are to be transferred to foreign registry, and secondly to reallocate our own flag ships in such a way as to make every cargo directly or indirectly useful. . . .[46]

Admiral Land proposed to transfer some forty Danish ships in American harbors to Panama to meet the presidential request. The disposition of these Danish ships presented a problem after the German invasion and conquest of Denmark in May 1940. The British at first had threatened to take any former Danish ships as prizes, but by mid-1941, they accepted American requisition of the ships as the most practical way to get them into service. However, the ships did not meet American standards for crew quarters; a further problem to be solved was provision for the Danish seamen aboard the vessels when the ships were interned. Land's plan for transfer of the ships to Panama to be operated with the existing Danish crews ran into serious opposition at the State Department. After discussions involving the legal adviser, Green Hackworth, Assistant Secretary Long conveyed the State Department objections to Admiral Land. Long, in spite of his Princeton education and long record of diplomatic service under Wilson and Roosevelt, retained some of the "show me" skepticism of his Missouri upbringing. When Admiral Land informed Long that the president himself requested the transfers, Long suggested that Roosevelt "may not entirely have understood the situation." Long reported on his conversation:

I proceeded to say that somebody was going to be made ridiculous some day if this plan went through, for it contemplated the use of American-owned vessels with title in the American company, sailing under the Panama flag, plying the North Atlantic on routes directly to England, and being equipped with guns. . . . It was such a subterfuge and such a probable fraud that the first time one of these vessels got sunk, the whole thing was going to be aired and those responsible for it were going to be made to look ridiculous.[47]

Labor unions also were suspicious of plans to requisition foreign vessels and to transfer them, taking the position that such ships should be placed under the American flag with American crews. The NMU fought the passage of the ship requisition bill in both houses of Congress, but the bill passed as Public Law 101, on 6 June 1941.[48]

Despite the objections of both labor unions and the State Department, Land went ahead with the plan under Public Law 101. Land notified Secretary Hull that the Maritime Commission had decided to use Panamanian registry for transatlantic and belligerent-zone transport of weapons, and that the commission intended to proceed to arm the ships.[49]

Long still objected, and noted that the whole scheme was not really needed. The plan, he felt, "was simply a subterfuge to avoid the restrictions of the Neutrality Act, and an unnecessary subterfuge at that." He pointed out that the Neutrality Act applied only to privately owned vessels. Since the requisitioned ships belonged to the commission, it could operate them directly to the war zone. Long argued, "The Neutrality Act does not restrict the Government of the United States from arming its vessels nor

The SS Sessa. *She was one of some forty Danish ships taken over by the United States Maritime Commission and then transferred to Panama under orders of Admiral Emory Land. The* Sessa *was torpedoed 18 August 1941 by U boat 38, precipitating a crisis in Panamanian-U.S. relations over the arming of such vessels. (Naval Photographic Center)*

from sending them anywhere it may choose to send them, carrying whatever it may choose them to carry."[50]

While the solution of public ownership and operation might have been legal, it certainly would have struck some strict interpreters of neutrality as a violation of the intent of the law and might have raised a public outcry similar to the November 1939 controversy. Yet, Land did not object to public ownership on the grounds that it would affront neutrality; nor did he object on grounds like Hoover's earlier ideological preference for private enterprise over public ownership. Land simply found that private operation was faster, and would not require the erection of a large-scale operations branch by the Maritime Commission on short notice.

The disagreement between the Maritime Commission and the State Department continued. In Long's temporary absence from the office in August 1941, Jesse Saugstad, the department's shipping expert who had taken a direct interest in the Danish ships and their crews, ordered that the arming of the ships be held up. When told that the president "had ordered it," Saugstad said that the State Department had nothing in writing regarding such an order. Barely holding down his sarcasm, Admiral Land addressed a "Memorandum For Honorable Breckinridge Long," to meet the need for something in writing:

> Pursuant to your request for a memorandum concerning the arming of such vessels and in confirmation of my oral advice to you the following statement is made: Several weeks ago the President, in a conference in his office at which Mr. Harry L. Hopkins, Maritime Commissioner H. L. Vickery and I were present, orally authorized the armament in this country of foreign flag vessels to be operated in combat zones. . . .[51]

Land added that the attorney general had approved the plan orally, and that the navy was ready to supply weapons for eighty-three Panamanian-registered ships.

Long accepted Admiral Land's assurances that the president had approved, and the arming proceeded. Nevertheless, members of the State Department continued to worry. In September, Long, Saugstad, and Hackworth met with Maritime Commission staff members to thrash out the whole matter. Since the press already was reporting the arming of the ships, Long pointed out, "It was necessary to become an advocate of the policy with which we had not been in sympathy," and therefore, the department sought a full explanation of the motives for the transfer and arming. The commission spelled out its objections to Long's idea of direct governmental operation in the war zones without merchant vessel registration.

–Retention of title by the commission allowed for later flexibility.

–The commission did not have the organization to operate ships directly and could not set up such an organization quickly.

–Since the ships were carrying mixed commercial cargoes, they needed bills of lading and other commercial bookkeeping.
–Therefore, the most efficient method of operation was the charter of the ships to experienced, large private ship operators.
–Private ship operators would not charter nonregistered ships since they encountered higher port charges for such government vessels.
–Under existing law, Panamanian-registered merchant ships could go to England, American-registered merchant ships could not.
–Therefore, government title, registry in Panama, and charter to private firms seemed the best solution.

Such ships, if unarmed, would be sitting ducks for torpedo attacks. Thus, they should be armed and should sail in convoy when that offered protection. Furthermore, the commission indicated, the ambassador of Panama had observed that "It would not be necessary for him to be officially advised on the subject." The armaments for the ships would be loaned by the navy to the commission, which paid for their installation on the ships at private dockyards. Neither Panama nor the United States had a law prohibiting the practice of arming Panamanian vessels in the United States. Merchant crews were instructed by the Coast Guard in the use of the weapons.[52]

Despite this full report, Long stuck to his position that the system was unsatisfactory: "In the first place, it is a subterfuge to evade the restrictions of the Neutrality Act and in the second place, it is not only unsafe to entrust American-owned vessels to incompetent defenders, but lacking in frankness, if not in honesty, to hide behind the flag of a friendly neutral nation."[53]

As a solution, Long recommended an amendment to the Neutrality Act to allow armed American merchant ships to operate in the combat zones. While Long's plan would avoid the "subterfuge," Admiral Land faced the immediate and pressing problem of getting tonnage onto the convoy routes to Britain in September and October 1941, while the Neutrality Act still prevented American tonnage from entering the war zone. His practical solution, while less than ideal, did represent a legal and operable means of implementing presidential policy while Congress discussed alteration of the law.[54]

By October 1941, Land agreed with Long that the Neutrality Act should be amended, and he frankly opposed the existing law. He damned the law "in about ten well-chosen four letter words" that the *San Francisco Chronicle* "edited for the breakfast table" down to "As far as I am concerned, it was a cowardly act."[55]

Meanwhile, however, it became clear that Panama was beginning to object, on much the same grounds as those outlined by Long, and as hinted at during the November 1939 debate by the then-President Arosemena. As Panamanian vessels were torpedoed and sunk, the pressures mounted. Several sinkings in August and September helped bring matters to a head (see table 11).

Table 11.
Panamanian-Registered Ships Torpedoed, August–September 1941

Ship	Former Name	Date Sunk	Position	U-Boat
Longtaker	(Sessa)	18 Aug. 1941	6126N 3050W	U 38
Montana	(Paula)	9 Sept. 1941	6340N 3550W	U 105
T. J. Williams		20 Sept. 1941	6134N 3511W	U 552
Pink Star	(Lundby)	20 Sept. 1941	6136N 3507W	U 552
I. C. White		26 Sept. 1941	1026S 2730W	U 66

Sources: Decimal 819.857, RG 59, USNA; Paul E. R. Scarceriaux, "Merchant Ships Lost Under Panamanian Flag During World War II," *Belgian Shiplover* 149 (1974): 93.

Although at least fifteen other Panamanian-registered ships had been sunk during the war prior to August 1941, the five listed in table 11 all were engaged in transatlantic supply to Britain or Iceland. The *T.J. Williams* and the *Pink Star* were both in the ill-fated convoy SC 44 when torpedoed. Roosevelt himself mentioned the loss of the *Sessa* in his 11 September 1941 speech announcing the shoot-on-sight policy laid down in response to the submarine attack on the USS *Greer*.[56]

On October 6, President Arnulfo Arias and the Panamanian cabinet took up the question of the sinkings of these vessels. The cabinet announced that henceforth it would not allow Panamanian-registered ships to be armed. On October 7, the Panamanian foreign minister instructed the Panamanian ambassador in Washington to inform shipowners that the registry of any merchant ships that had arms installed would be canceled. Later that day, the American ambassador, Edwin Wilson, sought an explanation of this action. The foreign minister stated that Panama could protest the sinking of its ships only if they were operating outside the German-declared war zones, and if they were unarmed. While complaints had been made to Germany about the *Montana* and the *Sessa* based on the ships' locations in noncombat zones (based, it turned out, on incorrect information regarding the German-declared combat zones), no complaint would or could be made on the *Pink Star* because it was in convoy when sunk or the *I.C. White*, which had been openly placed at the orders of the British government. The foreign minister pointed out that the United States had "given the lead" to Latin American governments by forbidding American-registered merchant ships from arming or going into combat zones. When Wilson protested that the American Neutrality Act was under debate for possible revision, the Panamanian foreign minister replied that Germany might respect American naval power and fear to attack armed U.S. merchant ships but that Panama's lack of a navy exposed it to attack.[57]

On the morning of the discussion, President Arias flew to Cuba for a short holiday with his mistress. Using his absence as a legal pretext, anti-Arias cabinet members and national guard officers planned a coup. After checking with Ambassador Wilson to see if the United States would object, they announced, October 10, that Arias was deposed on the grounds that he had abandoned the presidency without assembly approval.[58]

Arias's opponents needed only a word from the American ambassador that the United States would "abstain benignly" before launching the coup d'état, and they received that assurance. Among the various benefits that immediately accrued to the United States from the coup were a generally more pro-American atmosphere, reflected in open publication of English-language sections of local newspapers in Panama, and the rescinding of an Arias-inspired currency experiment. However, of far greater importance to the American war effort at the time, was the immediate reversal, the day after the coup, of the registry cancellation policy for armed ships. So crucial was that decision, that State Department officers thought it best to delay its announcement, lest the connection with the coup become too apparent. Thus, the State Department instructed Wilson, "It is indeed gratifying to the Department to note the decision of the Panamanian cabinet to cancel the recent action of the Government prohibiting the arming of Panamanian flag vessels. The Department is in full agreement that the cancellation may well be delayed for two or three days in order to minimize so far as possible the inferences which will be drawn therefrom by unfriendly propagandists." Meanwhile, the department expected "no administrative difficulties to the sailing of armed merchant vessels of Panamanian registry." The Panamanian cabinet made the policy formal and announced it on October 20. Land continued the arming of the ships without further Panamanian objection.[59]

The complex chronology of events surrounding the Panamanian coup and the ship registry cancellation policy during October 1941 is shown below:

October 6   Cancellation of registry for armed ships announced
October 7   Clarification of cancellation order to Ambassador Wilson
October 7   Arias's flight to Cuba
October 9   Inquiry to Ambassador Wilson if United States would object to coup
October 9   Overthrow of Arias by cabinet action
October 10   Reversal of ship registry cancellation order by Panamanian cabinet
October 13   U.S. request for delay in announcement of new policy
October 16   Secretary of State Hull denies part in coup
October 20   Public announcement of reversal in ship registry cancellation[60]

While the ship registry issue was far from the only cause of tension between the United States and Arias, its resolution was the most immediate and clear benefit to the United States from the overthrow of Arias. In response to congressional and public suspicions, Cordell Hull made an extensive announcement that the United States had "no connection, direct or indirect" with the coup. While it was apparently quite true that the United States did not "engineer" the coup, it is clear that the anti-Arias forces wanted to be assured of American willingness to stand aside during the forced resignation, and they timed the coup to coincide with a particularly tense crisis in relations, a crisis that had developed over the armed merchant ship question.[61]

In the months after the replacement of Arias by Ricardo Adolfo de la Guardia, a wide range of defense and canal issues were resolved in accord with American desires and needs. While Arias was regarded by American officials as pro-Nazi and a "nuisance," his resistance to American terms regarding opening new defense sites can be seen as an early outcropping of *panamenismo*. His removal cleared the way for later smooth negotiations on the bases. Major and minor details regarding ship registry also proceeded smoothly. Before the coup, German and Italian liaison officers could walk into the Seccion de Naves and obtain lists of newly registered ships. The office stopped the practice after the coup. As early as 16 October 1941, the new Foreign Minister Octavio Fabrega sought U.S. State Department help in preparing legal briefs to assist in framing diplomatic protests over ship sinkings, and within a week, the State Department turned the task over to private attorneys in the United States. By the end of the year, forty-one Panamanian ships had received weapons.[62]

The press of events through 1940 and early 1941 produced a policy of drift in the United States with regard to many maritime issues, but the apparently haphazard decisions revealed several patterns with long-range consequences for the evolution of flags of convenience. The sailors aboard the Danish ships had gone neglected for months while the British, the Maritime Commission, and the State Department tried to work out a policy decision for the ships. When the ships finally were requisitioned and used under the Panamanian flag, it became obvious, with the sinking of the *Sessa* and the *Montana*, that the vessels would have to go armed and in convoy if they were to be adequately protected. To demand that policy of Panama while U.S. law still prohibited such practices for American-registered ships showed a degree of contempt for Panamanian sovereignty that became more cynical and open with the pressure of each event. The 1939 predictions that the sinking of Panamanian-registered, American-owned ships could become a *casus belli* along the lines of the 1917 sinkings were borne out. When Roosevelt himself brought the sinking of the *Sessa*, along with the earlier sinking of the American-registered *Robin Moor* and the submarine encounter with the USS *Greer*, into his 11 September 1941 speech announcing the shoot-on-sight policy, he chose to classify the act as a provocative

German action. But, when President Arias presumed to forestall further attacks on Panamanian ships by attempting to enforce the same standards of neutrality that at the time were applied to American-flag vessels, he was regarded as "making a nuisance of himself." That American displeasure emboldened his political enemies sufficiently for them carefully to arrange his overthrow, with American sympathy and benign disinterest.

American policy makers in both the Maritime Commission and the State Department were willing, by the fall of 1941, to find in Panama a "convenient means of bypassing inconvenient laws of the United States."[63] While Congress eventually would alter the neutrality law, there was no need to wait, since American executive policy decisions could have the effect of decree in Panama. With the removal of Arias, the last barrier to the free exercise of that procedure was removed. American maritime officials now openly acted on the belief that they purchased many of the attributes of sovereignty, including management of details of registry and ship personnel, when they paid the registry fee that entitled their ships to fly the Panamanian flag. They had converted the system of commercial convenience established before 1939 into an adjunct fleet that would operate at the direction of the State Department on policies worked out by the Maritime Commission.

6

World War II

WITH THE ALTERATION of the neutrality law in November 1941, and with the declaration of war a month later, the neutrality-evasion motives for registry in Panama evaporated, yet the patterns, plans, and arrangements initiated during the neutrality period continued. The Maritime Commission continued to use and perfect the system of ship registry and the State Department continued to oversee and resolve a series of minor diplomatic snarls that arose in connection with Panama's world-wide shipping. While Panamanian diplomatic and policy-level cooperation seemed assured after the overthrow of Arias, difficulties in the operation presented by Panamanian officials gave both the Maritime Commission members and State Department officers reason to question the basic premises of the system. Out of those discussions emerged further clarification of the rationale for Panamanian registry, and the first appearance of the concept of "controlled" vessels, which would become part of the postwar dialogue over flags of convenience.

The Adjunct Fleet in Operation

In dealing with the Allies and the Axis on specific Panamanian-registered ships, the State Department kept up its usual formality and concern for correct procedure. When the British sought to requisition the *Oilshipper*, immobilized in the harbor of Istanbul, American State Department officers carefully kept tabs on the case, which involved a pro-Axis White Russian owner, abortive plans by the Panamanian government to requisition the ship, tentative Turkish agreement to buy the ship, and the claims of Turkish attorneys for fees. This case left a complex trail of claims and counterclaims not resolved until the 1950s, when dozens of secret documents relating to the file had to be cleared in advance of their scheduled opening in order to untangle the problem. In another case of potential Axis use, the American consul in Lisbon reported that the *Omega*, a suspicious Panamanian-registered ship, appeared to be serving the Axis under a Rumanian owner; and the consul cooperated in arranging for British sei- zure. In Marseilles, the Hamburg-American Lines purchased one of the old gun-and-refugee-runners, the *Dora*, to meet the Germans' desperate ship- ping shortage. In outposts such as Iceland and India, American consuls found themselves called upon to represent Panama in the absence of Panamanian consuls on issues such as crew-officer disputes, port facilities for damaged vessels, and regular shipping papers such as port clearances, harbor fee questions, and verification of crew lists. As usual in such hastily erected arrangements, local officers muddled through with little direction from a central office concerned with larger issues.[1]

Early in 1942, Roosevelt established the War Shipping Administration (WSA) and appointed Admiral Land to head the new agency as well as to retain his chairmanship of the Maritime Commission. Most of the direct operational aspects of shipping, including construction, acquisition, trans- fer, charter, agency and operational contracts, and routing, were taken over by the WSA. Admiral Land brought to the WSA the same decisive style that he had brought to the commission and he ran the war agency with the same impatience for bureaucratic or organizational delay that characterized his earlier work.

In the day-to-day administration of the Panamanian-registered shipping, the WSA met and rapidly solved a series of policy questions. The 1936 Merchant Marine Act was amended on 6 March 1942 to allow for a system of war-risk insurance for American vessels; by WSA General Orders 8 and 9, published in the *Federal Register*, the rates and categories of vessels eligible for the insurance were extended to cover American-owned ships registered in Central and South American countries.[2]

The effect of the WSA order extending the terms of war-risk insurance to Latin American countries was less widespread than the wording of the ruling suggested. A review of Latin American laws shows that only Pana- ma, Honduras, Nicaragua, Costa Rica, and Guatemala had provisions that allowed for alien ownership of vessels. The Venezuelan law of 1944 re- quired that 50 percent of the ownership of a vessel had to be Venezuelan, but that provision could be circumvented through the establishment of foreign-owned Venezuelan corporations. Honduras, which in the 1920s and 1930s had developed a small fleet largely under the ownership of United Fruit Company and other banana companies, vied with Panama to attract the flood of shipping revenue brought by WSA policies. In 1943, Honduras recodified its laws, incorporating features of Panama's code originally written to satisfy American demands. In particular, Section V,

Article 14 of the Honduras Organic Act of the National Merchant Marine, number 55 of 2 March 1943, allowed for cancellation of registry on grounds, including smuggling, almost identical to the terms of Panama's Law 54 of 1926. Both Costa Rica and Nicaragua also passed wartime revisions of their maritime codes to facilitate alien-owned registry. Minor convenience fleets began in both Honduras and Nicaragua, while ESSO holdings in Venezuela continued. Despite the war-risk insurance system that applied to them, in growth and size none of these fleets approached the Panamanian fleet, which exceeded 250 ships in mid-1942. While war-risk insurance represented a needed improvement in the system, it was by no means the element that stimulated the growth of Panama's fleet.[3]

Other WSA improvements in the system were put in operation as problems demanded resolution. As sailors were rescued from sinking vessels or were stranded in ports awaiting new berths while their ships underwent repairs, complex questions of the national status of Danish, Norwegian, Dutch, Belgian, and Canadian crewmen began to crop up. With State Department cooperation, Land worked out and authorized by WSA General Order 41, a system of I.D. cards for Panamanian crewmen. The card served such WSA-employed sailors as a single, standardized able-bodied seaman's certificate, and at times it served in lieu of a passport. The denial of the card also provided a means of excluding troublesome or politically dangerous crewmen from WSA employment.[4]

During the early months of the war, the adjunct nature of Panamanian shipping produced some casualties. The Coast Guard issued *Notices to Mariners* regarding hazards such as wrecks and minefields, but Panamanian-registered craft were not sent the notices. The oversight was recognized after ESSO's *J.A. Mowinckle* encountered a minefield off Cape Hatteras that had been detailed fully in a prior *Notice to Mariners*. Although the ship traveled in a coastal convoy, and although the minefield should have been guarded by patrol craft, a series of errors led to severe damage to the *J.A. Mowinckle*, as well as to a tug sent to bring the tanker into Hampton Roads.[5]

The management of Panama's system from Washington became routine and was widely accepted. The fiction that Panama's flag represented a separate sovereignty proved useful; yet, the reality of American operation and decision making was essential. The WSA continued the practice of setting rules and procedures for Panama's shipping, a practice that had been established during the neutrality period. When Grace Lines officers complained that secret routing information from ships' logs leaked to the enemy through Panamanian consuls who examined the logs in foreign ports, Land asked the State Department to obtain a Panamanian executive decree discontinuing the practice of ship log inspection by consuls and requiring only inspection of certificates of registry and crew lists. Executive Decree 283, dated 25 November 1942, was duly issued. The WSA established its right to review and approve or disapprove registry cancellations prior to Panamanian action. Article 13 of Panamanian Law 8 of 1925 required that any sale of Panamanian-registered ships to a foreign power be cleared by the executive. As long as Panama agreed to subordinate that power to the WSA, it provided for U.S. control. However, if Panama had chosen not to cooperate, the law could have provided an effective barrier to American control. Faced with manpower shortages aboard British and Dutch vessels, the WSA issued an order prohibiting further employment of British or Dutch seamen aboard Panamanian ships. The WSA began to deal directly with Panamanian consular officers in Miami and New York in order to facilitate transfers to Panamanian registry, and kept the State Department posted only as to major policy questions. From the WSA point of view, the direct dealings with the consuls cut red tape.[6]

In a variety of ports, the crews of Panamanian-registered ships presented local officials with crises ranging from the tragic to the absurd. In Sierra Leone, a ship's officer shot to death a crewman who ran amok aboard the *El Mundo*. In Port Said and Antofogasta, labor disputes delayed the sailings of the *Yorba Linda* and the *Loida*. In Shanghai, the discharged crewmen of the *Oradell* were stranded with no repatriation clause in their articles of employment. In Bombay, the Norwegian master of the *Ottio* refused to hire stranded American seamen, hiring only Norwegians. In Ciudad Trujillo, the crew of the *Typhoon*, formerly the Italian-owned *Colorado*, could not muster enough sober men to stand watch; according to their hard-drinking reputation, "they would drink paint if they could get it." In Karachi, three members of a Panamanian crew crashed a fancy-dress party at the YMCA, where one of them insulted the police commissioner's wife by urinating at her feet.[7]

Over 150 Panamanian-registered ships were sunk or captured during the war, and over 1,500 crewmen were lost. The first merchant ship of any registry sunk in American waters after the declaration of war was the Naess-owned *Norness*, 60 miles off Long Island, 14 January 1942. Since security prevented contemporary publication of statistics, compilations of the losses have been gleaned from archival and published sources. One careful tally by an independent modern researcher shows 158 Panamanian-registered ships sunk or taken by the Axis, representing 736,000 gross tons. More than half of the lost ships were less than 6,000 tons and most were older vessels built before 1921. By far the most valuable group of ships lost were the relatively modern tankers of the Panama Transport Company fleet. ESSO carefully submitted well-documented reports on each of its lost tankers to cancel the registry and to establish claims to war-risk insurance payments. In this roundabout fashion, the company at long last was able to bring home a part of the profits earned in Germany, profits that had been used for German construction of such ships as the *Harry G. Seidel* and the

Heinrich V. Reidemann, without ever paying American tax on those "earnings." Of the twenty ESSO ships registered in Panama lost in World War II, eight were among the original twenty-five transferred from Danzig in 1935. Later, the company compiled a detailed pictorial account of the adventures of its tankers under a variety of registries—*Ships of the Esso Fleet in World War II*, which recounted the often heroic actions of individual officers and men as they faced the hazards of the sea in wartime.[8] See table 12 for Panama Transport Company losses in World War II.

All the complaints by merchant seamen that their war service went largely unrecognized and despised by officials and public alike applied even more cruelly to the international conglomerate of crews and officers aboard the Panamanian ships working for the WSA. Nevertheless, staff members at both the State Department and the WSA made an effort to extend such recognition. Land developed a condolence letter sent to surviving widows and mothers of lost crewmen aboard both American and Panamanian vessels. Letters to Dutch relatives were sent to the government-in-exile in London for forwarding, while letters to Norwegian crewmen were forwarded through Norwegian shipping officials in the United States. Efforts to trace individual seamen who survived sinkings and to relay details of the

Table 12.
Panamanian-Registered ESSO Tankers Sunk, World War II

Ship	Tonnage	Date Lost	Former Registry	Sunk By
James McGee	9,859	21 June 1940	U.S.	mine
Charles Pratt	8,982	21 Dec. 1940	U.S.	U 65
Joseph Seep	7,088	25 Apr. 1941	U.S.	mine
T. J. Williams	8,212	20 Sept. 1941	U.S.	U 552
I. C. White	7,052	26 Sept. 1941	U.S.	U 66
W. C. Teagle	9,552	17 Oct. 1941	U.S.	U 558
Thalia	8,329	23 Feb. 1942	Danzig	(unknown)
Esso Copenhagen	9,245	25 Feb. 1942	U.S.	*Torelli*
Esso Bolivar	10,389	8 Mar. 1942	U.S.	U 126
Hanseat	8,241	9 Mar. 1942	Danzig	U 126
Penelope	8,436	14 Mar. 1942	Danzig	U 67
Heinrich V. Reidemann	11,020	17 Apr. 1942	Danzig	U 66
Harry G. Seidel	10,354	29 Apr. 1942	Danzig	U 66
Persephone	8,426	25 May 1942	Danzig	U 593
C. O. Stillman	13,006	6 June 1942	U.S.	U 68
J. A. Mowinckle	11,147	10 June 1942	Danzig	U 576
George Jones	6,914	11 June 1942	U.S.	U 455
Beaconlight	6,926	16 July 1942	U.S.	U 160
Leda	8,546	5 Nov. 1942	Danzig	U 160
C. J. Barkdull	6,773	10 Jan. 1943	U.S.	U 511

Source: Compiled from Decimal 819.857/282, RG 59, USNA.

The ESSO Bolivar, *registered in Panama, under tow after sustaining a torpedo hit. The 10,389-ton tanker was later sunk on 8 March 1942 by U boat 126. (Naval Photographic Center)*

death or injury of others occupied WSA and State Department officials as an essential part of wartime duty.[9]

While Panamanian officials cooperated in questions of ship registry cancellation and in issuing rules and regulations written by WSA staff, the system's rapid expansion and the flood of fees and revenues presented numerous opportunities for petty profiteering, and for viewing the operation as a business, not a bureau. WSA officers, like their chief, grew impatient with delays, and treated questions of graft as minor annoyances that should be cleared up in the interest of efficiency. The Panamanian consul in Miami charged double fees for operating after 4:30 in the afternoon, while the New York office refused to do business over the Christmas and New Year weekends. The New York office would not register small vessels in the 40- to 160-ton range, since the fees were too low. WSA officers indignantly suggested that Honduras might be more cooperative than Panama and would "waive any regulations" to receive the business.[10]

State Department Questions

One issue, which at first appeared to represent simply another detail that could be resolved through State Department liaison with Panama, brought the whole question of the continued use of the flag into serious discussion between Admiral Land and the State Department. In December 1942, Land requested that the State Department see to the elimination of the two dollar fee charged each seaman by Panamanian consuls when the men signed aboard ships. No such charge was made by corresponding American officials, and the fee was onerous to unemployed seamen—indeed, it smacked of a kickback for allowing the crewman to sign up. However, when the department requested that Ambassador Wilson in Panama arrange for the elimination of the practice, he advised against pursuing the matter. Wilson pointed out that the charge was a legal one, listed in the Consular Tariffs of Panama, and that fees represented important income for many consuls. "I strongly feel," he noted, "that we should not in any way jeopardize the good will and cooperation of Panamanian consular officers by depriving them of this slight remuneration."[11]

Some staff members at the State Department, including the specialists on shipping matters within the department, were outraged by this idea. Thomas Burke of the department's Division of International Communications told Breckinridge Long:

> I cannot go along with the view that because we continue to register foreign ships under foreign registry we should put up with practices that are not fair or reasonable. That attitude, unfortunately, has seeped too deeply into the thinking of a number of people in this Government. It has resulted in an accumulation of minor abuses, which, from time to time, have led to more important ones. As a matter of fact, the exorbitance of the charge in question is clearly apparent. It is a form of graft which should be discouraged. . . . I vigorously reject the implication that this Government or its people have to put up with petty graft merely because we register our ships under the Panamanian flag.[12]

Burke's outburst against a practice that, after all, was quite legal, is better understood against the background of an internal debate within the State Department. Members of the department, including Burke, had been waiting for such an issue over which to raise with the WSA a reconsideration of the whole Panamanian registry system. Earlier, in March 1942, Paul

Department of State, 1942. Seated in conference, left to right: Cordell Hull, Sumner Welles, Breckinridge Long, G. Howland Shaw, Adolf Berle, Green Hackworth, and Dean Acheson. Hull, Welles, Long, and Berle actively opposed the transfer to Panama of vessels confiscated by the United States. (Library of Congress)

Daniels of the American Republics desk had sent Burke a series of questions regarding Panamanian registry.

"What were the major reasons for adopting this procedure?" asked Daniels. "Now that Panama and the United States are co-belligerents in the war, what reasons continue to exist to justify the practice?" Burke reported that the reasons for the practice were to avoid American rules regarding construction and manning. The wage scales aboard the Panamanian ships were lower than American scales, he pointed out. The practice also allowed supply to belligerents not possible under American neutrality law. The system continued into the war period, he said, because confiscated ships transferred to Panama either would have to be rebuilt to meet American rules for crew quarters, or the rules would have to be waived.[13]

"Is control over the movements and operations of American-owned vessels facilitated by having such vessels registered in Panama, rather than the United States?" Daniels asked. Burke did not believe so—since the WSA exercised control through several mechanisms including ownership, voluntary cooperation of operating companies, and the ship warrant system, which routed cargoes. Burke believed expediency was the only justification for continuing the practice. Daniels accepted Burke's analysis, but noted, "It still seems curious to me for our Government to pass certain laws and adopt certain rules for the welfare of seamen and the safe operation of vessels and at the same time for the same Government to dodge those laws and regulations by registering the vessels which it owns under the flag of another country."[14] However, Daniels did not believe the issue should be raised with the Maritime Commission early in 1942. The chance to open the issue finally came with the two dollar fee issue, and Cordell Hull wrote directly to Admiral Land in February 1943 to inquire whether the coming of the war had not changed the circumstances so that it would be possible to return government-owned ships to American registry.[15]

In reply, Land reviewed the decision to place the Danish vessels requisitioned in 1941 under Public Law 101 into Panamanian registry. He argued that while the neutrality considerations at the beginning of the war in Europe "may have had in a certain few cases some minor influence on our decision," it was not the primary reason. Rather, there were technical, not policy reasons:

–The foreign ships requisitioned under Public Law 101 did not meet American-registry structural requirements and would have to be reconditioned in scarce shipyard space.
–The law required that displaced alien seamen be provided for, and retention of them seemed the best course.
–Registry in Panama saved time, manpower, and shipyard facilities.

Land pointed out that the shortages of manpower and shipyard space were even more severe in 1943 than in 1941, and that transfer back to the United

States, while preferable, should be delayed until it appeared to be in American interests.[16]

The Labor Issue

While Land's explanations quieted Hull's objections, other officers at the State Department continued to question Land's logic. In September 1943, the State Department's Division of International Communications once again raised the issue. Since American manning or space could be waived, some of Land's reasons for continuing the system seemed doubtful. J. B. Foster noted that the Maritime Commission by then was putting some American seamen aboard Panamanian vessels so that more experienced foreign crewmen from Panamanian ships could be released to serve on American ships. "Some of the men in the Department," noted Foster, "believe that the reasons given [in Land's memo to Hull] for continuing these ships under foreign flags do not hold water." At a meeting between Foster and WSA officer Huntington Morse, the latter provided a more candid analysis. "He [Morse] is of the opinion," reported Foster, "that it would be dangerous from an American labor viewpoint, especially in connection with union matters, to have the proposed changes made at present."[17]

Admiral Land, the Maritime Commission, and the WSA had earned a reputation with organized labor as serving the interests of the shipping industry. Land's opposition to labor was based on different premises than the antiunion position of corporate leaders. Land objected to organized labor not in the interest of corporate profit, but because he believed organizers and strikes would interfere in efficient production and in direct control of operations. Land recommended to Roosevelt that shipyard workers be prohibited from picketing and that unions be incorporated. Then, he believed, work stoppages and efforts to organize would be dealt with in a clean fashion—as illegal activity. Roosevelt calmly replied that such measures would be likely to arouse much labor opposition and to generate more trouble than they would resolve. Land tried to keep his opposition to organized labor under restraint, but in a public speech at a meeting of investment bankers at the Waldorf-Astoria, 19 October 1942, he suggested that "organizers" who interfered with the war effort were "guilty of treason." He later explained that he meant to include in his remark not just labor organizers but also political and pressure-group organizers, such as those working for the Ku Klux Klan. Nevertheless, Land had reflected correctly his view that labor unions were a potential threat to the war effort. Joseph Curran and other labor leaders used this speech to call for Land's resignation or dismissal. Land weathered this controversy, as he had many others, with his usual aplomb.[18]

Maritime Commissioner and War Shipping Administrator Admiral Emory Land, 1943. A tough-minded advocate of the merchant marine as an arm of defense, Land angered State Department officers and labor leaders by registering in Panama American-controlled vessels which did not meet U.S. standards. (Maritime Administration)

Although some members of the Maritime Commission were concerned over the high degree of Communist party recruiting through maritime unions and in particular, in the NMU locals and the radio operators' union, Land objected to labor unions because he viewed the efforts of the Maritime Commission and the WSA as essentially military operations with military functions. From that point of view, even labor organizations with conservative political leanings could represent only potential difficulty. Yet, by the early 1940s, Land had to operate against the background of considerable union recognition, organization, and legal and political achievement. New Deal labor legislation, including the National Labor Relations Act, which affirmed the right to collective bargaining, and the Maritime Labor Board, set up in 1940 specifically to guarantee bargaining rights for dockyard workers, longshoremen, and merchant seamen, were part of the improved labor climate. The Maritime War Emergency Board, set up on 19 December 1941, represented an effort to secure binding agreements among ship-owners, unions, the Maritime Commission, and later the WSA, on such matters as war-risk pay rates and war-risk insurance. To simplify potential labor grievances, the WSA extended the Maritime War Emergency Board's decisions as binding to Panamanian ships. Partly through such binding agreements, major maritime strikes and outbursts largely were avoided.[19]

The encouragement and support of legislation had strengthened unions; and the NMU, despite internal factional crises, some radical leaders, and perennial purges, was a strong political force that could not be ignored. The smaller AFL-related Seafarers' International Union (SIU) also grew in influence. When Huntington Morse of the Maritime Commission indicated that labor troubles would ensue if the Panamanian-registered former Danish ships were returned to American registry, he was probably correct. If the manning requirement had been waived to allow entire crews of foreign seamen to work, labor leaders would have been incensed at such overriding of a labor gain for American seamen that went back to the La Follette Seamen's Act of 1915. On the other hand, if the foreign crews had been dismissed, and American seamen had been employed, Public Law 101 regarding the provision for displaced alien seamen would have to be met in some other fashion, and American seamen would have had to live in quarters that did not even meet the 1915 standards. The waiving of those standards also would have been greeted with an outburst of labor dissent. The proposal suggested by the State Department, to return Panamanian ships to U.S. registry and to face the consequences of widespread waiving of American maritime labor standards, while eminently reasonable on the surface, would have thrown one more explosive element into the tense labor peace maintained under Land's administration. Given Land's disposition to avoid labor delays and his already-established reputation for opposition to labor activity, the avoidance of the issue by leaving the ships registered in Panama may well have been the wisest expedient.

For the reasons just described, one rarely spoken but important motive for Panamanian registry of American ships during World War II was similar to the motives openly discussed by W. L. Comyn for the transfer of the *Isonomia* and the *Ida* in 1922: the avoidance of American labor conditions. However, there was a major difference between the reasoning of Admiral-Orient Lines in 1922 and Admiral Land in 1942. Whereas the private companies had sought to maximize profits and to reduce costs in meeting foreign competition, the War Shipping Administration sought to maximize productivity and efficiency and to reduce delays. Yet, for American labor, the consequence was the same—the departure of ships from the American labor market. During the war years, the opposition of organized labor to "runaway ships" registered in Panama continued to simmer, to surface again, in reinvigorated form, in the immediate postwar years.

Much of the debate over registry in Panama between the State Department and the War Shipping Administration proceeded quietly, out of view of the public. Yet, the opinions enunciated in 1939 continued and were refined. Admiral Land argued that vessels in Panama were available and under control, and that strategy and expediency dictated that they remain there. The State Department continued to suspect subterfuge and dodge. Organized labor believed, with some reason, that a primary reason for the registry in Panama was escape from American labor's wages and conditions.

The WSA exercised control over Panamanian ships directly, working with Panama through the State Department only on questions such as consular relationships, requests for new Panamanian legislation, and dealings with third countries. But, operational control over ships proceeded without State Department, or even Panamanian, aid, through WSA charters directly from companies owning Panamanian-registered ships, or through agency agreements under which companies operated government-owned vessels registered in Panama. The mechanisms and extent of these operations, and the working system of control during the war, are detailed in chapter 11, which examines the development of the postwar "effective control" doctrine.

Yet the political positions, which had emerged over the efforts to evade neutrality and over the abortive efforts to secure cooperation from the Arias administration through State Department negotiations, persisted. Skeptics in the State Department, along with organized labor, viewed the system of Panamanian registry as a fraud. Admiral Land and the WSA believed the system offered practical solutions to specific shipping problems. For the corporations either operating their own vessels or serving as agents, the experiences with Panamanian registry provided a combination of positive features such as low operating costs, along with negative considerations such as bureaucratic control from Washington and a forced tolerance for sometimes extortionate Panamanian consular fees. Corporate officers looked forward to the restoration of peace and business as usual, when the negative features of the system somehow might be reduced.

7

The Origins of Liberia's Maritime Code, 1947–49

IN THE POSTWAR YEARS, several factors of international shipping competition encouraged larger-scale growth of the Panamanian merchant fleet. The European tonnage that had been destroyed during the war had to be replaced in order to build up the carrying capacity to meet peacetime needs. As European maritime powers rebuilt their fleets, several, including Britain and Norway, provided aid to ships of their own registries through programs of tax relief and subsidy. Further aid came in the generous sale of American war-built Liberty ships under the 1946 Ship Sales Act (60 Stat. 41), through which 1,113 ships were sold to foreign flags. American ship operators, who had dominated petroleum and cargo-carrying trades with Maritime Commission vessels during the war, naturally hoped to keep a strong position in the peacetime trade. With the rebirth and rebuilding of European shipping, however, American ship operators faced again the problem of international competition: how to maintain a dominant position in the market while paying American taxes and American labor rates. The operating subsidies of the 1936 Merchant Marine Act did not apply to tankers, whether owned by the oil companies as proprietary vessels, or operated by independent owners in the charter market, but only to passenger and cargo ships operating on established and scheduled lines and routes.

The war had exposed hundreds of business and government leaders to the system of business convenience under Panamanian registry, which had been tried out on a small scale in the 1930s. In the period from 1946 to 1948 that alternative appealed widely as American tanker owners utilized the flag to build a competitive position in the market. Since taxes would be paid only if and when subsidiary companies in Panama declared dividends to parent firms in the United States, earnings could be plowed back for years. This arrangement allowed for quick repayment of borrowed mortgage money; consequently, Panamanian-registered ships had an excellent position in the money market as they competed for loans. A Maritime Commission ruling restricting the sale of T-2 tankers only to American firms or those with American control was intended to aid this lucrative business. As tankers increased in size and cost, it became more crucial to have the ability to repay borrowed construction money quickly.[1] Of the ships sold under the 1946 act, 152 were registered in Panama; they were mainly American-owned tankers. Panama's total fleet increased from 268 ships in 1945 to 406 in 1946. By mid-1948, the fleet had grown to 515, with a total tonnage of about 3 million tons.[2]

Panama—Crises and Issues

As the fleet grew, it faced new crises. Opposition to the use of Panama's flag developed on two fronts: in American labor organizations, and among European shipowners, who immediately recognized the growing Panamanian tanker fleet as dangerous competition. By 1947, the labor protests became organized and focused on altering the Maritime Commission policy of freely accepting transfer applications for vessels sold under the act. The Maritime Trades Department of the American Federation of Labor complained directly to President Truman about the Panamanian fleet on several counts: the fleet had grown to twice its prewar size; Panama was not a "seafaring nation" and did not need the tonnage; the transfers were for purposes of saving taxes, hiring cheaper foreign crews, and avoiding inspection; the system put American seamen out of work. The union demanded that the commission plug the loopholes in the Ship Sales Act, loopholes that allowed "foreign or American speculators to grow fat at the American taxpayer's expense" and that depleted the American merchant marine. The union threatened to take steps "to close up all fink shipping halls which are used for shipping seamen to Panamanian vessels" and to boycott and picket Panamanian-flag vessels in American ports.[3]

Joseph Curran of the NMU also complained directly to Truman. He noted of the hundreds of transfers to Panama, "In most cases these transfers were made to dummy corporations. Actually the ships were controlled by American interests, with the profits from this cheaper operation accruing to these interests." Curran noted that Scandinavian seamen's unions had prohibited their members from manning Panamanian-registered ships, and that the boycott was expected to extend to other European unions. Erling Naess, one of the pioneers of the Panamanian registry system in the 1930s, began a new Norwegian-owned Panamanian line with the *Nortun* and encountered the union opposition of which Curran spoke. Naess argued with Norwegian labor leaders that not all Panamanian operators were bad, although he admitted that some maintained substandard ships. Norwegian labor did not accept his argument for a selective boycott against only irresponsible owners.[4]

Philip Murray, president of the CIO, wrote to President Truman complaining that the Panamanian flag had contributed to the loss of 16,000 maritime jobs in the period from 1945 to 1947. Much of the loss was due to European shipping growth, he admitted, but some came from the "runaway ships" in the fleets of Panama and Honduras, ships whose profits did not provide taxes to assist European reconstruction.[5]

Some of Truman's advisers warned of similar problems. In a report for the President's Scientific Research Board (a group of advisers attached to the Executive Office), Irving Ladimer spelled out the mounting arguments against allowing ship sales with transfers to Panama. Opposition and concern grew, he noted, among the Bureau of Internal Revenue, the Treasury Department, and congressional committees, as well as in the maritime unions. He pointed out that transfers would increase to meet competition, and that Panamanian subsidiaries would be beyond the legal control of the government. "Fly-by-night" operators would enter the trades, he feared, and profits would accumulate and go untaxed. Further, Greek companies buying American surplus ships and registering them in Panama avoided Greek taxes, placing more of a burden on the United States for aid to Greece. Ladimer recommended removing the tax relief to American corporations with vessels registered in Panama, limiting sales of ships only to maritime nations, limiting foreign sales of ships to bring shipping tonnages up only to prewar levels, and establishing a wage subsidy that would apply to tankers.[6]

Despite these criticisms and suggested reforms, the Maritime Commission held that its task was to dispose of the surplus fleet. As long as the ships were not needed in the American merchant marine, the potential revenue from foreign sales should be realized. Threatened with coming "block obsolescence" of the World War II fleet in the period from 1950 to 1960, the commission hoped to recover as much money as possible from the sales while the market held up. Foreign sales, including Panamanian sales, were an essential part of the ship disposal plan.

Labor opposition continued in Europe, as the International Transport Workers Federation (ITF) held meetings through 1948 and 1949 to consider boycotts against the Panamanian fleet. The ITF was a loose organization of some 300 unions in 46 countries, claiming four million members in teamster, maritime, railroad, longshore, fishing, and aviation unions. The diverse representatives of this international group had few issues on which they could find common ground; the hiring of nonunion and exploitable workers aboard Panamanian-registered ships, a practice that would undermine international standards, was one such issue. At three meetings, in July 1948 at Oslo, in November 1948 at Geneva, and in February 1949 at

London, the ITF cautiously took several actions against the Panamanian system. The group condemned the transfers both to Panama and to Honduras as "evasion of taxes, currency regulations and safety, social and labor standards," and established a committee to consider plans for a world-wide boycott of these ships of "spurious registry."[7]

The ITF agreed to suspend action on the boycott until the International Labor Organization (ILO) issued a planned report on Panama's shipping. The ILO was an agency founded under the League of Nations and inherited by the United Nations, consisting of governmental, labor, and business representatives from member nations. The ILO was not dominated by labor union members, but it took on the issue of Panama's merchant system because European shipping interests and governmental leaders also opposed the growth of Panama's registry. Representatives of those groups at the ILO agreed with the union representatives that the issue posed a threat to international labor standards and to the recovery of European shipping. The more conservative members of the group hoped that the study and report might bring about reform and forestall the possibility of widespread boycotting. Business and governmental leaders were not eager to see such an international example of effective direct action by labor groups. Although plans for the international boycott were stalled as the ITF awaited the ILO report, not issued until 1950, sporadic local boycotts and picketing were attempted against Panamanian ships in the United States and Europe.[8]

The Marine Fireman's Union organized one of the first boycott actions in Portland, Oregon, against the *Don Anselmo*, in April 1949. In response to the Portland action, the Panamanian embassy in Washington delivered a diplomatic protest to the State Department, calling the boycott and picketing "unfriendly acts" with the "purpose of depriving the Republic of Panama of its sovereign right to register ships." The Panamanian position was that the picketing was illegal under United States law, since it was not based on union representation of the seamen aboard the ship. The protest recalled the close links between Panama and the United States, in an attempt to suggest moral reasons for American support of Panama's shipping system, and reminded the United States of "the great amount of war material which was transported in Panamanian ships during the Second World War and which contributed in no small measure to the final victory of democracy over totalitarianism."[9]

Another threat to the advantages of Panamanian registry developed as Panama's politics entered a period of erratic change, and as the country showed signs of social instability and growing anti-American feeling. In December 1947, Panama City experienced a week of rioting, led by students who clashed with the National Guard. Stirred by anger over a proposed treaty extending for thirty years American control of bases occupied during the war, the protest took on a generally anti-American tone. The Panamanian Assembly rejected the treaty, and early in 1948, the United States evacuated bases it had occupied since 1940 and 1941.[10]

In 1948, the presidential elections in Panama created further turmoil. Arnulfo Arias ran for the presidency and claimed a victory, which Jose Remon, leader of the National Guard, refused to accept, placing both Arnulfo and Harmodio Arias in jail. The stability was short-lived; when Remon's preferred candidate, seventy-three-year-old Domingo Diaz, died in office in August 1949, Vice President Daniel Chanis attempted a showdown with Remon, a showdown that led to his own resignation and the elevation of Roberto Chiari to the presidency. When Chiari also refused to cooperate with Remon, the National Guard leader deposed him and placed Arnulfo Arias in power. Within a week, in November 1949, Panama had had three presidents. The outcome of all the changes was the return to power of Arias, who had a pro-fascist reputation, a high degree of popular support, and who had opposed Admiral Land's plan to arm merchant ships in 1941. While the State Department was willing to accept and deal with Arias, American shipowners were understandably concerned that the system might be no longer politically reliable or stable.[11]

A further difficulty with Panamanian registry, from the point of view of shipowners, was the continued system of consular fees. Where consular revenues were insufficient to maintain a self-defined decent style of life, consuls found reason to charge fees for every service rendered, including inspection of ship logs, approval of crew lists, overtime or weekend work, and signing crew members aboard vessels. While most such charges were fully legal, the opportunities for increasing revenue through defalcation and through unreported extra charges were as tempting in 1948 as they had been in 1919 in Vancouver, in 1928 in Bilbao, and in 1942 in Miami. The extensive consular system maintained by Panama around the world could not have been financed by the small country without the ship registry system. What shipowners saw as graft or corruption could be viewed as a revenue system for maintenance of the world-wide system of consuls, some of whom were political exiles, and some of whom regarded the positions as valuable patronage.

The conveniences of the Panamanian ship registry system for the hundreds of new shipowners in the period from 1946 to 1949 thus were marred by several considerations. Labor opposition led to scattered boycotts and serious threats of further action. Opposition by the established maritime states of Europe resulted in an unholy alliance of business, labor, and governmental agencies and led to a United Nations-sponsored investigation of Panamanian shipping through the ILO. The instability of the Panamanian government led to justifiable fears of anti-American excesses, possibly a Panamanian attempt to nationalize or confiscate shipping. The continued reliance of consuls on the system for revenue represented a burden of annoyances and delays that seemed a high price to pay for "convenience." Shipowners wanted an alternate flag.

Stettinius and Liberia

American owners in the oil tanker charter business searched for new means of maintaining competition with European fleets. Dissatisfied with Panama's conditions, they found an opportunity to develop a new merchant flag as a by-product of the plans of Edward R. Stettinius, Jr. for a system of privately directed economic aid to Liberia. Using private capital and public influence derived through his extensive contacts as a former corporation director and former secretary of state, in 1947 he organized Stettinius Associates—Liberia, Incorporated. His ambitious plans soon outreached available capital, but the Liberian ship registration system that he developed at that time rapidly grew far beyond its original scope. That system is the most important institutional survivor of the Stettinius corporate activities of the period, and eventually it brought Liberia to rank as the world's largest maritime power in total registered merchant tonnage.[12]

There were few members of Roosevelt's wartime cabinet who better typified enlightened corporate background and idealistic commitment than Stettinius. In 1926, he had headed welfare activities at General Motors, and by 1931, he took charge of the company's labor and public relations. In 1934, he moved to United States Steel, and by 1938, became chairman of the board of that corporation. Roosevelt recruited Stettinius into his administration, appointed him chairman of the War Resources Board in 1939, and in 1941, placed him in charge of the Lend-Lease program. In 1943, Cordell Hull brought Stettinius into the State Department as under secretary. In November 1944, Roosevelt appointed the handsome, prematurely white-haired, forty-four-year-old Stettinius as secretary of state. Stettinius earned a reputation for bringing in talented subordinates, for efficient administration, and for effective conduct of international meetings. Some observers, notably Senator Arthur Vandenberg, and later President Truman, thought Stettinius not sufficiently grounded in policy making or politics for the sensitive position, and he resigned shortly after Truman took office in 1945. Historian Walter Johnson demonstrated the longstanding basis of Stettinius's humanitarian concerns, pointing to his college career at the University of Virginia, where he neglected his studies to do charity and Sunday school work, and considered entering the ministry. As early as 1937, he had written that business should "be conducted with more statesmanlike emphasis on the welfare of all involved—employees, stockholders, consumers, and the public. . . ."[13]

As secretary of state, Stettinius led the American delegation to the Yalta conference, early in 1945. On his return, he made a brief ceremonial stopover in Liberia to officiate at the opening of the port of Monrovia, built with United States Navy assistance. While there, Stettinius noted the contrast between poverty and rich resources in the small country. As a former United States Steel executive, he was particularly attracted by newly discovered high-grade iron deposits.

Like Panama, Liberia had a special relationship with the United States. Founded in 1822 by black American settlers financed by the American Colonization Society, Liberia had grown from a string of isolated colonies of liberated American slaves and freemen into a self-governing common-wealth by 1839. In 1847, the commonwealth declared its independence and became the first republic in Africa. The 12,000 black settlers from the United States developed a stable government that, through careful di-plomacy, on the whole successfully withstood British and French efforts to annex its territory to their surrounding colonies. The descendants of the settlers were slow to admit the indigenous African population to equal citizenship, and government remained in the hands of a limited number of interrelated families. The country went into increasing debt to European bankers by the First World War. Liberian finances received a boost from a loan arranged by Firestone Company in 1926, to repay the foreign debt in exchange for rubber plantation concessions. Yet, the republic remained poor and underdeveloped through the 1940s.[14]

During the years of World War II, American officials took a renewed interest in the historic relationship between the United States and Liberia, which long had been emphasized by Liberian leaders as a buffer against European territorial encroachment, but which American policy makers largely had ignored for a century. Fears that West Africa would provide a "jumping off place" for an Axis invasion of the Western Hemisphere through Brazil, gave strategic reasons for this revived concern with Liberia. The United States built an airport, a seaplane base, as well as the breakwa-ter harbor dedicated by Stettinius, all as war measures. (See Map 2.)

Liberia had a number of striking parallels with Panama. Like Panama, Liberia had a small maritime tradition, but possessed no modern merchant fleet of its own. Both countries were tropical states of about one million population, each governed by a small, factionalized oligarchy with a long tradition of rule. In both cases, modern American concern was stimulated by considerations of global strategy and the geographic location of the nation. Like Panama, Liberia originally had been formed with American assistance; yet, both in fact had their own heritage of jealously defended independence, and each was fiercely proud of its sovereignty and national heritage in ways that Americans usually failed to recognize.[15]

As the first modern republic in Africa, Liberia had attracted the support and interest of black nationalists in the United States, precisely because its successful self-government provided a black-run alternative to white Amer-ican control, and because for a generation the republic, along with

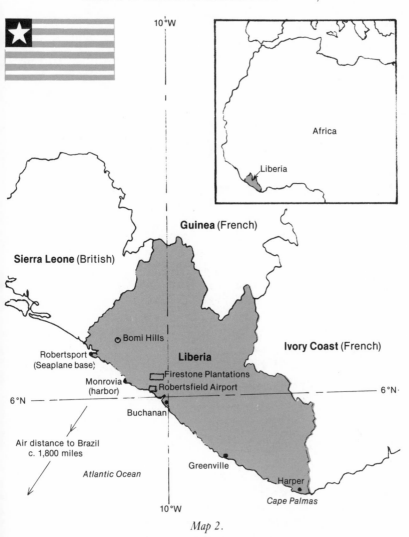

Map 2.

Ethiopia, represented the only self-ruled regimes in Africa. Nineteenth-century pan-African nationalists like Edward Blyden regarded Liberia as a model and base for anticolonialism. But Liberians, like Panamanians, knew that assistance from the United States was contingent upon treating American officials with expected deference.[16]

Careful manipulation of conflicting pressures long had been the hallmark of successful Liberian leadership. American interests and prejudices, European designs on the territory, indigenous pressure for more representation and participation, factionalism within the ruling elite—all these factors had been juggled with more or less success for a century.

The plans of Stettinius for private assistance would be welcomed—
Liberia's history of formation through private philanthropic enterprise and
its fiscal rescue by Firestone set ample precedents for such assistance.
Furthermore, President W.V.S. Tubman, elected in 1944 on an "Open
Door" platform, had promised to recruit foreign investment. While a
descendant of settlers, Tubman challenged the control of the country by
one faction of the elite and worked to build his own popular following,
political machine, and patronage clique. His opponents within the Liberian
elite hoped to unseat him in 1948. Tubman could benefit politically from
the promised investment, which would represent a notable administrative
achievement for him as he faced the upcoming elections for a second term.
Therefore, the development plans announced by Stettinius were supported
warmly by President Tubman.[17]

In 1947, Stettinius established his corporation to implement plans for
Liberian development. Stettinius Associates, starting with $1 million in
capital, of which he personally supplied $200,000, formed a profit-sharing
arrangement with the Liberian government. A subsidiary, Liberia Company, was to conduct actual operations in Liberia. Sixty-five percent of any
profits earned by Liberia Company were to be returned to the parent
corporation, with 25 percent to go directly to the Liberian government and
10 percent to be turned over to Liberia Foundation, a nonprofit organization devoted to Liberian educational, health, and welfare programs.
Stettinius hoped that if the plan succeeded, similar subsidiaries could be
established in Ethiopia, the Netherlands East Indies, Morocco, and French
West Africa.[18]

Liberia Company provided funding for exploration and start-up of further subsidiaries. Stettinius authorized studies of possible enterprises such
as diamond mines, cocoa and coffee plantations, fisheries and timber operations, as well as the eventual major export, iron ore. He ordered plans for a
highway network, electrification of Monrovia, water and sewage systems,
and construction of railroads. Such long-range plans attracted little outside
capital. Liberia Company participated in the management of the already-
established port of Monrovia in a seven-company consortium. Stettinius
Associates also helped reorganize the airport, originally built with United
States assistance, and set up Liberian International Airways with aid from
Pan-American Airways. During the war, American pilots had discovered
the iron deposits in the Bomi Hills, deposits that were so rich they deflected
compass needles in overflying aircraft. Wrangling over the iron exploitation
concessions delayed development of this resource until well after Stettinius's activities began. An independent iron concession finally succeeded in
obtaining a capital commitment from Republic Steel in 1949, through an
organization entirely separate from the Stettinius group of companies.[19]

Stettinius recruited a public relations firm to promote his Liberian
enterprises. As a result, from September 1947 through late 1948, over 500

news stories and 10 major magazine articles glowingly described his plans. The publicity emphasized the planned "three-way split" of profits, and the explicit concern with welfare. Several of the articles suggested parallels with the operations of the Rockefeller companies in Venezuela and of Aramco in Arabia. Observers noted that the "progressive capitalism" of Stettinius seemed a response to the ideas of Eric A. Johnston who, as head of the American Chamber of Commerce, urged American business to take such a course.[20]

Stettinius personally promoted what he conceived of as a new style of capitalist operation, informed with a social conscience, in nonprofit terms:

> When visiting Liberia during the war . . . I observed the great contrast between profuse, undeveloped natural resources on the one hand, and the needs of the people and the country on the other hand for improved living standards, health and education. . . . I believed that this condition could be remedied by applying American initiative.[21]

This statement in a press release reflected neither the profit consideration nor the military and strategic considerations brought out for other, more specialized audiences.

In a report to Liberia Company executives, Stettinius hinted at the profit possibilities that could spring from humanitarian concerns:

> There is no reason why a billion and a half people out of the two billion on earth should be suffering for want of food, clothing, or shelter. The Germans, Italians, British, and French can't do anything about this so it is a moral obligation for us to do something to help. . . . I asked . . . if Liberia would not be a good proving ground for this theory. We talked about Bomi Hills—everything mushroomed on that tiny little formula.[22]

Stettinius's interest in efficient organization of production meshed nicely with the new-found iron deposits at Bomi Hills.

In a brief for U.S. government aid to the Liberian effort, the organization stressed the inspiration of Roosevelt's New Deal programs behind the social aspects of the company plans, and then went on to summarize policy considerations such as "raw material interests" and the "strategic position of Liberia from the standpoint of U.S. protection of Panama Canal and Brazil." Stettinius referred to Liberia as America's "sole beachhead in Africa." He noted that if his company failed, "Communism, already at work in Africa, would rejoice."[23]

Writing the Law

It was in this context of American high resolve and Liberian eagerness for concrete, demonstrable results, that the plans for maritime registration developed. Late in 1947, shipowners asked Stettinius if Liberia had a system of ship registry and he replied that he did not know, but would look into it for them. In January 1948, E. Stanley Klein, an attorney for the corporation, reported "certain shipping interests had indicated a willingness to obtain registration under the Liberian flag." Thereafter, the idea of maritime registration remained on the agenda of Stettinius Associates. The work of developing a report and a draft of the proposed laws fell on Klein and James G. Mackey, secretary-treasurer of Stettinius Associates.[24]

Both Mackey and Klein also participated in another company, American Overseas Tanker Corporation (AOTC), established in September 1947. General Julius Holmes and Admiral William Halsey, both participants in Stettinius Associates, were also part owners of AOTC. This shipping company, with investments from Stettinius and other members of Stettinius Associates, borrowed funds and purchased eight surplus tankers from the U.S. government. Three of the tankers were sold immediately in a Chinese nationalist-financed corporation at a profit of $150,000 per vessel. The other five tankers were kept by AOTC, financed on a loan from Metropolitan Life Insurance Company, and operated with assistance from William Westerlund, president of Marine Transport Lines. The tankers were transferred to Greenwich Marine, an AOTC subsidiary established in Panama. The tankers then were chartered by this Panamanian subsidiary of AOTC to ESSO. The large profits of AOTC, collected in 1951 when the operating company was sold to Stavros Niarchos (although in the name of his American-citizen daughter), led to later congressional investigations, which revealed the complex arrangements, and to charges that the sales violated the Maritime Commission prohibition on the sale of tankers to foreign interests. In 1949, however, there was no public knowledge of the AOTC operation. From late 1947 through 1949, Stettinius and key aides who were actively involved in writing the Liberian Maritime Code were themselves quiet owners, through the entirely separate AOTC, of oil tankers registered in Panama.[25]

Several members of Stettinius Associates had served as State Department or wartime administration officials, and their contacts proved useful to the company as they developed the Liberian maritime law and other proposals. Joseph C. Grew, former ambassador to Japan, had been under secretary of state under Stettinius, and General Holmes had been appointed by Stettinius as assistant secretary. Both resigned the department in August 1945, after Stettinius's departure from State Department office. The president of Stettinius Associates, Blackwell Smith, had served in the Foreign Economic Administration during World War II.[26]

While some of the former colleagues from government service lent only their names, others were quite active. Grew provided considerable help with further contacts. In March 1948, he held what amounted to a sub-cabinet meeting at his home in Washington, D. C., a meeting attended by the secretaries of the army and the air force, the under secretary of the navy, an assistant secretary of state, and Brigadier General Edwin L. Siebert, deputy director of the newly formed Central Intelligence Agency (CIA). At this meeting, Stettinius, Grew, and Holmes explained the purposes and strategic importance of their operations in Liberia. They made clear that Liberia Company would be able to provide the CIA with information and reports, and that America's strategic interests in Africa would be well-served by the corporation. This explicit effort to enlist the support of top-level military and diplomatic officers came quite naturally to Stettinius While the meeting was private and its record was maintained on a confide. tial basis, it appears nothing illegal or improper was suggested. As will be seen, the effort to win support and endorsement of the military and the State Department did not entirely succeed.[27]

Between April and July 1948, the Stettinius group drafted the laws that would implement proposals to set up a corporation code for Liberia, and to form a service corporation through which foreign corporations could be established. While these plans moved along quickly, the maritime code took a month longer to prepare.[28]

Edward R. Stettinius, Jr., former secretary of state, established the Liberian maritime registry system as part of his plans for private development of Liberia. Known as a personable and effective administrator, Stettinius pushed American shipowners and oil companies to approve the system, then lobbied it through the Liberian legislature in the last two years of his life, 1948–49. (Library of Congress)

During this period, Stettinius viewed Liberian ship registration as a possible minor adjunct to his other Liberian enterprises. He noted that gasoline could be sold at a profit in Liberia for twenty-four cents a gallon, but that it cost sixty-five cents due to a cartel worked out by Shell, Sacony-Vacuum, and Texaco. "We must consider," he remarked, "the possibility of Venezuela oil brought in by tankers, under the Liberian flag to break the cartel and bring the prices down." Under such a plan, Stettinius Associates would directly set up Liberian-registered shipping for Liberian benefit. He envisioned a variety of other ways to utilize the maritime law. In August 1948, he looked into the possibility of transporting iron ore, calculating that one million tons of ore moved from Monrovia to Baltimore could be brought at a rate under three dollars per ton if the company used "liberty ships manned by officer personnel of some foreign nations such as Dutch, Scotch, etc., with the balance of the crew native Liberian boys, who would receive in the neighborhood of a dollar a day." Stettinius clearly understood the economic advantages of registration along Panamanian lines. Among other plans briefly suggested in this period was a proposal to set up a whaling operation under financing from Aristotle Onassis, using the Liberian flag. Onassis, the inveterate self-promoter, later incorrectly claimed credit for suggesting the whole Liberian merchant flag system to Stettinius.[29]

Members of Stettinius Associates began to line up registration business of other shipping lines even before drafting the legislation. Blackwell Smith remarked, "All of us should be asked to list ideas that we have picked up relative to possibilities of registration of fleets." Delta Shipping, Gulf Oil, the Ludwig interests, and the Onassis fleets all were approached.[30]

While the law was being drafted, Mackey, Klein, and Blackwell Smith spoke frankly of their ship registration enterprise as designed to lure shipping away from Panamanian registry. Shippers, they found, were "fed up to the backteeth with Panamanian demands." They saw the Republic of Panama's ship registry system as a profitable business whose trade could be acquired quietly by superior quality service, and accordingly, they maintained a degree of commercial security against the competition. Mackey investigated the steps that would be required to release a ship from Panamanian registry, requesting the information through his personal part ownership of the AOTC subsidiary in Panama, Greenwich Marine. Sidney de la Rue, a former State Department officer on the staff of Stettinius Associates, made quiet inquiries to determine the length of the Panamanian legislative session, out of concern with the timing of potential responses from that quarter. He carefully routed his inquiry through a bank to conceal the source of the question.[31]

By mid-1948, President Tubman of Liberia, as well as the officers of Stettinius Associates, grew anxious to get ship registration underway.

Tubman wanted visible results in the form of revenue and action to justify his arrangements with Stettinius. The corporation, for its part, wanted to show some revenue, in order to attract new investment, for salaries and travel expenses of the staff rapidly consumed the original funding. With both sides eager to get the law in operation, Mackey and Klein worked with considerable haste, simply copying comparable elements of the United States code, and quickly printing the resulting patchwork to be sent to Liberia.[32]

In reply to Liberia's complaints of inaction, Blackwell Smith promised revenue from the marine registration system within the year. By 21 July 1948, the Maritime Code of Liberia had been drafted, but a further delay was required. Mackey hesitated to send the draft to Liberia until it had been read, amended, and approved by officials of ESSO, including the maritime attorney, Robert P. Nash, and the director of maritime operations and member of the board, Bushrod B. Howard, who had presided over the Danzig-Panama transfer in 1935. Internally, members of the Stettinius organization saw nothing unusual or unreasonable about an American corporation participating in the drafting of legislation for the Liberian government to enact, legislation that later would affect the operations of that corporation directly.[33]

The delay on the Maritime Code in the early days of August can be attributed explicitly to the necessity of clearing it with major oil shippers. Stettinius himself, despite his crowded calendar, personally arranged to send galley proofs of the code to Howard of ESSO and to William Wester-lund, president of Marine Transport Lines. Stettinius noted, "Mr. Wester-lund is most anxious, as we are, to have Standard Oil committed as far as possible before passage of the legislation." The corporation group in Liberia working on passage of the laws grew impatient and cabled headquarters, asking for fifty copies of each piece of draft law, one for each legislator. In reply, Mackey sent copies of the Corporation Code, the charter for the International Trust Company, and a charter for the "Liberian Merchant Marine Company," but the Maritime Code itself was still in the hands of Nash and Westerlund. Final approval came on 12 August 1948, when Mackey noted, "Bob Nash and Bush Howard of Standard Oil yesterday gave me a 'green light' on the Maritime Code. This previously had been approved by Bill Westerlund and his associates, all of whom had page proofs."[34]

Mackey pointed out that ESSO officials felt particularly pleased because they expected ESSO to participate in the ownership of the ship registration company that would conduct Liberia's actual registry operations. Thus, ESSO officials counted on benefits from their own ship registry fees, as a proportion of them would represent revenue for the company, an arrange-ment reminiscent, in its outline, of the original Rockefeller rebate systems of the 1880s and 1890s. Mackey was pleased that ESSO officers seemed eager "to come over under the Liberian flag and avoid the Panama situation."[35]

As the Liberian legislature examined the codes and moved to enact them, Stettinius, Blackwell Smith, and other officers of the corporation followed the legislative moves carefully. De la Rue suggested to Smith, as a political tactic, that the loss of revenue from delays in passage of the Maritime Code could be mentioned to get some movement in Liberia. Smith complied, urgently claiming that the "opportunity that we have could pass in any 24 hours while we delay the authorization."[36]

The Liberian president and legislature changed the Maritime Code slightly, placing direct authority in the office of the secretary of the treasury, rather than the secretary of commerce, as the company-written draft had indicated. More significantly, the Liberian maritime commissioner, reporting to the secretary of the treasury, was to issue rules and regulations directly, without required consultation with the proposed Stettinius-organized contracting company, as the first draft indicated. Aside from these changes, the legislative-approved draft kept almost perfect fidelity to the original, even to the amounts of fees and fines. The Liberian legislature accepted the slightly rewritten code in November 1948, and Tubman signed it into law on 16 December 1948.[37]

Because the code was properly enacted, it had the same status, from an international point of view, as other national laws governing ship registry and flag use. The details of the code's authorship, as spelled out here, never were made public. Liberia's official position on the origin of the code has been that the country consulted with and drew on the experience of "the world's foremost admiralty law experts" to develop a modern law. Had it been known that those experts were members of the ship-owning group in the Stettinius organization and the ship management at ESSO, all involved in highly profitable tanker operations under Panama's flag, doubt might have been cast on their objectivity and independence. Nevertheless, the law, even though drafted in New York and Washington in the summer of 1948, was in fact, by December 1948, the Liberian Maritime Code.[38]

State Department Reaction

In contrast to the solicitude on the part of Stettinius and his executives in consulting with ESSO and Marine Transport Lines, the corporation did not provide the State Department with copies of the law for pre-editing or prior approval. Stettinius and other members of the corporation went through the motions of keeping the State Department posted on their activities, and expected that preliminary endorsement of their ideas in principle by high officials would be sufficient. However, opposition did develop at the State Department, at first taking the form of denial of rumors that state had "endorsed" the Stettinius ideas in detail. During the war State Department opposition to the Panamanian system had been based on the views of Berle, Long, and Hull that the system was a sort of subterfuge; such views persisted among State Department staff members long after the departure of that group of leadership. Middle-level policy makers and staff members at the State Department eventually decided that the drafts of the Liberian laws, especially the internationally significant Maritime Code, at least should be subject to a State Department-directed review. The corporation refused to wait, and urged the Liberian government to pass and implement the law without such prior review. The dispute grew heated as former State Department officers such as Stettinius, Holmes, and de la Rue impatiently tried to deal with current staff members in the department who, from their perspective, resented the assumption that Stettinius's private corporation was implementing what purported to be official policy, without going through channels. Little of the controversy surfaced at the time, but the intense struggle over State Department input into Liberian law eventually produced a full review of the Liberian Maritime Code early in 1949.

State Department staff members stiffly reminded de la Rue and Holmes that general discussions between Holmes and Assistant Secretary of State Norman Armour did not constitute clearance in the "technical sense used at the Department." To claim, in Liberia, that the code had approval of the State Department and that the Corporation Code had been cleared by the Federal Reserve Board, were severe, almost fraudulent, distortions. But, de la Rue said, he did not want to "clear every piece of legislation with the State Department before we discussed it with the Liberian Government." To do so would require time to get the "okay of at least four separate Offices and eleven of their dependent divisions." De la Rue did grudgingly supply the State Department with two copies of the ESSO-approved draft of the Maritime Code. The State Department, in advice to the chargé d'affaires in Monrovia, expressed concern over the "possibility that Libgovt may arrive at far-reaching decisions and agreements without taking time and care meticulously to examine proposals in all their aspects. . . ."[39]

The department hoped to study the proposals and send a report to Liberia, before the bills were to be introduced to the Liberian legislature. As it turned out, however, the American bureaucracy moved even more slowly than the fabled West African pace of the Liberian government. Although materials were referred by de la Rue to the State Department on 29 September 1948, the investigation was not initiated until January, and the report finally was issued and sent to Liberia in March 1949, three months after Liberia enacted the code. During this period, Secretary of State George Marshall was replaced by Dean Acheson, and the transition may have contributed to delays. The presence in the corporation of former State Department colleagues of Acheson, who had served as assistant secretary of state during Stettinius's tenure as secretary, may help explain a softening of State Department hostility toward the proposals before the final issuance of the report. While there is little evidence to indicate that Acheson thought highly of Stettinius himself, the influence of other former associates, such as Grew, may have had some impact. At least twice, Grew asked Acheson for help in improving the attitude of middle-level people at the State Department toward the corporation.[40]

The State Department was in a very awkward position regarding the Stettinius operation. Since so many members of the Stettinius group were former Roosevelt administration members, the corporation readily gave the impression that it had a quasi-official character. Furthermore, even though the department had to deny that the corporation acted in any official capacity, it could not deny that the overall plans did, in fact, conform to the direction of American foreign policy. Ambivalence over the organization's policies came through in instructions to the chargé d'affaires in Monrovia. While Liberia Company had received "no special approval and backing," the instructions pointed out, the State Department was interested in view of "its policy to encourage economic development of underdeveloped countries through private American capital." As a denial of endorsement, the statement left a very mixed impression.[41]

Middle-level policy makers at the State Department felt hesitant about their own role in attempting to edit legislation for Liberia, commenting, "This government is not in a position to tell another sovereign government what it should or should not do." On the other hand, it was felt that the department should "have the privilege of adequately reviewing the various schemes proposed by the company for the purpose of determining whether the proposals are good or bad for Liberia."[42]

No such Hamlet-like wavering affected the officers of the corporation as they not only wrote the legislation, but also suggested political tactics to spur its passage, and made suggestions to Tubman on dealing with American State Department interference. De la Rue suggested that Tubman ask the State Department to avoid a "political backfire" in Liberia by having the State Department review conducted entirely in the United States and issued to him as a confidential report. Tubman complied, and the review was kept quiet.[43]

The corporation officers anxiously sought to find out exactly who would be recruited to prepare the State Department review and report. Stettinius was relieved to learn the committee was to be headed by Francis Adams Truslow. A descendant of the presidential Adams family, Truslow had been elected March 1947 as president of the New York Curb Exchange, and

previously had served in World War II as president of the government's
Rubber Development Corporation. He personally was committed to ideas
of commercial expansion similar to those of Stettinius, having stated in
1947, "We must finance increased productivity in the rest of the world or
we cannot continue the trend in our export trade which we have enjoyed for
the last fifty years."[44]

As Truslow began his work, he uncovered a number of anomalies in the
Maritime Code, as passed by the Liberian legislature. Truslow called in de
la Rue early in the work to get an explanation of crucial elements that never
had been clarified properly. In particular, the aspect so much admired by
the officers of ESSO, the fact that the registration company would collect
the initial registration fee and the annual tonnage tax, was not properly
worked into the code.[45]

Truslow kept the corporation informed of his criticisms through de la
Rue, providing a chance for improvements to be worked out informally
before the final issuance of the report. Truslow advised de la Rue that a
bureau, with a commissioner and a number of deputy commissioners who
might be officers of the International Trust Company, would represent a
better arrangement than a subsidiary corporation acting as a contracting
agency. This change appears to have been relayed by the corporation
directly to Liberia, and implemented during contract negotiations. Truslow did not include it in his final report, but it was adopted through
maritime regulation, and later, by legislative amendment to the code. The
nature of this and other recommendations considered by Truslow suggest
that his liaison with de la Rue was a two-way process; some of the changes
he recommended were those already under discussion, as clarifications and
improvements, by company officials themselves.[46]

As Truslow worked on the Maritime Code, he came to the conclusion
that it had been drawn up hastily and that it reflected ignorance of both
maritime law and the international business of ship operation. Some of the
provisions seemed designed to apply only to American ships operating
under American law, reflecting the procedure of lifting some particular
passages verbatim from the United States 1936 Merchant Marine Act. The
Liberian code, as printed, also contained dozens of typographical errors,
some quite serious. He found the most important defect in the law, in his
opinion, to be the lack of provision for making or registering ship mortgages. He also warned that labor opposition to Panama's flag might indicate
that Liberia would encounter similar troubles. However, he never took the
stand that the idea of ship registration by Liberia was an improper or
inadvisable one.[47]

The American minister in Liberia grew impatient for the Truslow
report, which he hoped would be critical of the Stettinius operation, and he

requested it early in February. Secretary of State Dean Acheson replied personally, and asked the embassy to notify Tubman that the report was in preparation and would be forthcoming shortly.[48]

Truslow proved to be more of a diplomat then either the State Department officials or the corporation officers, since, by a combination of reasonable suggestions, gently phrased threats, and biting criticisms, he won the support of both groups for some of the ideas in his report. He threatened to submit the report without corporation support, indicating that the operation of the code might be greatly delayed in such a case. When he filed the report, he submitted to the State Department an extensive cover letter, which included explicit comments on the corporation's haste, confusion of purpose, and amateurish legal work. The cover letter, however, did not go to Tubman. The report, itself, simply spelled out suggested amendments to the codes and the rationale for each suggestion.[49]

Among other critiques in his covering letter, Truslow sardonically noted, "Perhaps the group was a little ashamed of the idea that it might be seeking profits." Truslow made very clear that he viewed profit-making as perfectly legitimate, and that he felt a profit orientation would benefit both Liberia and the corporation, if held to with diligence.[50]

The Truslow report recommended four substantive changes in the original company-drafted 1948 Maritime Code; in addition, the report suggested dozens of minor changes of wording and correction of typographical errors. Truslow proposed that instead of the vague term *documented* the term *registered* be used, and that the documentation of ships be clarified by reference to "certificates of registry." This clarification was not incorporated in amendments or modifications of the law through 1949. Truslow further recommended that the International Trust Company be given a contract to administer the registration of ships, and that the statute spell out that the company was not to be given power to issue rules and regulations. By the time of the formal issuance of his report, these changes already had been implemented through marine regulations issued by the commissioner in Liberia clarifying the relationship between the International Trust Company and the commissioner. Thus, no legislative action was required on this second suggestion. A provision to strengthen the Maritime Code to allow for liability protection for passengers was not accepted by the Liberians, perhaps as a further effort to keep costs under the Liberian flag at a minimum. The only substantive suggestion made by Truslow that clearly was accepted provided for registration and recording of ship mortgages, an essential addition in order to attract the new ships in the burgeoning tanker market. This amendment passed the Liberian legislature in December 1949, along with many minor typographical and wording changes pointed out by Truslow. The State Department's insistence on a full review thus ultimately had a quite minor impact on the law, primarily making it more serviceable, and giving official sanction to improvements suggested by the company. In a general republication of the laws of Liberia in 1956, the Maritime Code was edited again and republished, following the language of the 1949 editions and incorporating early marine regulations.[51]

Ship Registry as a Business

While the Truslow report was in preparation, in the period from 5 January through 28 February 1949, the corporation appointed George Schaeffer, a vice president of Chase National Bank who had worked in Panama for years, to set up offices in Liberia, incorporate the International Trust Company in Liberia, and obtain a contract between that company and the Liberian government to operate the ship registry system under the code. The contract worked out by Schaeffer provided that the company would deduct $.325 of every $1.20 per ton new registry fee collected as a fair and legal service charge for acting as a "quasi-official agent" of the Liberian government; the company would be exempt from any Liberian taxation because of that status. As Schaeffer worked on these details, he came to recognize that the ship registration enterprise promised to be the "one visible source of important income" for the whole Stettinius operation.[52]

Liberia's ship registry system, as designed by Mackey and Klein, improved upon by Truslow, and written in contract form by Schaeffer, represented a clear departure from the Panamanian system in several important respects, while it retained the features that attracted shipping to Panama's flag in the 1940s:

–The transfers and registry would be handled by the International Trust Company office in New York, rather than by a consular network.

–The system would be administered largely by International Trust Company employees, and not by the patronage-appointee nationals of the flag state.

–The system would be frankly funded by the 27 percent ($.325 of each $1.20) retention of fees, eliminating the necessity for irregular fee collection.

–The code was written carefully, by American corporate officers, to conform to American needs.

–Since the company-drafted code duly was passed by the Liberian legislature, it would have the status, in international law, of other national flag laws.

–No provision for Liberian inspection or control of ships, nor any requirement for Liberian seamen, was incorporated.

–Liberian registry would benefit from the same exemption from taxation and labor restriction found in Panama; in the tax-free environment, ship mortgages could be repaid on accelerated schedules out of earnings.

–Liberian-registered vessels could be owned by any citizen or corporate entity of any state in the world; Liberian incorporation was not required.

–Minor advantages could be found in the fact that all laws and transactions would be written in English; Liberia's currency was the American dollar.

Stettinius faced severe economic problems with his Liberian enterprises through late 1948 and early 1949, and he took several reorganization steps. To guarantee that the International Trust Company and its shipping operation would survive intact, in December 1948 he planned the establishment of a small proxy committee to run that operation. This most profitable of all the enterprises was not to be a subsidiary of the Liberia Company, which split its profits with the Liberian government under the "three-way" plan, but was to be separate corporation, with the tonnage fee-splitting arrangement to guarantee revenues to both the company and the Liberian government.[53]

Significantly for the future operation of the maritime registration business, Stettinius carefully provided for F. T. Lininger, who had served as his personal aide. Stettinius instructed Klein, "It is very important to me that Fred Lininger be dealt with in the Trust Company in a very fair and generous way. . . . Will you, as one of your Christmas deeds for me, say to the right person at the right time that we have made a commitment to Fred that he is to have a 'good' place in the Trust Company setup."[54] That commitment was honored, for Lininger was placed in charge of the International Trust Company, at first in the role of vice president, nominally under William Dennis, secretary of treasury in Liberia, who served as president. After reorganization and restructuring, Lininger served as deputy commissioner for maritime affairs for Liberia, as well as a senior vice president of the International Bank of Washington, which eventually took over ownership of International Trust Company. In the early transition months, Lininger diplomatically deferred what he called "important policy questions" to others in the organization, but he remained the senior manager of the operation.[55]

While Lininger acquired and held a place in the International Trust Company, which he administered for more than thirty years, Blackwell Smith and de la Rue, reputedly profligate spenders, were removed from active roles in the parent company, Stettinius Associates, as part of the economy drive. New financing of that operation was provided by Stettinius's brother-in-law, Juan Trippe, president of Pan-American Airways. The number of participating investors was kept below seventy in order that the corporation not be required to register with the Securities and Exchange Commission as a public corporation subject to reporting and regulation. The name Stettinius Associates—Liberia, Incorporated was replaced, and the newly financed organization emerged as Liberia Development Corporation. Stettinius informed Tubman personally that the removal of his own name from the organization implied no abandonment of the original goals. Liberia Development Corporation continued as a separate entity from the ship registry enterprise, International Trust Company, and the two organizations henceforth were completely independent of each other.[56]

To assist in financing, in 1949 Stettinius and Grew attempted to raise funds for the Liberia Development Corporation from the Export-Import Bank. They personally visited President Truman in February 1949, soliciting his help in influencing the bank. In another effort, they attempted to link the goals of the organization to Truman's point four program directing aid to Europe, but such aid came slowly, and when it did come, it by-passed the corporation. Thus the original aspiration of the corporation, to direct all phases of Liberian economic development, never was achieved. Stettinius's death in 1949 removed the elements of personal charm, vigor, and the reservoir of friendly contacts that Stettinius had brought to the operation.[57]

As the International Trust Company recruited ship registry business in its first years, it ran on a shoestring, drawing on reserves rather than showing a net gain, but earnings climbed with new registries. In 1954, the company was purchased by the International Bank of Washington, which, in turn, was purchased in 1956 by a corporate group headed by retired army General George Olmsted. Despite these changes in ownership, the operations continued to be run efficiently by Lininger.[58]

Although several companies, including Gulf Oil, the Farrell Lines, Delta Shipping, and the Ludwig-owned National Bulk Carriers, had expressed interest in Liberian registration in 1948, the first ship officially registered in 1949 under the new Liberian Maritime Code was the *World Peace*, a tanker owned by Stavros Niarchos and under charter to Gulf Oil. By the end of 1949, five ships had registered, and in 1950, the total climbed to twenty-two. Registration steadily increased; by 1955, Liberia surpassed Panama in tonnage, and in 1956, in number of ships registered. See table 13 for the comparative positions of the two fleets throughout this period.[59]

The Liberian Maritime Code was designed and put into effect with the assistance of several individuals and groups with considerable experience and knowledge of Panama's ship registry system. Schaeffer had headed Chase National Bank's Caribbean branch in Panama, and had been familiar with ship mortgages and with the working of that system since early in the 1920s. Allen Dulles, who worked with the group, was a partner in Sullivan and Cromwell, which still represented Panama and handled its fiscal affairs in the United States. Westerlund, consulted frequently in the planning stages, was a partner with Stettinius, Holmes, Klein, Mackey, and Admiral Halsey in American Overseas Tanker Corporation, which registered its

Table 13.
Merchant Flag Registries, Panama and Liberia, 1948–58

	Panama		Liberia	
Year	Number of Ships	Gross Tons	Number of Ships	Gross Tons
1948	515	2,716,468	2[a]	772
1949	535	3,016,227	5	47,314
1950	573	3,361,339	22	245,457
1951	607	3,609,395	69	595,198
1952	606	3,740,451	105	897,898
1953	593	3,906,901	158	1,434,085
1954	595	4,091,013	245	2,381,066
1955	555	3,922,529	436	3,996,904
1956	556	3,925,751	582	5,589,378
1957	580	4,129,029	743	7,466,490
1958	602	4,357,800	975	10,078,778

Source: Lloyd's of London, *Lloyd's Register of Shipping—Statistical Summaries*, 1948–58.
[a]These two ships were registered not under the Maritime Code, but by special arrangement in 1947.

vessels in Panama through Greenwich Marine. As president of Marine Transport Lines, Westerlund had handled transfers to Panama in the 1940s. Nash and Howard of ESSO had worked closely on the Panama Transport Company fleet registered there, and Howard personally had arranged a fifteen-year charter of the five AOTC tankers by ESSO.

Both Honduras and Costa Rica had attempted to compete with Panama through the 1940s, for the war and postwar use of convenient flags, but neither resorted to the development of a commercial enterprise to take over and run the system along business lines. Honduras had increased its fleet from 27 ships in 1939 to 82 in 1949, but the core of the registry remained United Fruit Company vessels. Costa Rica's fleet grew rapidly after 1949 to 123 ships by 1956, but the excessive registry of small vessels under that flag by arms and drug smugglers and the difficulty of collecting fees led the Costa Rican government to initiate reforms in 1958, reforms that resulted in the elimination of the entire system by 1962. Neither flag succeeded in competing with Panama, and neither attracted tankers, the mainstay of Liberia's growth.[60]

The Liberian flag registry enterprise, which did successfully compete and eventually surpass Panama's system, was unique in its origins. Frankly designed to meet the needs of American shipowners, the Liberian Maritime Code took the best ideas of the Panamanian arrangement, and avoided its worst aspects by substituting a well-run business organization for the unreliable consular network. Despite the disagreements between the State Department and the Stettinius organization over details and over claims of official endorsement, the careful base-touching in proper bureaucratic style proved very useful. Key individuals in the army, navy, State Department, CIA, in ESSO, and in the shipping community had been involved in the planning stages. Through crucial personal contacts available to Stettinius because of his spectacular careers in business and government service, large shipowners were ready to transfer their ships and to place newly built vessels under the Liberian flag. While never officially endorsed by the State Department, the creation of the code under the leadership of a former secretary of state, and its low-key review by a respected business leader under contract to the department, gave the organization and the Liberian registry system a degree of legitimization for American shipowners never achieved by Panama, which by the late 1940s had earned a reputation for corruption and instability. But, no sooner had the Liberian flag begun to attract registry, than it, along with Panama's flag, became the target of widespread, and now better-organized, attacks from labor organizations and from shipowners in traditional maritime states.

8

Investigations

IN THE DECADE OF THE 1950S, several international and national agencies launched major investigations into flags of convenience. Mounting pressure from European shipowners and the international labor movement for some action against Panama's system resulted in an official investigation by the International Labor Organization. In the United States, criticisms from American-flag ship operators and labor brought pressure on Congress, which, through several committees, conducted investigations into the motives, methods, and economic details of the flags of convenience.

The functions of these investigations, on both the international and the domestic American level, went beyond the simple gathering of information, statistics, and details of conditions. Opponents and critics of the system hoped to utilize the method of investigation as a weapon of attack, exposing what they perceived as deceptions and evasion of law. Panama responded to the international investigation with a range of diplomatic gestures and at least suggestions of reform. In the United States, corporate shipowners, particularly ESSO, Gulf Oil, and Mobil Oil, sent spokesmen to the committees in efforts to explain the economic benefits of the foreign registry. Those representatives tried to construe business benefits as necessary to American commercial survival in the competitive world of international commerce. Yet, many congressmen remained unconvinced and some expressed a skepticism that reflected the tone that Berle and Long had employed in 1939 and 1941.

Labor union officials, for their part, also employed rhetoric, exaggeration, argument, semantic devices, and statistical information in an effort to win Congress to their viewpoint. Despite the repeated gathering of data, the investigations launched by Congress did not result in legislation that would meet labor's basic demand for a prohibition on the transfer of ships to

Panama and Liberia. Instead, the investigations served as platforms for the expression of conflicting ideas about the system.

The survival of the two systems of flags of convenience in the face of such concerted attacks reflected both the utility of the systems themselves and the changed political atmosphere of the postwar decades. As the war-built fleet was sold, transferred, and dispersed from the United States, flags of convenience did, in fact, provide an opportunity for American-owned maritime enterprise under very favorable business conditions. After the First World War, American ownership of vessels had declined in the face of British, Japanese, and other subsidized and lower-cost operations. But, in the post-World War II period, a growing acceptance of multinational operations and the tactical uses of the Panamanian flag during the war had set precedents and contributed to a climate of opinion in business groups and in the government that made pragmatic justifications of the system acceptable.

While some journalists and congressmen continued to view the issue as a moral one, and saw the system as a deception, a dodge, and a subterfuge, the advocates of the flags found growing acceptance for their view that the issue was one of power and economics, not of ethics. Holding that American enterprise needed to expand abroad in order to provide markets and to preserve the American way of life, men like Stettinius and his circle of associates had followed the thinking of Eric Johnston of the Chamber of Commerce and Henry Luce, publisher of the Time-Life group of magazines. In 1941, Luce had written an editorial for *Life* magazine, "The American Century," in which he argued that in order to preserve the freedom of America and to avoid the oppression that he believed would be the consequence of a planned society, Americans would need to continue business and economic expansion abroad, to find markets and to protect the American system by building in the rest of the world a community of like-minded nations. To develop markets abroad would require the export of aid, know-how, and development skills, so that other nations would develop a taste for, and acceptance of, American products. Thus, the twentieth century would become the "American century." In a quiet way, Luce's essay had expressed and influenced the ideas of the generation of business leaders who worked in the government throughout the war years.[1]

In light of the widespread and sometimes unconscious acceptance of the principles of this American century ideology, the business and strategic justifications for flags of convenience met with increasingly wide positive reception. Use of the flags readily could be defended in terms that coincided with the assumptions of that viewpoint: American survival depended upon expanded U.S. participation in world commerce and expanded aid to less developed parts of the world. The systems would allow continued American presence in the world shipping market. If the procedure benefited some traditionally dependent underdeveloped states long associated with the United States, so much the better. Stettinius's system, with its humanitarian overtones, and the even less efficient Panamanian flag system, seemed appropriate mechanisms to implement the American century.[2]

Labor tried, rather unsuccessfully, to challenge that line of argument, while accepting the same ideology. It suggested that American-crewed vessels were of more strategic value than foreign-crewed vessels, and argued that the commercial benefits accruing to the companies operating under the foreign flags did not help the American economy. Furthermore, the unions argued, the owners did not aid but instead exploited Panama and Liberia and the foreign crews. Thus, the "American way of life," the union representatives contended, was injured, not sustained by the "PanLibHon" flags of convenience.

Panama, Liberia, and Honduras, with three distinct sets of ship registry laws, were similar in some respects. All three were underdeveloped, all three were dominated by existing American enterprises, and all had backgrounds of dependence on America. It was, perhaps, natural that all three should have been lumped together in the employment of the term *Pan-LibHon*, which emerged in the mid-1950s to describe the fleets of Panama, Liberia, and Honduras. The use of this term, apparently at first intended by journalists as a sort of shorthand code convenient for headlines, became a useful device for both critics and defenders of the systems. Since the term did not convey information but instead obscured it by implying that the three registries were fundamentally the same and by glossing over significant differences among the three systems, its use helped weaken criticism of the features of any one system. The term ignored the considerable efforts that had been expended to insure that Liberian law would be an American-directed improvement over specific flaws that shipowners perceived in the Panamanian system. Furthermore, the Honduran registry system was strikingly different from the other two. While the initial registry fee in Honduras was fifty cents per ton, only half the Panamanian fee, Honduras attracted little tonnage, since in fact the system was not really very convenient for most shipowners. Because Honduras expected actual manning of its ships by Hondurans, organized in a government-recognized union, and also required ownership to be vested in a Honduran corporation, the system had drawn only a scattering of owners besides the United Fruit Company, which had considerable interests in Honduras. But critics also found the term useful, since it suggested that the flaws or corruption of one registry could be found in all three. In the interest of having a "convenient" term, supporters and opponents alike used the expression *PanLibHon* throughout the 1950s, often ignoring the confusions it created.[3]

In contrast to earlier decades, in the 1950s information about flags of convenience was widespread, and many details of the system became exposed to public debate. But even so, as the international press and the United States Congress carried on discussions and investigations into the systems, and as law journals and economic newsletters published literally reams of material, there remained serious gaps in the presentations. In particular, few people understood or had access to information about the manner in which the Panamanian system had evolved during World War II, and the story of the origins of the Liberian maritime law remained largely unexplored in serious literature until the present work. The confusing mass of conflicting claims and the overwhelming pages of testimony created an information glut so formidable that few observers found their way through the verbiage to produce coherent or digested versions of the issues. The literature contained too much information about inconsequential contemporary detail and too little accurate explanation of crucial historical developments and institutional evolution.

Panama Reacts to International Pressure

Shipping companies and Panamanian officials made unsuccessful efforts to enlist the support of the State Department under both George Marshall and Dean Acheson through the late 1940s, in dealing with the pending actions by the ITF and in responding to the mounting complaints of labor groups in the United States. The National Federation of American Shipping sent a full report to the State Department in 1947, explaining the economic grounds for using both the Panamanian and Honduran flags at that time. Arguing that American shipowners had both the right and the duty to transfer their ships to the most profitable registry, the report argued that, "In any case, the shipping industry should not be singled out and barred from foreign investment. It is difficult as it is for our industry to meet foreign competition without accepting additional handicaps. Whenever it is economically or politically essential to invest in foreign flag operations we must exercise our right to do so." The attraction, the report pointed out, was quite different for American and for European shipowners. For Europeans, it was not a question of lowered costs: "Bedeviled by threats of nationalization, voyage licensing, currency controls, and a large number of other restrictions, Panama appears to them as a haven of refuge."[4]

The State Department's overseas representation of American shipowners registered under the Panamanian flag presented complex and distressing cases to the consular service. Dealing with a particularly offensive American owner who did not provide minimal facilities or food to crew or passengers, Consul J. W. Henry complained from East Africa. One of his problems, he noted, was that "few people, if any, understood that Panama is not a part of the United States." The confusion over the status of Panama, often regarded as an outlying territory of the United States, long had contributed to its attraction and its international success as the first flag of convenience. In Alexandria, Consul Raymond Buell protested, as had his predecessor, Russell, before the war. To back up his complaints to the department, he enclosed a news item from the local British newspaper in Egypt, a report that accused the growing number of Panamanian ships of flying "false colours." Buell remarked that American consular services to such ships required an increasing amount of time. Those services, he commented with a sense of offended rectitude, "do not appear to benefit the American Government, but they may well give the impression that the practice of registering vessels of foreign ownership under the Panamanian flag has the approval of our Government, regardless of the nature of the trade in which such vessels may be engaged."[5]

Panamanian requests for diplomatic policy support from the State Department were rejected firmly through the late 1940s. In a 1949 circular letter to all American diplomatic and consular officers throughout Latin America, Acheson made it clear that there was to be no official support for Panama's system, and that the union-shipowner dispute over Panama should be treated as any other interest group conflict. "It is the view of the United States Government that the possible boycott of Panamanian ships, which has been threatened from time to time by the ITF, is a problem that can be solved only by the unions and the owners involved. . . ."[6]

Panama's diplomats reacted to this position with a degree of pique. Miguel Amado, Panamanian representative to the Scandinavian countries, had the difficult task of dealing with the ILO, and sought United States assistance. He carefully explained that the opposition to the Panamanian flag derived not just from union pressures, but that the London and Geneva offices of the ILO represented governments as well, and that the British and Norwegian governments, acting in the interests of European shipowners, had used the ILO as a tool to bring pressure against the Panamanian system. Amado attempted to enlist American support against this European encroachment on Western Hemisphere rights, at the same time promising that the Panamanian government would look into genuine labor grievances. His appeal to Monroe Doctrine principles had no impact on the State Department's resort to propriety in the face of controversy.[7]

In response to the request for an investigation by the ILO, Panama called a maritime conference to be held in Panama, 30 March 1949, and invited shipowners and diplomatic representatives to recommend reforms to the government. A United Fruit Company representative at the conference believed that the meeting was intended "to preserve the status quo" and frankly admitted that a major attraction for United Fruit was escape from American labor disputes by having sixteen vessels registered in Honduras and Panama. A representative of ESSO came to argue against the proposed conference recommendation to adopt mild ILO labor standards; but the

Panama meeting approved the standards over his objections. Panama officials hoped to win American support by recommending reforms and by pointing to past collaboration. One Panamanian official at the conference confided, "For all practical purposes, the Panamanian merchant marine must be considered as an adjunct to the United States merchant marine, inasmuch as the majority of Panamanian-registered vessels are American-owned."[8]

While the conference served as a sounding board for United Fruit Company and ESSO opinions on Panama's flag, the delegates took some minor actions that seemed designed to conciliate labor. The conference delegates recommended, in addition to the adoption of the ILO standards, that the Panama Assembly regularize shipping registration, pass a Seafarers' Code, and indicate a willingness to respond to world opinion. Panama soon entered into negotiations with the ITF, negotiations that resulted in an agreement to welcome the ILO investigation.[9]

Ignoring pressure from shipowners and from Panama, the State Department had refused to offer any assistance beyond the usual consular work with individual vessels. Despite the logic of company appeals, and despite the effort by Panama to invoke hemispheric solidarity and to hint at reform in the face of European pressure, the department kept a hands-off attitude. The result was that Panama responded to the European criticisms, first by promoting token reforms, and then by accepting and cooperating with the ILO investigation.

The ILO Report on Panama

The ILO committee charged with the investigation met in four sessions through 1949. On instructions from the ILO Governing Board, the committee limited the scope of its investigation to the issues of safety and labor conditions aboard Panamanian ships, and chose to regard questions of taxation and currency-law evasion as beyond its scope. The traditional maritime states collectively were in a good position to use the investigation to discredit Panamanian registry, for they controlled the committee, which consisted of Hermann Vos, former minister of education of Belgium; A. G. Fenema, an employer's representative from the Netherlands; and A. Dagleish, a former union official from Britain.[10]

The committee reported on several obvious elements of the Panamanian fleet derived from shipping statistics: that its ships tended to be older, on the average, than fleets of the traditional maritime states; and that a "certain number of ships" registered in Panama were not up to the standards of maintenance and equipment required for classification by Lloyd's. More to the point, the report noted practical operating problems with Panama's system. On the majority of thirty ships examined at random by the committee, no copy of any Panamanian shipping laws was maintained. The laws themselves were scattered over several texts, and thus were difficult to collect.[11] The report described the working of Panamanian registry through consular representatives abroad, and pointed out the deficiencies of that system, deficiencies that had led to shipowner, as well as to labor, objections. The report reviewed the mixed record of the consular service in dealing with the ships, and pointed out complaints against particular consuls. The ILO report did not describe the machinery for American consular substitution for Panamanian consuls in specific ports, as detailed in this work, nor did it examine the earlier development of the fleet.[12]

The committee reported that, of the thirty vessels visited, twenty were over thirty years old. Lifeboats on most appeared to meet minimum standards, but the committee reported a host of problems with labor conditions, probably typical of Panamanian ships at that time. On most of the ships, crews worked under various articles of employment that offered little protection against dismissal, and that provided no schedule of overtime or holidays. Seamen rarely received workmen's compensation for injuries, or social security benefits. The crews lived in poor accommodations. Plumbing, as would be expected on ships of that vintage, was inadequate or nonexistent. The report concluded, "Panama has virtually no laws or regulations regarding safety of life at sea. . . . The legislation, of Panama concerning seafarers is inadequate. . . . This legislation, moreover, is frequently unknown to masters, and the Panama Consular Service has not been strong enough to secure its enforcement."[13]

Despite these harsh criticisms, the committee concluded that "Panamanian authorities now seem to be alive to the situation and to realize the responsibilities which a large merchant fleet implies." The report reviewed the measures that Panama had initiated, including proposals to reform and strengthen the consular service, to issue a labor code, and to consolidate existing laws.[14]

The ILO committee made twelve recommendations for improvement of the Panamanian system:
1. Passage of a labor law
2. Compilation of the law
3. Specific guarantees of rights in event of sickness, injury, or termination of contract
4. Adoption of regulations to give effect to load line and safety regulations
5. Concentration in one authority of all matters dealing with Panamanian-registered ships
6. Distribution of copies of the law to masters
7. Strengthening of the consular service
8. Arrangement for classification

9. Requirement for ship inspection
10. Verification of officers' certificates
11. Establishment of a disputes procedure
12. Adoption of a standard collective agreement[15]

Although phrased in nonpolemical terms typical of the ILO's tradition of responsible and balanced reporting on labor and social issues, the report was, by implication, a severe condemnation of the system along the lines complained of in the ITF protests. The fact that the two usually conservative members of such a tripartite committee, the representatives of employers and government, were from maritime states strongly opposed to Panama's system, explains the critical and almost muckraking implications of this particular ILO report. Despite Panama's cooperation in developing the investigation and report, and despite its gestures in the direction of reform, in the ILO report, maritime labor, backed by the shipowners and governments of Western Europe, had scored a propaganda victory against Panama's flag-of-convenience system.

Congressional Investigations in the 1950s

As the ILO investigations proceeded, the United States Congress began its own investigations into the ship transfer system, into flag-of-convenience practice, and into possible reform of American laws that allowed so many vessels to transfer to Panama and Liberia. The congressional inquiry was the first of a whole series extending over the next decade, none of which resulted in legislation directly affecting the system. Bills designed to place a limit on the system of ship transfer, or to force the return to the United States of American-owned vessels registered abroad were introduced rarely or died in committee.

The lack of congressional results in the form of legislation raises several important questions. What was the function of the inquiries? Why was no limiting or controlling legislation produced? Did Congress meet its responsibilities? Through the 1950s, congressional inaction reflected political and ideological deadlock over maritime issues, a deadlock that reflected a widespread impasse over maritime issues in American society; Congress limited its action to other functions besides the legislative one. Committees gathered information, developed terminology, conducted "oversight" of the transfer process, suggested minor reforms that could be implemented by executive action in the Maritime Administration, exposed and criticized abuses and weaknesses of the system, acted as a grand jury to develop evidence turned over to the Justice Department, and provided a platform for critiques and defenses of the system. The fact that Congress did not enact any laws opposing transfer to Panama or Liberia, while not an explicit endorsement of the system, did indicate that Congress would not attempt to change the status quo in any fundamental fashion. Implicitly, congressional legislative inaction served as such an endorsement.

The failure of Congress to come to grips with the issue and to pass any restrictive laws can be looked at as a symptom of the decline of labor's political influence since the mid-1930s. The passage of the Taft-Hartley Act (Labor-Management Relations Act) in 1947 over the veto of President Truman gave power to the National Labor Relations Board (NLRB) to declare injunctions in major strikes; right-to-work laws prevented the formation of union shops in several states. The drive against Communist subversion and espionage discredited many left-leaning labor leaders active in maritime unions. Despite the participation and powerful committee positions held by such prolabor political figures as Senator Warren Magnuson, these politicians could hope to do little more than express labor's objections to the system. On the other side of the deadlock, conservative members of Congress used investigative hearings to launch politically valuable inquiries into links between important Democratic leaders and scandals involving misuse of the ship transfer system.

Behind the political deadlock was the continuing conflict between the social justice and the national defense sides of American progressive orientation. While Congress generally accepted Henry Luce's concept that the American way of life would be preserved best by exporting its skills, know-how, food, and products, when national defense and social justice appeared to come in conflict over a specific policy issue, it was very difficult to choose between the two objectives. Congress, responsive to the divisions in American thought, could not resolve the Solomon's choice between two such fundamentally held sets of ideals. Reflecting American ambivalence, Congress faithfully represented its constituency, and, in that sense, met its responsibility.

The 1949–50 investigations in Congress showed the outlines of the coming decade's debate, opened topics, and developed new phrases and terms that clarified the discussion. The phrase *flags of convenience* itself first was introduced into the public record and became part of the language of the debate at a February 1950 hearing of the Senate Committee on Interstate and Foreign Commerce, when Joe Curran denied that the United Fruit Company had legitimate business connections with Honduras. "The reason," he claimed, "the company maintains its fleet under the Honduran flag is that it is a flag of convenience."[16]

The committee explored the motives for American corporate registry under the flags of Panama and Honduras, and the particular economic handicaps under which tanker operators worked. Without subsidies, tanker owners faced low-priced competition, which forced them either to lay up vessels, sell them abroad, or operate the ships under foreign registry. One independent oil dealer who did not wish to operate his ships under foreign flag described how he had been forced to sell his vessels and to rely on other foreign-registered suppliers. The report of the committee noted that such decisions "could well lead to a merchant marine wholly inadequate for trade and defense."[17]

The committee studied the question of the retention of profits abroad by corporations. Senator Magnuson viewed the procedure as a slightly scandalous system of tax evasion. Under the existing tax agreements, ESSO had been able to defer profits on Panama Transport Company earnings over the period from 1944 to 1949. When the Panama Transport Company declared and paid to the parent firm a dividend of $20 million in 1949 on the profits of that five-year period, the excess profit scale of war taxes had been removed. Thus, instead of paying a 50 percent tax rate, ESSO paid 38 percent, a savings of more than $2 million in taxes, by delaying payment until the more auspicious time. No such delayed-dividend procedure was available to shipowners operating under the American flag.[18]

The committee also examined a trade-out-and-build agreement that had been proposed to the Maritime Commission by ESSO. Under this arrangement, the company would agree to register four newly built ships within the United States, in exchange for permission to trade out, or transfer, an equivalent tonnage-capacity of six older ships to Panama. This arrangement struck Senator Magnuson as a form of "blackmail" or threat, and he repeated the point a number of times at the hearings. However, he grudgingly came to understand the position of the company that if the arrangement could not be made, the new vessels could be employed more profitably under the foreign flag, and the company would have to put them in the more profitable trade. The impact of the agreement on the merchant marine force of the United States would be to reduce the number of employed seamen, since the four new vessels to be registered in the United States employed fewer hands than the six older vessels transferred out. Maritime Commission members pointed out that if the trade-off were not permitted, the established practice of simply transferring new tankers abroad would continue. Since World War II, twenty-eight new tankers had been built and all had been transferred abroad. Legislation to prohibit transfer, or to require prior approval for transfer abroad of newly built ships, was not under consideration and such a power did not exist under the Merchant Marine Act of 1936.[19]

The secretary of defense designated the navy to represent the Defense Department's views regarding transfer to Panama, and Rear Admiral W. M. Callaghan testified. The navy believed that vessels transferred to Panama, Honduras, Liberia, Venezuela, or the Philippines should be regarded as "available" in case of emergency. Callaghan reviewed the origins of the policy in the period from 1939 through 1941. His testimony was cited in later investigations, and it served as the first official Defense Department statement to Congress of the endorsement of the concept of strategic convenience and its elevation to the level of semiofficial policy.

> There have been cases where defense considerations prompted the Government to approve the transfer of American vessels to foreign flag. Such a situation occurred during the period immediately preceding our entry into World War II when approval was granted by the Maritime Commission for the transfer of several dry cargo vessels to Panamanian registry as a means of relieving world shortage of tonnage and to carry American goods and supplies in certain areas. At that time, the Neutrality Act forbade the arming of American-flag vessels and restricted them from trading in certain parts of the world. The Commission's action had the concurrence of the Navy Department, and it may be recalled that the first ships that could be armed were in this category.[20]

Senator Magnuson responded, "I recall that. In that case, there were no restrictions under the Panamanian registry for trading; whereas we were bound by the Neutrality Act."

Callaghan proceeded, "That is correct. Similar conditions may arise in the future. There is an understanding with at least one of the Latin American governments which provides for the return to United States registry, at the event of an emergency, of American-owned vessels documented in that country. The Navy Department, therefore, considers that American-owned ships under the flag of such a country are potentially available on request of the United States Government in time of war."

Magnuson inquired, "What country is that?"

Callaghan replied, "That country is Panama."[21]

This colloquy contained a number of elements not pursued at the time because the day's session was coming to an end, but that gave practical reasons for congressional skepticism about the operation of the system. What was the nature of the understanding with Panama? Why was it with Panama alone? Was it appropriate to adopt a policy that would allow the Defense Department to counteract congressionally decided neutrality? The committee remained doubtful about the practical feasibility of the system, noting:

> While the Navy Department may consider as "available" vessels owned by American citizens operating under certain foreign flags, there are grave doubts in the minds of the members of the subcommittee as to the degree of reliability that can be hoped for from a foreign crew sailing a foreign flag vessel when given orders by the United States Government, especially if their sympathies or political interests are not in harmony with ours.[22]

It was not Admiral Callaghan, but a member of the Maritime Commission, Major General Phillip B. Fleming, who introduced the phrase *effective United States control* into the hearings and into public discussion of Panamanian registry. In reference to the ESSO proposal to register new tankers in the United States only if permitted to transfer a greater number of tankers out, Magnuson asked General Fleming, "Aren't we in an awful position when a company can come to the Maritime Commission with a club and say, 'unless you do this, we will do this?' "

Fleming demurred. He did not feel it was a threat, he said. "I voted for it, and I voted mostly because of a notation right here on the docket that the Military Establishment has consistently adhered to the principle that the transfer of United States tankers to Panama flag and registry to wholly-owned Panamanian subsidiaries of responsible United States companies constitutes effective United States control."[23]

Despite its rather full investigation of several aspects of the problem, the Senate committee made no specific recommendation for legislation, and the committee report explicitly noted the resulting indecision.

> The basic question and the one which is most in need of clarification of Congressional intent, is whether or not it is consistent with national policy and aspirations for American corporations or individuals to transfer merchant vessels to foreign flags, at the same time maintaining control and a financial interest in the vessel, for the purpose of avoiding the obviously higher American standards reflected in the cost of ship operation. The question is not one capable of an affirmative or a negative answer, but rather one which requires many qualifications and rationalizations.[24]

Rather lamely, the report recommended that the "shipowners, operators, and shipbuilders must cooperate to the end that the flight of ships to foreign countries, particularly the countries of convenience, be kept to the lowest practicable minimum." Despite its frank admission of deadlock on the issue, the committee had achieved a good deal both by obtaining a public statement from the Defense Department, a statement that made explicit the commitment of the Maritime Commission and the navy to the concept of strategic convenience, and by opening a discussion of the strengths and weaknesses of the idea. The introduction of the phrases *flags of convenience* and *effective United States control* provided terms for concepts that were to become central issues in maritime affairs over the next three decades.[25]

Onassis, Niarchos, and Kulukundis

By accident, another congressional investigation on a completely different topic uncovered the workings of the system employed by specific Greek ship operators to use Panamanian and Liberian registry to acquire control of ships that, under law, were to be sold only to American-controlled firms. Offhand testimony volunteered by "influence peddler" Joseph Casey during the course of an investigation into the administration of the Reconstruction Finance Corporation led to questions that exposed his involvement with Aristotle Onassis and Stavros Niarchos. Public knowledge of the operations then was developed in 1952 through the Permanent Subcommittee of Investigation of the Senate Committee of Government Operations, involving Senators Karl Mundt, Joseph McCarthy, and Richard Nixon. In the late 1940s Onassis, Niarchos, and Manuel Kulukundis all had sought ways to acquire surplus vessels sold under the 1946 Ship Sales Act, and each had worked out devices to cover his control with the legal cloak of American ownership.[26]

Since under the Ship Sales Act only American-controlled firms were allowed to purchase certain categories of vessels, particularly T-2 tankers, each of the Greek operators formed Panamanian corporations that nominally were owned by Americans, in majority. In each case, trusted American-citizen relatives of the Greek operators were among the majority stockholders along with a variety of figurehead Americans, such as Casey. With 40 to 49 percent of the ownership in the hands of the Greek financier, and another 10 to 20 percent in the hands of the American-citizen relative, actual control remained in the hands of the Greek shipowner. Through such corporate machinery, the "American-owned" company would purchase ships, either directly from the government, or from a recent American buyer of government vessels, and operate them under the registries of Panama or Liberia. Onassis built a fleet of nineteen ships through a group of interlocking companies; crucial ownership of stock was vested in his daughter, who was an American citizen. Niarchos acquired fourteen vessels, five of them from the American Overseas Tanker Corporation formed by Stettinius. Association between both Niarchos and Onassis and the recently deceased Democratic secretary of state who had presided at the Yalta conference was given a good degree of emphasis at the Republican-dominated committee investigation, although Stettinius's part in the creation of the Liberian system was not explored.[27]

The 1946 Ship Sales Act did not specify that vessels purchased from the government had to be *controlled* by American citizens or American interests, only that they had to be *owned* by American-citizen-controlled firms. Therefore, in a technical sense, the arrangements were within the law. However, the various schemes appeared to violate the intent of the law, and to provide a system for removing from American control ships regarded as valuable.

In 1953, under the administration of Dwight D. Eisenhower, the committee's findings were investigated by the Justice Department, and a plan was initiated to lodge both criminal and civil suits against the Greek operators. The criminal cases rested on charges of particular sharp practices that the Justice Department could prove, such as short-term deposits of large amounts of capital with "dummy" corporations so that they would appear well-founded during credit investigations, the use of subcharters from American-held companies to wholly Greek-owned companies in order to channel profits to the actual investor, and similar evidences of conspiracy. But, the legal constraints on American ownership, the main thrust of the senatorial concern and the focus of public indignation, had been obeyed completely.

The cases were difficult from the viewpoint of the Justice Department. For some suspected offenses, the statute of limitations had expired; further, the Maritime Commission earlier had investigated and approved the American ownership of the firms involved; an informal opinion from the Justice Department even had authorized the arrangements in outline. Nevertheless, the Justice Department issued warrants for the arrest of Onassis, Niarchos, and Kulukundis, and impounded their ships as they entered American ports. Through 1955 and early 1956, the Justice Department agreed to drop criminal charges against the Greek operators in exchange for cash settlements on the civil charges, although the department remained reluctant to characterize the payments as "deals" or out-of-court settlements. In the case of Onassis, a payment of $7 million was worked out.[28]

As Congress reviewed the cases, the Justice Department decision to settle for cash and not to prosecute disappointed particular congressmen. Nevertheless, the actions against the Greek operators served several political and psychological purposes. Onassis and the others took the attitude that they had "ransomed" their ships and themselves with the cash payments. But the focus of attention on Justice Department action against the three operators created a public impression that irregular and tangled schemes for foreign transfer of American vessels, needed for defense, had been worked out through the Panamanian and Liberian flags, but that the Justice Department had caught and reprimanded the offenders. In a process that had marked parallels to anti-Communist witch-hunt investigations of the period, the Greek operators were investigated, threatened with prosecution, and exposed to public criticism. Intended at first as a political exposé of the prior Democratic administration, these inquiries in the long run served a more general purpose. When the process was complete, the satisfaction of having discovered and exposed the wrongdoers served to express and channel both public and official anger over the deceptions inherent in flag-of-convenience registry, but did not substantially alter the system or penetrate to the core of the issue.[29]

Maritime Administration Response and Further Hearings

Congressional oversight, expressed through the 1950 hearings, resulted in a number of refinements in transfer rules. Under a presidential reorganization order, the duties of the Maritime Commission were turned over to a maritime administrator, serving as undersecretary of commerce, early in 1952. The Maritime Administration (MarAd) attempted to clarify and resolve problems of ship transfer and to regularize the system of effective United States control of vessels under "PanLibHon" registry. In July 1952, MarAd announced a new policy governing sales and transfers of ships to foreign registry, a policy that incorporated some of the earlier congressional criticisms.

The MarAd program strengthened specific controls on the transfer of vessels by restating the requirement that any ships approved for transfer had to be determined by the navy to be unneeded for national defense. Each request also would be cleared through the State Department, to verify that the transfer was consistent with foreign policy, and security checks of owners would be made through the ONI, the CIA, and the Office of International Trade. These policies were reaffirmations of practices that had been employed since the U.S. Shipping Board had scrutinized requests for transfer in the 1920s. All ships approved for transfer were subject to several specific new conditions: they could not trade in areas prohibited under Maritime Orders T-1 and T-2, which prohibited United States ships from trade with Communist powers; the owner would agree to sell or charter the vessel to the United States government or to a NATO government if requested; further changes of ownership or transfers would be subject to approval of the maritime administrator; and a surety bond of $25,000 to $250,000 would be posted to guarantee adherence to the conditions. Vessels over seventeen years old would be regarded as obsolete, and would be generally available for transfer, subject to the approvals and conditions outlined. Newer vessels could be transferred abroad under the regularized trade-out-and-build program, which would allow transfer of ships if the owner agreed to register in the United States a newly built ship of equivalent tonnage capacity.

The MarAd policy had regularized effective control; put on a regular footing the trade-out-and-build agreement suggested by ESSO; and reasserted security and policy controls to meet the objections of those who feared the ships would find their way into potentially dangerous or enemy hands. Ironically, the 1939 purpose of strategic convenience had involved a use of the Panamanian flag to avoid foreign policy restrictions in the Neutrality Act; the MarAd rules of 1952, which formally implemented the postwar system of effective control, made impossible such use of a convenient foreign flag for evasion of American official policy. Since the rules prohibited travel to the areas banned to U.S. ships, the system was designed to prevent evasion, rather than to foster it. It was logically impossible officially to endorse a policy that would allow for evasion of official policy.[30]

Despite the defusing of the political animosity directed against the system by scapegoating the Greek operators and regularizing the transfer arrangements after 1952, the basic charge leveled by labor representatives at committee hearings remained unanswered. "Runaway ships" continued to reduce American merchant marine employment. In 1954, Hoyt Haddock, executive secretary of the CIO Maritime Committee, attempted to marshall support for labor's position with appeals to defense considerations. Testifying before the Senate Committee on Interstate and Foreign Commerce, he pointed out the decline in the Greek merchant fleet, and suggested that the new policies of the Maritime Administration would result in a similar reduction of the American merchant marine to a few outmoded ships. "Despite the fact that we are at the brink of another terrible world war, our merchant marine is being methodically scuttled," Haddock claimed. By January 1954, he calculated, 346 ships owned by American firms were under the flags of Panama, Liberia, and Honduras, and another 72 were being constructed for registry under those flags.[31]

In 1957, the Senate Committee on Interstate and Foreign Commerce held further hearings, this time centering on bill S 1488, introduced by Senator Magnuson, which effectively would have put an end to flag-of-convenience registry by prohibiting the ownership of foreign-registered vessels by American parent companies. While the bill did not have any chance of being passed, as Magnuson himself admitted, its consideration provided an excellent opportunity for a clear-cut focus of the discussion of flags of convenience. After evaluating the workability of the guarantees for effective control of ships under Panamanian and Liberian flags as implemented by MarAd policies, the committee listened to a full explanation of the economics of the shipping situation by representatives of Mobil Oil, Gulf Oil, and ESSO.[32]

The senators, including the avowedly prolabor Magnuson, patiently and carefully followed the explanations offered by the companies, and obtained a full outline of the economic considerations that made the choice of Panamanian or Liberian registry profitable or "necessary" from the point of view of the major oil shippers. The representative of Mobil Oil, Charles Teitsworth, explained very candidly that operation costs per tanker of a 16,000-ton size were about $480,000 less per year under Panamanian registry than under American registry. Senator Magnuson pointed out that under that formula, the company probably could operate its six directly owned vessels and seven chartered ships for a total of about $5 million per year more, if they did it under the American flag. After all, if the cost was only $5 million, why could a company earning $250 million not afford to register vessels in the United States, Magnuson asked. Teitsworth explained that in addition to operating costs, the taxation rate of the United States would consume nearly 40 percent of each vessel's earnings. In

Panama, without taxes, it was possible to retain earnings for investment in other vessels; the acquisition of such amounts of capital for fleet expansion in the United States was difficult even for Mobil. The system allowed the generation of investment funds for shipping, while the American registry system did not.[33]

Teitsworth suggested that competition also explained the need for foreign registry, and claimed, "If you want to be in foreign business you must aim to be competitive and meet your competition on an equal footing because these margins on the sale of oil and oil products are pretty thin." However, Millard Gamble of ESSO pointed out that a two dollar per month, per *ton* increase in the cost of carrying oil in United States-registered tankers rather than Panamanian tankers, would be absorbed in the final sale without any increase in price to the consumer. It was not undefined "competition" that made foreign registry attractive; rather, it was the unrestricted opportunity provided under the tax-free environment to retain funds for ship construction purposes that drew the fleets of the major oil companies.[34]

Chairman of the Senate Committee on Interstate and Foreign Commerce, Warren Magnuson of Washington, led inquiries into the growing flag-of-convenience system as it came to dominate American oil-importing trade through the 1950s. (Senator Magnuson Collection)

Repeating concerns from earlier hearings, the committee members in 1957 again expressed doubts about the workability of the "effective control" principle. Gamble tried to reassure the senators on that point.

> The main reason for preferring, where practicable, to maintain ships under the flag of Panama in preference to flags of other foreign nations, is because of the close, cordial relationship between Panama and the United States and the flexibility permitted in the choice of crews. With this relationship and the careful screening exercised in employing and assigning crews, we are confident that these ships would be available to the United States in time of need.[35]

Gamble had not been in charge of the Marine Department of Standard Oil in August 1939, when ESSO had requested naval and State Department help in lining up military assistance to remove German crews from its Panamanian-registered tankers, nor in 1941, when President Arias had prohibited arming of United States-owned vessels under Panamanian registry. Gamble's apparent ignorance of those events was therefore excusable, although in retrospect, a review of such events casts doubts on the basis for his confidence.

The net results of the international and American investigations of flags of convenience had been to offer critiques that led to improvements in the systems, but not to their destruction, as desired by European competitors and American labor spokesmen. In response to the ILO charges, Panama enacted a labor code and supplied printed copies of its laws to shipowners and consuls. Partly in response to the growing complaints about Panama, Stettinius's group had developed the Liberian system. Congressional investigations provided for quite a range of minor administrative reforms in the United States, reforms that aided rather than hampered the systems: exercise of the "oversight" function of Congress led to improvements in the transfer system, and regularization of both "trade-out-and-build" and "effective control." The explanation of the positions of both labor and management through an exercise in symbolic politics took some pressure off the system; focus of discontent on Greek abuses of the system defused public antagonism. As Panama's slightly remodeled system and the American-designed and American-managed Liberian system continued to attract owners, American labor leaders sought to move the battle from what they perceived as the relatively ineffectual propaganda arena of Congress to direct action on the docks and to legal action in the courts. At the same time European shipowners, through their governments, sought international legal action against both Panama and Liberia.

9

Legal Assaults

IN THE LATE 1950s, American maritime unions and the governments of the traditional maritime states of Europe sought to prove in court their belief that both Panamanian and Liberian ship registry systems were subterfuges. Although they were mounted before different court systems and used differing tactics, both legal attacks on the systems worked from a similar premise: that flags of convenience were unethical legal fictions designed to escape the safety controls, social legislation, taxation, and maritime policies required by other nations. Several questions flowed from the fact that the *independent* sovereignties of both Panama and Liberia were assured, ironically, by their claims to special *dependent* relationships with the United States. Did their sovereign rights to enact their own maritime laws necessarily compel other nations to recognize those laws? Did registry of ships in these small nations free the ships from legal restraints of the nations of the owners, of the crews, or of the ports at which the vessels called? Was the "law of the flag" supreme over other laws that might apply?

In attacking the legal bases of flags of convenience, however, the maritime states of Europe and the maritime unions of the United States employed critically different tactics. The European maritime nations saw the flags as sheltering unfair competition and hoped to outlaw the systems, driving the ships registered under them back to the nations of ownership or to nations with strong maritime traditions. American unions, however, fought to extend American labor-law jurisdiction to American-owned vessels while they remained under the foreign flags—so that the crews could be organized and demand wages and treatment equal to those of American seamen. The difference in the tactics of the two forces that opposed the system would prevent effective cooperation between those opponents, for the British and other European governments would not look with favor on the extension of American laws and unions to American-owned ships under foreign registry, precisely because some vessels under their own flags were owned by American corporations. The precedent, if established, could lead to claims that the U.S. unions and laws had jurisdiction on some vessels under the British flag.

But American unions believed that if courts could be made to rule that the nation of ownership had jurisdiction over vessels in matters of labor law, then the flag itself no longer could provide a refuge. If the flag were ruled irrelevant, and the nation of ownership were given power to apply its standards to the crucial factors that determined operating costs, then the subterfuge would be so undermined that the flags no longer would attract shipping.

In response to legal attacks based upon such concepts, shipowners using the flags sought to restrict the issues before courts by focusing on well-defined cases in which the particular facts and situations could be defended on grounds of accepted principles of international and domestic law. By employing this well-established legal strategy of choosing to fight only on cases with "good facts," shipowners hoped to ward off the assaults mounted by both the European governments and American labor. For those owners who had come to depend on the advantages of Panamanian and Liberian registry, the battles were matters of economic life or death. The legal issues, although buried in masses of testimony, procedure, evidence, and decision, reflected a struggle for survival of the whole system of flags of convenience.

In the United States, the legal battles culminated twenty years after the issue had hardened in 1939 over the proposed transfer of nine United States Lines ships to Panama, and the issues necessarily went beyond narrow legal problems to larger matters of policy and politics. While in the United States, the struggle took on the characteristics of many earlier classic labor-management conflicts, both contending sides hoped to win by appealing to broader constituencies, and to show the relationship of the issue to matters of national policy along the grounds of the 1939 arguments. Thus, the U.S. court cases over flags of convenience tested not only the question of American labor-law jurisdiction over American-owned ships flying Liberian and Panamanian flags. The cases also involved debates over the modernized version of strategic convenience—"effective control" of the ships for military purposes—and the impact of such registries upon the American economy. Labor sought to convince the courts and the public that "runaway" ships not only cost seamen their jobs, but also cost the nation all the economic benefits of a merchant fleet. Management not only asserted the right to register vessels under foreign flags, it also claimed that the practice was necessary if American-owned ships were to compete in the world market. Liberia and Panama, claimed the owners, provided not "flags of convenience" but "flags of necessity."

International Forums

Several principles of international law were used by the owners of ships registered under the two flags to defend the systems in the 1950s. Since early in the nineteenth century, nations had extended recognition to the principle that other nations could grant nationality and flags to ships. This principle had been represented in bilateral treaties of Friendship, Commerce, and Navigation, called "FCN" treaties, in which two nations would agree to recognize each others' vessels and to admit them to port. By the twentieth century, the principles that each state could set for itself its rules and regulations governing the granting of nationality to ships and that these rules would be widely accepted were implemented and recognized through dozens of such bilateral FCN treaties. American attorneys representing Panama and Liberia argued that the "law of the flag" should take precedence over the law of the port or of the owner in determining nationality of vessels and jurisdiction over those vessels. The attorneys cited the principle developed through FCN treaties as the basis for flag recognition in international law.[1]

But a 1955 ruling by the International Court of Justice had the potential to undermine international legal acceptance of national policies governing the granting of flags. The challenging principle had been developed in a dispute between two unlikely antagonists—Guatemala and Lichtenstein—in the *Nottebohm* case. In this situation, Kurt Nottebohm, a German citizen resident in Guatemala, rapidly changed his citizenship to neutral Lichtenstein on the outbreak of World War II. When Guatemala seized his property as that of an enemy German, Nottebohm obtained a diplomatic protest from Lichtenstein. The International Court of Justice finally ruled in favor of Guatemala in 1955. The court declared there was no "genuine link" between Nottebohm and Lichtenstein, in that he had lived there only very briefly prior to the war, did no business there, and that his naturalization was secured artificially for the purpose of evading the confiscation of property. Without such a genuine link between citizen and nation of citizenship, Guatemala was correct in viewing Nottebohm as German. In effect, the court had ruled against what could have been called "citizenship of convenience."[2]

In 1956–58, Dutch and British lawyers hoped to extend to ships this principle of a "genuine link." In 1956, the International Law Commission, a group of international lawyers selected by the General Assembly of the United Nations, discussed whether the *Nottebohm* precedent should apply to ships, and whether some international agreement should be reached limiting the powers of states to grant nationality to vessels. The International Law Commission recommended that the issue of whether to require a genuine link between vessels and the state of registry be placed on the agenda of the planned Law of the Sea Conference to be held in Geneva in 1958. The commission recommended to the conference a provision that asserted that *"for purposes of recognition of the national character of a ship by other states*, there must exist a genuine link between the state and the ship." Such a view, if adopted, would represent an international vindication of the view that Panamanian and Liberian registries were subterfuges, since, like Nottebohm, many of the ships rarely or never visited their countries of "nationality" and had nothing to do with them except for the act of registration itself.[3]

In a hotly contested debate at the Geneva conference, representatives of the United States sided with Panama and Liberia in maneuvering to have the clause "recognition of the national character" weakened or removed. While the American State Department under Acheson had refused to take a stand during the Panama-ILO dispute, under John Foster Dulles, the department vigorously came to Panama's defense. Dulles's law firm, Sullivan and Cromwell, still represented Panama in the United States.

As adopted, the Law of the Sea Conference provision on the question finally read, "There must exist a genuine link between the State and the ship; in particular, the State must effectively exercise its jurisdiction and control in administrative, technical and social matters over the ships that fly its flag."

Successful American negotiation to remove the recognition clause had taken the teeth out of the proposal. The resulting agreement simply asserted the principle that a ship should be linked to its flag state, but defined the enforcement of regulations as evidence of the "link." After all, even Panama had made an effort to enforce its regulations, and the resulting formula, therefore, provided no challenge to the system. The forms of linkage between ship and nation employed in the traditional maritime states had included ownership by nationals, requirements that nationals be employed as crews, construction of the ship in the nation, or some combination of those requirements. The Law of the Sea Conference, by focusing on the enforcement of regulations as the linkage between ship and state, had defined the question in such a way that it would offer no challenge whatsoever to flag-of-convenience registries. The threat to use the conference to transfer to ships the Nottebohm concept of a genuine link had been forestalled successfully.[4]

When a case growing out of the establishment of the Intergovernmental Maritime Consultative Organization (IMCO) found its way to the International Court of Justice, the European traditional maritime powers once again aligned against the United States, Liberia, and Panama over the issue.

IMCO first had been planned in 1948, but it came into being only in 1958, after a total of twenty-one states had signed the convention establishing it as a specialized agency under United Nations auspices. As the organization held its opening meeting, the controversy over Panama and Liberia soon surfaced.[5]

The argument hinged on a minor organizational matter, but it took on world-wide significance in light of the ongoing legal and union actions over flag-of-convenience shipping; what might otherwise have been a detail of committee assignment became a major phase in the international struggle. According to Article 28 of the original IMCO convention, a Maritime Safety Committee was to be elected by the IMCO General Assembly. The committee would consist of fourteen members, representatives of "governments of those nations having an important interest in maritime safety, of which not less than eight shall be the largest shipowning nations." While it was difficult to determine exactly who "owned" some vessels, in terms of ultimate or beneficial ownership, it was clear that, measured in terms of registered tonnage, both Liberia and Panama were among the top eight maritime nations in the world. Liberia ranked third largest in 1959, with over ten million tons registered, and Panama ranked eighth, with over four million tons.[6]

In January 1959, the General Assembly of IMCO elected members to the Maritime Safety Committee, pointedly excluding both Panama and Liberia. There were several grounds for this decision presented by British, Dutch, Belgian, and Norwegian representatives during the debate over the issue:

–Neither Panama nor Liberia had any appreciable number of shipowners; the vessels in their registries belonged to nationals of other states. Thus, neither country could be called a "shipowning nation."
–The Maritime Safety Committee was to be drawn from those nations having an interest in safety. "Neither Panama nor Liberia was at the moment, in a position to make any important contribution to maritime safety," according to the British delegate.
–Since the convention that established IMCO called for an "election," the automatic selection of representatives of the top eight nations on grounds of tonnage could not have been the intent of the framers and signers of the convention. An "election" implied choice, not automatic selection.[7]

The European maritime states opposing Liberia and Panama hoped not only to raise these reasonable arguments against seating the two states on the committee, but also to make minor propaganda points against the legitimacy of the two countries as maritime nations. But, the issue provided an excellent opportunity to mount a legal defense of the two systems. It was a situation in which the "facts" of registry favored the flag-of-convenience cause. Both Panamanian and Liberian representatives at the assembly protested their exclusion from the committee, and, with support from the United States, obtained an agreement to submit the issue to the International Court of Justice.

In April and May 1959, the court met to discuss the issue, and it gave its formal ruling on 8 June 1960. In this case, written statements and oral arguments from the United States supported Panama and Liberia. Representatives from Italy, Holland, Britain, and Norway argued against the seating of Panama and Liberia on the committee, and asked that the court apply its own genuine link doctrine from the *Nottebohm* case to the IMCO case.

The International Court of Justice ruled against the traditional maritime states, holding that the assembly of IMCO did not hold its election properly when it excluded Panama and Liberia. The choice of representation to IMCO's Maritime Safety Committee, the court ruled, was, indeed, automatic, and the first eight nations chosen for the safety committee should be selected on the basis of registered tonnage alone. The decision stated, "Neither the nationality of stockholders of shipping companies nor the notion of a genuine link between ships and their country is a relevant test for determining 'shipowning nations.' "[8]

The decision on this rather minor organizational point served as the only test of the principles of flags of convenience before the International Court of Justice. The court did not examine the fundamental questions of international and maritime law, economic realities, and business history surrounding the legitimacy of such registries. The attorneys for Panama and Liberia had chosen the test case well, since the specific and narrow terms of the charter of IMCO restricted the court to interpretation of the language of that particular document. Yet, the decision could be touted as the "kiss of death" for the genuine link doctrine as applied to ships. Legal treatises and law journal articles, as well as legal experts working with the shipowning corporations, claimed a victory for the "law of the flag" over the principle of "genuine link." What had been a political position at the opening IMCO meeting, and the subject of careful diplomatic maneuvering, became, through the reassertion of scholars and the effective public relations of shipowners, enshrined as a dictum of international law.[9]

Labor and Management Prepare for Battle

While the European maritime states pursued their line of attack on flags of convenience through the international legal machinery, the international labor movement planned a more direct attack on the Liberian and Panamanian systems that allowed shipowners to escape the jurisdiction of the labor laws of Western Europe and the United States. The International Transport Workers Federation planned a four-day boycott, from 1 December through 4 December 1958, of selected ships registered under flags of convenience and owned by companies that had not signed contracts with ITF-affiliated unions. The boycott took place simultaneously around the world. While the ITF claimed that the boycott was a considerable success, owners and elements of the conservative press treated it as a failure, or at best a very mixed success. Low estimates held that 125 vessels were held up in the United States and some 38 in the rest of the world, while the ITF claimed that the boycott affected over 200 vessels world-wide.

In reaction to the threat of the boycott, shipowners organized a set of legal actions to enjoin the boycott—also with mixed success. In Holland, the boycott was declared illegal in Amsterdam, but allowed in Rotterdam, where it lasted one day. In Germany, precedents of damages and fines against labor unions prevented any boycott at all. In the United States, however, an appeal to the Federal District Court of New York by thirteen Liberian-registered and two Panamanian-registered companies resulted in a decision that the boycott was a legal labor dispute and, therefore, appropriately handled by the National Labor Relations Board (NLRB), not the courts. Therefore, unrestricted by any injunction in the United States, the boycott went ahead unmolested.[10]

Despite negative press comments, the immobilization of more than 100 Panamanian and Liberian ships in United States harbors encouraged American labor unions, and hardened the resistance of the companies. The employers formed the American Committee for Flags of Necessity (ACFN), and elected as its president, Erling Naess, the Norwegian shipowner who first had moved whaling ships to Panamanian registry in the 1930s. Naess, who had studied for a doctorate in economics in Britain in the 1920s, and had been a close student of George Maynard Keynes's theories, had succeeded in building a fifty thousand-dollar postwar investment into a multimillion-dollar shipping empire under the Liberian flag. He brought his considerable organizational and intellectual talents to the American effort, with funding provided by Mobil, ESSO, Standard Oil of California, Bethlehem Steel, and other corporations that owned ships registered in Liberia and Panama.

Under Naess's leadership, the organization recruited the public relations firm of William Fagen, and made a concerted and somewhat successful effort to win over the press. One of the more notable recruits was Raymond Moley of *Newsweek*, who published several editorials and syndicated columns suggesting the "flag of necessity" system as the solution to America's shipping dilemma. At first, Naess retained as attorney for the ACFN, John Koehler, former assistant secretary of the navy under Truman. Later, the firm of Donovan, Leisure, Newton, and Irvine took over the representation of the industry group. With the advice of such attorneys, the ACFN assisted individual companies in planning legal tactics.[11]

The unions, too, organized their efforts. The National Maritime Union and the Seafarers' International Union cooperated to set up a new organizing group, the International Maritime Workers Union (IMWU), specifically for the purpose of recruiting men aboard the American-owned Panamanian, Liberian, and Honduran vessels. In 1959, the ITF agreed to divide international labor jurisdiction aboard flag-of-convenience vessels, accepting the American labor position that ships should be organized not by unions of the crews' nationalities, but by unions in the nations of the ultimate owners. Authorized by the ITF to go ahead, emboldened by the success of the 1958 boycott and by the district court victory referring the injunction decision to the jurisdiction of the NLRB, and armed with the united approach of the IMWU, American organized labor embarked on a campaign of direct action, boycotts, pickets, and attempts to organize crews aboard flag-of-convenience ships over the four-year period from 1959 to 1962. With both sides so well-prepared and legally armed, the battle moved immediately from the docks to the courts.

As picket lines at docks in the United States immobilized scattered Panamanian and Liberian ships, the shipowners and the ACFN attempted to have the picketing stopped through court injunctions, or to sue the unions for damages. As organizers recruited crewmen aboard ships, distributed literature, and encouraged seamen to line up further members, some companies fired the men for union activity.

Both union and owner tactics depended on the answer to the question: Did the National Labor Relations Act apply to American-owned vessels registered under the flags of Panama and Liberia? If the law did apply, then firing workers for union activity would be illegal, the NLRB could hold elections, and the selected bargaining agents would have to be recognized by the shipowners. One of the main advantages or "conveniences" of the system would be destroyed if American labor rates and conditions were established under NLRB-enforced contracts. NLRB jurisdiction would put an end to one major motive for operation of American ships under the two flags.[12]

Shipowners seeking injunctions to prevent picketing ran into several legal obstacles. The Norris-La Guardia Act of 1932 and the Taft-Hartley Act of 1947 combined to make the use of injunction difficult. Under the 1932 act, the courts were prevented from applying injunctions to genuine labor disputes, although they still could prevent labor organizations from joining in "secondary boycotts" for political reasons, where the particular union had no direct interest. While shipowners argued that the picketing of "PanLibHon" ships was in the nature of a protest rather than an organizing drive, labor leaders claimed they planned to enlist the workers into the unions. Under the Taft-Hartley Act, the power to grant injunctions in cases of true labor disputes, as distinguished from political demonstrations, was restricted to the National Labor Relations Board. Even after six years of Republican administration, the Democratic appointees on the NLRB still held a majority, and tended to be prolabor.

Like the European attack through the International Law Commission and the International Court of Justice, the American labor position depended on assertions that a ship's true nationality derived from the genuine connections it had with the state of its owner, rather than the artificial connections with its flag state. For labor to insure NLRB jurisdiction, some American legal precedent for the "genuine link" theory would be required. The European use of the genuine link precedent from the *Nottebohm* case could not be applied in the United States, but the "balancing of contacts" principle from a 1953 Supreme Court case, *Lauritzen* v. *Larsen*, reflected the same principle. In that case, the Court denied jurisdiction to a foreign seaman seeking damages under American law for an injury aboard a foreign-owned and foreign-registered ship. The Court determined the issue of jurisdiction by weighing seven factors: the place of the wrongful act, the law of the flag, the allegiance or domicile of the injured party, the allegiance of the shipowners, the place of contract, the accessibility of the foreign forum, and the law of the forum—that is, U.S. law.[13]

Applying the balancing or weighing of contacts system developed in *Lauritzen* v. *Larsen* to a number of cases through the 1950s, district and appellate courts had ruled in several cases that a suit for damages under the Jones Act should proceed in the United States. The system was a practical and working tool to determine jurisdiction by evaluating the various national contacts of a ship with owner, crew, flag, and place of business. As lower courts decided on cases of jurisdiction over foreign-registered ships, the judges ruled in several cases that the "contact" of American ownership could outweigh the "contact" of foreign-flag registry. In *Zielinski* v. *Empresa Hondurena de Vapores*, the court determined that the contact of American ownership outweighed the contact of registry and flag. In *Bobalakis* v. *Compania Panamena Maritima San Gerassimo*, the judge went further and recognized that, even though the *company* was incorporated in Panama, the fact that the ship and the company both were owned in the United States outweighed that factor and gave the United States jurisdiction. In response to the company's claim that a foreign-incorporated subsidiary led to foreign jurisdiction over the ship, the judge commented that under that view, "An American owner might escape his statutory liability merely by interposing a foreign corporation between himself and the vessel, both of which, for all practical purposes, he owns. I do not believe that the law can be so easily baffled."[14]

These liability cases under the Jones Act, however, only established the fact that for individual crew claims for injuries, the contact of American ownership established American court jurisdiction. The NLRB sought to extend that principle of contact to an assertion of jurisdiction over labor union organization cases aboard American-owned vessels under Panamanian and Liberian flags.

In the *Peninsular and Occidental* case, the NLRB ruled against an American-owned Liberian corporation. The company operated the cruise ship *Florida* out of Miami to the Bahamas. It had registered the ship in Liberia for the express purpose of achieving lower operating costs on the same run it previously had conducted under the American flag. The company fired employees engaged in union activity and the NLRB took jurisdiction. The board found that, "P & O had full control of the vessel, was its beneficial owner, and was in fact the employer of its crew. . . . Clearly under such circumstances, the foreign incorporation of the nominal owner and operator of a vessel cannot bar the jurisdiction of the Act over an operation otherwise within the coverage of its provisions."[15] The board ordered the reinstatement of fired employees, a stop to unfair labor practices, and the arrangement of an election to determine a collective bargaining agent.

Through the late 1950s some judges in federal courts used logic similar to that of the NLRB in determining labor jurisdiction. In a case in Oregon, the judge issued an injunction against labor action, ruling that there was no American ownership to tip the balance in favor of American jurisdiction. However, he stated very strongly the principle that American ownership would create a case of American jurisdiction and NLRB powers:

> By subterfuge, the true ownership and nationality of a vessel [can be] disguised by having her registered and carrying the flag of some foreign country. . . . Now I have reached the conclusion that in determining the relationship of these parties that what flag any given bottom carried is not of importance. The question is, who are the true owners. . . .[16]

Opinions of this kind showed that American judges were beginning to treat Panamanian and Liberian registry as fictions.

In 1957, in *Benz* v. *Compania Naviera Hidalgo*, the Supreme Court indicated it would prefer that Congress clarify the complex questions of international relations involved in such jurisdictional disputes.

> For us to run interference in such a delicate field of international relations, there must be present the affirmative intention of the Congress clearly expressed. It alone has the facilities necessary to make fairly such an important policy decision where the possibilities of international discord are so evident and retaliative action so certain. We therefore conclude that any such appeal should be directed to the Congress rather than the courts.[17]

But, as has been shown, Congress remained stymied over the issue.

By 1959–60, without guidance from Congress, the federal courts and the National Labor Relations Board had moved toward a policy that would extend labor organization jurisdiction to flag-of-convenience shipping. The emerging policy contained several elements:

1. The balancing-of-contacts theory should be used to determine if a foreign ship came under American jurisdiction.
2. In weighing the contacts to determine jurisdiction, neither foreign incorporation, nor foreign registry, nor both, would preclude American jurisdiction if the ship was beneficially owned in the United States by a parent firm.
3. If the contacts showed American jurisdiction, then the courts would have power over Jones Act cases. The courts also could handle suits for damages growing out of labor disputes. However, as to questions of labor representation and injunctions against union picketing, the NLRB had jurisdiction.

This emerging policy, if carefully handled, provided an opportunity for labor unions to extend their activities and representation to flag-of-convenience shipping. Yet, a potential crisis between agencies of the government loomed as the courts and the NLRB were working toward an American application of the genuine link principle through the balancing-of-contacts procedure, while at the same time the State Department was fighting *against* the genuine link principle at the International Court of Justice in the IMCO case at the Hague.

In 1960, the NLRB moved ahead to make decisions favoring the unions, using the powers and jurisdiction established through the precedents of the previous few years. In May 1960, it ruled in *West India Fruit Company, Inc.* that it had jurisdiction. Applying the contact theory, the board found that the ship *Sea Level* never had been in a Liberian port, had no real connection with Liberia, and as a wholly owned American property, fell under United States jurisdiction. The board enjoined unfair labor practices aboard the ship, directed reinstatement of the fired crewmen, and ordered an election to determine the collective bargaining agent.[18]

In this landmark decision, the NLRB took on and dealt with a variety of arguments presented by the shipowners and drawn from international law. Liberia had signed an FCN treaty in 1938 with the United States. Under the treaty, the United States and Liberia mutually agreed to respect the jurisdiction of the flag state over the "internal order and discipline" in ships of each others' registry. As mentioned above, this sort of FCN treaty was one of the legal cornerstones for the theory that the law of the flag held supremacy over the laws of ports of call. However, when shipowners sought to rely on the FCN treaty as guaranteeing that Liberian law should prevail over the ship, the board pointed out that its jurisdiction over labor issues derived from the regulation-of-commerce power in the Constitution, and that labor matters considered by the board were not simply questions of "internal order and discipline" aboard ship referred to in the FCN treaties, but involved larger questions of commerce. Another argument against the power of the FCN treaty derived from a precedent the board traced back to the 1880s. The board showed that the Supreme Court had ruled in *Wildenhus's Case* that FCN treaties did not restrict jurisdiction to the flag state when events or crimes aboard the vessel threatened the security or public order of the port. Picketing and labor disputes, the board held, affected security and public order, as well as commerce. Furthermore, in responding to the argument by the shipowners that the flag was an emblem of foreign territory, the board recalled that the Supreme Court's decision in the *Cunard* case regarding Prohibition aboard ships had pointed out that ships were "territory" only metaphorically, and that ships often were subject to jurisdictions other than that of the flag state.[19]

The board voted, by a majority of three to two, to exercise labor jurisdiction in the *West India Fruit* case. The two minority dissenters argued that the board had exceeded its powers, not only over the law of the flag issue, but because the board had gone against the national policy of "effective control" as described by the Maritime Administration and the navy in hearings before Congress. But the majority of the NLRB held that while the Supreme Court had directed the board not to violate *congressional* intent or policy, it also had instructed the board not to be dictated to by other governmental agencies and boards that based their decisions on other legal obligations and powers. Since "effective control" never had become congressional policy, the majority of the board held, they need not adjust their own decisions to informally adopted policies of the Defense Department and the Maritime Administration.[20]

The ACFN reaction to the *West India Fruit* decision was to hold an "emergency meeting" the next day to discuss strategy. Naess and his associates were well aware that the future of flag-of-convenience operation could very well hinge on whether or not the NLRB's decision in the *West India Fruit* case was sustained by the Supreme Court. Naess recorded that ACFN members were quite worried that either the *West India Fruit* or the *Peninsular and Occidental* case would go to the Supreme Court for review. Each case had "an equally poor fact situation from our standpoint," Naess recalled. In both cases, American contacts of ownership and trade outweighed any connection between the vessels and the flag state, and if the Supreme Court followed its position from *Lauritzen* v. *Larsen*, the use of balancing contacts to establish labor jurisdiction would be vindicated and established as the law of the land.[21]

The ACFN would much prefer that cases involving the United Fruit Company go to the Supreme Court for review. United Fruit Company ships under the Honduran flag were not true flag-of-convenience vessels (despite the implication of their identity with Panamanian and Liberian ships in the use of the term *PanLibHon*), since they had extensive contacts with Honduras. The company's vessels called at Honduras, often carried Honduran cargoes, and were manned almost entirely by Honduran seamen, organized and represented through a Honduran labor union. Under either the international genuine link theory or the balancing-of-contacts procedure used in American courts, it would be possible to rule that United Fruit Company vessels were really Honduran and that the United States should have no jurisdiction. If the Supreme Court decided on United Fruit Company cases, then it might review, in the name of all PanLibHon shipping, the least typical but the most legitimate foreign-flag shipping under debate. The attempt to arrange for such "good facts" before the Supreme Court became the central ACFN tactic through 1961 and 1962. The ACFN members therefore were pleased when the NMU concentrated its efforts against the Empresa lines of United Fruit, and welcomed an NLRB battle on the safer ground of the Honduran flag.[22]

While the United Fruit Company case was before the NLRB, staff members at the White House made an effort to produce some coordinated policy out of the cross-purposes displayed by MarAd and by the Defense and State Departments on the one hand, and by the NLRB on the other. David Kendall, special counsel to President Eisenhower, directed his office to collect materials regarding the interagency conflict early in January 1959. Philip Areeda, assistant special counsel, was put in charge of the effort to obtain the viewpoints.[23]

Areeda pulled together for Kendall and the president a series of memoranda from the Maritime Administration, the navy, the State Department, the attorney general's office, and the NLRB explaining their positions. The Maritime Administration held that NLRB jurisdiction should not be applied to PanLibHon ships because, if flag-of-convenience shipping were exposed to American labor laws, the vessels probably would transfer to NATO powers, not to the United States. Under NATO flags, the ships would become available to the United States only in a general emergency involving NATO; even then, MarAd would have access only indirectly, through a merchant ship pooling plan. In lesser emergencies, involving the United States but no NATO powers, the ships would be unavailable. The navy shared this view and did not approve any plan to stimulate transfer from Panama or Liberia to European powers. The State Department's position was that the law of the flag should govern the vessels and that American interests lay with protecting the system of Panamanian and Liberian registry.[24]

The attorney general remained reluctant to become directly involved during the Eisenhower period, however. Assistant Attorney General George Doub pointed out on 3 February 1959, "I find no statutory authority or jurisdictional basis for the institution of an action by the Attorney General. . . . In agreement with Justice Clark's majority opinion in the *Benz* case, I feel that the shipowners' appeal should be directed to Congress rather than to the Executive or the Judiciary."[25]

In responding to Areeda's request for a statement of position, the NLRB's attorney recognized the issues presented by other agencies, but also pointed out that the board must concern itself with the condition of American seamen. He stated that for purposes of taxation, the ships might remain under foreign flag, but that legal authority over the working conditions of seamen aboard American vessels, even when registered abroad, should be in NLRB hands. Further, the board held, the conditions and legal arrangements under each flag varied, and should be subject to separate judgments and considerations.[26]

In April 1959, a White House meeting was held with representatives of the attorney general, the State Department, and the Defense Department. The representatives discussed and at first rejected a plan to have State and Defense submit memoranda to the attorney general for his use in preparing a brief for Justice Department intervention as a friend of the court in the United Fruit Company case before the NLRB. Areeda's office forwarded to the attorney general ACFN arguments urging participation of the government as a friend of the court, and spelling out reasons for denial of labor jurisdiction. The strategy of a brief from the attorney general's office was ordered directly by President Eisenhower, after discussions with Kendall. The Justice Department prepared a brief that asked for dismissal of jurisdiction and filed it with the NLRB on 18 November 1960, immediately after the election victory of John Kennedy over Richard Nixon, but prior to the inauguration of the new president.[27]

Despite this brief, in 1961, the NLRB decided in favor of the unions in the United Fruit Company case. Citing the balancing contact procedure from the *Lauritzen* case and the board's own decisions in the *West India Fruit* and *Peninsular and Occidental* cases, the board asserted jurisdiction over the ships of the United Fruit Company line in Honduras, despite the extensive Honduran contacts of the line. After proving that Empresa Hondurena was wholly owned by United Fruit and operated its ships under United Fruit's direct control, the board declared, "It follows, as we emphasized in our *West India* decision as we reemphasize here, that the particular flag or nationality of the vessels as such, plays no role in our determinations."[28] The board hoped to establish the idea that the contact of "parent" American ownership and administrative control would outweigh even such other contacts as organization under Honduran law, manning, extensive export trade, and local operations in Central America. Despite the possibility that the Honduran operation was not a "flag of convenience" at all, the NLRB asserted its jurisdiction. The company sought appeal to the Supreme

Court, leaving the continuing problem of interagency disagreement and the final legal showdown for the Kennedy administration to deal with.

The Supreme Court Decides

The cases that came before the Supreme Court included two *Hondurena* cases growing out of the NLRB's United Fruit Company decision, and a case involving the Italian-owned Incres line, operating under Liberian registry. In the *Incres* case, although the company operated from headquarters in New York, little other argument could be made for American "contacts," since the company was entirely owned and entirely crewed from Italy. The *Hondurena* and the *Incres* cases were to be heard together, indicating that the Supreme Court would come to grips with the major issues common to both cases. Amicus curiae briefs were filed by the governments of Panama, Liberia, Honduras, Britain, and Canada, and by Solicitor General Archibald Cox, representing the Kennedy administration's point of view.[29]

While the NMU concentrated its argument on the issue that "effective control" was a dubious policy, the issues in this final test case went far beyond the question of the workability of that concept. The NLRB had stated so clearly the argument for American jurisdiction over American-owned, foreign-registered shipping that even the British felt called upon to defend the supremacy of the law of the flag in the *Hondurena* and the *Incres* cases.

The British, despite their earlier position in opposition to Liberia and Panama at the IMCO meetings and at the International Court of Justice, argued in the United States Supreme Court in 1962 that the law of the flag should take precedence over the law of the owner. It was clear that if the United States exercised control over United Fruit Company ships, then American-owned British ships could become subject to the same jurisdiction. The British brief gave the practical historical reasons for the "subjection of vessels to the law of the flag state," and argued that "any assumption of jurisdiction which is in conflict with these principles can only be regarded as inimical to international trade."[30]

Solicitor General Cox's brief represented a very carefully thought-through position, which, while asking for the Court to reject the NMU position on the United Fruit Company ships and on the Italian-owned line, also asked the Court to leave open the question of possible NLRB jurisdiction over American-owned flag-of-convenience ships that had no connection with the flag state other than registry. The official position of the Kennedy administration, as reflected in the brief presented by Cox, was not the outright condemnation of labor jurisdiction for which the Eisenhower administration had argued in its brief to the NLRB in the same case in November 1960.[31]

Cox's brief implicitly utilized the contact principle and argued that the Court should deny NLRB jurisdiction in both the *Hondurena* and *Incres* cases, *based on the contacts in each case*. Cox distinguished between two classes of vessels: "those with significant links with the flag nation" and other, "truly flag of convenience vessels, flying the colors of a nation with which they have no substantial connection." Cox carefully used the term *flag of convenience* to apply only to the second category. He showed that *Hondurena* ships were in the first class, with substantial connections with Honduras, and that the United States should exercise no labor jurisdiction over them. The Incres ships were in the second class, true flag-of-convenience ships, but, since they were Italian-owned, the United States could claim no jurisdiction over them either. He warned the Court against "expressing any opinion upon the distinguishable issues that need not be decided until they require decisions." He recommended that there should be no NLRB jurisdiction over cases where there was a bona fide connection with the flag state; further, he advised against labor jurisdiction over true flag-of-convenience ships with no substantial link between the ship and the flag, *when the ownership and crew were foreign* to the United States. It should be noted that he did not ask for a ruling on flag-of-convenience cases where the contact between the United States and the ship was strong, as no such case was before the Court.

Cox also reviewed the Defense Department and European position that opposed "NLRB jurisdiction over any foreign flag vessels." He indicated that the protests filed by the foreign governments were not simply briefs by attorneys "but have been firmly conveyed to this government in diplomatic intercourse." Cox noted, "Application of the NLRB to these foreign-registered ships would be considered to be an affront to foreign nations and would have disturbing consequences."[32]

The new and precisely defined position, which would permit continued NLRB jurisdiction over American-owned ships under Panamanian and Liberian registry, was worked out by Cox after an interdepartmental committee meeting attended by President Kennedy and by representatives of the Departments of Commerce, State, Labor, and Defense. All the representatives, with the exception of Willard Wirtz, of the Department of Labor, agreed to recommend to the president opposition to NLRB jurisdiction on flag-of-convenience ships.

However, President Kennedy "dropped a bombshell" on the meeting, as Cox recalled later. Going to a bookshelf, Kennedy took down a collection of speeches and communications from his presidential campaign and read aloud from a telegram he had sent to Joe Curran at the NMU on 3 October 1960.

> I am especially interested and share your concern with your problems and in particular the "runaway ship" threat to the high standards which you and your union have fought for and established over the years. The "runaway ship," like its counterpart, the "runaway shop," is a hit-and-run operation which should be stopped.[33]

In the light of this statement, it would be awkward for the administration to ask for a Supreme Court decision that would place the "runaway ship" beyond the reach of American labor law.

After the meeting, Cox and Wirtz discussed the need to find a solution that was agreeable to everyone and that would avoid embarrassing the president. Cox then developed the brief, which departed from the previous administration's position and from the original interdepartmental committee recommendation, and which developed the formula that would "postpone the evil day when the Court would have to take a stand one way or the other" on the question.[34]

National Maritime Union leader Joe Curran (second from right, foreground) protests against the Panamanian-registered cruise ship Australis *and the flag-of-convenience system, 28 January 1968, in Port Everglades, Florida. (NMU* Pilot)

By asking that the Court rule only on the cases at hand and take no position on American-owned flag-of-convenience shipping, Cox honored the president's commitment to Joe Curran. Naess and the ACFN noted that Cox had attempted to "ride the fence" and that his policy would leave the door open to continued application of the contact theory. ACFN members were concerned and distressed, for the Supreme Court often took very seriously the advice of the administration as represented in briefs filed by the solicitor general.[35]

But, despite Cox's warning to limit the decision to the cases at hand, Justice Clark, in an opinion concurred in by the other seven justices participating, ruled 18 February 1963 on the broader question of the application of the National Labor Relations Act to the whole range of flag-of-convenience shipping. "We have concluded that the jurisdictional provisions of the Act do not extend to maritime operations of foreign-flag ships employing alien seamen," Justice Clark wrote.[36]

The Court noted that the cases raised issues "particularly high in the scale of our national interest because of their international complexion." But Justice Clark stated that the Court did not wish to deal with all the policy issues, but simply to decide whether Congress, in the National Labor Relations Act, had exercised its power to apply labor law to foreign-flag ships. The Court believed that, since Congress had not specifically indicated it intended jurisdiction of the act over foreign-flag vessels, the board should not apply the balancing-of-contacts procedure to such ships. The Court clearly indicated that Congress did have the power to extend labor jurisdiction in this field and it recommended, as it had in the earlier *Benz* case, that the parties should direct any further arguments to Congress. Although Justice Clark was careful to indicate that Congress could extend jurisdiction if it wished, and that the Court did not want to imply any "impairment of our own sovereignty or limitation of Congress" on the question of such jurisdiction, the ACFN greeted the decision as an outright and final American vindication of the "law of the flag," much as it had reacted to the International Court of Justice ruling in the narrow IMCO case.[37]

In spite of the presidential position, based on a minor campaign commitment, a crucial battle had been lost by the unions. Cox's potentially valuable distinction between the Honduran United Fruit Company situation and true flag-of-convenience shipping was not adopted by the Court, and the body of precedent that had worked out the balancing-of-contacts principle was ruled inapplicable to NLRB cases by the decision. Thereafter, the NMU and the SIU found themselves confronted with labor injunctions and damage suits and could not begin new pickets or boycotts without serious troubles in the courts. After 1963, labor cases won locally would encounter rebuffs on appeal, based on the simple and definitive nature of the *Incres-Hondurena* decision.

The battle between the conflicting views of flags of convenience, enunciated in 1939, had been fought through the 1950s and the early 1960s in several different institutional arenas. The State Department under Truman had continued a "hands-off" attitude on the grounds that the disputes were labor-management issues, and had refused to assist Panama in its battle with European shipowners through the ILO. But in the mid-1950s, when British, Dutch, and Norwegian opposition to the system focused on the international legal forums of the International Law Commission, the Law of the Sea Conference, IMCO, and the International Court of Justice, then the State Department, under Dulles, came to the defense of the system.

In the United States, the view that the system represented a set of subterfuges began to emerge both in the lower courts and in several NLRB decisions. By 1961, the board even had ruled that the Honduran vessels of the United Fruit Company should come under American labor law. It appeared labor's argument that the systems sheltered "runaway ships" would win the backing of the courts and the NLRB. The evolution of the balancing-of-contacts procedure gave a legal expression to the skeptical view, and threatened to destroy one of the main advantages of Panamanian and Liberian shipping from the viewpoint of American shipowners.

The failure of Congress to deal with the issues surrounding flags of convenience left the question to the judicial and the executive branches to resolve. The fundamental differences among the executive agencies were thrashed out in subcabinet meetings under both Eisenhower and Kennedy, with similar approaches considered by each. Both administrations were inclined to accept the position, advocated by the Defense Department and the ACFN, that the systems were strategically convenient and commercially necessary; but in Kennedy's case, the campaign commitment to labor required a tactic that would forestall the issue. The Court, faced with congressional inaction and executive department hesitancy, made its decision. Despite the care taken by Cox in presenting the executive branch's position to the Supreme Court, the mechanisms that had evolved for piercing the veil of foreign incorporation and convenient flag registry were swept aside in the Court's concerns not to exceed explicit congressional intent or to disturb international harmony.

By 1963, shipowners successfully had met both international and American legal challenges, and had cleared the way for expansion of Liberian and Panamanian registries, limited only by the vagaries and needs of the shipping markets.

10

Environment and Energy

In the period following the *Incres-Hondurena* Supreme Court decision in 1963, the fleet registered in Liberia grew with phenomenal rapidity, outstripping even its remarkable earlier growth. Having surpassed Panama in both numbers and tonnage by 1956, the Liberian flag overtook those of both Great Britain and the United States in 1966, when it became the largest registry in the world. (See table 14.)

The causes of the rapid growth in Liberia's registry could be found in the conjunction of a favorable legal environment and pressing economic conditions. With the advantages of no taxation and lower operating costs, shipowning corporations in the United States and elsewhere sought the flag with the best legal arrangements. Freed from the challenge of American labor, endorsed by the United States Supreme Court and the International Court of Justice, administered by an efficient American corporation, and defended by an effective pressure group in the ACFN, the Liberian system provided ideal conditions for registry.

Profits of the large independent operators under the Liberian flag could be plowed back into innovative shipping ideas. Naess pioneered in the development of the Oil-Bulk-Ore carrier that allowed for highly profitable triangular and quadrilateral trades. Instead of filling cargo tanks with sea water for ballast, the combination carriers could carry a cargo of grain or other bulk product on return trips to oil-producing countries. Ludwig invested in the "jumboized" tanker—a tanker in which the midsection and bottom were removed and replaced. The lengthened and deepened ship would be converted from a large 50,000-ton vessel to a 100,000-ton behemoth.[1]

The closing of the Suez Canal in 1967 for an eight-year period guaranteed the economic usefulness of the jumbo carrier and launched a competitive

Table 14.
Merchant Flag Registries, 1960–78

	Liberia			Panama		
Year	No. of Ships	Tonnage in Thousands	Percentage of World Tonnage	No. of Ships	Tonnage in Thousands	Percentage of World Tonnage
1960	977	11,282	8.7	607	4,236	3.3
1965	1,287	17,539	10.9	692	4,465	2.8
1968	1,613	25,720	13.2	798	5,097	2.6
1970	1,869	33,297	14.6	886	5,646	4.8
1975	2,520	65,820	19.2	2,418	13,667	4.0
1978	2,523	80,191	19.8	3,640	20,749	5.1

Source: The Economist Intelligence Unit, Ltd. *Open Registry Shipping.*

increase in size. Unrestricted by the limit of canal depth, tanker operators found that economies of scale on the voyages around the Cape of Good Hope from the Persian Gulf to Europe continued with the increases of size, and tankers of an unheard-of scale were planned and constructed. The growth continued even after the reopening of the canal, and the huge vessels avoided the canal route. Each year saw the arrival of another "largest" tanker as Niarchos and Onassis competed for sheer size. Vessels between 150,000 and 300,000 tons became common by the early 1970s. The designation "supertanker," once attached to the 50,000-ton range, no longer seemed appropriate, and the new giants were dubbed Very Large Crude Carriers (VLCCs). Planned vessels in the 500,000-ton range and larger were to be called Ultra Large Crude Carriers.[2]

A combination of low oil prices from Middle Eastern sources; increased use of automobiles in the United States, Western Europe, and Japan; and universal consumption of a range of petroleum products increased world dependence on petroleum supplied by sea. In both Europe and Japan, oil consumption increased despite substantially higher prices on gasoline and other petroleum products than those prevailing in the United States. Tanker rates climbed as demand increased. Great fortunes were built by the adventurous independent tanker owners; many of those who succeeded took advantage of a variety of competitive devices permitted under Liberia's law. Men who had pioneered Panamanian ownership in the 1930s and 1940s emerged as the giants of the shipping industry in the 1960s. Naess, Ludwig, Onassis, and Niarchos all continued their empire-building under the Liberian flag, and were challenged by younger rivals from Pakistan and Hong Kong.[3]

A smaller class of independent tanker owners grew up with direct ties to certain oil companies. Several firms were organized by oil company executives, and those firms received contracts from the corporations managed by their owners. Such arrangements had all the finesse of the devices worked out by the Credit Mobilier construction firm that built the Union Pacific Railroad in the nineteenth century. Profits, instead of being earned by the widely held company, would be consumed in charges to the closely held firm owned by the managers of the larger company. Profit would be channeled to dividends earned by the small company owned by the managing group.[4]

More quietly, the large fleets of the multinational oil companies grew, with ESSO still leading the group. The major oil companies arranged a similar diversion of profit to shipping subsidiaries that were owned wholly by the parent firm; but in such systems, the profits accumulated would benefit the corporation as a whole, rather than a narrow circle of executives. Economists regarded this practice by the multinational oil companies as "transfer pricing," a sophisticated term for a simple practice. The companies could count as a business cost to the American refining operations charges for shipping crude oil from the Middle East to American ports. Since profits of the Liberian operation were not taxable, and could be retained from year to year, the practice allowed earnings in the tax-free environment to be increased by "transferring" high prices to the taxable U.S. environment. In effect, the artificially high prices charged for ship-

The Arietta Livanos, *a 285,000-ton tanker, was one of dozens owned by the Greek families of* Onassis, Niarchos, *and* Livanos. *These fleets earned fortunes through the relatively tax-free registry of Liberia. (Naval Photographic Center)*

ping allowed more profits to be accumulated where they would not be subject to taxes.

From time to time, oil company executives denied that such practices explained their attraction to the flags of convenience, and claimed that they set shipping prices by competition that was reflected in international average rates and standards. Critics responded that those average rates themselves were established by the high proportion of prices set artificially by the companies shipping oil on their own vessels. Corporate officials would not release detailed information regarding their internal pricing decisions for oil transport. It was clear, however, that such prices were multiples of actual shipping costs in the boom years of the late 1960s and early 1970s. The practice developed by ESSO in the 1920s, building a fleet in Danzig out of earnings from transportation, had carried over to Panama and to Liberia as ESSO enlarged its fleets and other companies emulated its system.[5]

In the struggle to reduce costs and increase the profit margins in the tax-free environment, individual and corporate owners sought to man their vessels with inexpensive crews, but they were aware that they could go too far. Clearly, it would not pay to invest $20 to $40 million in a vessel, another $2 to $4 million in cargo, and then place the ship in the hands of officers and crew members who would run the ship into danger or fail to comply with the pressing demands of arrival and departure schedules, documentation, loading, handling, and dozens of minute administrative details that would allow for profitable employment of such huge investments. American, Canadian, German, British, and Scandinavian crews and officers, while they provided an excellent pool of skill from which to select, had the disadvantage of high salary and wage expectations. The less developed economies of Greece and Italy, with their rich reservoirs of seamen and nautical experience, could provide the best of both worlds—sophistication in the technology of modern shipping, but wage scales that would allow a company to man a first-class supertanker or VLCC for $250 thousand to $1 million less per year than an American or Canadian crew would require. As the Liberian fleet expanded, so did employment of Italian and Greek officers and crews. World War II veterans who had served as junior naval officers found their careers advancing rapidly; soon the senior posts of command on the largest vessels that ever had plied the seas were in the hands of former coastal vessel officers. Liberia issued licensing regulations that made the practice easier; Liberian officers' certificates would be granted automatically to holders of equivalent masters', mates', and engineers' certificates from the traditional maritime nations. Men of talent and diligence found those qualities rapidly and generously rewarded in the burgeoning oil company and independent tanker fleets.[6]

The Politics of Disaster

The growth of Liberia's fleet encountered severe challenges over the decade from 1967 through 1977. A series of accidents at sea, groundings, and oil spills brought the Liberian system to world attention and brought several modifications to the system. The oil-importing nations found themselves immersed in the politics of disaster, simultaneously facing sudden popular protest, technological problems of an apparently insurmountable nature, and legal and financial issues of a new magnitude.

Three Liberian-registered tankers forced the British and American publics to view flags of convenience as potential threats to the environment and as challenges to the world order. The *Torrey Canyon* wrecked in 1967 off Britain's Cornish coast; the *Ocean Eagle* broke in half in San Juan harbor, Puerto Rico, in 1968; and the *Argo Merchant* grounded off Nantucket in the winter of 1976. The names of these Liberian ships were the first to enter the vocabulary of world affairs.

Each of these Liberian tankers produced a disastrous oil spill, and each provoked frantic political and legal maneuvers designed to place or to evade responsibility for the accidents. Each event formed the basis for investigative studies, both by journalists and by experts, designed to respond to questions posed by governments and by the public.

Despite the growing importance of sea transport of petroleum to the world's economy, the mechanisms of the tanker business had remained a mystery to the informed public. As news writers began to describe the disasters, they discovered layers of information that needed to be digested, verified, and presented rapidly, to meet news deadlines. Journalists explained the complex and unfamiliar arrangements of tanker charters, the various national schemes of subsidy and tax credits, the confidential pricing practices of the multinational oil firms, the fluctuations in independent tanker rates, and the network of international legal practices and relationships previously little discussed beyond the circle of the ship operators themselves. Several journalists, realizing the futility of presenting these complicated issues in the format of a news or magazine article, wrote books, a few of which became best sellers. The inquiries of journalists in turn became briefs for the political debate growing out of the disasters.[7]

The popular interest in news stories, televised reports, and book-length accounts of the crises was stimulated by several new developments in public attitudes through the 1960s and 1970s. Disasters at sea and spilled oil themselves were not new events—ships had foundered on rocks for centuries, and spilled oil had been an emblem of wealth since the gushers of the nineteenth century. But, by the 1960s, drastic changes in public attitudes made the combination of sea disaster and oil spill a matter of agonized concern. The control of oil by an often secretive group of five American and two European corporations focused populist discontents upon this form of corporate wealth. In the case of ocean oil spills, that concern coincided with the growing world concern with the natural environment. Conservation had been a powerful political movement both in Europe and in the United States since the first decade of the twentieth century. By the 1960s, the reasons for its original elevation to a political issue had grown; frustration with the pace of urban life, industrialization, and the growth of massive impersonal institutions all helped explain longstanding psychological and social roots of such concerns. Politically, one could strive conservatively to preserve the preindustrial and natural environment and at the same time, in the name of the people, couple that gesture with a socially conscious attack on special interests.[8]

As the questions of pollution and environmental protection aroused more concern, the technical nature of petroleum pollution came into question. Oil industry scientists claimed that oil in the sea would disperse and decay naturally. But, some independent scientists believed oil would persist and contaminate the life chain in the seas for decades. The chemical composition of petroleum was toxic and carcinogenic, but oceanographers and chemists debated whether the toxicity would persist in sea water, and precisely how carcinogenic specific quantities of petroleum traces would be in seafood.[9]

When the Liberian-registered tankers foundered on the rocky isles off Britain, in the harbor of Puerto Rico, and on the shoals of Nantucket, the impact was a complex interplay of business, law, diplomacy, journalism, mass psychology, and scientific debate whose repercussions seriously threatened the very survival of flags of convenience.

The *Torrey Canyon*

The disaster that befell Captain Pastrengo Rugiati, his crew, and their vessel the *Torrey Canyon* on the morning of 15 March 1967 was the most widely recounted of all the disasters. The accounts focused on the precise details of Rugiati's behavior that morning; they showed how a combination of pressures, inattention to details, and personal interaction led to a fateful series of human errors. The master was concerned with bringing his 100,000-ton, 30 million-gallon cargo of Kuwait crude oil into Milford Haven harbor in Wales on a high tide, to meet schedules demanded by the Union Oil Company, and he was slightly out of sorts. As the ship neared a fateful decision point off the Scilly Islands at the tip of Cornwall, he delayed his decision as to the course a few minutes too long, and failed to communicate his intentions clearly to his helmsman and his watch officers. When he finally ordered a bearing change that would take the huge vessel through the relatively narrow 6 mile wide passage in the islands, the ship did not answer the helm, but continued ahead, grounding on Pollard Rock. The failure to respond, Captain Rugiati discovered a moment before the impact, was due to the setting of the helm on the "control" or automatic, rather than the manual, option.[10]

The ship was too large and too well impaled on the rocks to salvage, its cargo was too difficult to recover in the seas that rose the next morning, and the 100,000 tons of cargo spilled into the sea and began to wash ashore. It became the largest oil spill at sea in history to that date.

Once he subdued his panic, Captain Rugiati reacted responsibly. He signaled distress, and as salvage and British official observers arrived, he welcomed them and stayed with his ship to help organize salvage attempts. Despite the apparent dangers of fire or explosion, he left only after it became apparent that salvage efforts were unavailing. Yet, he was burdened with a sense of failure—it was, after all, his responsibility to have controlled the ship and planned its course, and the errors that had led to the grounding had been his errors. The dignity with which he accepted blame did him credit in the eyes of both mariners and the British public. Journalists reported wide sympathy for him; yet his career was ruined.[11]

Behind the responsibility of the individual for the mechanics of the accident lay even more crucial questions of legal and diplomatic responsibility. On one level was the issue of liability. Who was to pay for the damage the vessel brought? On another level was the question of the political authority over the ship. Who would make crucial technical decisions about the wreck—whether to try to salvage it, to destroy it, to abandon it? Who would decide on methods to clean up the spill and choose between detergents and dispersal agents, which might sink the oil?

The rapid spread of the ship's "black tide" to the scenic shores and coves of Cornwall, and across the English Channel to Brittany in France, endangered the rich fishing grounds of that coast and left no time for contemplating such issues of higher responsibility. The British Navy, acting on direct orders of Prime Minister Harold Wilson, proceeded to use available detergents to wash down rocks and harbors, while French volunteers spread straw and raked up the beaches in France. The detergents, claimed representatives of the oil industry, were highly toxic and killed organisms more widely than the crude oil itself, which, the companies reminded the public, was a "natural product." On 18 March 1967, the British government decided to destroy the wreck by bombing and to ignite the remaining crude oil cargo with jet fuel and napalm. However, by the time the decision was made, much of the spill had washed ashore, and the more flammable and volatile components of the crude oil had evaporated, making it difficult to ignite or sustain a fire in the remaining cargo. Nevertheless, the Royal Air Force claimed it had destroyed 40,000 tons. Eventually, after fifteen days, still leaking oil, the battered hulk of the ship slipped off the rock into deeper water.[12]

In attempting to resolve the financial question of who should pay for the cleanup costs, Britain sought out the owners of the *Torrey Canyon*. A group of Union Oil Company executives and associated attorneys owned the vessel through a Bermuda corporation, Barracuda Tanker Company. The company proved difficult to deal with, claiming that, since the oil spill derived from errors of the master, not from any fault or knowledge of the owners, the liability of the company was limited to the remaining salvage value of the vessel. An American court accepted that logic, and held the $8.40 million British claim and a French claim of $7.64 million could be attached only to the one lifeboat, recovered in damaged condition and worth perhaps $50. The British and French governments thought otherwise, and proceeded to issue writs for the arrest of either of two sister ships belonging to Barracuda Tanker Company, the *Lake Poularde* and the *Sansinena*. The owning company carefully avoided scheduling either ship into a British or French port where such writs could be served. But, the British were able to detain the *Lake Poularde* on 15 July 1967, in Singapore. That ship, worth some $17 million, could not miss its schedule, and the owners agreed to post a bond covering the British damage claim against the *Torrey Canyon* in order to obtain permission for the *Lake Poularde* to leave Singapore. As she steamed out of the harbor, a French officer on a launch chased her to serve another writ, but the tanker escaped. In April 1968, the French secured a settlement for damages through a similar arrest of the same ship in Rotterdam.[13]

The question of responsibility could endanger the continued use of the Liberian flag itself. The appointed deputy maritime commissioners of Liberia in the United States worked to preserve the system against the legal and public relations assaults that followed the *Torrey Canyon* disaster. As they did so, however, they drew attention to the fact that the Liberian ship registry system was administered by employees of the International Trust Company. In Genoa, Italy, the Liberian Maritime Commission held an inquiry into the causes of the *Torrey Canyon* wreck and proceeded to question the officers. Although the commission never released a transcript of the hearing, a purloined copy of the proceedings provided journalists with further grounds to criticize the system.[14] According to the possibly inaccurate transcript of the hearing, Captain Rugiati, unrepresented by counsel, took responsibility for the errors and the commission ordered his Liberian license suspended. The private hearing and the reports of its procedure seemed to outside observers to serve as another proof of the artificial nature of the Liberian system. One author argued that Liberia sought to protect the owners by placing responsibility on the captain, while another contended that an additional purpose was to divert criticism from the Liberian system itself. A French maritime writer, Captain L. de Vaisseau Oudet, argued forcefully that the hearing demonstrated the essentially private and corporate nature of Liberian registry. He held that those officials acted in the interests of the companies that had created and sustained the system. They were blind to injustices they perpetrated or to the bias they reflected, because they were, in effect, part of the corporate structure that itself was responsible for the ships. Without access to the details of the creation of the system, Oudet intuitively concluded that the system was essentially an extension of the American system of corporations. Oudet's critique overlooked some of the complexities of the relationship between shipowners and the Liberian registry system, but he suggested a real connection few observers had emphasized.[15]

The argument that flags of convenience were systems of subterfuge was given a new aspect by the events following the wreck of the *Torrey Canyon*. Prime Minister Wilson indicated that his first reaction to ships of such registry was to regard them as sailing under a suspect arrangement, with poor safety enforcement. The British view of such flags had its roots in dealings with the clandestine trades of the 1930s and 1940s under Panama's flag. But Wilson admitted that the safety and maintenance records of the Liberian vessels of the late 1960s were of a high quality, and showed the inaccuracy of his first reaction. The actual subterfuge lay, he noted, not in evasion of safety measures, but in the opportunity such registries created to evade responsibility and liability for damages. To clarify the issue of liability for oil damage from wrecked tankers in the future, the British called for an emergency meeting of IMCO to draw up an agenda for a conference that would produce an international convention requiring liability insurance by tanker owners to cover future incidents.[16]

The preliminary IMCO meeting, held in London on 5 and 6 May 1967, considered a variety of proposals ranging from technical issues such as ocean speed limits, traffic separation patterns, and rules demanding more navigational aids on tankers, to a requirement for compulsory liability insurance and a rule holding shipowners responsible for damage without consideration of the degree of shipowner negligence. While the discussions proceeded, the major oil companies entered a voluntary agreement that provided for a $10 million fund to pay for oil damage cleanup by governments and a supplementary agreement that extended the coverage to $30 million for damages to third parties. In 1969, at the full meeting of the IMCO conference in Brussels, two international conventions were agreed upon. One convention required compulsory insurance for tankers covering oil spill damages up to a maximum of $14 million. The limit was set on the advice of the London ship insurance market that insurance with higher limits could not be purchased. The second convention provided for armed intervention on the high seas in cases of oil pollution casualties. The British cabinet had hesitated to order the Royal Air Force to fire on the *Torrey Canyon* since, technically, the vessel was on the high seas, and the attack could be viewed as an act of war against the flag state. While some legal authorities had argued convincingly that existing precedents for self-defense allowed the attack, the question was legally debatable, and the delay had allowed for the escape of oil and the evaporation of much of the flammable part of the cargo. Both conventions went into force in 1975. Critics of the liability convention pointed out that the limitation on liability aided tanker owners, since it was quite conceivable that a major oil spill in a resort area, through damages to tourist trade, could result in losses of business far in excess of the limited amount.[17]

The *Ocean Eagle*

A test of the reaction to such an oil spill in a tourist economy was provided on 3 March 1968. The channel past Morro Castle into San Juan harbor, Puerto Rico, is scenic, narrow, relatively shallow, and obstructed by bars and previous wreckage. When the slightly overloaded 18,000-ton *Ocean Eagle*, carrying a cargo of oil for Gulf Oil from Venezuela to a refinery in Puerto Rico, approached the passage, the master Stelios Galaris, had doubts of his ability to run the gauntlet in the 15-foot swells and force-four winds. But, when Harbor Pilot David Gonzales tried to come aboard, the master did not slow the tanker to allow boarding. As the tanker ran aground in the quieter waters of the channel, Gonzales boarded, to find the crew and officers in a state of panic.[18]

The controversy over the accident focused on the failure of the pilot to board the tanker outside the passage. The pilot's launch had no radio for communication with the ship; boarding in a moderate sea was difficult or impossible; no clear system of visual signals was employed between the launch and the tanker. While the oil had been owned by one subsidiary of Gulf Oil for sale to another subsidiary, the ship itself was owned by a small organization, Trans-Ocean Tankers Corporation, under charter to Gulf's shipping subsidiary, Kupan Transport. Cleanup operations were undertaken by the Army Corps of Engineers, and questions of liability for the damages went unresolved.

Owners of resort hotels fronting the beaches tried to minimize publicity of the oil spill. Even as oil was plowed off the hotel beaches at the hotel owners' expense, local tourist agencies denied the seriousness of the event, to avoid cancellations of previously booked reservations. The vessel broke in half, blocking the harbor entrance, and only after a week of repeated attempts could the two sections be towed to sea for scuttling.[19]

Despite the grounding of the *Ocean Eagle* in United States territorial waters, the accident had far less media impact in the United States than had the *Torrey Canyon*. The use of booms to contain the spilled oil, and the experiments with the use of various detergents provided useful experience to the Coast Guard, but public attention did not linger on the crisis. Partly because of the distance of the event from the media centers in New York, and partly out of local officials' deference to commercial insistence that the disaster not be overplayed, reporters found it difficult to gather details, and the crisis did not evoke the national concern that had swept Britain the year before.[20]

The *Argo Merchant*

It was the wreck of the *Argo Merchant*, 15 December 1976, on the shoals south of Nantucket that riveted American public interest on the question of Liberian registry and its growing dominance of oil imports. Again, the officers were responsible, but, in addition, the ship's second-rate equipment discredited the efforts of the major oil companies to claim a superior safety record, maintenance schedule, and precautionary standard aboard Liberian vessels. In contrast to the *Torrey Canyon*, the *Argo Merchant* had inadequate radar, no direction finder, and an unreliable fathometer. Further, the officers displayed a lack of navigation skills that posed a danger to the vessel, themselves, and the ports to which they brought the ship.

Coast Guard inspectors knew the *Argo Merchant* was a dangerous ship, with a record of some eighteen minor incidents and collisions. The Coast Guard command planned to detain the vessel outside Boston harbor for inspection and possible detention for compulsory repair of equipment. But, before the ship could reach the inspection point, it ran hard aground on the shoals and began to leak its 29,000-ton cargo of heavy industrial fuel.

The ship's master, Georgios Papadopolous, claimed he had passed the Nantucket lightship without seeing it, and that then he had incorrectly interpreted the ship's radar by 180°, heading away from the lightship, instead of toward it. He had ignored fathometer readings as he entered shallow waters—since the depth did not agree with his incorrectly deduced position. When he signaled distress, he could not give his position accurately, but reported a number of incorrect coordinates over a several hundred square-mile area. He denied that he intentionally had attempted a shortcut through shallow waters. Whatever his intentions, he made serious errors of seamanship, and had lost his vessel.[21]

The impact of the *Argo Merchant* accident in the United States was both parallel to, and distinct from, the impact of the *Torrey Canyon* in Britain. Sustained press and television coverage of the accident for two weeks reflected and generated public concern, adding to the developing public perception of the Liberian flag as a subterfuge. Carefully researched newspaper articles explored the background of tanker economics and ownership,

The Argo Merchant *aground on shoals off Nantucket, 27 December 1976. The wreck of this Liberian-registered tanker and the danger of its spilled oil renewed U.S. public concern over flag-of-convenience issues. (Elaine Chan, National Oceanic and Atmospheric Administration)*

uncovering the ship's owner, the small Thebes Shipping Company owned by resident-alien Greek nationals in New York. Other exposés revealed the record of poor equipment and dubious officer qualifications, and placed responsibility for the accident on both the owners and the Liberian registry system itself.[22]

The press and public concern shaped the official response, as it had in Britain. The *Argo Merchant* provided a test of the Coast Guard's strike force capability built up from the *Ocean Eagle* experience. As in the case of the *Torrey Canyon* accident, high seas prevented any effort to pump oil to other vessels. The Coast Guard did a competent job of rescuing the crew, destroying the ship, and tracking the oil spill as it dispersed away from fishing grounds, far into the Atlantic. In response to the licensing and equipment inadequacies of the ship, the Coast Guard launched an increased inspection program. Within one year, the Coast Guard visited 2,650 ships, reporting more than 50 percent with violations of safety standards. A computerized record of all polluting incidents reported to the Coast Guard was developed, navigational aids were added to the list of items checked, and inspections were conducted in contiguous waters, not simply within the territorial 12-mile limit. The accident strengthened the hand of the

Coast Guard in its requests for increased budget to meet its new missions under the 1972 Port and Waterways Safety Act, by providing an excellent example of the dangers to which the nation could be exposed if strong enforcement of the law were neglected. Coast Guard and environmental protection advocates relied on the traditional right of the law of the port to take precedence over the law of the flag on questions of public order and safety.[23]

Economic Considerations

At the time the *Argo Merchant* went down, the independent tanker owners faced a problem of world tanker surplus. In 1973, the successful moves of the Organization of Petroleum-Exporting Countries (OPEC) in increasing oil prices and limiting shipments to Western supporters of Israel had engendered the "oil crisis" in Western Europe and in the United States. The result was a cut in consumption at the very time when jumboized tankers and VLCCs of the 200,000- to 300,000-ton range were coming into the market. When oil consumption fell by a small percentage, the leverage principle that had worked in favor of the independent tanker owners in the boom times of the 1950s and 1960s now worked in reverse. A 10 percent cut in tanker need had resulted in a catastrophic fall in short-term charter rates, as the major oil companies relied on their own vessels and cut off contracts with the independents as soon as possible. Shipowners continued to face fixed charges such as mortgage payments and maintenance costs. The Independent Tanker Owners' Association (Intertanko), headquartered in Oslo and chaired by Erling Naess, who had left his position with ACFN in 1968, struggled with a variety of ship retirement schemes and devised several measures, none too successful, to reduce the surplus. The *Argo Merchant* accident, Naess claimed, provided public pressure for the retirement of marginal vessels, pressure that was welcomed by the larger independent and oil-company fleets.[24]

Intertanko had encountered a variety of legal and business obstacles to its various tanker-reduction schemes. By leaving ships in ports longer for repairs and classification, by slow steaming to reduce deliveries and bring down ship fuel costs, and by increased scrapping of older vessels, owners had hoped to cut the surplus cargo capacity. But, such measures of reduction meant that each individual owner would lose opportunities for carrying the decreased cargoes. Cooperation was required, but difficult to arrange. When possible, owners of combination carriers individually could switch from oil transport to grain and other bulk carriage, but soon the rates for those cargoes declined as ships previously employed in oil trade switched into the dry bulk trades, creating a surplus tonnage in that category as well. Several vessels were anchored and used as fixed storage facilities for petroleum, but the cost per ton of storage aboard a tanker was considerably higher than that for on-shore storage.[25]

One of Naess's proposals was to take advantage of world concern with tanker pollution incurred in tank cleaning and ballasting. He pointed out that those vessels that contained their oil slops from tank washings needed port facilities for discharge of the oil-water mix. While some ports had special reception facilities for such waste, many ports did not. Thus, in the name of a viable antipollution measure, tankers could be retired to serve as reception facilities in smaller ports. Intertanko lobbied for legislation that would require such facilities, but without much success, through 1977. Again, on a strictly business basis, the cost of maintaining the tanker as a storage facility mitigated against this device for the reduction of the tanker surplus. Intertanko members believed aroused public concern over pollution might increase the chances of imposing the system legislatively.[26]

More direct plans for voluntary vessel retirement, arranged between independent tanker owners and the oil companies, ran into specific legal obstacles. American oil companies, which owned the largest part of the tanker tonnage, would not cooperate in voluntary vessel retirement schemes, since the United States Justice Department held such agreements to be in restraint of trade and illegal. Naess claimed that what the Justice Department regarded as illegal, the Coast Guard and the public would achieve under the plans for enforcement of safety regulations. Naess hoped that the climate of aroused opinion after the *Argo Merchant* would save the tanker market. By forcing marginal operators out of the American trade, the larger operators, both the multinational company subsidiaries and the large independents with their higher capital resources for improvements and modern equipment, might find a protected market.[27]

Naess hoped to utilize concerns with oil pollution in several other ways to strengthen the position of his own fleet. In reaction to American outrage at the leaking *Argo Merchant*, Naess supported plans for requiring double bottoms in tankers, plans that had been discussed since the *Torrey Canyon* incident. While some owners, such as ESSO, had regarded double bottoms as potentially dangerous, since the space provided would entrap gasses, might fill with water on collision, and would represent an unneeded capital outlay, others had experimented with double bottom and double hull construction. Many of Naess's own Oil-Bulk-Ore carriers were constructed with double bottoms and with segregated sea water ballast tanks. Naess admittedly planned to turn public antipollution concerns and political pressures to business advantage by securing laws that compelled owners to retrofit tankers with such features. Since segregated and dedicated ballast tanks would not require the use of cargo tanks to carry sea water ballast, they would avoid the discharge of oily water ballast into the sea or into shore holding facilities. Even without regulations requiring such a measure as an antipollution device, the equipment had a competitive advantage in that it allowed slightly faster turnaround time at ports, since tank washing stages could be avoided and clean sea water ballast could be discharged directly into harbors without the delay of discharge into holding facilities. While double bottoms had no such advantage, Naess hoped that legislation requiring them would place his previously equipped vessels in a strong competitive position. However, as these plans were under discussion in 1978, his son, Michael Naess, acting as manager of the firm, worked out the sale of the whole shipping line owned by Naess to the British Peninsular and Oriental group for $205 million; Erling Naess accepted retirement from the battle to write his memoirs.[28]

On a larger scale, the Federation of American-Controlled Shipping (FACS), the successor to ACFN, reacted in a similar, but slightly less obviously self-interested fashion. Testifying at the Liberian Marine Board of Investigation convened to investigate the *Argo Merchant* wreck, Phillip Loree, chairman of the FACS, submitted eight recommendations. FACS documents noted that the lawyers for the Thebes Shipping Company, owners of the *Argo Merchant*, strongly opposed the recommendations. Since FACS tended to be controlled by the largest shipowning corporations, the organization could endorse reforms of Liberian law and regulations that would strengthen their advantages in the limited tanker market. Loree and the FACS recommended:

1. Full disclosure of ownership of each Liberian vessel to the Liberian authorities
2. A rule requiring owners to give evidence of financial responsibility
3. A program by which Liberia would identify and investigate vessels with high casualty records
4. A program of increased inspection by Liberia of *all* vessels under its registry
5. A rule requiring all new Liberian registries to be contingent on inspection of the vessels
6. Rules requiring deck officers to be proficient in radar observation, navigation, and in pollution rules
7. Regularized rules for holding investigations of casualties
8. Ratification of the 1974 Convention for the Safety of Life at Sea (SOLAS-74)[29]

Each of the FACS-recommended reforms of the Liberian system was in fact implemented over the next two years. The International Trust Company perfected its system of inspection, enforced upgraded requirements for licensing, and obtained Liberian ratification of the SOLAS-74 convention. At its offices in Reston, Virginia, the International Trust Company set up computer-accessible records on each vessel in its registry, and began a program of warnings and cancellations of casualty-prone or low-grade vessels. To insure that the inspections of vessels were, indeed, conducted by qualified and trustworthy inspectors, trust company executives themselves investigated the credentials of the maritime licensing and engineering groups conducting the ship inspections.[30]

The responsiveness of both individual owners like Naess and the FACS organization to the public concern with pollution stands in marked contrast to the reaction of the same organization to the assaults of labor in the previous decade. Yet, it is clear that in this case, as in many other situations, specific business interests could advance their own positions by sponsoring reforms that coincided with widespread public concerns. Both large and small operators had shared an interest in opposing the extension of the NLRB rules to their vessels, but only the larger and better-financed corporations would benefit from heightened technical specifications and improved inspection, safety, and licensing requirements. In this way, the politics of disaster served to sort out and point up divisions among owners of flag-of-convenience shipping, in a way not disclosed when they stood together against organized labor.

Congressional Assaults

As the dependence of the United States upon imported oil increased, the significance of the flag-of-convenience system to the American national economy became more and more pronounced. By 1977, the United States imported about 48 percent of the oil it consumed. Only some 3.5 percent of the oil entered the United States in American-registered ships, while about 58 percent came in on Liberian and Panamanian ships. Of these vessels, approximately 85 percent of the tonnage, or about one-half of the total imported oil, came on flag-of-convenience ships owned by the oil companies.[31]

Despite President Nixon's announced "Project Independence," which aimed at energy self-sufficiency for the United States by the 1980s, it was clear by the mid-1970s, that American dependence on imported oil still was increasing, not decreasing. Any comprehensive approach to the energy supply question in the United States therefore necessarily involved a consideration of flags of convenience.[32]

In two major legislative efforts, Congress attempted to establish a system of U.S.-flag ship quotas for oil imports. The Energy Transportation Security Act of 1974 (HR 8193) would have required that 50 percent of all imported oil enter the United States aboard U.S.-registered vessels. After extensive hearings that probed the workings of flags of convenience, the bill passed both houses of Congress despite administrative opposition and extensive lobbying by multinational oil firms. The bill was vetoed by

President Ford in 1974. The Energy Transportation Security Act of 1977 (HR 1037) began with a more modest plan, to build in stages to a requirement that 30 percent of imported oil enter aboard American-flag vessels. President Carter, after reviewing conflicting advice from various agencies, including MarAd, navy, transportation, state, and labor, proposed that the bill be modified to work from a requirement that 4.5 percent of imported oil enter on U.S.-flag ships in the first year, to an import quota of 9.5 percent by 1983. The planned growth of the quota by 1 percent per annum would be gradual and would require a steady increase in American-built and American-registered tonnage.[33]

The bill was supported by a surprising range of opinion groups, including the National Maritime Union and other maritime unions, the American Legion, organized and individual American-flag shipowners, the National Farmer's Union, small oil refining companies, the shipbuilding industry, some academic critics of the oil companies, and both the navy and MarAd. But the 1977 bill failed on the floor of Congress by a vote of 257 to 165.[34]

The American Petroleum Institute (API) testified against both bills, as did Phillip Loree, who testified for FACS, and Erling Naess, who testified for Intertanko. The API and individual oil companies mounted an extensive newspaper advertisement campaign, encouraging letters to congressmen in selected districts, to generate the appearance, and the reality, of public opposition to both bills.[35]

Advocates of both bills saw the legislation as a frontal attack on the systems of flags of convenience, and a way to bring some of the benefits of shipping back to the United States. While economic projections and statistics offered by advocates and opponents of the bills tended to obfuscate, rather than to clarify the issues, the lines of argument were clear.[36] Supporters of both bills claimed several national benefits:

1. The reduction of dependence on foreign-flag energy imports would reduce the risk of a potential oil transportation boycott, which could have effects similar to the oil export embargo of 1973–74.
2. Jobs on ships would be increased, as would jobs in shipbuilding, component, and supporting industries.
3. The marine environment would be easier to protect with direct control over licensing and maintenance of more vessels.
4. The United States position in international balance of payments would benefit as shipping charges to foreign-based companies would be reduced.
5. Subsidy costs under the 1970 Merchant Marine Act, which had extended both construction and operating subsidies to bulk carriers, would be reduced.
6. Tax revenue loss from oil company practices of using foreign vessels would be reduced.

7. The shipbuilding industry would be strengthened with long-range benefits to national security.

The API and the FACS countered each of these arguments, claiming the supposed benefits derived from incorrect calculations. Further, the API

The 500,000-ton Ultra Large Crude Carrier Atlantic, *owned by Exxon and registered in Liberia, "lightering" to a smaller vessel, itself a supertanker by the standards of a decade earlier. Owners of such huge ships claimed an excellent safety record, despite the increased risks imposed by sheer size. No U.S. mainland port could accommodate the* Atlantic. *(Exxon Corporation)*

and oil company representatives suggested several national interest arguments against the two bills: (1) increased costs of importation on American-flag ships would be passed on to the American consumers; and (2) American vessels had a poorer safety record than Liberian vessels, and thus more pollution, not less, might result from the act. Oil company testimony suggesting these lines of argument was met by congressmen who questioned the honesty of the concern that oil companies displayed for protecting the consumer from increased prices; few took seriously the argument that pollution would increase under the acts. Lines of argument that carried more weight in influencing Congress were introduced less directly than through API testimony at the hearings. Newspaper advertising campaigns centered in New England stressed fears of oil shortages, which might be accelerated by import quotas. Erling Naess testified that import quotas might set off an international chain reaction of protectionist legislation, and protests against the 1977 bill were filed by Belgium, Denmark, Finland, Great Britain, Greece, Holland, Italy, Japan, Norway, and Sweden.[37]

Supporters of the legislation attributed both the veto of the 1974 bill and the congressional defeat of the 1977 bill to the "very slick" campaigns of the "oil lobby." While the pollution issue and the energy crisis aroused massive public concern with the flag-of-convenience systems, the shipowning corporations that carefully had nurtured and constructed those systems were richly experienced in dealing with public pressure and discontent. The API and FACS representatives had been in the business longer than many of the government officials with whom they dealt, and they displayed ingenuity in turning public concerns to their own purposes. Concern with rising oil prices and shortages, defense of the environment, and fears of special-interest legislation, all would appear ideal political rallying points for opposition to the power of the multinational oil firms and their supporting businesses and associations. Yet, the multinational defenders of flag-of-convenience shipping turned each of those concerns to their own purposes. Fears of increases in price and of oil shortages that might result from more use of American-flag vessels stimulated thousands of letters to congressmen. Those congressmen and federal administrators who supported the bills found themselves charged with working in the special interests of the shipbuilding industry and the American-flag shipping companies, and in the interests of the maritime labor unions. Statistics regarding safety records of the various flags were presented to show that the larger VLCCs under Liberian registry carried more cargo safely than did the smaller vessels registered in the United States. The control of information regarding private business decisions prevented fully informed discussion of costs, pricing, and the effects of regulation and tax systems on oil prices. The challenges to the flag-of-convenience systems posed by fears of pollution and by concern with the control of energy supply had been met and forestalled by the end of the decade through the political use of those very fears.[38]

Presidential Initiatives and Coast Guard Actions

While Congressional supporters of the cargo preference bills failed to establish a system that would guarantee increased use of American-flag vessels, a more direct line of attack on the ocean pollution problem had far greater success. In response to the national concern following the *Argo Merchant* spill and the sequence of other accidents through the winter of 1976–77, President Carter issued on 17 March 1977, a seven-point list of proposals to Congress to deal with the question of oil pollution of the seas. His proposals, which came to be called the "Presidential Initiatives," derived from White House staff studies, and called for a diverse and interrelated group of measures that would reduce both operational oil pollution and the hazards of tanker transport. His message asked for:

1. Ratification of the International Convention for the Prevention of Pollution from Ships—the MARPOL-73 convention
2. Reform of ship construction and equipment standards, including requirements for double bottoms, segregated ballast tanks, inert gas systems to reduce the likelihood of explosion, and improved radar and steering equipment
3. Improvement of international inspection and certification of tankers
4. Improvement of crew and officer standards, both in the United States and internationally
5. Development of a tanker boarding program and a marine safety information system
6. Approval of a comprehensive liability system
7. Improvement of federal agencies' abilities to respond to oil spills[39]

The vigorous actions by the Coast Guard, the Environmental Protection Agency (EPA), the State Department, and Congress in response to the proposals over the period from 1977 to 1980 represents, collectively, one of the unsung achievements of the Carter administration. The Coast Guard improved its monitoring and inspection systems, and established stricter rules regarding radar use and crew qualifications. Both the EPA and the Coast Guard improved their ability to respond to polluting incidents, and established procedures for interagency cooperation among officials dealing with spills on location. The State Department, with Coast Guard officers serving as technical experts, proposed that IMCO convene an international conference on tanker safety and pollution prevention. The conference, held in February 1978 in London, endorsed a range of new requirements that the United States planned to implement through government regulation, even before the new agreements formally came into force. The actions of the conference took the form of "protocols" altering two earlier conventions, the Convention for the Safety of Life at Sea, 1974 (SOLAS-74) and the International Convention for the Prevention of Pollution from Ships, 1973 (MARPOL-73).[40]

While the technical aspects of the approved protocols were complex in detail, the conference's most notable measure in dealing with the question of oil pollution from collisions and groundings was to require dedicated water ballast tanks on the sides and bottoms of oil carriers. These tanks, not to be used for the transport of oil, would never present problems of discharge, as they would carry only sea water for ballast. While the double bottom proposal suggested in the "Presidential Initiatives" was not accepted, the dedicated ballast tanks, when strategically located, would protect interior cargo tanks in much the same fashion, without some of the risks associated with double bottoms. Other regulations that required crude oil washing of cargo tanks, inert gas systems, improved steering capabilities, and radar and emergency drills also were approved at the 1978 London conference, and implemented in the United States through the federal rule-making procedure by the Coast Guard.[41]

The improvements and technical changes, required both by regulation and by treaty, were scheduled to go into effect through the early 1980s, and older vessels would be equipped with the new features. Both the spectacular type of pollution caused by collisions and groundings, and the much more widespread, but less newsworthy, operational pollution from tank washing and ballasting would be reduced over a period of about three years. Even though Liberian representatives were present at the conference and agreed to the new protocols, it was clear that the United States, through exercise of "the law of the port" was prepared to implement the changes on ships of foreign registry even in the absence of international agreement.

While the measures were comprehensive, and represented the best "state of the art," their implementation was achieved without challenging the bases of the flag-of-convenience system itself. In the public eye, flags of convenience had become associated with unsafe, colliding, or sinking vessels as a result of the *Torrey Canyon*, the *Ocean Eagle*, the *Argo Merchant*, and in 1978, the *Amoco Cadiz*. Many smaller but still newsworthy incidents had confirmed that association. But for oil companies and major independent tanker owners, lax pollution control or safety regulation had not been major "conveniences" of the Liberian flag. The absence of income tax and the freedom to hire low-cost or nonunionized crews had remained the major attractions of the Liberian flag for the major oil carriers. Therefore, the political danger of the pollution issue, from the point of view of the largest users of the Liberian flag and the International Trust Company, was *not* that it would result in public demands for costly alteration and new construction of vessels to conform to regulations. Rather, the danger to the system had derived from the fact that public concern could lead to demands for the transfer of the cargoes to the "traditional maritime flags," those with more stringent taxation and labor laws, as visualized in the defeated 1974 and 1977 cargo preference bills.

The implementation of the "Presidential Initiatives" and the 1978 London conference approval of the protocols could be seen as victories for the point of view of the larger firms. The effects of the reforms on the oil transport business would be to reduce the risk of loss, to drive some marginal and "surplus" tankers from the field, to reduce both pollution and the political attention brought by pollution, and to allow the preservation and continuation of the flag-of-convenience system.

The pollution and energy-supply issues, however, had resulted in increased congressional and public concern with all aspects of the oil transport business. Congressional opponents of flags of convenience had developed many insights into the operation of the system, and took credit for planting suspicions about the reliability of effective control in both MarAd and navy circles. By the mid 1970s, personnel in both of those agencies did question the viability and the logic of the concept with new intensity. The strategic convenience rationale for the system became the subject of criticism, analysis, and reconsideration.

11

Effective Control Doctrine under Fire

As HAS BEEN SHOWN, during the public and legal debates over the Panamanian and Liberian flags of convenience, the defenders of the flag systems received considerable assistance at crucial points from the endorsement of the system by the defense establishment. The policy of "effective United States control," it was claimed, made it in the national interest to support the systems of registry. Under the premises of this doctrine, vessels owned by American firms and registered in Liberia, Panama, or Honduras were under effective control of the United States and could be called upon in times of military emergency. The policy had been a boon to the defenders of flags of convenience in their public and congressional debates in that it provided official sanction and justification for the system. Yet the concept had been formulated, not through public debate, but in an evolving internal planning document of the Joint Chiefs of Staff in the period from 1945 through 1947. While the debates over "PanLibHon" registry moved from Congress to the courts, quiet discussion within MarAd, the Navy Department, and the Department of Defense proceeded to elaborate, refine, and explore the strengths and weaknesses of the concept. Such critiques, however, have not examined the historical roots or evolution of the concept systematically. This chapter is devoted to an analysis of that background, through an examination of available primary documentation, and in the light of themes already presented in this book.

The evolution of the effective control concept is a case of the conversion of a practical operating system, developed during World War II, into a strategic planning doctrine. That conversion of practice into doctrine proceeded in a hasty fashion, governed by the necessities of the moment and limited by the constraints of military decision-making procedure. Even as the planning doctrine was developed, the facts of the World War II operating system were buried, and to an extent the facts now are buried deeper, in the files of the Navy Department and the War Shipping Administration. Some of those documents give an outline of the origins of the term and the concept itself.

World War II Origins of Effective Control

As was shown in chapter 6, vessels registered under the Panamanian flag during World War II provided an adjunct fleet whose details were administered by the WSA under the direction of Admiral Land. What the postwar advocates of the effective control doctrine did not fully consider, however, was that the World War II Panamanian fleet was only one of several such adjunct fleets, and that it clearly was designed to serve as a temporary military expedient, not as a long-range system. The procedures of wartime effective control could be viewed as a system of "tactical convenience."[1]

It was the practice of the WSA to indicate in its reports those vessels that were sailing directly under the United States flag, and to append to such listings, or to include within the lists, vessels "under U.S. control" but flying other flags. Thus, for example, a list published by the WSA in January 1945, showed over 3,800 merchant vessels under U.S. control, including some 3,500 ships under the American flag and 315 vessels under a variety of other flags, as shown in table 15.[2]

The designation *U.S. control* meant simply what it said in such reports. The vessels so designated were under the control of the WSA either through a "Time Charter Agreement" in which the WSA or the Maritime

Table 15.
Foreign-Flag Vessels Listed as "Under U.S. Control"
by the WSA, January 1945

Flag	Number of Vessels	Flag	Number of Vessels
Panama	121	Mexico	4
Norway	73	Belgium	4
Netherlands	33	Britain	3
Honduras	23	Argentina	3
Venezuela	18	Yugoslavia	3
France	11	Switzerland	2
Greece	8	China	2
Poland	5	Cuba	1
		Sweden	1
		Total	315

Source: "Vessels Not on the Navy List," January 1945, CNO Files, Naval Operational Archives.

Commission chartered the vessel from the owning company, or under a "General Agency Agreement," through which a WSA-owned vessel or a vessel requisitioned for use was operated by a company as an agent for the government. U.S. control over the ships was exercised in fact through those contracts, charters, and agreements, not through any control over all of the vessels under the flag of the state in question.

Each of the groups of vessels under the foreign flags had its own history of entry into U.S. control. Norwegian-flag ships were responsible to the American-headquartered Norwegian Trade and Shipping Mission. Belgian, Polish, and Dutch vessels remained under the flags of their governments-in-exile. Fleets managed by the British War Shipping Ministry clearly were not under U.S. control, but under British control. The three ships under British flag in the list of U.S.-controlled ships were American-owned, and the British accepted WSA control in their cases.[3]

When Denmark was invaded, its government was overrun. Unlike those of Belgium, Norway, Holland, and Poland, members of the Danish government were not able to escape to establish a government-in-exile. Thus, more than 400 Danish vessels were regarded by Britain as under German control and subject to British seizure. In the United States, 40 vessels flying the Danish flag could not leave harbor without the threat of British seizure. The Danish ambassador worked out with the State Department and the Maritime Commission an arrangement under which the vessels would be taken over for use by the United States government, which would pay the owners the equivalent of a fair charter rate for their use. Admiral Land was able to regularize the takeover of the Danish ships through Public Law 101 of June 1941. To provide employment for the crews, he arranged that the vessels be operated by American companies, and registered in Panama, to the discomfort of Assistant Secretary of State Long. Nevertheless, the 40 vessels were transferred, then armed, and several, including the *Sessa* and the *Montana*, were sunk in convoy, precipitating the crisis over the Arias administration.[4]

When Italy entered the war, there were twenty-eight vessels of Italian registry in American harbors. Following orders, the Italian crews damaged the engines of the vessels, hoping, through sabotage, to make the ships unusable. After some hesitation, the Coast Guard seized the ships and arrested the crews, under World War I sedition laws that prohibited damage to vessels in American harbors. Most of the ships were repaired and transferred to Panamanian registry by the Maritime Commission. Further additions to the Panamanian fleet came from a group of sixteen Finnish vessels. Altogether, ninety-seven ships of foreign registry were taken over prior to February 1942, as shown in table 16.[5]

Of the ninety-seven vessels, seventy-seven were placed under Panamanian registry. The others were placed in service directly by the army, the

Table 16.
Ships Taken by Maritime Commission, 1941–42

Original Flag	Number Taken	Number Placed under Panamanian Registry
Denmark	40	30
Italy	28	27
Finland	16	15
France	8	3
Romania	1	0
Germany	3	1
Estonia	1	1
Totals	97	77

Source: "Vessels under the Control of the War Shipping Administration," 21 March 1942, CNO Files, Naval Operational Archives.

navy, or the Maritime Commission and operated as government vessels without documentation under a flag, since flag registry and documentation were required only for vessels operated by private companies. After experimenting with several charter arrangements, the WSA settled on the system of agency agreements for operating the seventy-seven ships.

An examination of the ship lists and the records of Panamanian ship casualties during the war reveals that at one time or another about 200 Panamanian vessels were under the control of the United States through agency agreements and through government charter from companies that already owned Panamanian-registered vessels. Due to continual casualties and several additions to those fleets, however, the total at any one time designated as under U.S. control fluctuated in the range of 100 to 130 vessels.[6]

However, the Panamanian registry during the war years included many vessels not under U.S. control, including some of those with prior registries from European, Chinese, and Japanese owners, and some owned by Americans. Prior to the outbreak of the war, Panamanian sources had shown a total of 240 vessels under their flag; over 20 were sunk before the United States entered the war, but the remaining fleet included the wide range of European, Asian, and American ownership developed during the 1930s. State Department and WSA problems with possible Axis use of ships such as the *Oilshipper* and the *Janko*, clandestine-trade use of the *Parita* and the *Struma*, and uncontrolled uses of American-owned but Panamanian-registered ships such as the *Daylite*, all revealed the variety of the vessels under Panamanian registry.[7]

With these facts in mind, it is clear that when the WSA referred to Panamanian-flag merchant ships as under U.S. control, the agency referred to *a specific segment* of the total Panamanian registry, not to the whole range of vessels under that flag, nor even to the whole range of American-owned vessels under the flag. *United States control of ships under the Panamanian flag extended specifically and only to vessels that, through either time charter or agency agreement, were operated directly for the War Shipping Administration.*

In May 1944, the WSA listed 127 Panamanian ships afloat that were under U.S. control. The sources of those ships are shown in table 17.[8]

The effective control fleet in World War II was simply a designation that meant direct control. But the term did not imply that all of the particular states issuing the flags were especially reliable. The designation applied to various anomalous small groups of ships such as Yugoslav vessels operated for the WSA, vessels flying the flag of the Polish government-in-exile, two ships transferred to Switzerland from Spain and employed to take approved cargoes of petroleum to Spain, and groups of American-owned ships under contracts from Honduras, Venezuela, Mexico, Argentina, and other nations. During the war some of those nations, such as Argentina and Yugoslavia, had relations with the United States that could not possibly have formed the basis for an assessment of political reliability.[9]

One consequence of the agency agreements to operate the WSA-controlled vessels under the flag of Panama was to expose a host of Amer-

Table 17.
Sources of Panamanian Vessels under U.S. Control, May 1944

I. Vessels under General Agency Agreements		
Survivors of the groups requisitioned for use previously Danish, Finnish, Italian, etc.	44	
Confiscations as a result of war seizures, February 1942–May 1944	22	
Total		66
II. Vessels under Time Charter Agreements, owned by U.S. companies		
ESSO	22	
Balboa and United Fruit	6	
Vikingen (Naess group)	2	
Socony	4	
Standard Oil of California	2	
Atlantic Refining	3	
Texaco	1	
Grace Lines	1	
Other companies	20	
Total		61
Total of both categories		127

Source: "Vessels under the Control of the War Shipping Administration," 15 May 1944, CNO Files, Naval Operational Archives.

ican companies that had had no previous experience under the Panamanian flag, to the conveniences of that registry. Among those companies was Marine Transport Lines, headed by William Westerlund. Under the 1946 Ship Sales Act, hundreds of ships were transferred to Panamanian registry as American owners and operators like Westerlund took advantage of the conveniences of freedom from taxation and labor regulation that had been established in the prewar era, and to which they had been exposed by the WSA agency system.[10]

Conversion of Effective Control from Tactic to Doctrine

A crucial stage of maritime planning came during the war, when the navy and other services established a postwar demobilization plan. The navy plan at first was derived in something of a vacuum, with little input from other agencies. However, by the end of the war, Chief of Naval Operations Admiral Horne received advice from a variety of private and published sources as to the optimum size of a postwar merchant marine. This plan calculated on a need for some 9 to 16 million tons of active shipping to sustain American trade, with another 10 million tons of shipping in reserve. The tentative plan worked out by the navy envisioned a "Five Pool" plan, including an active trading category; an active reserve fleet for transfers in and out; a group transferred to allies for their needs; a fourth group in long-term inactive ("mothballed") reserve; and a fifth group to be scrapped. The actively trading vessels, it was visualized, should be sufficient to carry 50 percent of American import and export trades.[11]

Such judgments coincided with the predictions and expectations of other agencies, including the WSA. In calculating the amount of shipping that should be placed in a reserve for fighting future wars, the newly emerging nuclear strategies of the postwar era were a source of difficulty for the navy not only in planning but also in projecting future strategy, budget requests, and weapons systems. In an atomic blitz, what part could a civilian merchant marine play? Clearly, there would not be the required lead time to build a fleet such as had been built in World Wars I and II.[12]

Navy planners, however, did not fully accept the nuclear exchange scenario as the only possible one for future military engagements. The merchant fleet was to have several functions in long-range strategies. Following classic Mahan-inspired reasoning, a large merchant marine provided for a strong commercial network, and itself would serve as a basis for national prosperity. That concept continued to be demonstrated in naval thinking. Thus, a strong merchant fleet could serve as a deterrent to potential aggressors, who would recognize a viable merchant fleet as one of the assets of a powerful nation. For more direct naval uses, it was clear that a good reserve of fleet oilers and supply ships would be required to aid a military effort; yet, in a major war, the normal trade routes would be interdicted and the vessels freed from commercial trade would more than supply the needs of the military.[13]

The first use of the term *effective control* in thinking about the strategic considerations of merchant reserves and resources grew not out of naval planning directly in the CNO's office, but out of plans developed at the Joint Chiefs of Staff (JCS), chaired at that time by Admiral William Leahy. A specialized committee of the Joint Chiefs, the Joint Military Transportation Committee (JMTC), submitted to the JCS in 1945 a plan for future needs of the merchant marine. This document, JCS 1454/1, was modified as circumstances and pressures required. In developing JCS 1454, the phrase *effective United States control* at first was used to indicate the total reserve fleet available to the United States, including both vessels under the U.S. flag and those under foreign flag. Therefore, in 1945, the term and its use followed the practice of World War II, indicating a variety of registries that would provide ships under American control. In a 1946 revision of JCS 1454, to illustrate the principle, reference was made to the Norwegian arrangements during the war period.[14]

However, after the passage of the 1946 Ship Sales Act, and the vastly increased sales of vessels to foreign registry, including Panama, the JCS modified the plan extensively. In the 1947 revision, JCS 1454/11, the Joint Chiefs developed a firmer definition of *effective control*, a definition that noted the difficulties of such registries.

> The term "effective control" . . . appears to be inadequately defined. . . . Except through agreement there are no legal means by which the United States can regain control of a United States merchant vessel, the registry of which has been transferred to another country. From a legal standpoint, therefore, it can be considered that the only time a vessel is under absolute "effective United States control" is when it flies the United States flag.[15]

Nevertheless, the Joint Chiefs were willing to accept the Panamanian precedent. In doing so, however, they looked to the 1939–41 experience, not to the more recent war years during which control actually had operated.

> There are certain countries in this hemisphere which, through diplomatic or other arrangements, will permit the transfer to their registry of United States ships . . . and allow United States citizens or corporations to retain control of these vessels. Prior to entry of the United States into World War II, United States vessels were transferred to Panamanian registry for the purpose of rendering aid to the Allies. Such a case . . . can be considered to be within the meaning of the term "effective United States control."[16]

The new JCS definition concluded with a set of guidelines for determining "effective control," guidelines that were based on the political relationship between the nation of registry and the United States.

> The primary consideration in determining whether or not a United States merchant ship registered under a foreign flag would still be under "effective United States control" are: the practice followed in the past with regard to transfer of United States merchant vessels to foreign registry; the status of diplomatic relations between the United States and the foreign country concerned; the foreign country's relations with countries opposed to our system of government or foreign policy; the proximity of the foreign country to the United States and the stability of its government.[17]

This extensive definition revealed the development of JCS thinking and the degree to which it departed from WSA practice. Instead of drawing on that practice, the statement derived its precedents from the attempt to evade the Neutrality Act. By 1947, the logic and the details of the neutrality debates had faded from memory. The policy of that period was seen simply as a system of aiding the Allies. The view of neutrality held by Land and Roosevelt, that it meant that the United States should stay out of the war while aiding the Allies, had become, in retrospect, a respectable and official view; the opposing argument, that the country should act in an abstractly neutral fashion, and aid neither side, had been discredited as "isolationist." The strategic convenience justification of aid through the mechanism of Panamanian registry had been decided against publicly by Roosevelt in November 1939, and had been revived quietly by Land through Maritime Commission rulings that allowed tankers to transfer to existing companies in Panama—the Berle solution. But, it was incorrect to regard those methods of evading the neutrality policy as an exercise of effective control as the tactical practice had developed during the war.[18]

The faulty premise led to some logical problems. Because the system of evading neutrality—as publicly proposed and then quietly implemented by Land from 1939 through 1940—had depended upon the political support of Panama, rather than upon the more truly effective contractual relationships of the war period, the system had been very difficult to operate. That political support had wavered when Arias had refused to allow the arming of the merchant vessels, and the system nearly broke down. The fortuitous coup d'état in Panama helped the United States out of the situation of political opposition by Arias, although the very fortuitous nature of the coup proved an embarrassment to the State Department, which repeatedly denied any direct American connection with the overthrow. The faulty basis of the 1939–41 neutrality evasion system, a blind trust in the political allegiance of Panama, had been demonstrated. Yet, that coup, and its close relationship to the armed ship issue, was forgotten. The JCS misreading of the neutrality period was excusable, given the degree of confusion about the evolution of the practice and the tendency in the postwar period to regard the pro-Allied version of neutrality as the *correct* version. The more realistic and practical wartime methods of exercising control, such as agreements and time charter contracts, were recognized in passing in the JCS paper, but were not emphasized as the meaningful precedent. In short, by falling back on the concept of political control through a friendly government, the JCS came up with a system for regarding as available in reserve a group of vessels whose reliability essentially depended on demonstrably unreliable political considerations rather than on contractual ones.

The JCS decision as well as earlier details of WSA practices remained concealed from public, or even scholarly, scrutiny through a combination of classification and filing methods. The JCS effective control doctrine itself remained a matter that quietly was put in the files and that was not discussed publicly for several years.

The Political Realities of Postwar Effective Control

The 1947 document had suggested that effective control would apply to nations in the Western Hemisphere. The process by which Liberia was judged to be an appropriate addition as an effective control nation is revealed specifically in further declassified records of the JCS. On 30 June 1948, three months after the "subcabinet" briefing by Stettinius Associates held in Joseph Grew's home, Acting Secretary of the Navy W. John Kenney inquired of the Chief of Naval Operations whether permission could be granted to transfer the five tankers belonging to American Overseas Tanker Corporation from Panama to Liberia. As has been shown, AOTC was owned by Stettinius and several of his close associates who were engaged in writing the Liberian Maritime Code through 1948. The CNO referred the question to the Joint Chiefs who asked for analysis from their own Joint Military Transportation Committee.[19]

While approving transfer to Liberia, the committee hoped to stabilize control of the ships in writing, and recommended that specific agreements be secured from both the owners and the government to allow for return of ships to U.S. registry in an emergency. The concept that control implied potential return to the United States was a clear departure from World War II WSA practice, hinted at in the 1947 JCS document but asserted specifically and explicitly in the 1948 JMTC report. The WSA had not returned vessels to the United States, it had transferred vessels *to* Panama, and then had exercised control through contracts. But, the JMTC visualized control as the potential for return to the United States of vessels registered in a politically reliable state. In the case of Liberia, such control was to be enforced with specific agreements. Analyzing the reliability of Liberian registry even before the registry law was written, the JMTC conducted its analysis entirely on the basis of political and strategic factors, following the themes of Liberia's relationship with the United States that characterized the view held by the Stettinius organization. "In a sense," noted the committee report, "the Republic of Liberia is a ward of the United States."[20]

Disposing of the potential argument that only Western Hemisphere states met the guidelines suggested in the 1947 JCS plan, the committee noted, "The location of the country with relation to the United States has no bearing on this question. Tankers whether under U.S. or foreign registry are engaged in world-wide petroleum service and, in fact, may never contact the ports of the country of registry." But, lest that assertion suggest that Liberia's location was entirely irrelevant to its relationship, the report spelled out Liberia's geopolitical virtues, repeating some of Stettinius's personal ideas: "Situated at the point where the distance to South America is the shortest, Liberia is strategically important to the defense of the United States." To demonstrate further America's strategic interest and stewardship over Liberia, the report listed the building of the Freeport of Monrovia with Lend-Lease Act funds and U.S. Navy assistance, the construction of Roberts Field airport by the U.S. Army, and Stettinius's highly publicized plans for development.[21]

While reflecting some close acceptance of ideas held by the Stettinius group, the final JMTC report did *not* reflect several specific points of information about the group itself. The committee did not report that AOTC was owned by Stettinius, that Stettinius's organization was writing the maritime code, nor that the proposed "Liberian Merchant Marine Company," of which JMTC members were aware, was to be set up and run by Stettinius's staff members in an American-based corporation. The record does not reveal whether these omissions resulted from the committee's ignorance of the facts, or from a decision not to include those points in its report. But the rather careful measures taken within the Stettinius organization to keep such aspects of the development quiet at the time suggest that the JMTC had no access to the information.

The Joint Chiefs of Staff accepted the JMTC's recommendations, and three months prior to the passage of the Liberian Maritime Code, 21 September 1948, recommended to the CNO, "In the event the Maritime Commission invites your comments . . . that you interpose no objections to the transfer . . . ." The JCS did ask that the Chief of Naval Operations impose the condition that owners and the Liberian government both agree to the return of the vessels in time of emergency, as the JMTC had suggested.[22]

Thus, even before the law had been approved in Liberia, Stettinius's group had secured military acceptance of Liberia's status as an effective control country, using the group's own AOTC ships as the test case. As it turned out, the AOTC vessels remained under Panamanian registry so the conditions to be imposed were not put in effect, but the test case had established a military endorsement of the system.

When events through 1948 and 1949 placed the political reliability of Panama in doubt in military circles, it had not been difficult for Stettinius and Grew to develop legitimate top-level support in the National Military Establishment for their plans for an American-designed system of registry under the flag of Liberia. The kind of resistance to and skepticism about the plan that developed in the mid-level offices of the State Department was not matched in any of the staff work that contributed to the JCS decision to regard Liberia as an effective control country. The only hint of suspicion was the Joint Chiefs' planned insistence on placing in writing, in the case of Liberia, the shipowners' obligation to return the vessels in time of emergency.

The doctrine of effective control, developed in the 1947 JCS document and expanded in 1948 to include Liberia, was reflected in annual revisions of merchant ship mobilization plans worked out by the JMTC for the Joint Chiefs of Staff through the mid-1950s. *Effective control* had become subtly transformed from a term that described a tactical operating system of contract control under the WSA into an established designation for a list of countries under whose flags theoretically available, American-owned ships were registered. Honduras was accepted as an effective control state; Venezuela and Costa Rica were added to the list, and later removed; and the Philippines temporarily was considered for inclusion on the list. In 1954, on request of the Greek government, the JMTC in a peremptory, and far less analytic review, approved the inclusion of Greece in the list of effective control countries. But, the decision, which confused NATO control and effective control, was not recognized in MarAd reports, or in future calculations of effective control strengths. Panama, Liberia, and Honduras remained as the core group of designated countries.[23]

The principle of effective control helped defense establishment planners to show as available to American use, a total vessel strength regarded as somewhat closer to projected needs than the American-registered fleet by itself would provide. Thus, tabulations of the JMTC in 1952 showed 165 of 695 available tankers as registered under foreign flags, defined as "selected Panamanian, Honduran, Venezuelan, and Liberian flag vessels owned by U.S. citizens." Even considering such foreign-registered shipping, however, American-controlled tanker tonnage would become insufficient to carry expected civilian and military traffic in the event of planned mobilization under various scenarios of predicted attack.[24]

The first official discussion of the doctrine outside the highly classified internal reports of the Joint Chiefs of Staff took place in the testimony of

Admiral Callaghan and General Fleming before the Senate Committee on Interstate and Foreign Commerce in 1950. At that time, in explaining the permission given to transfer ESSO vessels from the United States to Panama, General Fleming noted a reference on the Maritime Commission docket that the vessels going to Panama under American ownership were regarded as under "effective control." Both General Fleming and Admiral Callaghan relied, somewhat inaccurately, on the official JCS analysis of the origins of the system as outlined in JCS 1454/11 to give a sketch of the history of the practice. Callaghan had asserted incorrectly that there was a written agreement with Panama to return vessels. In point of fact, no treaties or agreements existed with Panama, Liberia, or Honduras to insure return of the vessels.[25]

The political reliability of the Tubman regime, which had served as the basis for the JMTC analysis and the JCS decision, did not become the subject for congressional or public debate. Tubman's repeated reelection to office through the 1950s seemed to insure the reliability of the nation. The Tubman administrations, although autocratic, did, in fact, provide stability over an extended period. The efficient management of the American offices of the International Trust Company under Lininger, and under the eventual ownership of General George Olmsted, was about as "effective" a control system as could be imagined, although the American nature of the Liberian operating system itself was not advanced as part of the public defense of the system's reliability.[26]

The opponents of the system through the 1950s and 1960s continued to point to its flaws, and concentrated on several weak points in the system. Would the crews be reliable on such ships? Could the governments of such countries interpose their authority between the American owner and the vessel itself? Could owners be counted upon to obey the orders or directives of U.S. governmental authorities if they were to conflict with orders from the flag-granting state?

Such questions persisted. The Maritime Administration made several efforts over the 1950s and the 1960s to regularize and tighten up the system in order to cover such eventualities. The practice of issuing war-risk insurance to foreign-registered vessels under general agency and time charter agreements had been established by wartime WSA regulations. In 1950, the regulation was enacted as law, through an amendment to Section 902 of the 1936 Merchant Marine Act, which made available the extension of war-risk insurance contracts to Panamanian, Honduran, and Liberian vessels. The insurance contracts provided that the purchaser would make his ships available in time of emergency.[27]

The Maritime Administration recognized the underlying difficulty that control would be ineffective without contractual as well as political controls, and developed a series of specific contracts in an attempt to guarantee the availability of the ships. Unlike the agreements made during the war, however, these contracts and "letters of intent" were cast in a conditional mood, spelling out what would take place *if* an emergency developed, rather than representing a present or immediate contract for services as did the wartime charters and agreements. Thus, the workability of the obligations would be demonstrated only if an emergency were declared and mobilization were attempted, but no such mobilization ever was announced and the conditional contracts never were invoked.

In 1959, Assistant Secretary of Defense Perkins McGuire spelled out in a memorandum to the White House staff the fundamental handicap facing the system and the measures that had been employed to overcome it. "From a purely military point of view," he stated, "it would be preferable that all American-owned shipping be documented under U.S. flag. Under such circumstances each ship would be immediately and unquestionably available to the United States in the event of an emergency. Such an ideal situation does not exist." Despite the explicit JCS evaluation of both Panama and Liberia as politically reliable, Secretary McGuire asserted that the availability of the ships was "not founded on governmental treaties or governmental assurances." Instead, practical reliance was placed on "assurances" from the American owners. To show that assurances would have legal force, McGuire listed the contract stipulations of the trade-out-and-build agreements, which made the ships transferred out subject to requisitioning authority under Section 902 of the 1936 act. Further legal controls, he indicated, included denial of war-risk insurance, and the powers under the Standby Ship Warrants Act, which could "increase the problems on non-conformist shipping" by denial of port facilities for their support or repairs. Ultimately, however, McGuire indicated that military force would be the most trusted guarantee of effective control: "PanLibHon countries possess negligible capability to intercept, seize, or protect shipping on the high seas. Consequently, these countries are not in a position to expropriate American property afloat nor to dispute U.S. assumption of control over selected shipping." In describing the mechanisms of control for the White House in 1959, Maritime Administrator Clarence Morse outlined the same factors suggested by McGuire: contracts, letters of intent, and the ultimate reliance on force, if necessary.[28]

Despite such methods, conformity to American policy remained an issue. In response to pressure to clarify the availability of vessels, Liberia issued a maritime regulation allowing for the exercise of control over Liberian ships by foreign governments, on permission of the Liberian maritime commissioner. Trade to Communist China and Soviet bloc nations by vessels registered under the flags of Panama, Honduras, and Liberia, along with much larger numbers registered under NATO flags, was noted in monthly secret reports of the Office of Naval Intelligence directly to the Joint Chiefs during the period of the Korean War. The ONI noted the growth of a "Greek cartel" with ships registered in Panama and Britain, as well as vessels believed dominated by Chinese Communist interests as particularly active in such trades. In partial remedy of the practice, the Liberian government in 1951 issued a maritime regulation prohibiting Liberian-registered vessels from trading with Communist-bloc countries, but the ONI reports showed continued trade under that flag on a small scale through 1953. Panamanian-flag trade with the Eastern bloc continued to flourish, as did trade under NATO flags.[29]

Ultimately, as suggested in JCS 1454/11, any ship would be controlled only as effectively as the government of the flag state wished. Maritime Administration reports and analyses published in maritime interest journals, including the *United States Naval Institute Proceedings*, reflected the potential loopholes in the system, even after concerted attempts, on the part of Liberian and American authorities, to plug them.

The Military Establishment Discusses Effective Control

In published and confidential reports over the period from the early 1950s through 1970, staff members of the office of the CNO, retired admirals, maritime administrators, and members of the Defense Department's civilian administration prepared analyses of effective control over flag-of-convenience ships. While many of their statements seemed intended to defend the system, most recognized the potential difficulties in the system and reflected a kind of reconciled acceptance of the system as the best available way of developing a mobilization plan for merchant vessels.

Several recurrent elements can be found in a review of these published and unpublished commentaries. In 1954 and 1961, Admiral Land reiterated his assertions that the Panamanian system had provided a means for aiding the Allies during the neutrality period, thus recalling the premises on which he had argued publicly in 1939 against the prevailing view of neutrality. Some other exponents of the system repeated this theme, but none reviewed the actual nature of the 1939 controversy, in which Land's and Roosevelt's views had been considerably ahead of the letter of the neutrality law.[30]

Other themes in the military defenses of effective control included a reassertion that the vessels under PanLibHon registry would be more reliable than ships under the registries of NATO countries. Vessels registered in the Netherlands, Norway, or Britain would be subject to requisition and control by those NATO powers; in the event of a major war involving NATO countries, the ships would be requisitioned by the flag states and then would be available only from a NATO pool. In the event of a limited-scale war, NATO ships would not be available without the consent of the flag state. Publicly reported trade of Norwegian ships with the Soviet Union and with Communist China was noted as evidence of the unreliability of such registries.[31]

Several analyses of previous reliability were presented, but those that examined the evidence from World War II incorrectly asserted that Panamanian-registered vessels had been taken over and made available to the government. They overlooked the fact that about half the operating fleet in Panama under U.S. control during the war had resulted from U.S. seizures of foreign-flag vessels transferred there for reasons of tactical convenience. Rather, the comments usually referred to the model of the ESSO fleet as typical of the WSA practice.[32]

During the Korean War Panamanian- and Liberian-registered tankers were available through a Voluntary Tanker Pool sponsored by the American oil companies that owned them, but "effective control" methods of utilizing those vessels did not come into play. The tankers were neither transferred back to the United States, nor were they attached to a nationally mobilized fleet in the sense that the WSA fleet in World War II had been under a central authority. Assertions of the availability of vessels during the Vietnam war were made in reports in 1970; but such ships simply had been engaged in commercial trade on short-term government contracts.[33]

Despite the efforts to explain and defend the origins and workings of the system, most naval writers continued to express some reservations about the system. Vice Admiral Ralph Wilson, who had served on the Federal Maritime Board, successor agency to the Maritime Commission, gently suggested his reservations in 1963: "Immediately following World War II, the concept of effective U.S. control was born of necessity in the minds of Defense Department planners as the only practicable and valid means of meeting serious emergency deficiencies in readily available American owned shipping. It has consistently proved to be a necessary planning expedient since that time.. It has never been claimed that the concept of effective U.S. control gives the United States an ironclad hold over these ships." In confidential as well as public forums, Wilson recognized the system as less than ideal.[34]

In a carefully researched article published in 1970 in the *United States Naval Institute Proceedings*, Lieutenant (jg) Sidney Emery concluded with a balanced assessment of the system's reliability. "Though the experience in applying the theory is thin at best, the Vietnam conflict has produced some suggestive results. Not a single crew has ever protested against sailing its ship to Vietnam. Yet, all is not sunny in the effective control picture. . . ." Emery spelled out the contrast between doubtful reliability and high expectations: "Owners are not excited about diverting their vessels from profitable commercial contracts to government charters. . . . In truth, it was initially a makeshift theory, devised to get more ships built in the U.S.

without putting them under subsidy." Emery noted that in some Department of Defense assessments of vessel availability, effective control became a seductive concept since it improved the impression of readiness. "Offices of Emergency Transportation and Emergency Planning, which work directly for the President, have alluded to EUSC lifting capacity as to surround the . . . ships with an aura of reliability." Since effective control never really had been tested, Emery warned, enthusiasm for the system was ill-advised.[35]

At the Maritime Administration, shipping research specialists Irwin Heine and Muriel Coe published two analyses of the fleet, in 1960 and 1970. Their reports, like Lieutenant Emery's, reflected doubts about the availability of vessels. In the 1960 report, the MarAd authors hinted at the distinction between World War II practical WSA control and the looser planning concept of the postwar era. In a brief, penetrating historical comment, reflecting documentation from the JCS, the 1970 report presented the outlines of the original JCS decision and rightly traced the policy to its inception. In both reports, the statistical analysis of the numbers of vessels available under effective control was quite conservative.[36]

Retired Rear Admiral Walter Ford showed the same concerns in a 1970 essay for *Shipmate*, the U.S. Naval Academy alumni magazine. He believed that the effective control fleet "does not provide a solution to the inadequacies in the general and specialized segments of the American Merchant Marine. There is no dispute over the fact that the carriage of general cargo under emergency conditions presents a continuing, and under present circumstances, an insoluble problem."[37]

The inherent flaws of effective control as a postwar military policy derived from the classified nature of military planning itself. Military planners rightly were accustomed to develop war plans and alternative responses to crisis situations in secret, and to keep strict classification and control over distribution of such internal documents limited to those with a need to know. But to the extent that planning involved civilian merchant vessels and matters of foreign policy or labor relations, it was not possible to explain adequately decisions and actions based on planning doctrine without discussing before Congress and the public, the premises of that doctrine. Yet, the confidential and closed procedure by which JCS decisions were reached and recorded prevented, until much later declassification of the records, a truly informed presentation of the issues.

It was often a simple, practical matter. An admiral or general testifying before Congress would not bring specific documents like JCS 1454/11 or the JMTC report on Liberia to the meetings; by the time these documents were ready for declassification, they long ago had passed from the operational files available for staff work to the archival system. In a practical sense, the security system surrounding military planning, in this case at

The Liberian-registered Esso Copenhagen, *theoretically part of the U.S. effective control fleet. Built in 1970, the 112,763-ton vessel has a cargo capacity of nearly 2 million barrels. (Exxon Corporation)*

least, was a self-imposed handicap that prevented military men from expressing the origins of their own doctrines, from explaining the factors that contributed to the doctrine's evolution, and from developing even in internal debates, an analysis that was based on the record.

Direct review of the records of the JMTC reveals that the changing members of that group were not familiar with the details of earlier decisions by their predecessors on the same committee. Thus, in 1954, the JMTC review of the Greek request to be regarded as an effective control state was approved without reference to the previous acceptance of Liberia; the analysis did not reflect an understanding of the ongoing distinction between effective control as defined in JCS document 1454/11 and the NATO pool of available vessels. The incorrect assumption that Panama and Liberia had signed agreements with the United States permitting takeover of vessels persisted even after the JMTC discovered and reported that no such agreements existed. The limited circulation of JCS documents, combined with their voluminous nature, appeared not only to stand in the way of informed discussion with outside agencies and the services in general, but also to obstruct effective and clear internal decision-making. The difficulty lay in the fact that the military planning process, originally designed to reach difficult and secret decisions quickly, was simply unsuited to the quasi-legislative role it played in the creation and development of the postwar effective control principle.[38]

The Survival of Effective Control

While the logic and premises of effective control had been the subjects of considerable public criticism by labor and labor-oriented congressmen for thirty years, the Defense Department, the navy, and MarAd all continued to question its efficacy, its extent, and its usefulness, especially in documents intended for internal naval audiences. Much of the literature on the defense and MarAd explanations of the system was devoted to the rather elaborate contractual arrangements that had been put together to make control over the vessels less dependent upon the political reliability of the flag states. Despite explicit awareness of the untried nature of such arrangements, and despite the tendency to fall back on reliance upon the threat of extralegal force and seizure, despite constant and scrupulous review of the actual numbers of ships available, the military support for the system persisted in communications to other agencies. Why should such an unreliable assertion of control have been accepted in 1947, and why did it persist, with the force of doctrine, in the light of such awareness of its obvious shortcomings? The answer lies in the pressures upon the military through the period, pressures created by the decline of the American merchant marine.

Economic factors continued to reduce the American merchant marine fleet and the proportion of American trade carried under the flag. In 1947, most of the U.S. maritime oil trade was protected by cabotage, since it required voyages from the Texas-Gulf area to the Northeast. But, with the growth of Middle Eastern oil sources in the 1960s, oil companies were motivated for economic reasons to build supertanker fleets under any flag they preferred. By the late 1960s, new entries in the flag-of-convenience list appeared, as Cyprus and Singapore experimented with systems that attracted Greek and Chinese owners. Such new convenient flags were not considered for the list of U.S. effective control flags, however. Economic factors continued to reduce the need for, and the proportion of trade carried by, American-flag ships.[39]

Even in the mid-1950s, it was clear to naval planners that U.S. registry would be unable to provide the reserve fleet required in an emergency. The spectre of obsolescence for the mothballed fleet of merchant ships haunted the planners even as the ships were placed in reserve. This inactive reserve tonnage had proved useful in the case of the Korean War; but, by the 1960s, such vessels were difficult to recommission, inefficient, almost impossible to crew, and not reliable as a source for merchant transport to Vietnam.[40]

The active operating fleet of American-owned vessels in Panama and Liberia did provide a convenient alternative to the bleak picture of inadequacy in the face of shrinking sea power. Other planning alternatives remained as unacceptable as they had been in 1947. To rely on allies who could deny requests for shipping was unwise. To attempt to force through Congress legislation that would require a large fleet in the United States would be fruitless, as such an effort would encounter powerful opposition. Operating a dry cargo and tanker fleet sufficient for civilian needs directly through the navy or Military Sea Transport Service budget would deprive other programs more essential to the naval mission. To plan on the basis of a totally inadequate fleet also was unacceptable. By contrast to such difficult alternatives, the makeshift concept of effective control, however fraught with problems, was attractive.[41]

The 1970 Merchant Marine Act, passed with the support of the Nixon administration, envisioned a shipbuilding program and subsidies for tankers in addition to the long-established subsidies for cargo liners and passenger vessels. Rear Admiral Ford hoped that the new subsidies would provide a domestic alternative to the effective control fleet. However, when the subsidies produced little growth and the proportion of trade carried in the American-flag registry continued to decline, effective control, despite its shortcomings, remained the only substitute for the classic Mahan-inspired strengths of national sea power. As Admiral Elmo Zumwalt (CNO, 1970–74) pointed out in his memoirs, military planners remained reluctant to describe a state of readiness that revealed vulnerability. Effective control at least reduced the appearance of unpreparedness.[42]

Panama and Liberia Assert Their Autonomy

By the 1970s, fundamental changes in world and local politics placed the concept of effective control, when based on the political reliability of Panama and Liberia, in serious jeopardy. With certain parallels to the independence displayed by the Chiari regime in the 1920s and the Arnulfo Arias regime in the 1940s, Panama in the 1960s began to move toward exerting sovereignty over the canal, a move that culminated in renegotiated treaties signed in 1979. Active and retired naval officers viewed the coming loss of U.S. control over the canal and the Canal Zone as dangers to American defenses.[43]

Liberia, too, demonstrated a steady growth of independent behavior, at first less obvious from a naval point of view. While thirty-five African states attained their independence over the years from 1957 to 1968, President Tubman, as one of the elder statesmen of Africa, attempted to play a leadership role. He hosted Organization of African Unity meetings in his nation, and joined with Ethiopia in International Court of Justice actions against South Africa over control of Southwest Africa (Namibia). Tubman's international role has been judged by outside observers as an effort to counteract criticisms that his regime was a narrow-based oligarchy, unrepresentative of the indigenous-descended majority of his nation. The political "Africanization" of Liberia had begun. By the early 1970s, Liberia had staked a claim for a leadership position in the community of Afro-Asian states, and on a number of United Nations issues relating to African affairs, had voted with those states in opposition to a United States position.[44]

In the case of the politics of both Panama and Liberia, the developments of the 1960s were well within local traditions. Panama's political history long had been marked by outright rejection of the American view of Panama's role as a colony—challenges to American control were not the exception in Panamanian politics, but the underlying rule. Similarly, Liberia's sensitivity to the politics of surrounding African territories had a long tradition. In a quiet, but persistent fashion, Liberia had represented the aspirations of African people for self-government against the colonial powers, and several spokesmen, like Edward Blyden, had used the country's unique origins to lay claim to leadership of Pan-African movements in the nineteenth century.[45]

On the death of Tubman in 1971, his vice president (and son's father-in-law), William H. R. Tolbert, took over the republic. At his inauguration, Tolbert dramatically symbolized the new order—instead of the traditional top hat and tails that had characterized ceremonial occasions in Liberia since the mid-nineteenth century, he wore an African bush jacket suit, which soon became the preferred garb of the many Afro-American settler-descended government employees in the republic. But, more importantly, Tolbert continued and expanded the policies of third-world international leadership initiated by Tubman.

On the outbreak of the Yom Kippur War in October 1973, Tolbert issued Executive Order IV prohibiting Liberian-registered vessels from supplying arms to Israel for the duration of the war. While the action could be regarded as only symbolic, in that the war ended before affected vessels could test the application of the order, the decision on Tolbert's part demonstrated an interdiction of control over the effective control fleet, an action that the U.S. Navy long had feared might occur. When compared to the embargo placed by OPEC on oil supplies to U.S. forces during the war, Liberian independence of U.S. policy was a minor, but noticeable, concern to naval and other military analysts. In vain, business supporters of the system pointed out that Tolbert supplemented the order with an exemption to vessels under commitment to the United States. The exact legal implications and logistic effect of the original publicized order and the quietly announced exemption went untested. However, the net political effect of the action was to assert the alignment of Liberia with the African, Islamic, Eastern bloc, and Asian states supporting Egypt and Syria in that war.[46]

Some of those who long had opposed flags of convenience, including union representatives, congressmen who advocated cargo preference legislation, and representatives of American-flag shipping, were quick to point to the unreliability of the Liberian fleet in the light of Tolbert's Executive Order IV. In addition, however, a growing number of active and retired naval officers reflected a new tone of doubt in the system created by the Liberian action and by the changed international climate of the 1970s.[47]

Testifying before Congress in 1974, Rear Admiral (Ret.) Albert Mumma noted:

> Concerning the availability and use of flag of convenience vessels in time of peace and in time of crisis, it has become evident in the last several years that there is an increasing disregard for international law. The effectiveness of U.S. ownership . . . has become moot in view of the expropriations and decisions for control which occurred. . . . There is little basis today for believing that a U.S. owned vessel under a foreign flag and manned by a foreign crew would always remain available to the United States in time of crisis.[48]

Maritime Administrator Robert Blackwell quoted Admiral Zumwalt's preference for American-registered tankers over those of other flags, and noted that the increased likelihood of OPEC participation in the ownership of tankers, a stated objective of several of the oil-exporting countries, made reliance on United States-registered tankers preferable from a strategic perspective. While not specifically directing his comments against the effective control vessels of Liberia and Panama, Blackwell suggested the growing sense, in maritime planning circles, that reliance upon foreign registry was dangerous in the changing world of oil politics.[49]

In 1977, Rear Admiral Penrose L. Albright, who earlier had been asked by Admiral Zumwalt to activate and reorganize the Naval Reserve Association, stated, "We do not believe that we should be dependent upon the fleet of flags of convenience to meet our requirements in a wartime situation. Something needs to be done."[50]

As the contracts expired that required effective control vessels to be available, and as the war-risk insurance covering vessels in this group ended in 1975, Defense Department spokesmen, as well as FACS representative Phillip Loree, suggested that the vessels of the fleet could be called upon, not through the obligations of contracts, but through "voluntary pledges" on the part of the owners. In the light of oil company compliance with OPEC directives prohibiting supplies to U.S. naval vessels, such assurances were viewed with considerable doubt by congressmen whose politics ranged from the prolabor position of John Murphy of New York, chairman of the House Committee on Merchant Marine and Fisheries, to the independent and skeptical orientation of Republican Congressman John Anderson of Illinois, who noted that the companies themselves asserted a degree of sovereignty in deciding which orders they would obey.[51]

While the 1973 order of the Tolbert administration can be seen as a major factor contributing to the growing naval and congressional doubts about the effective control system, the roots of that objection went much deeper. Effective control always had been regarded by naval planners as a reluctantly accepted expedient, a second-best system. The doctrine always had relied on a sterile political stability that required a negation of the two nations' sovereign independence. An awareness that flags of convenience were based on a type of deception had been one of the bases for criticisms for strategic convenience in 1939, and frequently had been a minor theme in military suspicions of effective control through the postwar years. For naval men who preferred hard-headed realism to falsely based optimism, the Liberian order provided a solid argument for reconsidering the doctrine of effective control itself.

Liberia's political stability through the Tubman period had derived partly from a network of political spies who reported directly to the president. Tolbert had relaxed that system, and arrests and detentions for political opposition had decreased. Nevertheless, Tolbert continued the same system of political rewards to a narrow elite that had characterized the Tubman regime. A coterie of relatives and friends continued to profit from patronage, nepotism, and outright corruption, bribery, and theft. Despite

The Esso Japan, *built in 1976, is a VLCC of 192,679 tons with a cargo capacity of over 3 million barrels. Until recently such Liberian-registered vessels were assumed to be part of the U.S. effective control fleet. In light of Liberia's stance during the 1973 Arab-Israeli conflict and the 1979 coup in Liberia, the effectiveness of U.S. control is less certain. (Exxon Corporation)*

such obvious warning signs that the system was based on an unstable foundation, most Liberian and American observers were surprised by the coup d'état and assassination of Tolbert and other high-ranking officials, led by a group of enlisted men from Liberia's army in April 1980. It was, after all, the first nonconstitutional change of government since 1871, and prior faith in the republic's stability had seemed very well founded. One of the first actions of the new regime was to send assurances to the International Trust Company that the ship registry system would not be disturbed. Since the shipping system had provided some 7 to 12 percent of government revenues over the decade of the 1970s, the new government was careful not to endanger the lucrative source of support. Nevertheless, International Trust Company officials in the United States anticipated that members of the shipping community would express some fears about the new regime, since it clearly seemed inclined, through summary courts-martial and executions, to overthrow and destroy elements of the conservative elite that long had governed the country. The International Trust Company hoped to allay shipowners' fears as the continued operation of the registry system demonstrated that, whatever domestic reforms might be implemented, the government of Liberia was still a reliable and stable one. Despite the company's official optimism, it was clear that defenders of the flag-of-convenience system no longer could claim the tradition of political stability and the conservative elite-dominated regime as an "asset." While the new regime did stabilize over the months immediately following the coup, the future was not at all assured, and the long-range reasons for doubting the political reliability of Liberia, present even in the days of Tubman and Tolbert, now were made more obvious and critical, and would affect shipowners as well as military policy makers.

The concept that Panama or Liberia had sufficient sovereignty to issue merchant flags, but insufficient sovereignty to exercise control over the ships under those flags, had been assumed from the beginning. Shipowners originally sought to have both states issue flags without laying claim to some of the other attributes of national sovereignty, such as labor legislation or taxation. But, the independent stand of Panama on the canal and of Liberia on its third-world commitments gave renewed evidence that both countries were entirely capable of developing foreign policies that were quite independent of American positions. Just as Joseph Grew wrongly had believed that Ricardo Alfaro would yield on the seizure of the *Federalship*, and Emory Land had believed that Arnulfo Arias would accept without objection the arming of the vessels under his country's flag, only to be disillusioned, so the refusal of W.H.R. Tolbert to let his flag supply Israel had contributed to a renewed disillusionment. Panama and Liberia both had demonstrated that reliance upon the lack of willingness to assert sovereignty was a weak reed upon which to depend in times of international military crisis. From the point of view of the two flag states, surrender of sovereignty over ships on business matters had been a reasonable exchange for tonnage revenues, but the international use of their flags in political and military situations was quite another matter. By 1980, it was clear that neither nation had ever fully accepted the American premise that her sovereignty was for sale.

Epilogue

THE SUBJECT OF THE ORIGINS of flags of convenience reflects the contrast between two kinds of history—*remembered* history present in the minds of participants long after the event, and *actual* history, the day-to-day events and practices, often forgotten when they have little glamour. This book has attempted to weave the two strands together, to illuminate the well-known and oft-told side of the story with a contrasting look at the lesser-known, detailed side of daily events. The pragmatic wisdom and critical observations that might have been drawn from a study of the more obscure but practical side of the record frequently were missed by contemporaries.

Thus, for example, the Harriman transfers to escape the Dougherty ruling on Prohibition long have been regarded as the first transfers of U.S. ships to Panama, rather than the actual and more mundane first Shipping Board-approved transfers for reasons of administrative convenience. Harriman's continued use of the flag for business reasons, after the "libertarian" reasons had been rendered moot by the Supreme Court, was never part of the public story. Later, Joseph Grew derived satisfaction from what he perceived as the backing-down of Alfaro and the Panamanian government over the *Federalship* and other smugglers; in point of fact, a look at the diplomatic correspondence and the court cases reveals that Panama did not yield on principle, but retained her jurisdiction over the decision of whether or not to cancel smuggling vessels.

The actual establishment of the ESSO fleet in Danzig and its reasons for transferring to Panama were not matters of contemporary public interest. When ESSO historians felt called upon later to justify the 1935 decision, they described factors of opposition to Naziism, factors that were politically suitable in the postwar period in which the interpretation was published. Yet the real reasons for transfer had had very little to do with ideology. The choice of Panama's flag had been a practical business matter; again, the decision was a forgotten, mundane, and less-than-glamorous process. Similarly, the tense moments for ESSO managers as they lost European-flag tankers and nervously arranged to exchange German crews for Allied crews aboard Panamanian-registered tankers were ignored in the postwar emphasis on the dramatic and real courage of ESSO mariners who fought under several flags to take fuel to the Allies during the war.

Of greater consequence was the hardening of opinion during the first great public debate over convenient flags—the neutrality debate of 1939. While Admiral Emory Land lost the fight in that the specific vessels he had planned to transfer to Panama were shifted to Belgium instead, the lines of argument had become established. Once overcome, the problem revealed by the refusal of Arias to accept U.S. control could be ignored. Later, when the JCS established "effective control" as a planning doctrine, it was the neutrality debate that was remembered, not the actual wartime operating agreements and time charters, which in fact had been the only proven precedents for practical effective control. Thus, Land, although he had lost the argument in 1939, and had seen political reliance on Panama challenged by Arias in 1941, won in the long run. His view that the flag could provide a system of politically based strategic convenience provided the logic upon which the JCS designed its system of effective control. In the short span of ten years, the facts of hard experience and daily practice were forgotten in favor of the drama of debate, and supporters and critics alike sounded variations on the 1939 rhetoric through the hearings and court cases of the 1950s and 1960s.

The design and development of a Liberian registry system that would improve upon and compete with the flag of Panama proceeded quietly as a business arrangement, and was presented to contemporaries as an exercise in American reform and modernization of an African state. When the JCS considered whether Liberia should be regarded as an "effective control country," the analysis was built rather quickly on an impressionistic summary of Liberia's historic connections with the United States, its political leanings, and its geopolitical position, as presented in publicity by the Stettinius group. The motives, procedures, and structure of the actual operating system were not subjected to examination. The review of the system conducted for the State Department by Francis Truslow became utilized as an internal document of suggested improvements, not as a public critique. The steady growth of the registry business, and its efficient superiority to the randomly assembled Panamanian collection of decrees, laws, and consular structure, did not become the object of public scrutiny. The custom-made, tax-free legal environment proved hospitable to the registry of tankers as the world economy became more and more dependent upon petroleum transport by sea. Only when oil spills and energy economics created new arguments, and when the system of effective control began to face the changing international political environment of the 1970s, did the long-harbored suspicions of navy men about the reliability of the system bring about serious reevaluation of the premises of effective control.

The short memory of public figures for events in which they themselves had participated need not surprise us, for individual memory, like all historical thought, is consciously and unconsciously selective. The account that is retold and thus remembered is rarely one that reflects defeats, setbacks, or decisions taken for reasons of necessity or profit rather than idealism. The story of flags of convenience has been particularly afflicted with such intentional editing and casual forgetfulness by its participants, for the registry of vessels under foreign flags was by definition frequently a matter of profit, necessity, or convenience, rather than of patriotism or ideals. It is for such reasons that the two strands of publicly remembered drama and forgotten day-to-day operation lie so intricately interwoven through the records of the past, and that their examination becomes the obligation of later generations of observers.

Notes

Abbreviations Used in the Notes

DDEPL   Dwight D. Eisenhower Presidential Library, Abilene, Kansas
ERS   Edward R. Stettinius, Jr., Papers, Manuscript Department, University of Virginia Library, Charlottesville, Virginia
FRUS   *Foreign Relations of the United States*
HHPL   Herbert Hoover Presidential Library, West Branch, Iowa
HSTPL   Harry S Truman Presidential Library, Independence, Missouri
LOC   Library of Congress, Manuscript Division, Washington, D.C.
NavOpArch   Operational Archives, Naval History Division, Navy Yard, Washington, D.C.
USNA   United States National Archives, Washington, D.C.
RG   Record Group—to designate collection at the National Archives

Notes to Introduction

1. In the *Muscat Dhows* case, the Permanent Court of Arbitration held that sailing dhows registered under the flag of France, but owned by subjects of the Sultan of Muscat, legally were entitled to the French flag, despite a British protectorate over Muscat. The precedent has been used to justify unilateral decisions of states to extend their merchant flags to vessels of foreign ownership. Scott, *Hague Court Reports* 93 (1916):8.

2. Dwight Syfert, "The Liberian Coasting Trade, 1822–1900," *Journal of African History* 18 (1977):217; German Arciniegas, *Caribbean*, pp. 420–21, 435, 441–43.

Notes to Chapter 1

1. 4 March 1912, Decimal 819.851; 3 October 1913, Decimal 819.851/1; Honduras fostered maritime communication to overcome travel problems, 1912, Decimal 713/16, RG 59, USNA.

2. Law 63 of 1917, dated 5 December 1917; Commercial Code of 22 August 1916.

3. 7 November 1922, Decimal 819.851/3, RG 59, USNA.

4. See Walter LaFeber, *The Panama Canal* for a review of American assumptions. Contemporary view by former American Minister to Panama William J. Price, "Influence of the United States on Central American Progress," *Current History* 26 (1927):871.

5. Lawrence O. Ealy, *The Republic of Panama in World Affairs*, pp. 40–41, 59–62.

6. Jeffrey Dorwart, "The Mongrel Fleet: America Buys a Navy to Fight Spain, 1898," *Warship International*, in press, 1980; William R. Braisted, *The United States Navy in the Pacific, 1909–1922*, p. 471.

7. Jeffrey J. Safford, *Wilsonian Maritime Diplomacy, 1913–1921*, p. 92; Darrel H. Smith and Paul Betters, *The United States Shipping Board*, p. 99; Arthur E. Cook, *A History of the United States Shipping Board*, pp. 71–74; Walter Albrecht Radius, *United States Shipping in Transpacific Trade, 1922–1938*, pp. 14–17.

8. 42 Stat. 957 (Tariff Act of 1922); strengthened bureau: Edward Nash Hurley, *New Merchant Marine*, p. 223; Cook, *History of the United States Shipping Board*, pp. 51–52.

9. Safford, *Wilsonian Maritime Diplomacy*, pp. 68–76, 83–87, 92–95, 141–67.

10. 38 Stat. 1164 (La Follette Seamen's Act).

11. Gerald R. Jantscher, *Bread Upon the Waters*, p. 46; Paul M. Zeis, *American Shipping Policy*, chapter 10.

12. William S. Benson, *The New Merchant Marine*, pp. 176–77.

13. 41 Stat. 988 (Jones Act of 1920), Section 9.

14. Decimal 418.11 G 65/36; 418.11 G 65/41, RG 59, USNA.

15. Burlingham to State, 8 December 1919, Decimal 704.1900/6, RG 59, USNA. For the issues in the war, see Charles David Kepner and Jay H. Soothill, *The Banana Empire*, pp. 87–89.

16. Decimal 418.11 G 65/12241, 418.11 G 65/13, 418.11 G 65/3, 418.11 G 65/60, RG 59, USNA.

17. Decimal 418.11 G 65/1, 418.11 G 65/60, RG 59, USNA.

18. Ealy, *Panama in World Affairs*, pp. 59–62, 53–55.

19. Decimal 418.11 G 65/39, RG 59, USNA.

20. L.F.E. Goldie, "Recognition and Dual Nationality," *British Yearbook of International Law* (1963):220–83; Boleslaw Adam Boczek, *Flags of Convenience*, p. 106.

21. 1091–1253, RG 32, USNA; Smith and Betters, *United States Shipping Board*, pp. 42, 55, 68, 79.

22. 1091–1252, RG 32, USNA; Minutes, United States Shipping Board, vol. 11, 4599, 3 June 1922, 1091–1253, RG 32, USNA.

23. *New York Herald*, 1 October 1922.

24. Ibid. Robert Dollar had argued since 1914 that no profit could be made in Pacific trade without using Chinese crews. Report on manning and wage scales, in Roy H. Morrill and E. C. Plummer Papers, LOC.

25. 7 November 1922, Decimal 819.851/3; 8 June 1923, Decimal 819.851/5, RG 59, USNA.

26. The form of the ship's articles in use in the mid-1920s indicated the legislative history of the required provisions. The copy reviewed is in Decimal 819.863, RG 59, USNA.

27. 17 April 1923, Decimal 819.863, RG 59, USNA.

28. 1091–905 *Tunica*, RG 32, USNA ; Docket File, *Tunica*, 7 6.2 T83, RG 32, USNA; Decimal 819.801/4, 819.863, 819.863/2, RG 59, USNA.

29. Geist to State, 10 December 1923, Decimal 819.863/2, RG 59, USNA.

30. Carr to Jaeckel, 26 November 1923, Jaeckel to State, 15 January 1924, Decimal 819.863/2, RG 59, USNA.

31. Decimal 819.867, 819.867/1, RG 59 USNA.

32. Terry Coleman, *The Liners*, pp. 40–58; John Malcolm Brinnin, *The Sway of the Grand Saloon*, pp. 340–41, 433–34.

33. Harriman's prohibition-evasion as the initial motive is repeated in the literature on the subject. See, for example, Sidney W. Emery, "The Effective United States Control Fleet," *United States Naval Institute Proceedings* 96 (May 1970):160.

34. Charles Robert Vernon Gibbs, *Passenger Liners of the Western Ocean*, pp. 380–82.

35. *New York Times*, 7 October 1922, p. 2; Proceedings of the United States Shipping Board, November 1922, RG 32, USNA; 1091–5555, RG 32, USNA.

36. Proceedings of the United States Shipping Board, 1 November 1922, RG 32, USNA; 1091–5555, RG 32, USNA; Cunard et al. v. Mellon et al., 262 U.S. 100 (1922).

37. *New York Times*, 27 October 1922, p. 3, 11 November 1922, p. 22.

38. *New York Times*, 10 November 1922, p. 2.

39. Ibid.

40. Proceedings of the United States Shipping Board, 1 November 1922, 1091–5555, RG 32, USNA.

41. Interviews with George D. Woods, p. 3; with Allen Dulles, p. 43; with Eustace Seligman, p. 5; with David Hawkins, p. 7; with W. Averell Harriman, p. 3; Dulles correspondence, Morales to Dulles, 6 June 1917; Dulles to Morales, June 1917; Clipping File, Box 404, *New York World*, 5 March 1921, 6 March 1921; in the Dulles Oral History Collection, Firestone Library, Princeton University, Princeton, New Jersey. On the Dulles perspective, see Leonard Mosley, *Dulles: A Biography of Eleanor, Allen and John Foster Dulles and Their Family Network*; and Townsend Hoopes, *The Devil and John Foster Dulles*, pp. 25–28, 35–36.

42. *New York Times*, 6 December 1922, p. 2.

43. Jaeckel to State, 15 January 1924, Decimal 819.863/2, RG 59, USNA.

Notes to Chapter 2

1. Decimal 819.801/2; Orr to Carr, 15 December 1922, Decimal 819.801/3, RG 59, USNA.

2. Passages cited in the Panamanian laws were Article 61 and Articles 1077 through 1533 of the Commercial Code; Articles 494, 553, and 589 of the Fiscal Code; and Law 63 of 1917, dated 15 December 1917.

3. South to State, 2 February 1925, Decimal 819.032/103; revenues: 23 March 1927, Decimal 819.00/1342; press notice of rates: Decimal 819.851/7; intention to attract registries: Decimal 811.114 *Chasina*/5, RG 59, USNA.

4. Gunsaulus to State, 21 June 1923, Decimal 819.864/orig., RG 59, USNA.

5. Convention between the United States and Panama for the Prevention of Smuggling of Intoxicating Liquors, signed at Washington, 6 June 1924, proclaimed 19 January 1925.

6. Decimal 811.114 *Chasina*/14, RG 59, USNA.

7. Decimal 811.114 *Federalship*/7; Decimal 811.114 *Chasina*/11, RG 59, USNA.

8. Decimal 811.114 *Chasina*/5, RG 59, USNA; the new law was Law 54 of 1926.

9. Decimal 811.114 *Federalship*, bulky file, RG 59, USNA; see also Malcolm Francis Willoughby, *Rum War at Sea*, pp. 83–85.

10. Decimal 811.114 *Federalship*, RG 59, USNA.

11. Decimal 811.114 *Federalship*/45, RG 59, USNA.

12. Alfaro to State, 30 October 1926, Decimal 811.114 *Chasina*, RG 59, USNA.

13. Decimal 811.114 *Federalship*/71; Decimal 811.114 *Hakadata*/21, RG 59, USNA.

14. United States v. Ferris et al. 19 F 2d 925 (*Federalship* case); Ford v. United States 10 F 2d 339 (*Quadra* case).

15. Willoughby, *Rum War at Sea*, p. 85.

16. United States v. Schouweiler 19 F 2d 387 (*Hakadata* case, incorrectly transcribed as "*Hakadate*").

17. Decimal 811.114 *Hakadata*/22, RG 59, USNA.

18. Ford v. United States 10 F 2d 339; 19 May 1927, Decimal 819.00/1354, RG 59, USNA.

19. Decimal 819.00/1369; Decimal 811.114 *Chasina*, RG 59, USNA.

20. Decimal 811.114 *Helori*, RG 59, USNA.

21. Decimal 819.00/1359, RG 59, USNA.

22. Decimal 811.114 *Federalship*/29, RG 59, USNA.

23. Lawrence O. Ealy, *The Republic of Panama in World Affairs*, pp. 53–67, 72–75.

24. Decimal 811.114 *Hakadata*/49, RG 59, USNA.

25. Decimal 811.114 *Chasina*/22; Decimal 811.114 *Federalship*/29, RG 59, USNA.

26. Decimal 819.00/1363; Decimal 811.114 *Federalship*/33; Decimal 811.114 *Federalship*/82, RG 59, USNA.

27. Decimal 819.00/1366, RG 59, USNA; Ealy, *Panama in World Affairs*, p. 64.

28. Grew: Decimal 811.114 *Federalship*/88; Alfaro: Decimal 811.114 *Hakadata*/22, RG 59, USNA.

29. Decimal 819.00/1373, RG 59, USNA.

30. Decimal 811.114/4641, RG 59, USNA.

31. Consular Instruction 442, 21 January 1916, Decimal 704.1900; 17 January 1928, Decimal 195.1/1523, RG 59, USNA.

32. 17 January 1928, Decimal 195.1/1523, RG 59, USNA.

33. Decimal 711.192/30a; Decimal 711.192/72, RG 59, USNA.

34. Decimal 819.00/1356; Decimal 811.114 *Federalship*/98, RG 59, USNA.

35. Decimal 819.00/1126; 29 May 1923, Decimal 819.863, RG 59, USNA; in 1937, Panama's Foreign Office regularized the procedure for American consular representation of Panama's interests and established a list of specific cities at which U.S. representation was desired. See Decimal 819.85/1-1449, RG 59, USNA.

36. Examples of the procedures *Maspeth II*, April 1924, Decimal 1091.8403; *Viking*, October 1927, Decimal 1091.9979, RG 32, USNA.

37. Motives of the transfers, *Maspeth II*, Decimal 1091.8403; *Centralia*, Decimal 1091.9038 (Order of Transfer 2208); *Lincoln Land*, Orders of Transfer, vol. 6, 1584;

Viking, Decimal 1091.2879; *Buckhannon*, Decimal 1091.3919; *City of Para*, Orders of Transfer, vol. 6, 1567, RG 32, USNA. See also Lloyd's of London, *Lloyd's Register of Shipping*, 1926.

38. Orders of Transfer, vol. 6, 1583, *Lebanon; Oronite*, Decimal 1091.3154, RG 32, USNA.

39. U.S., Congress, House, Committee on Merchant Marine and Fisheries, *Hearings on HR 8361*, 71st Cong., 27 June 1930, pp. 131, 152, 179. See Mira Wilkins, *The Maturing of Multinational Enterprise*, pp. 96–98; and Charles David Kepner and Jay H. Soothill, *The Banana Empire*.

40. *New York Times*, 10 December 1922, p. 6.

Notes to Chapter 3

1. Like other assumptions about the system, the neutrality-evasion point is rarely subject to independent verification. See "PanLibHon Registration of American-owned Merchant Ships: Government Policy and the Problem of the Courts," *Columbia Law Review* 60 (1960):711–37.

2. Hoover to Benson, 5 March 1921; Hoover to Coolidge, 21 August 1923, Commerce Files, HHPL.

3. Hoover to Barneson, 5 January 1923; Hoover to Coolidge, 2 February 1923, Commerce Files, HHPL.

4. Hoover to Congressional Committee, "Oral Testimony," 22 January 1924, Commerce Files, HHPL; Clinton Doggett, "The Hoover Plan for Dissolution of the Shipping Board," *Nautical Gazette*, 26 December 1931.

5. Plummer to Hoover, 27 October 1925, Commerce Files, HHPL. Plummer to Hoover, 2 October 1925, Morrill-Plummer Papers, LOC.

6. Coolidge to Hoover, 12 March 1924; Gregg to Hoover, 28 May 1924; O'Connor to Hoover, 7 June 1924; Hoover to O'Connor, 25 June 1924; Report of Committee, 29 December 1924; Gregg to Stokes, 1 August 1925; Chamber of Commerce Report, September 1925; Gregg to Hoover, 18 November 1925, Commerce Files, HHPL.

7. O'Connor to Hoover, 23 September 1931, Presdential Files; Hoover Speech, 24 October 1923, Commerce Files, HHPL. Hoover's ideas are summarized in a letter to Congressman Wallace White, 4 November 1925, Commerce Files, Box 390—Merchant Marine, HHPL.

8. 45 Stat. 675 (Merchant Marine Act of 1928), Title III and Title IV.

9. Sixth Merchant Marine Conference, 4 January 1933, Subject File, Merchant Marine, Presidential Papers, HHPL.

10. Senator Royal Copeland at Sixth Merchant Marine Conference reviewed the variety of subsidies in the laws of the maritime nations at that point.

11. *United States Naval Institute Proceedings*, vol. 53, no. 26, 1927.

12. *New York Times*, 30 December 1935, p. 1.

13. 49 Stat. 858 (Merchant Marine Act of 1936), Title II, Sections 201–214.

14. Emory S. Land, *Winning the War with Ships*; Frederic C. Lane, *Ships for Victory*, p. 30.

15. Merchant Marine Act of 1936, Title V, Sections 501–508.

16. Merchant Marine Act of 1936, Title VI, Sections 601–608; Title IX, Sections 902, 903.

17. Grace Lines sales: Domestic and Foreign Commerce, 518-Panama, RG 151, USNA; Hanson to Richey, 14 September 1929, Presidential Files, Subject Merchant Marine—1929, HHPL.

18. Doswell testimony: U.S., Congress, House, Committee on Merchant Marine and Fisheries, *Hearings on HR 8361*, 71st Cong., 27 June 1930, pp. 128–79.

19. Ibid. p. 131.

20. Charles David Kepner and Jay H. Soothill, *The Banana Empire*, p. 202; Jenkins on S. 628: 5 January 1933 at the Sixth Merchant Marine Conference. Other support for the bill outlawing mail contracts to foreign-flag operators: flyer, Middle West Foreign Trade Committee, Presidential Files, Subject, Merchant Marine—1931 (dated 8 April 1931), HHPL.

21. Kepner and Soothill, *The Banana Empire*, pp. 205–6.

22. Doswell testimony, 71st Cong., p. 179.

23. George Sweet Gibb and Evelyn Knowlton, *History of Standard Oil Company (New Jersey), 1911–1927*, p. 270. One of these DAPG reparations vessels later was transferred to the United States; it was the *Pawnee*, which then became one of the first vessels transferred to Panama in 1922. See chapter 1.

24. Report of Work Done December 1920, Memel and Danzig, 15 May 1920, Reparations Commission—Maritime Services of, QQ Reparations Commission, RG 45, USNA. Right to register under the Danzig flag: John B. Mason, *The Danzig Dilemma*, pp. 65, 326; Gibb and Knowlton, *History of Standard Oil, 1911–1927*, pp. 270–71; John Basset Moore, "Legal Brief for Standard Oil: Beneficial Ownership," in *Collected Papers of John Basset Moore*, 5:237, 293–98.

25. Vessels not deliverable, 14 August 1920, QQ Reparations Commission, RG 45, USNA; Mason, *The Danzig Dilemma*, p. 62.

26. Hague to Benson, 23 October 1923, vol. 6, Orders of Transfer, appl. 1691, RG 32, USNA. Two of the vessels, the *J. A. Mowinckle* and the *Orville Harden*, were built in Monfalcone, Italy; one, the *Peter Hurll*, was built in Britain; the rest of the new ships were German-built. See Standard Oil Company of New Jersey, *Ships of the Esso Fleet in World War II*, pp. 210, 363, 511. See also Felix Riesenberg, *Sea War*, p. 119, noting the use of blocked marks to build ships.

27. Henri Goldberg, *Le Port du Dantzig*, p. 122; Lloyd's of London, *Lloyd's Register of Shipping*, 1930–31, vol. 2, p. 1159; Kurt Peiser, *Danzig's Shipping and Foreign Trade*, pp. 10–11.

28. Henrietta Larson, E. H. Knowlton, and C. S. Popple, *History of Standard Oil Company, (New Jersey), 1927–1950*, pp. 207, 215. In the light of ESSO's active supply and cooperation with I. G. Farben through 1941, claims of concern over Nazi politics in the mid-1930s were clearly the result of postwar hindsight. See Joseph Borkin, *The Crime and Punishment of I. G. Farben*, pp. 96–102, 108–15; and William Stevenson, *A Man Called Intrepid*, pp. 308–9.

29. Larson et al., *History of Standard Oil, 1927–1950*, p. 207; on local Nazi party in Danzig, see Christoph M. Kimmich, *The Free City*, p. 116.

30. Sentfleben: Decimal 660c.116/185; complaints by ESSO and other oil companies regarding Polish customs administration: 8 March 1935, Decimal 660c.116/10; Bruins to State, 4 December 1934, Decimal 660k.116, RG 59, USNA.

31. Larson et al., *History of Standard Oil, 1927–1950*, p. 217.

32. ESSO's requests and action: Decimal 819.855/2, 819.855/6 through /9; Schoenfeld to State, on treaty, 29 October 1939, Decimal 819.843/1, RG 59, USNA.

33. Atlantic Refining Company, in a less spectacular move, had placed two new tankers, the *Brunswick* and the *Winkler*, under Panamanian registry even prior to the larger-scale ESSO transfer, *Lloyd's*, 1930–31. See also, for Norwegian operations, Erling Naess, *The Great PanLibHon Controversy*, pp. 2–4.

34. Foreign and Domestic Commerce, 518-Panama, 15 January 1931, 4 February 1931, RG 151, USNA.

35. Taxation covered in 55 Stat. 1363 (International Agreements other than Treaties, Jan.–March 1941); Agreements between United States of America and Panama with regard to mutual recognition of ship measurement certificates, Exchange of Notes, 17 August 1937, in 50 Stat. 1726 (International Agreements other than Treaties); see also, on measurement, Decimal 819.855/1 and 819.855/2, RG 59, USNA. The 1941 exchange of notes regarding mutual exemption of taxation indicated that the original Panamanian exemption dated back to 2 March 1936, Executive Resolution 33-bis.

Notes to Chapter 4

1. Doolittle (Bilbao) to State, 18 December 1931, H-MC 800.866/62/199, RG 59, USNA; Beltza, *El Nacionalismo Vasco*, p. 205; the company owning the *Pilar*, the *Santa Marta*, and the *Ignacia Aguado* worked in the coal trade to Italy but was bankrupt by 1933, Rafael Gonzalez Echegaray, *Cincuenta Anos de Vapores Santanderinos*, p. 161.

2. Decimal 819.85/2, 819.86/3, RG 59, USNA.

3. Stefan Riesenfeld, "Sovereign Immunity of Foreign Vessels in Anglo-American Law," *Minnesota Law Review* 25 (1940):1–65. Sota y Aznar: *New York Times*, 29 September 1937, p. 12.

4. Andreas Georgiou Laimos, *The Greeks and the Sea*, quoting Kyriakides, p. 201.

5. Shantz (Athens) to State, 14 November 1939, Decimal 819.851/29, RG 59, USNA.

6. P. L. Perdicas, "History and Outline of Greek Maritime Law," *Transactions of the Grotius Society* (Papers) 25 (1939):40–45.

7. The competition between Onassis and Kulukundis over this story is discussed in Nicholas Fraser et al., *Aristotle Onassis*, pp. 50–51. The Onassis version is repeated elsewhere; a fictionalized account appears in Nicholas Gage, *The Bourlotas Fortune*, pp. 265–66. A similar restriction in American law provided for emergency exemption from the manning rule while in foreign ports, but Greek law did not include such an exemption at that time.

8. Derived from a review of *Lloyd's Register of Shipping*.

9. Erling Naess, *The Great PanLibHon Controversy*, pp. 1–2; Erling Naess, *Autobiography of a Shipping Man*, pp. 34–38.

10. Naess, *The Great PanLibHon Controversy*, p. 2. The *Tai Ping Yang*, the *Tai Shan*, and the *Granville* all were registered in Panama prior to the Naess ships.

11. White to Davis, 15 April 1933, Decimal 811.7619 Playa/1, RG 59, USNA.

12. Norman J. Padelford, *International Law and Diplomacy in the Spanish Civil Strife*, pp. 14–15.

13. W. H. Davis, "The Naval Side of the Spanish Civil War, 1936–1939," *United States Naval Institute Proceedings* 66 (June 1940):803–23; D. P. O'Connell, *The Influence of Law on Sea Power*, pp. 115–21.

14. *New York Times*, 5 February 1939, p. 35; *New York Times*, 28 February 1939, p. 35; ONI report: Confidential Memo L-118, 16 November 1938, Decimal 819.851/29, RG 59, USNA.

15. Wolf: Decimal 856.85/72; Emmet to State, 12 May 1937, Decimal 856.85/69 (on *Hordena*); Emmet to State, 9 June 1937, Decimal 856.85/71; 856.85/70 and 856.85/72; related companies 711.011 Lic. Wolf, Rudolf/1 through /57 /51, RG 59, USNA.

16. Shantz (Athens) to State, 14 November 1938, Decimal 819.851/34, RG 59, USNA.

17. Ibid. Shantz collected this evidence specifically in order to prove the illegal and cynical uses of the flag by Davaris. Thus, he may have characterized Davaris in the dialogue as slightly more criminal than he was in fact.

18. Shantz request, Decimal 819.851/29, RG 59, USNA.

19. Ehud Avriel, *Open the Gates*, p. 54. The use of Panama's vessels for refugee smuggling continued through Israeli independence in 1948.

20. Wadsworth to State, 3 June 1959, Decimal 867n.55/176; Steger press report: Decimal 867n.9111/229; State Department pressure on Panama: Decimal 867n.55/194, RG 59, USNA. By 1940 denial of service was regularized: Latimer to State, 1 February 1940, Decimal 819.851/59; Cole to State, 25 May 1940, Decimal 819.851/62, RG 59, USNA.

21. Avriel, *Open the Gates*, pp. 116–17; Steger to State, 21 September 1939, Decimal 867n.55/196; Honaker to State, Decimal 819.857/133, 27 February 1942, RG 59, USNA. The file Decimal 819.857/100 through /165, RG 59, USNA, details the political repercussions of this tragedy.

22. Navy concern with fishermen: Puleston to State, 18 October 1934; Vogemann: Decimal 819.851/10; Japan and China: Decimal 819.853/2, 894.852/11; China: Decimal 195.1/700 through /1750.0, RG 59, USNA.

23. Russell to State, 2 February 1934, Decimal 819.86/2, RG 59, USNA.

24. The *Dora*: Decimal 819.863/6; debate over service to the *Beme*: Decimal 819.851/32; Division of Foreign Service Administration to Republics of the Americas, 10 December 1938, Decimal 819.851/26; Near Eastern Affairs to Foreign Service Administration, 16 December 1938, Decimal 819.851/27, RG 59, USNA.

25. The *Josiah Macy*: Dodge to Dunn, 10 December 1936, Decimal 852.00/4145, RG 59, USNA; the *Norseman*: Padelford, *International Law and Diplomacy in the Spanish Civil Strife*, pp. 663 ff; the *Hordena*: Decimal 852.00/6294, RG 59, USNA.

26. Abbott to Bullitt, 6 August 1938, Decimal 195.2/3554, RG 59, USNA; the *Nantucket Chief*: Padelford, *International Law and Diplomacy in the Spanish Civil Strife*, p. 173; Decimal 195.2/3535, /3562B, /3564, /3581, RG 59, USNA; the Arcon Steamship Company: Decimal 195.2/3548, RG 59, USNA; on Texaco: Joseph L. Thorndike, "Cap Rieber," *Life* (1 July 1940), pp. 60–68; Ladislas Farago, *The Game of the Foxes*, p. 399.

27. Naess, *The Great PanLibHon Controversy*, p. 2.

28. Flexer to State, 3 May 1938, Decimal 819.851/25, RG 59, USNA. This is the earliest reference to "convenient flags" encountered in the course of research for this work.

29. 15 January 1937, Decimal 819.855/2; Campanole Report, 3 September 1936, Decimal 819.85/3, RG 59, USNA.

30. Goldman: Naess, *The Great PanLibHon Controversy*, p. 2; Naess, *Autobiography*, p. 41; Fabrega: Decimal 819.857/117, RG 59, USNA; *New York Times* notices scattered, 23 August 1936, 29 August 1937, 5 September 1937, 29 September 1937, 6 January 1939.

Notes to Chapter 5

1. U.S., Congress, Senate, Special Committee Investigating the Munitions Industry ("Nye Committee"), 73d Cong., 1934; Walter Millis, *The Road to War*; Neutrality Act of 1935, 49 Stat. 1081; Neutrality Act of 1937, 50 Stat. 121.

2. "Cash-and-Carry" Neutrality Act, 54 Stat. 4, 4 November 1939.

3. William Langer and S. Everett Gleason, *The Challenge to Isolation*, p. 235.

4. Ibid., p. 232. Scapegoat sensation applied to earlier neutrality legislation as well: *Marine Journal*, 15 January 1936, p. 9. Both the Propeller Club and the National Foreign Trade Conference opposed the Pittman bill, see *Marine Journal*, 15 October 1939, pp. 8, 16.

5. Henrietta M. Larson, E. H. Knowlton, and C. S. Popple, *History of Standard Oil Company (New Jersey), 1927–1950*, p. 393.

6. Hackworth to State, 10 March 1937, Decimal 195.2/3488, RG 59, USNA.

7. Langer and Gleason, *Challenge to Isolation*, pp. 212-13; *The Diary of Adolf Berle* (Microfilm, Roosevelt Library, Hyde Park, 1977), Roll 1, Frame 1147, 30 September 1939; "chastity belt": *Berle Diary*, Roll 2, Frame 362, 17 February 1940; Roll 2, Frame 418, 12 March 1940; text of the Declaration of Panama: *FRUS*, 1939, volume 2, p. 100.

8. *FRUS*, 1939, vol. 5, pp. 60–62, 67; Decimal 800.852/207a RG 59, USNA; Samuel F. Bemis, *The Latin American Policy of the United States*, pp. 363–64; Welles to Berle, 28 August 1939, Decimal FW 819.864/4, RG 59, USNA; British attitude toward declaration: *Berle Diary*, Roll 1, Frames 1148, 1151, 30 September 1939; Frame 1153, 2 October 1939.

9. W. H. Shephardson and William Scroggs, *The United States in World Affairs*, p. 208, suggested that the provision "evoked considerable discussion" later. This essay interpreted the transfer provision of the declaration as setting precedents for transfers from the United States to Panama, rather than from Germany to Latin American neutrals.

10. Totals transferred compiled from Standard Oil Company of New Jersey, *Ships of the Esso Fleet in World War II*.

11. Ibid., p. 63; Decimal 819.851/39, /40, RG 59, USNA.

12. Embassy to State, 2 September 1939, Decimal 819.851/39; Welles to Berle, 28 August 1939, Decimal FW 819.864/4, RG 59, USNA. Despite these crises, cf. use of the incident as example of effective control: U.S., Congress, Senate, Committee on Interstate and Foreign Commerce, Subcommittee on Merchant Marine and

Fisheries. *Hearings on Ship Transfers*, 85th Cong., 1st sess., April 1957, p. 79; and Ainsworth to Areeda, 20 February 1959, Areeda Papers, DDEPL.

13. Standard Oil, *Ships of the Esso Fleet in World War II*, p. 300.

14. *Life*, 1 July 1940, p. 67; however, Rieber became engaged in German espionage and propaganda efforts as part of the price of his vessels. See Ladislas Farago, *The Game of the Foxes*, pp. 399–412. Rieber's activities were well known in State Department and intelligence circles, as well as receiving a favorable press in the Luce publications. Thornburg to Acheson, 18 July 1941, Decimal 819.852/37a, RG 59, USNA. See also William Stevenson, *A Man Called Intrepid*, p. 115.

15. Larson et al., *History of Standard Oil, 1927–1950*, p. 392.

16. Decimal 819.8591/25, /29, /42, RG 59, USNA; Larson et al., *History of Standard Oil, 1927–1950*, pp. 394–95.

17. Lee: *New York Times*, 9 November 1939, p. 10; editorial: *Marine Journal*, 15 November 1939, p. 7; goozlefixers: *Marine Journal*, 15 December 1939, pp. 9–10; Taylor: *New York Times*, 29 December 1939.

18. Land address, "Off the Cuff," 17 November 1939, before the Society of Naval Architects and Engineers, in Speeches-23, Land Papers, LOC.

19. *New York Times*, 7 November 1939, p. 2.

20. *New York Times*, 8 November 1939, p. 1.

21. Destroyers for bases: Mark Lincoln Chadwin, *The Warhawks*, pp. 74–108; on scrap ships: Division of American Republics, internal memorandum, 7 November 1940, Decimal 819.852/9, RG 59, USNA.

22. Kirk to State, 11 November 1939, Decimal 195.1/1806; Kirk to State, 11 November 1939, Decimal 195.1/1805; Kirk to State, 8 November 1939, Decimal 195.1/1796, RG 59, USNA.

23. Boake Carter: NMU minutes, 16 January 1940, Baarslag Collection, HHPL. Tom Connally: *New York Times*, 7 November 1939, p. 22; Bailey to Roosevelt, 10 November 1939, Land Papers, LOC.

24. *Berle Diary*, Roll 1, Frames 1155–1156, 3 October 1939.

25. *Berle Diary*, Roll 1, Frame 1232, 6 November 1939.

26. Cordell Hull, *Memoirs of Cordell Hull*, 1: 698.

27. *New York Times*, 9 November 1939, p. 22. Arthur Krock commented specifically on this issue in *New York Times*, 8 November 1939, p. 22; 10 November 1939, p. 22; 12 November 1939, Section IV, p. 3.

28. Pillsbury to Duggan, 7 November 1939, Decimal 195.1/1826, RG 59, USNA.

29. Curran to Hull, 7 November 1939, Decimal 195.1/1790, RG 59, USNA.

30. Curran to Roosevelt, 16 November 1939, Decimal 195.1/1814; Burke to Hull, 8 November 1939, Decimal 195.1/1794; Jurich to Hull, 9 November 1939, Decimal 195.1/1807; Deal to Hull, 9 November 1939, Decimal 195.1/1808; Scully to Land, 13 November 1939, Decimal 195.1/1811, RG 59, USNA. *New York Times*, 7 November 1939, p. 22.

31. Dawson to State, 9 November 1939, Decimal 195.1/1801, RG 59, USNA.

32. *Berle Diary*, Roll 2, Frame 49, 11 November 1939.

33. *Berle Diary*, Roll 2, Frames 50–51, 12 November 1939.

34. Curran to Roosevelt, 16 November 1939, Decimal 195.1/1814, RG 59, USNA; NMU minutes, entries for 16 January 1940 and for 24 June 1941, Baarslag Collection, HHPL.

35. Hull, *Memoirs*, 1:699–700; *New York Times*, 17 December 1939, p. 42.

36. NBC Interview, Speech File, 18 November 1940, Land Papers, LOC; "America's Shipping Lifeline: The Merchant Marine as Naval Auxiliary," *Marine Journal*, 15 December 1940.

37. *Berle Diary*, Roll 2, Frame 255, 17 November 1939; Roll 2, Frame 289, 17 January 1940; Roll 2, Frames 321–322, 27 January 1940; Roll 2, Frame 367, 27 February 1940.

38. Survey of correspondence: 11 December 1939, Decimal 195.1/1822, RG 59, USNA; Berle on "eating cake": *Berle Diary*, Roll 1, Frame 1232, 6 November 1939; Chadwin, *The Warhawks*, p. 83.

39. *New York Times*, 9 November 1939, p. 22.

40. Decimal 819.852/10; Dawson to State, 7 February 1941, Decimal 819.852/14, RG 59, USNA.

41. The Greeks cooperated as well by prohibiting transfer to Panama, by a "Decree-Law" of 30 March 1940, in Reed (Athens) to State, 11 April 1940, Decimal 819.851/61; Wadsworth to State, 25 May 1940, Decimal 819.851/64; Latimer to State, March 1940, Decimal 819.859/26, RG 59, USNA.

42. Land to Hull, 30 July 1941, Decimal 819.852/39; Panamanian order: 12 September 1941, Decimal FW 819.852/57, RG 59, USNA.

43. *Janko* to Yokohama: Decimal 819.8591/13; Dutch position: Decimal 819.8591/59; Hull to Saugstad, 29 September 1941, Decimal 819.8591/60; Norwegian position: Decimal 819.8591/61, RG 59, USNA; Long to Welles, 3 October 1941, Box 196, Long Papers, LOC; also filed in Decimal 819.8591/62, RG 59, USNA.

44. Spanish transshipments: Scott to State, 28 February 1941, Decimal 819.8591/25; Texaco: Welles to Wilson, Decimal 819.852/37A; *Daylite*: September and October 1941, Decimal 819.851/80 through /85; scrap ship policy: Division of American Republics, internal memo 7 November 1940, Decimal 819.852/9, and passim through Decimal 819.852/5a through 819.852/27; Finnish ships: Decimal 819.851/85½ through 819.851/94, RG 59, USNA; United Fruit: *FRUS*, 1939, vol. 5, p. 79, ref. to Decimal 862.852/51, RG 59, USNA; *FRUS*, 1940, vol. 5, p. 410, ref. to Notter to Duggan, 21 March 1940, Decimal 862.852/82, RG 59, USNA.

45. Division American Republics internal memorandum, 22 September 1941, Decimal 891.841/83; 819.851/100, RG 59, USNA. In 1940 and 1941, however, officials within the State Department realized that the "adjunct fleet" concept was unreliable and depended on the good will of Panamanian officials. Warnings of the dangers of reliance in 12 April 1941, Decimal 819.852/25; Dawson to State, 7 February 1941, Decimal 891.852/14; Dawson to State, 11 December 1940, Decimal 819.852/6, RG 59, USNA.

46. Roosevelt to Land, 30 April 1941, Presidenial Memoranda, Box 4 (Added Materials), Land Papers, LOC.

47. Long to Welles, 17 June 1941, Box 196, International Communications, Belgian-Danish shipping, Long Papers, LOC.

48. 8 May 1941 entry in NMU minutes, Baarslag Collection, HHPL.

49. Land to Hull, 4 August 1941, Decimal 819.8595/17, RG 59, USNA. The decision was taken by the Maritime Commission on 24 July 1941.

50. 11 August 1941, Subject File: State Department International Communication, General Files, Long Papers, LOC.

51. Saugstad's interest: *Berle Diary*, Roll 3, Frame 273, 23 July 1941. Authoriza-

tion in writing: "Memo to the Honorable B. Long," 12 August 1941, Decimal 819.8595/3, RG 59, USNA.

52. Memorandum of conference: 23 September 1941, Decimal 819.8595/18, RG 59, USNA.

53. Ibid.

54. Ibid.

55. Land himself liked this press notice, *San Francisco Chronicle*, 23 October 1941; he clipped it for his scrapbook: Scrapbook, Box 3, Land Papers, LOC.

56. Berle on *Sessa*: *Berle Diary*, Roll 3, Frame 320, 6 September 1941; Roll 2, Frame 336, Frame 383, 9 September 1941; Roll 2, Frame 392, 11 September 1941; Roll 2, Frame 402, 15 September 1941. See also Robert Sherwood, *Roosevelt and Hopkins*, p. 370. While the *Montana* and *Sessa* had not been armed, the *Pink Star* was armed, but the gun unmanned; there was considerable confusion in the record over the degree to which the ships had been armed: Decimal 819.857/9a, Decimal 819.857/*Pink Star* 4 through /*Pink Star* 7, RG 59, USNA.

57. Wilson to State, 7 October 1941, Dispatches 314, 315, Decimal 819.8595/9; Dispatch 319, Decimal 819.8595/11; incorrect data on *Sessa's* location: Decimal 819.857/*Sessa* 19a, RG 59, USNA. The United States Neutrality Act was not modified to allow arming of U.S. ships until 17 November 1941: 55 Stat. 764.

58. Walter LaFeber, *The Panama Canal*, pp. 97–98. While LaFeber did not refer to the ship issue in his analysis of the coup, Lawrence O. Ealy, *The Republic of Panama in World Affairs*, p. 110, noted the connection, but without access to State Department papers still classified at the time of his writing.

59. Wilson to State, 11 October 1941, Decimal 819.8595/20A; State to Wilson, 13 October 1941, Decimal 819.8595/20A, RG 59, USNA; Long to Welles, 9 October 1941, File 197, Long Papers, LOC; pencilled memorandum, 13 October 1941, File 197, Long Papers, LOC.

60. Decimal 819.8595, RG 59, USNA.

61. Hull's denial: Press Release 500, 16 October 1941, Division of American Republics, Box 191, Long Papers, LOC; *New York Times*, 17 October 1941; Berle thought the coup not U.S. responsibility: *Berle Diary*, Roll 3, Frame 479, 10 October 1941. Since-declassified O.S.S. report indicates Berle correct: OSS R&A Report 147, RG 59, USNA.

62. Ricardo Adolfo de la Guardia took over after a transition through Ernesto Jean de la Guardia (no relation), who was given the post of ambassador to the United States. The Seccion de Naves had begun to refuse Axis requests for information even prior to the coup: Muccio to State, 1 October 1941, Decimal 819.851/81; Fabrega: Wilson to Duggan, 16 October 1941, and Barber to Wilson, 23 October 1941, Decimal 819.857/49, RG 59, USNA. Total armed ships: Samuel E. Morison, *History of United States Naval Operations in World War II*, vol. 1, *The Battle of the Atlantic*, p. 416. Army G-2 saw the armed ship policy as "the first definitely cooperative action taken by the new administration," see Carter to War Department, 19 October 1941, Decimal 819.8595/13, RG 59, USNA. A rather minor benefit was the closing of all Japanese businesses, see Decimal 819.5034/67, 819.00/2244, RG 59, USNA.

63. Convenient means: Morison, *Battle of the Atlantic*, p. 297. The same view was reflected in a slightly more contemporary account: Gilbert Cant, *The American Navy*

in World War II, p. 189n, who defined Panamanian registry as a "legal fiction which proved convenient in circumventing the provisions of the Neutrality Act."

Notes to Chapter 6

1. *Oilshipper* case: Wilson to State, 4 December 1941, Decimal 819.852/96; the case continued passim through Decimal 819.852/196 to 819.852/299, RG 59, USNA, perhaps a classic in "red tape." The *Omega*: Decimal 819.852/147, /153, /183, /225A; the *Dora*: Decimal 819.857/208; consular representation: Decimal 819.857/222, RG 59, USNA.

2. The regulations extending war-risk insurance to Latin American states were WSA directives, not legislation: *Federal Register*, 7 February 1942, p. 823, Section 243.1; 19 June 1942, p. 4593, Section 301.7g and Section 301.8a; 19 August 1942, p. 6545, Section 302.22. The law itself simply made "American-owned" ships eligible for the insurance, without reference to flag or registry, in 54 Stat. 689 of 29 June 1940.

3. John G. Kilgour, "The EUSC Program," in *The United States Merchant Marine*, regarded war-risk as the "centerpiece" of the system of control. See chapter 11 for details of the operating system.

4. I.D. card system, Decimal 819.63/39, /42; 819.8608/1, RG 59, USNA.

5. Edwin P. Hoyt, *U-Boats Offshore*, pp. 166–72; War Diary, Eastern Sea Frontier, 7/42 VII, NavOpArch.

6. Ship logs: Decimal 819.853/11 through /14; prior control on cancellations: Decimal 819.853/17 of 21 April 1944; Article 13: Decimal 819.85/93; Dutch and British employment forbidden: Decimal 819.863/16; direct dealing with consuls: Decimal 819.853/17, 819.851/178, RG 59, USNA. In spite of cooperation, Panama did not wish to endanger revenue, still viewed as the system's main function: Muccio to State, 20 June 1942, Decimal 819.852/176, RG 59, USNA.

7. Crew problems: the *El Mundo*, 10 March 1942, Decimal 819.8632/1; The *Yorba Linda*, 9 November 1942, Decimal 819.863/18; the *Loida*, 19 February 1943, Decimal 819l863/22; the *Oradell*, Decimal 819.864/10; the *Typhoon*, Decimal 819.863/14; "Fracas at the YMCA," Decimal 819.863/19, 819.86/29, RG 59, USNA. A gruesome case of cannibalism among the survivors of the *Donerail* was reported in Abbott to State, 23 April 1942, Decimal 819.857/150, RG 59, USNA.

8. ESSO loss reports, as of 14 June 1943, in Decimal 819.857/282, RG 59, USNA. The reports were requested by Panama in order to remove the ships from the registry: Decimal FW819.857/259, RG 59, USNA. Excellent, but not definitive: Paul E. R. Scarceriaux, "Merchant Ships Lost Under Panamanian Flag During World War II," *Belgian Shiplover* 149 (1974): shiplist no. 693; submarine losses in Jürgen Rohwer, *Die U-Boot-Erfolge der Achsenmächte, 1939–1945*.

9. Condolence letter system and services to Panamanian seamen: Hull to Cunningham, 8 August 1942, Decimal 819.857/222, RG 59, USNA.

10. Hunt-Falck conversation, 8 January 1943, Decimal 819.862/4, RG 59, USNA. The overtime and optional holiday hours were specifically legal under Panama's law, although by U.S. standards, the practice may have seemed improper. Article 108 of the Consular Tariffs of Panama, Decree 41 of 1935 specified the

holiday rules. State was unaware of this fact, it appeared. Jorge Fabrega, trans., *Consular Tariff of Panama*, pp. 28–29.

11. Wilson to State, 24 December 1942, Decimal 819.862/4, RG 59, USNA. The fee also dated from 1935 and was specified by Article 24, Decree 199, Fabrega, *Consular Tariff*, p. 23.

12. Burke to Long, 12 January 1943, Decimal 819.851/118, RG 59, USNA.

13. Burke-Daniels correspondence: Daniels to Burke, 24 March 1942, Decimal 819.851/118; Burke to Daniels, 14 April 1942, Decimal 819.851/119, RG 59, USNA.

14. Ibid.

15. Hull-Land inquiry, 24 February 1943, Decimal 819.851/141A, RG 59, USNA.

16. Land to Hull, 2 March 1943, Decimal 819.851/142, RG 59, USNA.

17. Foster-Morse conversations, 14 October 1943, 29 October 1943, Decimal 819.851/150, RG 59, USNA; State Department staff had been looking for grounds on which to reopen the issue: Cabot to Bonsal, 2 August 1943, Decimal 819.851/145, RG 59, USNA.

18. Land's proposed legislation: Land to Roosevelt, 23 June 1941; Roosevelt to Land, 9 July 1941, Land Papers, LOC. Speech, Land Papers, General Correspondence, October 1942, LOC. Land's position was well known. See Frederic C. Lane, *Ships for Victory*, pp. 302–3.

19. Maritime Labor Board, 52 Stat. 955, 55 Stat. 259; Land to Hull, 3 March 1943, Decimal 819.86/33 regarding inclusion of Panamanian ships under Maritime War Emergency Board, RG 59, USNA.

Notes to Chapter 7

1. Boleslaw Adam Boczek, *Flags of Convenience*, pp. 28–29, 59–60. The transfers were warmly supported in the Maritime Commission, against union objections: CIO Maritime Committee, to "All Unions in the CIO Maritime Committee," 6 March 1947 and 27 March 1947, OF Misc., Truman Papers, HSTPL.

2. Lloyd's of London, *Lloyd's Register of Shipping, Summary of Statistics*.

3. Owens to Truman, 1 April 1947, OF 99 Misc., Truman Papers, HSTPL. The labor opposition to Panama's flag was widespread and could be documented endlessly from widely available news and labor publications. The archival material cited here is chosen by way of illustrating commonly used arguments. Ferdinand Smith to Truman, 29 August 1945, OF 798, Truman Papers, HSTPL. Boczek, *Flags of Convenience* devoted a chapter to labor opposition, pp. 64–88.

4. Curran to Truman, 21 November 1947, OF 99 Misc., Truman Papers, HSTPL; Erling Naess, *The Great PanLibHon Controversy*, pp. 8–10.

5. Murray to Truman, 17 December 1947, OF 99 Misc., Truman Papers, HSTPL. "Runaway ships" was a pun on "runaway shops," industries that left unionized northern states for nonunionized southern states.

6. Ladimer to Kingsley, 11 April 1947, OF 126 Misc., Truman Papers, HSTPL. The National Federation of American Shipping prepared a report that reached similar conclusions, 17 April 1947, "Research Report No. 7" in Decimal 819.85/

4-1747, RG 59, USNA. By 1949, Panama appointed more consuls to handle the "illicit trade" in the Mediterranean, Guerra to State, 26 March 1949, Decimal 819.85/3-2649, RG 59, USNA.

7. Boczek, *Flags of Convenience*, pp. 65–68; O. W. Pearson to Steelman, 15 April 1949, OF 99 Misc., Truman Papers, HSTPL.

8. ILO report: International Labour Office, *Conditions in Ships Flying the Panama Flag*.

9. O. A. Vallarino to Acheson, 18 April 1949, OF 99 Misc., Truman Papers, HSTPL.

10. Walter LaFeber, *The Panama Canal*, pp. 96–98.

11. Larry LaRae Pippin, *The Remon Era*, pp. 17–19. Continued use of refugee vessels to Palestine under the Panamanian flag made the news and caused difficulties for Panama through early 1948. See Ehud Avriel, *Open the Gates*. Panamanian requests for State Department help on the issue appeared unavailing in Decimal 819.85/1-2448, 819.85/3-2548, RG 59, USNA.

12. The following account appeared in Rodney Carlisle, "The American Century Implemented: Stettinius and the Liberian Flag of Convenience," *Business History Review* 14 (1980):175–91.

13. Stettinius's business and government career is reviewed by Walter Johnson in "Edward R. Stettinius, Jr." in Norman Graebner, ed., *An Uncertain Tradition*, Stettinius quoted, p. 212. Arthur Vandenberg, Jr., *The Private Papers of Senator Vandenberg*, pp. 167, 191. Harry S Truman, *Memoirs*, vol. 1, p. 14.

14. Charles Henry Huberich, *The Political and Legislative History of Liberia* is the definitive constitutional history of the colonial and early period. But see note 39 below.

15. In 1947, two American-owned ships, under a Farrell subsidiary, engaged in rubber trade from river ports to the sea coast. They were registered under a special agreement with the Liberian government, and show up in some accounts as the first ships registered in Liberia. This was true in a sense, but they were not registered under the code that attracted tonnage away from Panama.

16. Rodney Carlisle, "Self-Determination in Colonial Liberia and American Black Nationalism," *Negro History Bulletin* 36 (1973): 77–83 and Rodney Carlisle, *The Roots of Black Nationalism* explore the attraction Liberia held for American black nationalists and African Pan-Africanists.

17. Stephen Hlophe, "A Class Analysis of the Politics of Ethnicity of the Tubman and Tolbert Administrations in Liberia," a paper given at the Liberian Studies Association, 2 April 1977, Macomb, Illinois. See also Martin Lowenkopf, *Politics in Liberia* on the factionalism in the elite. Extensive materials on Stettinius Associates are found in the Edward R. Stettinius, Jr., Papers, Manuscript Department, University of Virginia Library, Charlottesville, Virginia, hereafter cited as ERS. Material cited here is used by permission of the Curator of Manuscripts, University of Virginia Library. Report on Tubman's political problems: W. K. Trimble to B. Smith, 24 June 1948, Box 789, ERS.

18. Specific reference to non-Liberian efforts: Morocco, Sulzberger to Chancerelle, 4 June 1948, Box 790; Ethiopia, Smith to Haile Selassie, 19 July 1948, Box 789; Netherlands East Indies, de la Rue to Stettinius, 7 July 1948, Box 789; French West Africa, de la Rue to Stettinius, 14 July 1948, Box 789, ERS.

19. Robert Christie, an independent operator who obtained the early iron concession, resisted Stettinius's encroachment on what he viewed as his ground, as did
Harvey Firestone.

20. Articles appeared in *Time, Life, National Geographic, Ebony,* and *Readers Digest,*
among others. Connection with Rockefeller: *New Haven* (Connecticut) *Journal
Courier,* 14 February 1949. Stephen E. Fitzgerald, "The Public Relations Program
of the Liberia Company: An Interim Report," 9 July 1948, Box 789, ERS. Eric
Johnston's impact: see William Appleman Williams, *Tragedy of American Diplomacy,*
pp. 176, 181.

21. "Original Press Release," 27 September 1947, Box 767, ERS.

22. Report on meeting, 21 April 1948, Box 791, ERS.

23. Memorandum, "Points in Connection with the U.S. Public Interest in the
Liberian Program," 15 February 1949, Box 797, ERS. Earlier drafts in the same box
indicate that Stettinius himself participated in drafting the memo.

24. Shipowner approach to Stettinius: interview, author-Lininger, February
1979; first documented reference: Stettinius to Smith, 31 December 1947, ref.
conversation with E. S. Klein, Box 767; memorandum of meeting, 6 January 1948,
Box 790; "Weekly Assignment Report," 5 March 1948, Box 791, ERS.

25. U.S., Congress, Senate, Committee on Government Operations, Permanent
Subcommittee of Investigation, *Hearings on Sale of Government-Owned Vessels,* 82d
Cong., 18 February 1952, pp. 1, 24–26, 33–36, 40, 135–36. This committee linked
Stettinius and the AOTC investors to the "Casey group," a network of associates
headed by a former congressman involved in "influence peddling." The investments
in AOTC were nominal; most of the capital was acquired through mortgage against
guaranteed charter revenue; the leverage allowed for very high profits on investments.

26. *New York Times,* 18 August 1945, p. 1; 27 September 1947, p. 6.

27. Memorandum of meeting at Grew's home, 13 March 1948, Box 790, ERS.
Julius Holmes, Grew, Klein, and M. D. Franz talked directly with Assistant
Secretary of State Norman Armour and with Under Secretary of the Navy W. John
Kenney, 10 May 1948: Holmes to Sulzberger, 11 May 1948, Box 790, ERS.

28. Memorandum to His Excellency, the President of the Republic of Liberia, 5
April 1948, Box 790, ERS.

29. Report by Stettinius, 21 April 1948, Box 791; Stettinius to Smith, 5 August
1948, Box 791, ERS. See Nicholas Fraser, et al., *Aristotle Onassis,* pp. 101–14.

30. S. B. Adams to Sulzberger, 22 April 1948, Box 790; Smith to Stettinius, 14
July 1948, Box 793; Gulf: de la Rue to Lininger, 27 January 1948, Box 797; Ludwig:
de la Rue to Lininger, 28 January 1949, Box 797; Onassis: Stettinius to Kadow, 28
October 1948, Box 767, ERS.

31. De la Rue to Lininger, 24 January 1949, Box 797; Mackey to Franz, 30
November 1948, Box 793; de la Rue to Green, Franz, Klein, and copy to Stettinius,
16 December 1948, Box 793, ERS.

32. Trimble to Smith, 24 June 1948, Box 789, ERS; copying of comparable U.S.
codes: Truslow report, Francis Adams Truslow, *Report on the Corporation Code of
Liberia, the Maritime Code of Liberia and the Act Establishing the International Trust
Company of Liberia,* 10 March 1949, p. 80, Decimal 882.516/3-1049, RG 59, USNA.

33. Smith to Dennis, 10 June 1948, Box 790; Loucheim to Stettinius, 21 July
1948, Box 789; Mackey to Smith, 29 July 1948, Box 791, ERS.

34. Memorandum of conversation, by Stettinius, 3 August 1948, Box 791; Franz to Stettinius, 4 August 1948, Box 791, ERS.

35. Mackey to Frantz, 4 August 1948, Box 791; Mackey to Smith, 13 August 1948, Box 796, ERS.

36. Trimble to Smith, 16 November 1948; Trimble to Stettinius, 24 November 1948; Mackey to Smith, 29 November 1948; Smith to Trimble, 14 December 1948; Stettinius to Harley, 17 December 1948; Trimble to Smith and Stettinius, 16 December 1948, all in Box 793, ERS. De la Rue to Smith, 13 August 1948, Box 796; Smith to Trimble, 13 September 1948, Box 796, ERS.

37. Mackey to Smith, 29 November 1948; Trimble to Smith and Stettinius, 16 December 1948, Box 793, ERS. The company draft of the law, in print, is in Box 791, ERS, and is entitled, "Draft of an Act Repealing 'Part 19, Sections 916 to 928, Inclusive of the Revised Statutes of the Republic of Liberia' and Establishing a Maritime Code of Law for the Republic of Liberia." The legislative-approved version signed into law in December is in Box 793, ERS, in mimeographed form, and entitled "Draft-Maritime Code as Accepted by Government" on cover sheet and "Draft of an Act to Establish a Maritime Code," on the first page. The crucial variations appear in Title I, Sections 3 and 4 of both versions.

38. Republic of Liberia, *Liberia—25 Years as a Maritime Nation*, p. 6.

39. S. B. Adams to Palmer, 31 December 1947, Decimal 882.5034/12-3147, RG 59, USNA; Holmes to Sulzberger, 11 May 1948, Box 790, ERS; meeting summarized in State Department office memorandum, Satterthwaite to Nitze, 12 October 1948, Decimal 882.5034/10-1248, RG 59, USNA. Stettinius to Smith, 2 August 1948, Box 793, ERS. American writing of Liberian commercial law had been a dream of Sidney de la Rue, and he had recommended it after a stay in Liberia as general receiver of customs; see Sidney de la Rue, *Land of the Pepperbird*. According to legend, Liberia's constitution itself had been written by Harvard Professor Samuel Greenleaf in 1848. Recent research suggests that, while a draft of the constitution was prepared in the United States, Liberians drafted their own document without any influence from Greenleaf's draft, which arrived later (Robert S. Brown, "Struggle for Power: The Opposition to Independence, 1839–1847"). However, the legend of American authorship of the constitution was alive and well in 1948, reiterated in Huberich, *The Political and Legislative History of Liberia*.

40. Covering letter with Truslow report, 25 March 1949, Decimal 882.516/3-1049; Grew to Acheson, 5 March 1949, Decimal 882.50/3-549; Grew to Acheson, 31 July 1949, Decimal 882.50/7-3149, RG 59, USNA. However, Stettinius had been on excellent personal terms with Marshall, even presenting him with prize turkeys on holidays. No such personal warmth existed between Stettinius and Acheson. Interview, author-Lininger, February 1979.

41. Quoted in State Department office memorandum, Satterthwaite to Nitze, 12 October 1948, Decimal 882.5034/10-1248, RG 59, USNA.

42. State Department memorandum of conversation, 24 August 1948, Decimal 882.5034/8-2448, RG 59, USNA.

43. De la Rue to Smith, 14 December 1948; Smith to Trimble, 17 December 1948, Box 793, ERS.

44. State Department memorandum of conversations, Allen Dulles-Sims, Decimal 882.5034/1-549, RG 59, USNA; Dulles was a good informant, for he notified Stettinius the same day: memorandum of telephone conversation, Stettinius-Allen

Dulles, 5 January 1949, ERS; State Department memorandum, Lovett to American Legation, 10 January 1949, Decimal 882.516/1-1049, RG 59, USNA; Truslow background and statement: *New York Times*, 3 March 1947, p. 32, and 3 October 1947, p. 40.

45. De la Rue to Lininger, 18 January 1949, Box 797, ERS.

46. De la Rue to Lininger, 21 January 1949, Box 797, ERS.

47. De la Rue to Stettinius, 11 February 1949 and 19 February 1949, Box 797, ERS.

48. State Department telegram, Acheson to American Embassy, Liberia, 4 February 1949, Decimal 882.516/1-1049, RG 59, USNA.

49. State Department memorandum, Sims to Satterthwaite, 7 March 1949, Decimal 882.5034/3-749, RG 59, USNA.

50. Truslow to Thorpe, Decimal 882.516/3-1049, RG 59, USNA.

51. Comparison of the December 1948 version of the law in Box 793, ERS (note 37 above), and the Truslow report in Decimal 882.516/3-1049 (note 32, above), reveals the four areas of disagreement. In the Truslow report, the suggested changes were: registration, p. 38; no delegation of rule-making power, p. 36; liability, p. 57; filing of liens, p. 47. Comparison of Truslow's suggestions with the 1956 code shows only the filing of liens incorporated in the legislation (Republic of Liberia, *Liberian Code of Laws of 1956 Adopted by the Legislature of the Republic of Liberia March 22, 1956*, vol. 2, pp. 811–12, Article 22, Section 106). Minor typographical corrections and contributions were incorporated in June and December 1949, as indicated through the 1956 annotated version of the code. Truslow's suggestion regarding "certificates of registry" was made part of the law by amendments made in 1958 and 1969, reflected in Sections 55 and 56 (Republic of Liberia, *Liberian Maritime Law*, pp. 11–12).

52. Smith to Klein, December, Box 793; Mackey to Schaeffer, 22 December 1948, Box 793; Mackey to Trimble, 6 January 1949, Box 797; Mackey to V. Rodriguez of Sullivan and Cromwell, 7 January 1949, Box 797; Schaeffer to Lininger, 17 January 1949, Box 797; Mackey to Schaeffer (n.d.), Box 797; Mackey to Franz, 5 January 1949, enclosing contract, Box 797, ERS. The rate was reduced to $.24 per $1.20 in a 1976 revision of the contract, but the system of contracting work to an American-based company is still in effect (interview, author-Frank Wiswall, January 1979). Schaeffer on income: Schaeffer to Lininger, 17 January 1949, Box 797, ERS. Schaeffer was correct. From 1949 to 1975, the International Trust Company earned at least $22 million from the ship registry, while Liberia earned over $60 million from new ship registry tonnage fees alone. A 1979 analysis placed the republic's earnings between 5.8 percent and 12.5 percent of annual Liberian government receipts over the period 1971–78 (International Maritime Associates, *Economic Impact of Open Registry Shipping*, pp. iii–13). The income was slow at first; see note 59, below.

53. Stettinius to Grew, 18 December 1948, Box 793, ERS. Under the fee-splitting arrangement, Liberia's earnings were considerably higher than they would have been under the original Liberia Company "three-way" division of profits. Thus the alteration on this count was clearly to the advantage of the republic, not the company.

54. Stettinius to Klein, 24 December 1948, Box 793, ERS.

55. Mackey to Franz, 5 January 1949, Box 797; Lininger to Green, 24 January 1949, Box 797, ERS; interview author-Lininger, February 1979.

56. State Department memorandum of conversations, Nitze-Morton, 13 April 1949, Decimal 882.5034/4-1349; Morton-Gorlitz, 7 November 1949, Decimal 882.5034/11-749; Morton-Moose, 11 May 1949, Decimal 882.5034/5-1149, RG 59, USNA. Stettinius to Green, 18 December 1948, Box 793; Cromwell to Bane, 7 January 1949, Box 797, ERS.

57. Truman to Gaston, chairman of Export-Import Bank, 28 February 1949, Box 797, ERS. On point-four: Thorp to Acheson, 28 March 1949; Truman to Acheson, 22 March 1949; Truman to Grew, 4 March 1949, PSF-Liberia, HSTPL; some duplicated in Decimal 840.50 Recovery/3-3349, RG 59, USNA.

58. Interview, author-Lininger, February 1979.

59. Registration of *World Peace* in Republic of Liberia, *Liberia—25 Years as a Maritime Nation*, p. 5; interview author-Lininger, February 1979. The total of five ships reflected in the 1949 tally by Lloyd's was an incomplete figure gathered for the June report. While the operation moved along slowly at first, by December 1949, thirteen large ships and several smaller ones had registered with a total tonnage of 128,000 tons. At $.325 per ton, if all revenue was collected, the tonnage would have yielded the company only $41,500 by the end of the first calendar year of operation. The Liberian government would have recovered some $112,000 by the end of 1949. Figures derived from reports by Ambassador Dudley in Decimal 882.851/8-2549, 882.851/10-1149, and 882.12-2949, RG 59, USNA. Some legal observers attributed Liberia's attraction to such factors as currency and language common with the United States, and "familiar American phrases" in the law of Liberia, without analysis of the origin of those phrases (Arnold Knauth and Christopher Knauth, *Benedict on Admiralty*, 6:334).

60. Boczek, *Flags of Convenience*, pp. 13–15.

Notes to Chapter 8

1. Henry Luce, "The American Century," *Life*, 17 February 1941, pp. 61–65. American century "ideology" is discussed in William Appleman Williams, *The Tragedy of American Diplomacy*, pp. 180–81, 199–200; see also Lloyd Gardner, *Architects of Illusion*, pp. 22–23.

2. Rodney Carlisle, "The American Century Implemented: Stettinius and the Liberian Flag of Convenience," *Business History Review* 14 (1980): 175–91.

3. The term *PanLibHon* itself is discussed in "PanLibHon Registration of American-owned Merchant Ships: Government Policy and the Problem of the Courts," *Columbia Law Review* 60 (1960): 711–37.

4. McCullogh to Longstreet, 17 April 1947, Decimal 819.85/4-1747, RG 59, USNA.

5. Henry to State, 15 May 1947, Decimal 819.85/5-1547; Buell to State, 23 October 1947, Decimal 819.851/10-2347, RG 59, USNA.

6. "Circular Airgram to American Diplomatic and Consular Officers in the Other American Republics," 5 October 1949, Decimal 819.85/10-549, RG 59, USNA.

7. Memorandum of conversation, Asst. Secretary Miller-Miguel Amodo, Decimal 819.85/10-1449, RG 59, USNA.

8. Guerra to State, 11 April 1949, Decimal 819.85/4-1149, RG 59, USNA.

9. Guerra to State, 26 March 1949, Decimal 819.85/3-2649; resolutions in Decimal 819.85/5-1649, RG 59, USNA. International Labour Office, *Conditions in Ships Flying the Panama Flag*, p. 5.

10. International Labour Office, op. cit., pp. 1–2.

11. Ibid., pp. 8–11.

12. Ibid., pp. 11, 23–25.

13. Ibid., pp. 29–36, conclusions, p. 39.

14. Ibid., p. 40.

15. Ibid., pp. 41-42. In 1951 Panama issued an English and Spanish edition entitled *Consular Tariff of Panama*, edited and translated by Jorge Fabrega, which compiled related codes covering fees charged by consuls. The Panamanian Labor Code, Act 67 of 1947 (11 November 1947) was ordered to be printed in a special edition, in Spanish, and apparently funded by the ILO (International Labour Office, *Codigo de Trabajo, Edition Extra-official*), but neither law was amended to take into account the recommendations. Beyond the two publications of existing codes, little was done to implement the ILO *Report*.

16. U.S., Congress, Senate, Committee on Interstate and Foreign Commerce, *Merchant Marine Study and Investigation*, 81st Cong., 2d sess., hearings pursuant to Senate Resolution 50 and on S. 2786, 27 February 1950, p. 542. Hereafter *Senate Study*, 1950.

17. Ibid., p. 66.

18. Ibid., p. 538.

19. Ibid., p. 68. Magnuson continued to regard the system as blackmail since under the law, ESSO could register its new tankers directly under Panamanian flag without permission from the Maritime Commission. The company would register them in the United States only if permitted to transfer more vessels out. Thus it was their "threat" to place new ships out of U.S. registry that forced the commission to allow the transfer of older vessels. Magnuson adhered to this view and reiterated it in 1957 (U.S., Congress, Senate, Committee on Interstate and Foreign Commerce, Subcommittee on Merchant Marine and Fisheries, *Hearings on Ship Transfers*, 85th Cóng., 1st sess., on S. 1488, 1957, p. 135). Some companies did not accept the arrangement: National Bulk Carriers in Maj. Gen. Phillip Fleming to Steelman, 7 February 1950, OF 99, Truman Papers, HSTPL.

20. *Senate Study*, 1950, p. 628.

21. Ibid.

22. Ibid., p. 73.

23. Ibid., p. 610.

24. Ibid., p. 69.

25. Ibid., p. 74.

26. *New York Times*, 13 March 1951, p. 1; 1 April 1951, p. 1; 13 March 1951, p. 1; 30 March 1951, p. 1. See U.S., Congress, Senate, Committee on Government Operations, Permanent Subcommittee of Investigation, *Hearings on Sale of Government-Owned Vessels*, 82d Cong., 18 February 1952. See Nicholas Fraser et al., *Aristotle Onassis*, pp. 100–14.

27. The Justice Department investigation was reviewed in 1957: U.S., Congress, House, Committee on Merchant Marine and Fisheries, *Study of Vessel Transfer*,

Trade-in and Reserve Fleet Policies, 85th Cong., 1st sess., 1957, pp. 70–120, 168, 186–88.

28. Ibid., p. 199.

29. The fact that Onassis had proposed to the Saudi government that it establish its own flag registry system, under which Onassis would operate and which would be guaranteed a proportion of Saudi oil export carrying trade, had caused an outburst of antagonism against him by the major international oil firms (see Fraser et al., *Aristotle Onassis,* pp. 132–53). For a suggestion that Nixon's "persecution" of Onassis was at the instigation of the oil companies, see Jim Hougan, "Prelude to Watergate: The Plot to Wreck the Golden Greek," *Playboy,* September 1978, pp. 95–98 et seq. The eventual creation of such a registry by the Saudis after the successes of OPEC can be seen as part of the revolt of the oil-producing states against the corporations (see H. P. Drewry, *The Involvement of Oil-Exporting Countries in International Shipping,* pp. 1–2).

30. These and other problems with the premises of effective control are examined in chapter 11.

31. U.S., Congress, Senate, Committee on Interstate and Foreign Commerce, Subcommittee on Commerce, *Investigation of Federal Maritime Administration, Transfer to Foreign Flag, S. 173,* 83d Cong., 2d sess., 1954, p. 40.

32. U.S., Congress, Senate, Committee on Interstate and Foreign Commerce, Subcommittee on Merchant Marine and Fisheries, *Hearings on Ship Transfers,* 85th Cong., 1st sess., on S 1488, 1957. Hereafter *Ship Transfer Hearings,* 1957.

33. *Ship Transfer Hearings,* 1957, pp. 27–28.

34. Gamble's testimony: *Ship Transfer Hearings,* 1957, p. 70. It should be noted that 1 ton of crude oil yielded about 311 gallons of final product, including gasoline and heating oil. Therefore, two dollars per month per ton would add less than one cent to the cost per gallon of fuel refined from crude transported by sea. Since that fuel would compete with wholly domestically produced fuel, however, the price would be diluted even more. Since in the 1950s, U.S. refineries as a whole were obtaining 80 to 90 percent of their supply from domestic wells, the price truly could be absorbed. However, when imports increased in later years, the proportion of shipping cost in final product would be marginally higher. That subject became hotly debated in 1977 hearings on HR 1037, discussed in chapter 10.

35. *Ship Transfer Hearings,* 1957, p. 74.

Notes to Chapter 9

1. Boleslaw Adam Boczek, *Flags of Convenience,* p. 95.

2. Ibid., pp. 116–19. See also David Renton, *The Genuine Link Concept and the Nationality of Physical and Legal Persons, Ships and Aircraft,* pp. 41–50, 103–10; and Nagendra Singh, *Maritime Flag and International Law,* p. 44. *ICJ Reports* (1955): 4.

3. Boczek, *Flags of Convenience,* pp. 215–42, 246–65.

4. Ibid., pp. 272–74.

5. "Constitution of the Maritime Safety Committee of the Intergovernmental Maritime Consultative Organization," Advisory Opinion, 8 June 1960, *ICJ Reports* (1960): 150–78.

6. Ibid.

7. Ibid.

8. Ibid.

9. Erling Naess, *The Great PanLibHon Controversy*, pp. 120–25. L.F.E. Goldie showed that Boczek misread and exaggerated the significance of the IMCO decision in "Recognition and Dual Nationality: A Problem of Flags of Convenience," *British Yearbook of International Law* (1963):220–83. To interpret the decision as international law reflected Boczek's pro-flag of convenience orientation.

10. Afran Transport Company et al. v. National Maritime Union, 43 LRRM 2311 U.S. District Court, S.D.N.Y. (14 November 1958).

11. W. E. Fagen, "Knight and Dragon: Slogans vs. Information," *Public Relations Journal* 20 (August 1964):20; Naess, *The Great PanLibHon Controversy*, pp. 58–59; memorandum of conversation, 27 January 1959, Areeda Papers, DDEPL.

12. The use of the NLRB to establish labor jurisdiction over flag-of-convenience vessels had been discussed as a possible tactic at the NMU as early as 1941: W. M. Standard, memorandum, 21 October 1941, Foreign Flags File, NMU Research Department, New York.

13. "PanLibHon Registration of American-owned Merchant Ships: Government Policy and the Problem of the Courts," *Columbia Law Review* 60 (1960):711; Lauritzen v. Larsen, 345 U.S. 571 (1953).

14. Lauritzen v. Larsen, 345 U.S. 571 (1953); Zielinski v. Empresa Hondurena de Vapores, S.A. 113 F. Supp. 93, S.D.N.Y. (1953); Bobalakis v. Compania Panamena Maritima San Gerassimo, 168 F. Supp. 236, S.D.N.Y. (26 November 1958).

15. Peninsular & Occidental Steamship Company and Green Trading Company and Seafarers International Union of North America (Case 12-CA-235), 132 NLRB 10 (10 July 1961).

16. Fianza Cia. Nav. S. A. v. Benz, 43 LRRM 2682 (4 December 1958).

17. Benz v. Compania Naviera Hidalgo, 353 U.S. 138 (1957).

18. West India Fruit Company, Inc. (Case 15-CA-1454) 130 NLRB 343 (1960).

19. West India Fruit, 130 NLRB 343 (1960); Wildenhus's Case, 120 U.S. 1-12 (1886); Cunard Steamship Co. et al. v. Mellon et al., 262 U.S. 100 (1923).

20. West India Fruit, 130 NLRB 343 (1960).

21. Naess, *The Great PanLibHon Controversy*, p. 100.

22. Ibid.

23. "Informal Chronology," Areeda Papers, Box 12, Folder 5, DDEPL.

24. Gardner Ainsworth to Areeda, 11 February 1959; Clarence Morse to Areeda, 9 February 1959; Chief of Naval Operations Office to Areeda, 7 February 1959, Areeda Papers, DDEPL.

25. George Doub to David Kendall, 23 February 1959, with enclosure, Areeda Papers, DDEPL.

26. Stuart Rothman to Kendall, 25 August 1959, Morgan Papers, DDEPL.

27. Areeda to Doub, 4 December 1959, Areeda Papers, DDEPL. Brief of the United States, Intervenor, as Amicus, (NLRB Cases 15-CA-1454, 12-CA-255, 21-RC-415, 2-RC-10379) NLRB jurisdiction, Suitland Depository, USNA.

28. United Fruit Company and National Maritime Union of America AFL-CIO (Case 2-RC-10379) 134 NLRB 287 (15 November 1961).

29. Naess noted that *Incres* and *Hondurena* were "the two most favourable cases fact-wise, as viewed by [the ACFN]" (*The Great PanLibHon Controversy*, p. 100).

NMU brief, *Supreme Court Briefs*, 372 U.S. 10 (1963). The decision to fight on the *Incres* case was taken on the grounds that in management, Incres was in fact a U.S. firm. Attorneys and union executives did not perceive this case as a risk to their strategy: draft brief submitted "To the International Maritime Workers Union," on the *Incres* case, NMU Research Department files, New York.

30. British brief, *Supreme Court Briefs*, 372 U.S. 10 (1963).

31. Solicitor General's brief, *Supreme Court Briefs*, 372 U.S. 10 (1963).

32. Ibid.

33. Interview, author-Archibald Cox, November 1979; Kennedy had consulted *The Speeches of Senator John F. Kennedy, Presidential Campaign, 1960, Part I, Freedom of Communications*. U.S., Congress, Senate, Committee on Commerce, Subcommittee of the Subcommittee on Communications, *Final Report, Pursuant to 395*, 86th Cong., 1961, p. 1075; the telegram, dated 3 October 1960, was read at the NMU convention and therefore also reported in *NMU Proceedings, 12th National Convention, NMU of America of the AFL-CIO, 1960* (New York: NMU, 1960), p. 53.

34. Interview, author-Cox, November 1979.

35. Naess, *The Great PanLibHon Controversy*, p. 106.

36. Supreme Court decision in the *Incres-Hondurena* cases: 372 U.S. 10 (1963).

37. Ibid. Naess, *The Great PanLibHon Controversy*, p. 110. Naess called the decision "a complete victory for the flags of convenience shipowners" (Naess, *Autobiography of a Shipping Man*, p. 158). L.F.E. Goldie showed that the decision should not be interpreted so comprehensively in his review of Boczek, *Flags of Convenience*, in *International and Comparative Law Quarterly* 12 (1963):989–1004.

Notes to Chapter 10

1. Erling Naess, *Autobiography of a Shipping Man*, pp. 120–32, 146–48; Jeffrey Potter, *Disaster by Oil*, pp. 2–5.

2. See Noel Mostert, *Supership*.

3. H. P. Drewry, *The Role of the Independent Tanker Owners*, pp. 1–6.

4. Such operations by company-executive groups are reported in the case of Union Oil executive ownership of Barracuda, *New York Times*, 14 February 1977, p. 14; and in the case of a Mobil Oil group, "Samarco," in *Washington Post*, 30 November 1979, setting up operation under Saudi flag.

5. Zenon S. Zannetos, "Some Problems and Prospects for Marine Transportation of Oil in the 1970s," (Conference paper), Alfred Sloan School of Management, Massachusetts Institute of Technology, Cambridge. Zannetos predicted such a procedure in 1970, but suggested corporations overlooked profit potential of shipping; Stanley Ruttenberg spelled out the practice in testimony, U.S., Congress, House, Committee on Merchant Marine and Fisheries, Subcommittee on Merchant Marine, *Energy Transportation Security Act of 1974 (HR 8193)*, 93d Cong., 1974, pp. 630–80.

6. One such analysis, based on figures from FACS, appears in "The 'Flag of Convenience' Fleet: Not All Bad and Getting Better," *Marine Engineering Log*, August 1978.

7. *New York Times*, 13 February 1977, p. 1; 14 February 1977, p. 14; works by Cowan, Petrow, Potter, Mostert (see bibliography) were part of the journalist-authored literature.

8. Robert Engler, *Politics of Oil* and *The Brotherhood of Oil*, and Anthony Sampson, *The Seven Sisters* all contributed to the public awareness of oil company politics. Reactions to disaster, controlled by API financing of conference, reflected in American Petroleum Institute, *Proceedings, Joint Conference on Prevention and Control of Oil Spills*, 15–17 December 1969, henceforth *1969 Proceedings*.

9. For contrast of positions on oil as dangerous to marine environment, see *1969 Proceedings*, p. 343 for the "safe" argument; cf. U.S., Maritime Administration, *Shipboard Guide to Pollution-Free Operations* for the "dangerous" argument.

10. *Torrey Canyon* accounts in Richard Petrow, *In the Wake of the Torrey Canyon*, published in Britain as *Black Tide*; and Edward Cowan, *Oil and Water*. The best account from a mariner's viewpoint, is in L. de Vaisseau Oudet, *In the Wake of the Torrey Canyon* pp. 12–23.

11. Oudet, *In the Wake of the Torrey Canyon*, pp. 24–27.

12. Narrative compiled from Oudet, Petrow, and Cowan. Oil company position on detergents, *1969 Proceedings*, p. 343.

13. Petrow, *In the Wake of the Torrey Canyon*, pp. 228–32.

14. Oudet, *In the Wake of the Torrey Canyon*, pp. 24–27; L.F.E. Goldie, in review of four works concerned with *Torrey Canyon*, *Journal of Maritime Law and Commerce* 1 (October 1969):155–65.

15. Oudet, *In the Wake of the Torrey Canyon*, pp. 11, 35–36; Petrow, *In the Wake of the Torrey Canyon*, pp. 184, 189–90; Cowan, *Oil and Water*, pp. 188, 192.

16. Cowan, *Oil and Water*, p. 190; Oudet, *In the Wake of the Torrey Canyon*, pp. 48–55. Oudet suggested that the European viewpoint was widespread and hinted at its roots.

17. IMCO and tanker owners' reactions to *Torrey Canyon*: Petrow, *In the Wake of the Torrey Canyon*, p. 238; U.S., MarAd, Office of Technology Assessment, *Oil Transportation by Tankers*, pp. 72–79; Edward Duncan Brown, *The Legal Regime of Hydrospace*, pp. 159–74; Gerald Moore, "Legal Aspects of Marine Pollution Control," in R. Johnston, ed., *Marine Pollution*, pp. 605–16, 619n; Robert Shinn, *The International Politics of Marine Pollution*, pp. 65–75.

18. *Ocean Eagle* account: Jeffrey Potter, *Disaster by Oil*, pp. 45–102. *New York Times*, 4 March 1968, p. 1; 5 March 1968, p. 1; 8 March 1968, p. 2; 29 March 1968, p. 81; 5 April 1968, p. 92. Beaches were being cleared a full week after declared "all clear."

19. Potter, *Disaster by Oil*, pp. 63–64.

20. Ibid.

21. *Washington Post*, 30 December 1976; *New York Times*, 30 December 1976, pp. 10, 22; 31 December 1976, pp. IV–1, I–9.

22. The impact of the *Argo Merchant* was heightened by explosions, collisions, and groundings of several other Liberian-registered ships over the following few weeks: *Sansinena* exploded 17 December 1976; *Oswego Peace*, oil spill, 24 December 1976; *Olympic Games*, oil spill, 24 December 1976; *Universe Leader*, grounded, 4 January 1977. The press gave emphasis to these events partly because ship incidents had become "good copy."

23. U.S., MarAd, Office of Technology Assessment, *Oil Transportation by Tankers*, pp. 6–7. In the world debate over the extent of territorial seas, U.S. maritime opinion was divided. The inspection issue tended to align the Coast Guard with east coast fishing interests and environmental groups in favor of extension of territorial

limits as against naval interests preferring the traditional limits. See Mark W. Janis, *Sea Power and the Law of the Sea*, pp. 10–18. Specific use of the *Argo Merchant* Coast Guard performance as an argument for increased budget, see Senator Edward Brooke, 22 March 1979, in U.S., Congress, Senate, Committee on Appropriations, *Coast Guard Resource Needs for Responding to Oil Spills, Fiscal Year 1979*, 95th Cong., 2d sess., Special Hearing, 1979.

24. Naess, *Autobiography*, pp. 200, 237.

25. Ibid., pp. 230–36; H. P. Drewry, *U.S. Oil Imports, Policies and Tanker Shipping*, p. 58.

26. Naess, testimony, U.S., Congress, House, Committee on Merchant Marine and Fisheries, Subcommittee on Merchant Marine. *Energy Transportation Security Act of 1977 (HR 1037)*, 95th Cong., 1977, p. 570. Hereafter *Hearings on HR 1037*.

27. Naess observed, "The *Argo Merchant* did the work for me" (*Autobiography*, p. 238).

28. Naess, testimony, *Hearings on HR 1037*, p. 570; Naess sale was July 1975, but he continued some Intertanko political work for at least two years after the sale.

29. FACS multilith publication, 31 March 1977.

30. Interview, author-Frank Wiswall, International Trust Company, Reston, Virginia, January 1979.

31. Drewry, *U.S. Oil Imports*, pp. 1–10, 29.

32. Ibid.; Nixon speech given 7 November 1973, text in *New York Times*, 8 November 1973, p. 32.

33. Conflicting advice, *Hearings on HR 1037*, p. 459.

34. Ibid., pp. 545–50.

35. API publicity, Ibid., p. 465.

36. FACS use of statistics, Ibid., pp. 237 ff.

37. Review of testimony from both bills and a summary of the issues on the 1974 bill, HR 8193, is presented in Drewry, *U.S. Oil Imports*, pp. 56–59.

38. Interview author-Larry O'Brien, Chief Counsel of House Committee on Merchant Marine and Fisheries, December 1979.

39. U.S., Department of Transportation, United States Coast Guard, *Background and Summary Regarding the International Conference on Tanker Safety and Pollution Prevention Held in London, England, 5–17 February 1978*, pp. 3–4.

40. U.S., Department of Transportation, United States Coast Guard, *Final Regulatory Analysis and Environmental Impact Statement, Regulations to Implement the Results of the International Conference on Tanker Safety and Pollution*, pp. 21–31.

41. Ibid.

Notes to Chapter 11

1. See chapter 6.

2. "Vessels Not on the Navy List. Merchant Vessels Under U.S. Control," January 1945, QS-1, Confidential, CNO Files, NavOpArch.

3. Erling Naess, *Autobiography of a Shipping Man*, pp. 95–100.

4. Danish shipping : Miscellaneous Office Files, Box 17, Lot 146, E/TRC/5 D; "The Danish Shipping Question," 9 April 1940–9 June 1942, Miscellaneous Office Files, Box 21, 58D-54-EUR/BND, RG 59, USNA.

5. "The taking of Italian, German and Danish Merchant Vessels in Ports of the United States in Protective Custody by the U.S. Coast Guard," World War II Histories and Historical Reports in U.S. Naval History Division, NavOpArch. "Report No. 190–92: Vessels under the Control of the War Shipping Administration," 21 March 1942, QS–1, Secret, CNO Files, NavOp Arch.

6. Several ship lists have been cross-tabulated to reach these conclusions. In addition to data from "Vessels Not on the Navy List," (note 2, above), and from "Report No. 190–92" (note 5, above), loss data were derived from Jürgen Rohwer, *Die U-Boot-Erfolge der Achsenmächte, 1939–1945*; Paul E. R. Scarceriaux, "Merchant Ships Lost Under Panamanian Flag During World War II," *Belgian Shiplover* 149 (January 1974); and from "British and Foreign Merchant Vessels Lost or Damaged by Enemy Action During Second World War, From 3 September 1939 to 2 September 1945," B.R. 1337, NavOpArch.

7. Panamanian total derived from two State Department memoranda: Muccio to State, 28 April 1941, Decimal 819.852/27, RG 59, USNA, which showed vessels lost or transferred away from Panama to that date; and Andrews to State, 26 April 1941, Decimal 819.852/29, RG 59, USNA, transmitting a list of vessels "definitively registered." Considering loss records cited in note 6, above, the prewar fleet may have been between 240 and 255 at its high point. The Panamanian chief of Consular and Shipping Bureau himself had no idea in 1945 how many vessels under the flag survived the war: Latimer to State, 3 September 1945, Decimal 819.857/9-1345, RG 59, USNA.

8. "Report 190–92: Vessels under the Control of the War Shipping Administration," 15 May 1944, QS–1, Secret, CNO Files, NavOpArch.

9. Swiss flag discussed in Capt. A. S. Pickhart, ONI, to State, 15 December 1942, in Miscellaneous Office Files, Box 17, Lot 141-E/TRC/SD, RG 59, USNA.

10. Particular agency agreements with companies were listed in "Report 190-92: Vessels under the Control of the War Shipping Administration," QS-1, Secret, CNO Files, NavOpArch.

11. "Analysis and Recommendations concerning Surplus Shipping and Postwar Strategic Reserve of Merchant Tonnage," Prepared in Office of Chief of Naval Operations by Naval Transportation Service (Op-39), June 1945, in Horne to Forrestal, 8 August 1945, A-16 EN, Secret, CNO Files, NavOpArch. This report had an extensive bibliography reflecting awareness of other agencies' plans. "Data for Naval History—Second World War, History of Op-05 for September, 1944," in QW-20, Secret, 2 October 1944, CNO Files, NavOpArch; Forrestal to Admiral King, 15 May 1945; King to Forrestal, 16 May 1945, QS-1, Secret, CNO Files, NavOpArch, showing Navy access to WSA plans.

12. Long to Hull, 22 November 1943, enclosing "Report of the Special Committee on Shipping: Basic Principles of United States Post-War Merchant Shipping Policy," approved 23 October 1943, in Miscellaneous Office Files, Box 18, 57D-165 E/TRC/SH, RG 59, USNA. Nuclear dilemmas, see Vincent Davis, *Postwar Defense Policy and the U.S. Navy, 1943–1946*.

13. For the Mahan influence in naval planning, see Vincent Davis, *The Admirals Lobby*, pp. 106–12.

14. JCS 1454/1 is discussed and revised through 1946 in CCS 540 (8-9-45) Sec. 2, RG 218, USNA.

15. JCS 1454/11, 11 October 1947, CCS 540 (8-9-45) Sec. 3, RG 218, USNA.

16. Ibid.

17. Ibid.

18. See chapter 5.

19. The Liberian report is JCS 1454/15, in CCS 540 (8-9-45) Sec. 4, RG 218, USNA. W. John Kenney to CNO, 30 June 1948, RG 218, USNA. Kenney had met with the AOTC owning group on 10 May 1948, Holmes to Sulzberger, 11 May 1948, ERS. For conference at Grew's home, see chapter 7.

20. JCS 1454/15, CCS 540 (8-9-45) Sec. 4, RG 218, USNA.

21. Ibid.

22. JCS to CNO, 21 September 1948, CCS 540 (8-9-45) Sec. 4, RG 218, USNA. The JMTC recommendations for insisting upon agreement to return vessels were incorporated later in permissions to transfer ships out granted by U.S. authorities. Further, the Liberians, by marine regulation (not treaty) agreed to such conditions in cases of particular vessels. Maritime Regulation 1.41, in Republic of Liberia, *Liberian Maritime Regulations*.

23. Inclusion and exclusion of Venezuela and Costa Rica: Clarence Morse to Areeda, 9 February 1959, Areeda Papers, DDEPL. Greece: correspondence and report, 137/3, 14 October 1954 through 7 December 1954, CCS 540 (8-9-45) Sec. 16, RG 218, USNA.

24. "Inventory of U.S. Controlled Tankers," Appendix "G" to Enclosure "B," 31 December 1952, CCS 540 (8-9-45) Sec. 14, RG 218, USNA. In 1948, a similar analysis showed only Panamanian and Honduran ships in addition to U.S. vessels, "Study of Merchant Ship Requirements and Availability for National Security," CCS 540 (8-9-45) B.P. 48-50, RG 218, USNA. Transfer out of older ships to provide stimulus to shipbuilding: Forrestal to Vandenberg, 11 February 1948, CCS 540 (8-9-45) Sec. 4, RG 218, USNA.

25. U.S., Congress, Senate, Committee on Interstate and Foreign Commerce, *Merchant Marine Study and Investigation*, 81st Cong., 2d sess., Hearings pursuant to Senate Resolution 50 and on S. 2768, 27 February 1950, p. 628. A search for treaties or agreements revealed none by 1954, CCS 540 (8-9-45) Sec. 15, RG 218, USNA.

26. Olmsted: interview author-Lininger, February 1979; International Bank, *Annual Report, 1977, International Bank*, Form 10-K, on file with Securities and Exchange Commission.

27. War-risk insurance was authorized during World War II under act of 29 June 1940 (54 Stat. 689); it was repealed 25 July 1947 (61 Stat. 449), 1950 U.S., *Code Cong. Service*, 3592. It was reestablished on a stand-by basis by act, 7 September 1950 (64 Stat. 773), which expired in September 1975, and was reenacted in 1976, to expire again, October 1979, 46 USCA, Section 1281. Effective control American-owned vessels were admitted to the insurance program by administrative actions. The power to requisition Panamanian-registered ships under Section 902 of the 1936 Merchant Marine Act had not been employed during the war; rather, charters had been used. The owners had refused to accept Section 902 requisition: William Radner to Carl McDowell, 17 November 1950, Radner Papers, HSTPL. Acceptance of war-risk insurance under the 1950 act included an acceptance of the power to requisition under Section 902, but that power never was tested.

28. McGuire to Areeda, 4 April 1959, Areeda Papers, DDEPL; Morse to Areeda, 9 February 1959, Areeda Papers, DDEPL.

29. Greek "cartel": ONI Report, March 1953, CCS 540 (8-9-45) Sec. 15, RG 218,

USNA. The ONI reports showed an average of five to fifteen Panamanian vessels trading with Communist-bloc nations monthly; Liberian vessels were very rare in the reports. Liberian rule allowing control: enacted in 1960, Section 1.41 in Republic of Liberia, *Liberian Maritime Regulations*; regulation prohibiting trade to Communist bloc: enacted in 1951 Section 1.40 (previously 1.51), *Liberian Maritime Regulations*.

30. Emory S. Land, "The Merchant Marine of Panama as an American Asset," *United States Naval Institute Proceedings* 80 (July 1954): 726–29; address by Emory Land, "The Fleet of American-Controlled Foreign Flag Ships: Its Importance to American Business and Industry, Both at Home and Abroad," May 1961, Hot Springs, Virginia, Speeches and Writings File, Land Papers, LOC.

31. Ainsworth to Areeda, 11 February 1959, "Supplementary Information Regarding Flags of Convenience," in Areeda Papers, DDEPL. The issue had been discussed at a National Security Council meeting, noted Rhymes (Op-404B) to Adm. Arthur Radford, 28 January 1959, Areeda Papers, DDEPL.

32. Vice Admiral Ralph E. Wilson (Ret.), "Is the Present Fleet of 'Flags of Convenience' Shipping Necessary to Meet National Security Requirements under Present Maritime Laws," in Marvin Fair and Howard C. Reese, eds., *Merchant Marine Policy*, pp. 73–85.

33. Korean and Vietnam reliability assessed in Walter C. Ford, "Active and Available Merchant Ships Are Growing in Importance in the Navy: Emergency Sealift Planning," *Shipmate*, May 1970, pp. 2–9.

34. Wilson to Senator Butler, 21 February 1959, Areeda Papers, DDEPL; Wilson, "Is the Present Fleet Necessary," cited above, note 32.

35. Sidney W. Emery, "The Effective United States Control Fleet," *United States Naval Institute Proceedings* 96 (May 1970):160.

36. Irwin Heine and Muriel Coe, *An Analysis of the Ships Under "Effective U.S. Control" and their Employment in the U.S. Foreign Trade During 1960*; *Effective U.S. Control of Merchant Ships: A Statistical Analysis, 1970*.

37. Ford, "Active and Available Merchant Ships."

38. JCS decision process, see Lawrence J. Korb, *The Joint Chiefs of Staff*, pp. 18–19, 21–23, 180.

39. The high proportion of protection through cabotage was noted in JCS 1454/11 of 1947 and the 1948 revision extending the principle to Liberia. Cabotage still was regarded as protecting a large tanker "nucleus" under the U.S. flag in, "Staff Analysis of Policy Issues Regarding Federal Assistance to the Merchant Marine," 14 January 1953, p. 29, Dennison Papers, HSTPL. Reviews of the Cyprus, Singapore, and other minor flags of convenience can be found in "OECD Study of Flags of Convenience," *Journal of Maritime Law and Commerce*, 4 (January 1973):243 f.

40. Ford, "Active and Available Merchant Ships."

41. The makeshift and less than ideal solution was a theme noted in works by Wilson, Ford, Emery, noted above.

42. Elmo R. Zumwalt, *On Watch*, pp. 461–64.

43. On canal and related literature, see Walter LaFeber, *The Panama Canal*. Officers opposing new canal treaties, U.S., Congress, House, Committee on Merchant Marine and Fisheries, *New Panama Canal Treaty Hearings*, 95th Cong. (Serial

95-13), 17 August 1977, p. 2. See also Paul Ryan, "Canal Diplomacy and U.S. Interests," *United States Naval Institute Proceedings* 103 (January 1977):43–53.

44. Martin Lowenkopf, *Politics in Liberia*, pp. 154–61.

45. Traditions of independence: Panama, see chapter 1; Liberia, see chapter 7.

46. Comments and text of the executive order: U.S., Congress, House, Committee on Merchant Marine and Fisheries, Subcommittee on Merchant Marine, *Energy Transportation Security Act of 1974 (HR 8193)*, 93d Cong., 1974, pp. 329, 670–73. Hereafter, *Hearings, HR 8193*.

47. *Hearings, HR 8193*, pp. 324–29, 670–73.

48. Ibid., p. 284.

49. Ibid., pp. 24–25.

50. U.S., Congress, House, Committee on Merchant Marine and Fisheries, Subcommittee on Merchant Marine, *Energy Transportation Security Act of 1977 (HR 1037)*, 95th Cong., 1977, pp. 387, 372–86 passim.

51. Ibid., pp. 256–60.

Bibliography

Primary Sources

U.S. National Archives

Decimal Files, Record Group 59. These files for both Panama and Liberia, open through 1949, are in the Diplomatic Branch of the U.S. National Archives. Organized by country and subject, the "851" through "863" files for both countries covered ship registry and shipping questions. Thus, 882.85 through 882.863 provided material on Liberian shipping, for the relatively short period 1947–49, while 819.851 through 819.863 yielded extremely rich materials on Panamanian shipping from the 1920s through 1949.

Record Group 218, in the Modern Military Branch of the archives, included records for the Joint Chiefs of Staff, cleared and open through 1957. Record Groups 32 and 151 in the Economic and Social Branch included Shipping Board records through 1930.

Library of Congress

The Manuscript Division of the Library of Congress has several collections that proved extremely valuable, including the papers of W. S. Benson, Emory Land, Breckinridge Long, E. C. Plummer, and Kermit Roosevelt. By far the richest were the Land and Long papers for the neutrality and World War II periods.

Navy Yard

The Operational Archives at the Naval Historical Division of the Navy Yard, Washington, D.C., yielded great amounts of information about the WSA-Navy Department relationships during World War II.

Presidential Libraries

The Herbert Hoover Presidential Library in West Branch, Iowa; the Harry S Truman Presidential Library in Independence, Missouri; and the Dwight D. Eisenhower Presidential Library in Abilene, Kansas, all yielded useful materials. The Hoover library was strongest for providing insight into the views of Hoover himself on the problem of reorganizing the Shipping Board. The Truman library yielded some details that supplemented State Department and other information for the late 1940s and early 1950s. At the Eisenhower library, the Areeda papers proved valuable for insights into the culmination of labor-management fights in the courts, and for naval and MarAd positions in that conflict. The *Berle Diary*, published on microfilm by the Roosevelt library at Hyde Park, New York, gave excellent insights into the neutrality debates of 1939–41.

University and Other Collections

At the University of Virginia Library, the Edward R. Stettinius, Jr., Papers gave the corporate side of the formation of the Liberian maritime code in an excellent and meticulously organized collection that told the day-by-day story. Other archives consulted included the Dulles Oral History Collection at Princeton University; the Joseph Grew papers at Harvard University; administrative files in the jurisdiction of the National Labor Relations Board and the Maritime Administration stored in the Suitland repository of the National Archives, the records of the National Maritime Union at the union headquarters in New York City, the records of the Liberian Maritime Commission in Monrovia, and the National Archives of Liberia under the jurisdiction of the Foreign Ministry, Monrovia.

Many mimeographed and multilithed publications of limited circulation found in the archives are cited only in the notes, as they are rarely available as publications in general libraries. In addition to the primary materials found in archives, other classes of contemporary records proved quite useful, including court cases, congressional investigations, and legislation itself. Such materials are cited in the text notes.

Quantitative Data

From a variety of published and archival sources, data bases of Panamanian-registered ships in the 1920s and in the 1930s were constructed and verified against the entries in Lloyd's of London and in memoranda from Panamanian sources in Record Group 59 at the National Archives. This process yielded some discoveries, reflected in the text and presented in tables, such as the following: (1) very few U.S. vessels registered in Panama in the 1920s; (2) Spanish ships, not Greek or Norwegian, were the first European-owned ships registered in Panama; (3) through the 1930s, European-owned ships were more numerous in the Panamanian registry than American-owned ships; (4) the major American owners of Panamanian registry in the 1930s were the banana and petroleum companies. These and other quantitative discoveries developed from the data base shaped the direction of the political analysis undertaken for that period. For the 1920s and 1930s no previous statistical work had sketched the outlines of the Panama fleet; the quantitative work therefore provided a take-off point for subjective and conventional historical analysis, but not an end in itself. For the more modern period, the excellent analyses of ownership patterns by H. P. Drewry Shipping Consultants of London, indicated below in the list of secondary sources, and statistical presentations developed by both advocates and critics of Liberian registry, made unnecessary the compilation of raw data required for the earlier decades.

Secondary Sources

The following list includes books and articles, both contemporaneous with the events discussed, and historical materials and memoirs written after the event. Readers wishing to pursue closely a particular topic may want to consult both the bibliography and the notes.

Abbazia, Patrick. *Mr. Roosevelt's Navy: The Private War of the U.S. Atlantic Fleet, 1939–1942.* Annapolis: Naval Institute Press, 1975.

Agirotto, Enrico. "Flags of Convenience and Sub-standard Vessels: A Review of the ILO's Approach to the Problem."*International Labor Review* 110 (1974): 437.

Albion, Robert Greenhalgh. *Naval and Maritime History: An Annotated Bibliography.* Mystic, Conn.: Munson Institute of American Maritime History, 1972.

Albion, Robert Greenhalgh and J. B. Pope. *Sealanes in Wartime: The American Experience.* New York: Norton, 1942. Reprint. Hamden, Conn.: Archon, 1968.

Alexandersson, Gunnar and Goran Norstrum. *World Shipping: An Economic Geography of Ports and Seaborne Trade.* New York: Wiley, 1963.

American Committee for Flags of Necessity. *The Role of Flags of Necessity.* New York: American Committee for Flags of Necessity, 1962.

American Petroleum Institute. *Proceedings, Joint Conference on Prevention and Control of Oil Spills.* New York: American Petroleum Institute, 1970(?).

Anderson, Robert Earle. *The Merchant Marine and World Frontiers.* Ithaca, N.Y.: Cornell University Press, 1945. Reprint. Westport, Conn.: Greenwood, 1978.

————. *Liberia, America's African Friend.* Chapel Hill: University of North Carolina Press, 1952. Reprint. Westport, Conn.: Greenwood, 1976.

Arciniegas, German. *Caribbean: Sea of the New World.* New York: A. A. Knopf, 1946.

Armstrong, Arthur J. "Bitumin in the Waters of Babylonia: The Impact of Recent Legislation on the Limited Liability Act of 1951." *Judge Advocate General's Journal* 26 (1972): 215.

Avriel, Ehud. *Open the Gates: A Personal Story of "Illegal" Immigration to Israel.* London, New York: Atheneum, 1975.

Azikiwe, Nnamdi. *Liberia in World Politics*. 1934. Reprint. Westport, Conn.: Greenwood, 1970.

Baker, G. W., Jr. "The Wilson Administration and Panama, 1913–1921." *Journal of Inter-American Studies* 8 (1966): 279.

Ball, Joseph H. "Some Problems of American Shipping." *ICC Practitioners' Journal* 17 (1949): 96.

Barker, James R. and Robert Brandwein. *United States Merchant Marine in National Perspective*. Lexington, Ky.: Heath, 1970.

Baty, T. "The Free Sea: Produce the Evidence." *American Journal of International Law* 35 (1941): 227.

Beichman, Arnold. "Red Phantom Fleet Sails Under Panama Flag: Boycott War Looms." *New Leader*, 15 April 1950.

Beltza. *El Nacionalismo Vasco: 1876–1936*. San Sebastian, Spain: Editorial Txerto, 1976(?).

Bemis, Samuel F. *The Latin American Policy of the United States*. New York: Harcourt Brace, 1943.

Benson, William S. *The New Merchant Marine: A Necessity in Time of War, a Source of Independence and Strength in Peace*. New York: Macmillan, 1923.

———. "Our New Merchant Marine." *United States Naval Institute Proceedings* 52 (October 1926): 1941.

Berguido, Carlos. "The Rights of Seamen on a Ship Under Panamanian Registry." *Temple Law Quarterly* 19 (1946): 458.

Berguido, Carlos and Jorge T. Fabrega. *Manual for Masters and Seamen on Ships under the Panamanian Flag*. Philadelphia, 1949.

Betters, Paul and Darrel H. Smith. *The United States Shipping Board*. Washington: Brookings Institution, 1931.

Bixler, Raymond W. *The Foreign Policy of the United States in Liberia: 1819–1955*. New York: Pageant Press, 1957.

Bjork, Robert D. "Shipowners' Limitation of Liability and Personal Injuries: A Need for Re-evaluation." *Tulane Law Review* 48 (1974): 376.

Boczek, Boleslaw Adam. *Flags of Convenience: An International Legal Study*. Cambridge, Mass.: Harvard University Press, 1962.

Bolin, Luis. *Spain, the Vital Years*. London: Cassell, 1967.

Borchard, Edwin M. *Neutrality for the United States*. New Haven, Conn.: Yale University Press, 1940.

———. "War, Neutrality and Non-Belligerency." *American Journal of International Law* 35 (1941): 618.

Borkin, Joseph. *The Crime and Punishment of I. G. Farben*. New York: Free Press, 1978.

Bowett, D. W. *The Law of the Sea*. New York: Oceana, 1967.

Brady, Frank. *Onassis, An Extravagant Life*. Englewood Cliffs, N.J.: Prentice-Hall, 1977.

Braisted, William R. *The United States Navy in the Pacific, 1909–1922*. Austin: University of Texas Press, 1971.

Brinnin, John Malcolm. *The Sway of the Grand Saloon: A Social History of the North Atlantic*. New York: Delacorte Press, 1971.

Brown, Edward Duncan. "The Lessons of the *Torrey Canyon:* International Law Aspects." *Current Legal Problems* (1968): 113.
————. *The Legal Regime of Hydrospace.* London: Stevens, 1971.
Brown, Robert S. "Struggle for Power: The Opposition to Independence, 1839–47." Paper given at Liberian Studies Conference, Burlington, Vt., April 1980.
Brown, Seyom and Larry Fabian. "Diplomats at Sea." *Foreign Affairs* 52 (1974): 301.
Buell, R. L. "Panama and the United States." *Foreign Policy Reports*, 20 January 1932.
————. "The New American Neutrality." *Foreign Policy Reports*, 15 January 1936.
Bullock, C. U. "Angary." *British Yearbook of International Law* (1922): 99.
Burns, F. Bradford. "Panama's Struggle for Independence." *Current History* 66 (1974): 19.
Butte, W. L. "Controlling Marine Pollution: World Task or National." *Stanford Journal of International Studies* 8 (1973): 99.
Campbell, John and Phillip Sherrard. *Modern Greece.* New York: Praeger, 1968.
Cant, Gilbert. *The American Navy in World War II.* New York: John Day, 1943.
Carlisle, Rodney. "Self-Determination in Colonial Liberia and American Black Nationalism." *Negro History Bulletin* 36 (1973): 77.
————. *The Roots of Black Nationalism.* Port Washington, N.Y.: Kennikat, 1975.
————. "The American Century Implemented: Stettinius and the Liberian Flag of Convenience." *Business History Review* 14 (1980): 175.
Carrell, William Pfingst. "A Study of American-owned Vessels Under the Flags of Panama, Honduras and Costa Rica." Master's thesis, University of Virginia, Charlottesville, 1962.
Carse, Robert. *Rum Row.* New York: Rinehart, 1959.
————. *The Long Haul: The U.S. Merchant Service in World War II.* New York: Norton, 1965.
Ceres, Albert F. "Merchant Marine: National Necessity." *United States Naval Institute Proceedings* 53 (1927): 570.
Chadwin, Mark Lincoln. *The Warhawks: American Interventionists Before Pearl Harbor.* New York: Norton, 1970.
Clark, Earl W., Hoyt S. Haddock, and Stanley J. Volens. *The U.S. Merchant Marine Today: Sunrise or Sunset.* Washington: Labor-Management Maritime Committee, 1970.
Coleman, Terry. *The Liners: A History of the North Atlantic Crossing.* London: Allen Lane, 1976.
Colombos, Constantine J. *The International Law of the Sea.* 6th ed. New York: McKay, 1967.
Committee of Inquiry into Shipping. *Report (Rochdale Report).* London: H. M. Stationery Office, 1970.
Cook, Arthur E. *A History of the United States Shipping Board and Merchant Fleet Corporation.* Baltimore: Day, 1927.
Cowan, Edward. *Oil and Water: The Torrey Canyon Disaster.* New York: Lippincott, 1968.
Cummins, Phillip A. "Oil Tanker Pollution Control: Design Criteria vs. Effective Liability Assessment." *Journal of Maritime Law and Commerce* 7 (1975): 169.

Curran, Joe and Paul Hall. "Modern Piracy." *American Federationist*, January 1959.

Currie, David P. "Flags of Convenience, American Labor and the Conflict of Laws." *Supreme Court Review* (1963): 34.

Dalton, A. C. "A National Merchant Marine Is Vital to Our Security." *United States Naval Institute Proceedings* 53 (October 1927): 1065.

Dalton, George. "History, Politics and Economic Development in Liberia." *Journal of Economic History* 25 (1965): 569.

Daly, John. *The Role of the Joint Chiefs of Staff in National Policy*. Washington: American Enterprise Institute, 1978.

Daniels, Josephus. *The Wilson Era: The Years of War and After, 1917–1923*. Chapel Hill: University of North Carolina Press, 1946.

———. *The Cabinet Diaries of Josephus Daniels, 1913–1921*. Edited by E. David Cronon. Lincoln: University of Nebraska Press, 1973.

Davies, J. Clarence, III. *The Politics of Pollution*. New York: Pegasus, 1970.

Davis, M. S. "Ports and Waterways Safety Act of 1972: An Expansion of the Federal Approach to Oil Pollution." *Journal of Maritime Law and Commerce* 6 (1975): 249.

Davis, Vincent. *Postwar Defense Policy and the U.S. Navy, 1943–1946*. Chapel Hill: University of North Carolina Press, 1962.

———. *The Admirals Lobby*. Chapel Hill: University of North Carolina Press, 1967.

Davis W. H. "The Naval Side of the Spanish Civil War, 1936–1939." *United States Naval Institute Proceedings* 66 (June 1940): 803.

Degler, Stanley, ed. *Oil Pollution: Problems and Policies*. Washington: Bureau of National Affairs, 1969.

de la Rue, Sidney. *The Land of the Pepperbird*. New York, London: G. P. Putnam's Sons, 1930.

Diebold, William J. "The Wartime Use of Shipping." *Foreign Affairs* 19 (1941): 751.

Dix, James and Aron Suna. "The Control of Pollution by Oil Under the WQIA–1970." *Washington and Lee Law Review* 27 (1970): 278.

Doggett, Clinton. "The Hoover Plan for Dissolution of the Shipping Board: Its Pros and Cons." *Nautical Gazette*, 26 December 1931.

Dollar, Robert. "American Merchant Marine." *Atlantic Monthly*, September 1927.

Dorwart, Jeffrey. "The Mongrel Fleet: America Buys a Navy to Fight Spain, 1898." *Warship International*, in press.

Doud, Alden Lowell. "Compensation for Oil Pollution Damage: Further Comment on the Civil Liability and Compensation Fund Conventions." *Journal of Maritime Law and Commerce* 4 (1972): 525.

Drewry, H. P. *U.S. Oil Imports, 1971–1985: Repercussions on the World Tanker and Oil Industries*. London: Drewry Shipping Consultants, 1973.

———. *Market Conditions and Tanker Economics*. London: Drewry Shipping Consultants, 1976.

———. *The Tanker Crisis*. London: Drewry Shipping Consultants, 1976.

———. *The Involvement of Oil-Exporting Countries in International Shipping*. London: Drewry Shipping Consultants, 1976.

———. *The Role of the Independent Tanker Owners*. London: Drewry Shipping Consultants, 1976.

————. *U.S. Oil Imports, Policies and Tanker Shipping.* London: Drewry Shipping Consultants, 1978.

Duff, Ernest A. "The United Fruit Company and the Political Affairs of Guatemala, 1944–1954." Master's thesis, University of Virginia, Charlottesville, 1957.

Dulles, Allen W. "Cash and Carry Neutrality: The Pittman Act." *Foreign Affairs* 18 (1940): 179.

Ealy, Lawrence O. *The Republic of Panama in World Affairs: 1903–1950.* Philadelphia: University of Pennsylvania Press, 1951. Reprint. Westport, Conn.: Greenwood, 1970.

————. *Yanqui Politics and the Isthmian Canal.* University Park: Pennsylvania State University Press, 1971.

Eberle, E. W. "The Sea-Borne Commerce of the United States." *United States Naval Institute Proceedings* 53 (October 1927): 1060.

Economist. "Flying the Liberian Flag." *The Economist,* 7 September 1957.

————. "Boycott for PanHonLib." *The Economist,* 22 November 1958.

————. "Shipping Boycott: Mixed Success." *The Economist,* 6 December 1958.

————. "Striking Foreign Flags." *The Economist,* 24 June 1961.

————. "Chasing the Runaways." *The Economist,* 24 February 1962.

————. "Nationality Goes to Court." *The Economist,* 2 March 1963.

————. "Shipping: British Flag of Convenience?" *The Economist,* 19 March 1966.

————. "Liberia: Plugging Some Leaks." *The Economist,* 8 May 1971.

The Economist Intelligence Unit, Ltd. *Open Registry Shipping.* London: The Economist Intelligence Unit, 1979.

Ellis, Lewis E. *Republican Foreign Policy: 1921–1933.* New Brunswick, N.J.: Rutgers University Press, 1968.

Emery, Sidney W. "The Effective United States Control Fleet." *United States Naval Institute Proceedings* 96 (May 1970): 160.

————. "The Merchant Marine Act of 1970." *United States Naval Institute Proceedings* 97 (March 1971): 38.

Engler, Robert. *The Politics of Oil.* New York: Macmillan, 1961.

————. *The Brotherhood of Oil.* Chicago: University of Chicago Press, 1970.

Fabrega, Jorge, trans. *Consular Tariff of Panama: Decree 41 of 1935.* Panama, 1951.

Fagen, W. E. "Knight and Dragon: Slogans vs. Information." *Public Relations Journal* 20 (August 1964): 20.

Fair, Marvin and Howard C. Reese, eds. *Merchant Marine Policy.* Cambridge, Md.: Cornell Maritime Press, 1963.

Fairplay. "Prospect of Tanker Shortage." *Fairplay,* 17 September 1970.

Farago, Ladislas. *The Game of the Foxes.* New York, London: McKay, 1971.

Fehrenbach, T. R. *FDR's Undeclared War, 1939–1941.* New York: McKay, 1967.

Feis, Herbert. *The Spanish Story: Franco and the Nations at War.* New York: A. A. Knopf, 1948.

Flourney, Richard W., Jr., and Manley Hudson. *A Collection of Nationality Laws of Various Countries as Contained in Constitutions, Statutes and Treaties.* Oxford: Oxford University Press, 1929.

Forbes, John D. *Stettinius, Sr.: A Portrait of a Morgan Partner.* Charlottesville: University Press of Virginia, 1974.

Ford, Walter C. "Active and Available Merchant Ships Are Growing in Importance in the Navy: Emergency Sealift Planning," *Shipmate*, May 1970.

Foreign Policy Association. "Neutral Rights and Maritime Law." *Foreign Policy Association Information Series*, 16 March 1928.

Forster, M. "Civil Liability for Shipowners for Oil Pollution." *Journal of Business Law* (1973): 23.

Frankel, Ernst G. and Henry S. Marcus. *Ocean Transportation*. Cambridge, Mass.: MIT Press, 1973.

Fraser, Nicholas, Philip Jacobsen, Mark Ottaway, and Lewis Chester. *Aristotle Onassis*. Philadelphia: Lippincott, 1977.

Frischauer, Willi. *Onassis*. London: Bodley Head, 1968.

———. *Millionaires' Islands*. London: Joseph, 1973.

Frye, J. "Oil, Superships and the Oceans." *Oceans* 7 (1974): 48.

Gage, Nicholas. *The Bourlotas Fortune*. New York: Holt, Rinehart and Winston, 1975.

Gallagher, Thomas Michael. *Fire At Sea: The Story of the Morro Castle*. New York: Rinehart, 1959.

Gardner, Lloyd. *Architects of Illusion: Men and Ideas in American Foreign Policy, 1941–1949*. Chicago: Quadrangle, 1970.

Garner, James W. "The Transfer of Merchant Vessels from Belligerent to Neutral Flags." *American Law Review* 49 (1915): 321.

Gatewood, R. D. "Sea Power and American Destiny." *United States Naval Institute Proceedings* 53 (October 1927): 1070.

Gibb, George Sweet and Evelyn Knowlton. *History of Standard Oil Company (New Jersey), 1911–1927: The Resurgent Years*. New York: Harper, 1956.

Gibbs, Charles Robert Vernon. *Passenger Liners of the Western Ocean*. New York: Staples Press, 1952.

———. *The Western Ocean Passenger Lines and Liners, 1934–1969*. Glasgow: Brown, Son and Ferguson, 1970.

Gill, Crispin. *The Wreck of the Torrey Canyon*. New York: Taplinger, 1967.

Gillespie, Joan. "A New Role for Growing Liberia: Strong Economy Bolsters President Tubman's Position in Africa." *New Leader*, 18 January 1960.

Gold, Edgar. "Pollution of the Sea and International Law: A Canadian Perspective." *Journal of Maritime Law and Commerce* 3 (1971): 13.

Goldberg, Henri. *Le Port du Dantzig: Son Developpement Depuis le Traite de Versailles*. Lausanne, 1934.

Goldberg, Joseph Phillip. *The Maritime Story: A Study in Labor Management Relations*. Cambridge, Mass.: Harvard University Press, 1958.

Goldie, L.F.E. "Recognition and Dual Nationality: A Problem of Flags of Convenience." *British Yearbook of International Law* (1963): 220.

———. "Flags of Convenience: Review of B. A. Boczek, *Flags of Convenience*." *International and Comparative Law Quarterly* 12 (1963): 989.

———. "International Principles of Responsibility for Pollution." *Columbia Journal of Transnational Law*, Fall 1970.

———. "Liability for Oil Pollution Disasters: International Law and the Delimitation of Competencies in a Federal Policy." *Journal of Maritime Law and Commerce* 6 (1975): 303.

Gonzalez Echegaray, Rafael. *Cincuenta Anos de Vapores Santanderinos.* Santander, Spain: Industria y Navegacion de la Provincia, 1951.

Greer, T. V. "Mercantile Potpourri Called Panama." *Journal of Inter-American Studies,* August 1972.

Grew, Joseph C. *Turbulent Era: A Diplomatic Record of Forty Years, 1904–1945.* Freeport: Books for Libraries Press, 1970.

Haag, Alfred H. "The Lack of Modern Tonnage a Severe Handicap in the Expansion of our Foreign Trade and National Defense." *United States Naval Institute Proceedings* 53 (October 1927): 1090.

Hamilton, Thomas J. *Appeasement's Child: The Franco Regime in Spain.* New York: A. A. Knopf, 1943.

Hanson, E. P. "United States Invades Africa," *Harper's,* February 1947.

Harbridge House. *The Balance of Payments and the U.S. Merchant Marine.* Boston: Harbridge House, 1968.

Harolds, L. R. "Some Legal Problems Arising out of Foreign Flag Operations." *Fordham Law Review* 28 (1959): 295.

Harris, Bravid W. "Liberia Is America's Responsibility." *Forth,* February 1949.

Harvard International Law Journal. "Oil Pollution of the Sea" (Comment). *Harvard International Law Journal* 10 (1969): 316.

Harwood, Michael. "Oil and Water." *Harper's,* September 1978.

Healy, Nicholas J. "The International Convention on Civil Liability for Oil Pollution Damage." *Journal of Maritime Law and Commerce* 1 (1970): 317.

Hedrick, Basil C. and Anne K. Hedrick. *Historical Dictionary of Panama.* Metuchen, N.J.: Scarecrow Press, 1970.

Heine, Irwin and Muriel Coe. *An Analysis of the Participation of U.S. and Foreign Flag Ships in the Oceanborne Foreign Trade of the United States, 1937, 1938, 1951–1960.* Washington: Government Printing Office, 1962.

———. *An Analysis of the Ships Under "Effective U.S. Control" and their Employment in the U.S. Foreign Trade During 1960.* Washington: Maritime Administration, 1962.

———. *Effective U.S. Control of Merchant Ships: A Statistical Analysis, 1970.* Washington: Government Printing Office, 1970.

Herring, George and Thomas Campbell, eds. *The Diaries of Edward R. Stettinius, Jr., 1943–1946.* New York: New Viewpoints, 1975.

Hess, Wilmot N. *The Amoco Cadiz Oil Spill.* Washington: Government Printing Office, 1978.

Higgins, Alexander Pearce and C. J. Colombos. *The International Law of the Sea.* London: Longmans Green, 1943.

Hlophe, Stephen. "A Class Analysis of the Politics of Ethnicity of the Tubman and Tolbert Administrations in Liberia." Paper read at Liberian Studies Association, Macomb, Ill., 2 April 1977.

Hohman, Elmo Paul. *History of American Merchant Seamen.* Hamden, Conn.: Shoestring Press, 1965.

Hollick, Ann L. and Robert E. Osgood. *New Era of Ocean Politics.* Baltimore: Johns Hopkins University Press, 1974.

Hoopes, Townsend. *The Devil and John Foster Dulles.* Boston: Little Brown, 1973.

Hougan, Jim. "Prelude to Watergate: The Plot to Wreck the Golden Greek." *Playboy,* September 1978.

Howard, Bushrod B. "Tankers in the War, and Postwar Trends." In *America's Postwar Merchant Marine Forecast, The Marine News*. New York: *Marine News*, 1944.

Hoyt, Edwin P. *U-Boats Offshore*. New York: Stein and Day, 1978.

Huberich, Charles Henry. *The Political and Legislative History of Liberia*. 2 vols. New York: Central Book Company, 1947.

Hull, Cordell. *Memoirs of Cordell Hull*. 2 vols. New York: Macmillan, 1948.

Hurley, Edward Nash. *The New Merchant Marine*. New York: Century Company, 1920.

———. *The Bridge to France*. Philadelphia: Lippincott, 1927.

Hutchins, John G. B. *The American Maritime Industries and Public Policy, 1789–1914: An Economic History*. Cambridge, Mass.: Harvard University Press, 1941.

Ickes, Harold. *Fightin' Oil*. New York: A. A. Knopf, 1943; Westport, Conn.: Hyperion, 1976.

International Bank. *Annual Report*. Washington: International Bank, 1977.

International Labour Office. *Codigo de Trabajo, Edition Extra-official*. Montreal: International Labour Office, 1951.

International Labour Office. *Conditions in Ships Flying the Panama Flag: Report of the Committee of Enquiry of the International Labour Organization. (May–November, 1949)*. London: International Labour Office, 1950.

International Maritime Associates. *Economic Impact of Open Registry Shipping*. Washington: International Maritime Associates, 1979.

Janis, Mark W. *Sea Power and the Law of the Sea*. Lexington, Ky.: Heath, 1976.

Jantscher, Gerald R. *Bread Upon the Waters: Federal Aids to the Maritime Industries*. Washington: Brookings Institution, 1975.

Jenks, C.W. "Nationality, the Flag and Registration as Criteria for Demarcating the Scope of Maritime Conventions." *Journal of Comparative Legislation and International Law* 19 3d ser. (1937): 245.

Jessup, P. C. *The Law of Territorial Waters and Maritime Jurisdiction*. New York: G. A. Jennings Company, 1927.

———. "Diversion of Merchantmen." *American Journal of International Law* 34 (1940): 312.

———. "The Geneva Conference on the Law of the Sea: A Study in International Law-Making." *American Journal of International Law* 52 (1958): 730.

———. "The United Nations Conference on the Law of the Sea." *Columbia Law Review* 59 (1959): 234.

Johnson, D.H.N. "Nationality of Ships." *Indian Yearbook of International Affairs* 8 (1959): 13.

———. "IMCO: The First Four Years (1959–1962)." *International Comparative Law Quarterly* 12 (1963): 31.

Johnson, Walter. "Edward R. Stettinius, Jr." In Norman Graebner, ed. *An Uncertain Tradition: American Secretaries of State in the Twentieth Century*. New York: McGraw Hill, 1961.

———. "E. R. Stettinius, Jr." In Walter Johnson, ed. *Roosevelt and The Russians: The Yalta Conference*. 1949. Reprint. Westport, Conn.: Greenwood, 1970.

Johnston, Eric. "Our Merchant Marine in the Changing World: China a Great

Potential Area for Future Foreign Trade." In *America's Postwar Merchant Marine Forecast*, *The Marine News*. New York: *Marine News*, 1944.

Karmel, Roberta S. "Labor Law, International Law and the PanLibHon Fleet." *New York University Law Review* 36 (1961): 1342.

Keeton, G. W. "The Lesson of the *Torrey Canyon*: English Law Aspects." *Current Legal Problems* 1 (1968): 94.

Kendall, Lane C. *The Business of Shipping*. Cambridge, Md.: Cornell Maritime Press, 1973.

Kepner, Charles David and Jay H. Soothill. *The Banana Empire: A Case Study of Economic Imperialism*. New York: Vanguard, 1935. Reprint. New York: Russell and Russell, 1967.

Kilgour, John G. *The United States Merchant Marine: National Maritime Policy and Industrial Relations*. New York: Praeger, 1975.

———. "Effective United States Control?" *Journal of Maritime Law and Commerce* 8 (1977): 377.

Kimmich, Christoph M. *The Free City: Danzig and German Foreign Policy, 1919–1934*. New Haven, Conn.: Yale University Press, 1968.

Klotz, J. C. "Are Ocean Polluters Subject to Universal Jurisdiction: Canada Breaks the Ice." *International Lawyer* 6 (1970): 706.

Knauth, Arnold and Christopher Knauth. *Benedict on Admiralty*. 7th ed., Vol. 6. New York: Matthew Bender, 1969.

Knox, Dudley Wright. *The Eclipse of American Sea Power*. New York: *American Army and Navy Journal*, 1922.

Knudson, Olaf. *The Politics of International Shipping*. Lexington, Ky.: Heath, 1973.

Korb, Lawrence J. *The Joint Chiefs of Staff*. Bloomington: Indiana University Press, 1976.

LaBarge, Richard Allen. "Impact of the United Fruit Company on the Economic Development of Guatemala, 1946–1954." In Richard Allen LaBarge, Wayne M. Clegern, and Oriol Pi-Sunyer. *Studies in Middle American Economics*. New Orleans: Middle America Research Institute, Tulane University, 1968.

LaFeber, Walter. *The Panama Canal: The Crisis in Historical Perspective*. New York: Oxford University Press, 1978; revised, 1979.

Laimos, Andreas Georgiou. *The Greeks and the Sea*. London: Cassell, 1976.

Land, Emory S. *Winning the War with Ships*. New York: R. M. McBride, 1958.

———. "The Merchant Marine of Panama as an American Asset." *United States Naval Institute Proceedings* 80 (July 1954): 726.

Lane, Frederic C. *Ships for Victory: A History of Shipbuilding Under the U.S. Maritime Commission in World War II*. Baltimore: Johns Hopkins Press, 1951.

Langer, William and S. Everett Gleason. *The Challenge to Isolation: The World Crisis and American Foreign Policy, 1937–1940*. New York: Harper, 1952.

———. *The Undeclared War, 1940–1941*. New York: Harper, 1953.

Langley, Lester D. "U.S.-Panamanian Relations Since 1941." *Journal of Inter-American Studies*, July 1970.

———. "World Crisis and the Good Neighbor Policy in Panama, 1936–1941." *Americas*, October 1967.

Lansing, Robert. *Notes on Sovereignty from the Standpoint of the State and the World*. Washington: Carnegie Endowment for International Peace, 1921.

Larson, Henrietta M., E. H. Knowlton, and C. S. Popple. *History of Standard Oil Company (New Jersey), 1927–1950: New Horizons*. New York: Harper, 1971.

Lawrence, Samuel A. *United States Merchant Shipping Policies and Politics*. Washington: Brookings Institution, 1966.

League of Nations. "The Comparative Study of National Laws Governing the Grant of the Right to Fly the Merchant Flag." *League of Nations Official Journal* 12 (1931): 1631.

Leonhardt, Hans Leo. *Nazi Conquest of Danzig*. Chicago: University of Chicago Press, 1942.

Levine, Herbert S. *Danzig: Hitler's Free City*. Chicago: University of Chicago Press, 1973.

Lewis, M. M. "The Free City of Danzig." *British Yearbook of International Law* (1924): 89.

Liebenow, J. Gus. *Liberia: The Evolution of Privilege*. Ithaca, N.Y.: Cornell University Press, 1969.

Lilly, Doris. *Those Fabulous Greeks: Onassis, Niarchos and Livanos*. New York: Cowles Book Company, 1970.

Literary Digest. "Mediterranean Fleets and Italian Oil." *Literary Digest*, 18 January 1936.

Lloyd's of London. *Lloyd's Register of Shipping*. London: Lloyd's, 1919–79 (annual).

———. *Lloyd's Register of Shipping: Statistical Tables, 1978*. London: Lloyd's, 1978.

Lowenkopf, Martin. *Politics in Liberia: The Conservative Road to Development*. Stanford, Calif.: Hoover Institution Press, 1976.

Lowry, P. D. "Shipowners and Oil Pollution Liability." *McGill Law Journal* 18 (1972): 577.

Luce, Henry. "The American Century." *Life*, 17 February 1941.

McCain, William David. *The United States and the Republic of Panama*. Durham, N.C.: Duke University, 1937. Reprint. New York: Arno, 1970.

McCann, Thomas P. *An American Company: The Tragedy of United Fruit*. New York: Crown Publishers, 1976.

McCoy, F. T. "Oil Spill and Pollution Control: The Conflict Between State and Maritime Law." *George Washington Law Review* 40 (1971): 97.

McDonald, Eula. "Toward a World Maritime Organization." *Department of State Bulletin* 18 (1948): 99.

McDougal, W. S. and W. T. Burke. "Crisis in the Law of the Sea: Community Perspective vs. National Egoism." *Yale Law Journal* 67 (1958): 539.

McDougal, W. S., W. T. Burke, and I. A. Vlasic. "Maintenance of Public Order at Sea and the Nationality of Ships." *American Journal of International Law* 54 (1960): 25.

McDowell, Carl E. and Helen Gibbs. *Ocean Transportation*. New York: McGraw Hill, 1954.

Mackay, Donald. "The Declaration of London in Relation to Neutrals and Contraband." *Central Law Journal* 80 (1915): 252.

McNair, A.D. "The Requisitioning of Merchant Vessels." *Journal of Comparative Legislation and International Law* 27 (1945): 68.

McNamee, Luke. "The Farmer and the Merchant Marine." *United States Naval Institute Proceedings* 53 (October 1927): 1062.

Mahan, Alfred Thayer. *The Influence of Seapower on History.* 1890. Reprint. New York: Sangamon Press, 1957.

Mance, Sir Harry Osborne. *International Sea Transport.* New York: Oxford University Press, 1945.

Manson, P. "Shipping Board's Money Losses." *Nation,* 15 November 1922.

Marine Engineering Log. "The 'Flag of Convenience' Fleet: Not All Bad and Getting Better." *Marine Engineering Log,* August 1978.

Mason, John B. *The Danzig Dilemma: A Study in Peace-Making by Compromise.* London: Oxford University Press, 1946.

Mason, John Brown. "The Status of the Free City of Danzig under International Law." *Rocky Mountain Law Review* (1933): 85.

May, Stacy and Galo Plaza. *The United Fruit Company in Latin America.* Washington: National Planning Association, 1958. Reprint. New York: Arno, 1976.

Mellander, G. A. *The United States in Panamanian Politics: The Intriguing Formative Years.* Danville: Interstate Printers and Publishers, 1971.

Melville, John H. *The Great White Fleet.* New York: Vintage, 1976.

Mendelsohn, Allan I. "Maritime Liability for Oil Pollution: Domestic and International Law." *George Washington Law Review* 38 (1969): 1.

———. "The Public Interest and Private International Maritime Law." *William and Mary Law Review* 10 (1969): 783.

———. "Ocean Pollution and the 1972 UN Conference on the Environment." *Journal of Maritime Law and Commerce* 3 (1971): 385.

Metaxas, Bas N. *The Economics of Tramp Shipping.* London: Athlone Press, 1971.

Meyers, H. *Nationality of Ships.* The Hague: Nijhoff, 1967.

Millis, Walter. *The Road to War: America 1914–1917.* Boston: 1935. Reprint. New York: Fertig, 1970.

Milsten, Donald E. "Enforcing International Law: U.S. Agencies and the Regulation of Oil Pollution in American Waters." *Journal of Maritime Law and Commerce* 6 (1975): 273.

Moore, Gerald. "Legal Aspects of Marine Pollution Control." In R. Johnston, ed. *Marine Pollution.* New York: Academic Press, 1976.

Moore, John Basset. *The Collected Papers of John Basset Moore.* Vol. 5. London: Oxford University Press, 1945.

Morison, Samuel E. *The Battle of the Atlantic,* Vol. 1 of *History of the United States Naval Operations in World War II.* Boston: Little Brown, 1947.

Morrow, Jan. "The International Status of the Free City of Danzig." *British Yearbook of International Law* (1937): 114.

Morse, Clarence G. "A Study of American Merchant Marine Legislation." *Law and Contemporary Problems* 25 (1960): 57.

Mosley, Leonard. *Dulles: A Biography of Eleanor, Allen and John Foster Dulles and Their Family Network.* New York: Dial Press, 1978.

Mostert, Noel. *Supership.* New York: A. A. Knopf, 1974.

Naess, Erling. *The Great PanLibHon Controversy.* Epping, England: Gower Press, 1972.

———. *Autobiography of a Shipping Man.* Colchester, England: Seatrade Publications, 1977.

National Research Council. "The Role of the U.S. Merchant Marine in National Security." (Walrus Report). Washington: National Academy of Sciences, 1959.

Neuman, Robert. "Oil on Troubled Waters: The International Control of Marine Pollution." *Journal of Maritime Law and Commerce*, January 1971.

Nielsen, Fred K. "The Lack of Uniformity in the Law and Practice of States with Regard to Merchant Vessels." *American Journal of International Law* 13 (1919): 1.

Norwegian Shipping News. "Liberia Regains Tanker Lead." *Norwegian Shipping News*, 5 March 1964.

Novick, Sheldon. "Ducking Liability at Sea." *Environment*, January, February 1977.

O'Connell, Dennis M. "Reflections on Brussels: IMCO and the 1969 Pollution Conventions." *Cornell International Law Journal* 3 (1970): 161.

O'Connell, D. P. *The Influence of Law on Sea Power*. Manchester: Manchester University Press, 1975.

OECD. *Maritime Transport 1971. A Study by the Maritime Transport Committee*. Paris: Organization for Economic Cooperation and Development, 1972.

Orr, David W. and Marvin S. Soroos, eds. *The Global Predicament: Ecological Perspectives on the World Order*. Chapel Hill: University of North Carolina Press, 1979.

Oudet, L. de Vaisseau. *In the Wake of the Torrey Canyon: Reflections on a Disaster*. London: Royal Institute of Navigation, 1972.

Overstreet, Luther M. "The Merchant Marine, Its Value in Peace and War." *United States Naval Institute Proceedings* 53 (October 1927): 1094.

Padelford, Norman J. "International Law and the Spanish Civil War." *American Journal of International Law* 31 (1937): 237.

———. "Foreign Shipping During the Spanish Civil War." *American Journal of International Law* 32 (1938): 264.

———. *International Law and Diplomacy in the Spanish Civil Strife*. New York: Macmillan, 1939.

"PanLibHon Registration of American-owned Merchant Ships: Government Policy and the Problem of the Courts." *Columbia Law Review* 60 (1960): 711.

Peiser, Kurt. *Danzig's Shipping and Foreign Trade*. Danzig: A. W. Kafemann, 1930.

Perdicas, P. L. "History and Outline of Greek Maritime Law." *Transactions of the Grotius Society* (Papers) 25 (1939): 40.

Petrow, Richard. *In the Wake of the Torrey Canyon*. New York: McKay, 1968; simultaneously published in Britain as *Black Tide*.

Phelps, Edith M. *American Merchant Marine: Debaters' Handbook Series*. New York: Wilson, 1920.

Pippin, Larry LaRae. *The Remon Era: An Analysis of a Decade of Events in Panama, 1947–1957*. Stanford, Calif.: Institute of Hispanic American and Luso-Brazilian Studies, 1964.

Plummer, Edward C. "Merchant Ships and the Navy." *North American Review* 224 (1927): 505.

Popper, David. "American Neutrality and Maritime Rights." *Foreign Policy Reports*, 1 January 1940.

Popperwell, Ronald G. *Norway*. New York: Praeger, 1972.

Popple, Charles S. *Standard Oil Company (New Jersey) in World War II*. New York: Standard Oil Company, 1952.

Potter, Jeffrey. *Disaster by Oil: Oil Spills—Why They Happen—What They Do—How We Can End Them.* New York: Macmillan, 1973.
Pratt, Fletcher. "Commerce Destruction, Past and Future." *United States Naval Institute Proceedings* 54 (1934): 1513.
Price, William J. "Influence of the United States on Central American Progress." *Current History* 26 (1927): 871.
Radius, Walter Albrecht. *United States Shipping in Transpacific Trade, 1922–1938.* Stanford, Calif.: Stanford University Press, 1944. Reprint. New York: Greenwood, 1968.
Reisman, W. M. "Sanctions and Enforcement." In Cyril Black and Richard Falk, eds. *The Future of the International Legal Order.* Vol. 3. Princeton, N.J.: Princeton University Press, 1971.
Renton, David. *The Genuine Link Concept and the Nationality of Physical and Legal Persons, Ships and Aircraft.* Cologne: 1975.
Republic of Liberia. *Liberian Code of Laws of 1956 Adopted by the Legislature of the Republic of Liberia March 22, 1956.* Ithaca, N.Y.: Cornell University Press, 1957.
Republic of Liberia. "Board of Investigation (Into Torrey Canyon)." *International Legal Materials* 6 (1967): 480.
Republic of Liberia. *Liberian Maritime Regulations.* Monrovia: International Trust Company, 1972.
Republic of Liberia. *Liberian Maritime Law.* Monrovia: International Trust Company, 1973.
Republic of Liberia. *Liberia—25 Years as a Maritime Nation.* Monrovia: International Trust Company, 1975(?).
Rienow, Robert. *The Test of the Nationality of a Merchant Vessel.* New York: Columbia University Press, 1937.
Riesenberg, Felix. *Sea War: The Story of the U.S. Merchant Marine in World War II.* New York: Rinehart, 1956. Reprint. Westport, Conn.: Greenwood, 1974.
Riesenfeld, Stefan. "Sovereign Immunity of Foreign Vessels in Anglo-American Law: The Evolution of a Legal Doctrine," *Minnesota Law Review* 25 (1940): 1.
Rohwer, Jürgen. *Die U-Boot-Erfolge der Achsenmächte, 1939–1945.* Munich: J. F. Lehmann, 1968.
Ryan, Paul. "Canal Diplomacy and U.S. Interests." *United States Naval Institute Proceedings* 103 (January 1977): 43.
———. *The Panama Canal Controversy: U.S. Diplomacy and Defense Interests.* Stanford, Calif.: Hoover Institution Press, 1977.
Safford, Jeffrey J. "Edward Hurley and American Shipping Policy: An Elaboration on Wilsonian Diplomacy, 1918–1919." *Historian* 35 (1973): 568.
———. *Wilsonian Maritime Diplomacy, 1913–1921.* New Brunswick, N.J.: Rutgers University Press, 1977.
Sampson, Anthony. *The Seven Sisters: The Great Oil Companies and the World They Shaped.* New York: Viking, 1975.
Sankawulo, Wilton. *Liberia and African Unity.* n.p., 1972.
Saugstad, Jesse E. *Shipping and the State: France, Germany, Japan, Italy, Spain, Great Britain, United States.* Washington: U.S. Shipping Board Bureau of Research, 1928.
———. *Shipping and Shipbuilding Subsidies.* Washington: Government Publications Office, 1932.

Savage, Carlton. *Policy of the United States Toward Maritime Commerce in War.* Washington: Department of State, 1936.

Scarceriaux, Paul E. R. "Merchant Ships Lost Under Panamanian Flag During World War II: Tentative List." *Belgian Shiplover* 149 (1974): 93.

Schachter, Oscar and Daniel Serwer. "Marine Pollution: Problems and Remedies." *American Journal of International Law* 65 (1971): 84.

Schmidt, F. "Ships Flying Flags of Convenience." *Arkiv for Sjørett* (Norway) 12 (1972): 77.

Schultz, Charles R. *Bibliography of Periodical Articles on Maritime and Naval History.* Mystic, Conn.: Marine Historical Association, 1972.

Scott, James Brown. *The Declaration of London, February 26, 1909.* New York: Oxford University Press, 1919.

Scroggs, W. O. "Oil for Italy." *Foreign Affairs* 14 (1936): 523.

Shell Briefing Service. "Conserving our Environment." Shell Briefing Service, July 1970.

Shepardson, W. H. and William Scroggs. *The United States in World Affairs.* New York: Harper Brothers for the Council on Foreign Relations, 1940.

Sherwood, Robert. *Roosevelt and Hopkins.* New York: Harper, 1948.

Shils, E. B. "The Flag of Necessity Fleet and the American Economy." *Labor Law Journal* 13 (1962): 151.

Shils, E. B. and Sidney Miller. "Foreign Flags on U.S. Ships: Convenience or Necessity?" *Industrial Relations* 2 (1963): 131.

Shinn, Robert. *The International Politics of Marine Pollution.* New York: Praeger, 1974.

Simmonds, K. R. "The Constitution of the Maritime Safety Committee of IMCO." *International Comparative Law Quarterly* 12 (1963): 56.

Singh, Nagendra. "International Law of Merchant Shipping." *Academie de Droit International, Recueil des Cours* 107 (1962): 1.

———. *Shipowners.* London: Stevens, 1967.

———. *Maritime Flag and International Law.* Leyden: Sitjhoff, 1978.

Smith, Darrel H. and Paul Betters. *The United States Shipping Board: Its History, Activities and Organization.* Washington: Brookings Institution, 1931.

Smith, Myron J., Jr. *The American Navy, 1919–1941: A Bibliography.* Metuchen, N.J.: Scarecrow Press, 1974.

Solow, Herbert. "Those Resourceful Greek Shipping Men." *Fortune,* October 1953.

Sørenson, Max. "Law of the Sea." *International Conciliation* 520 (November 1958): 205.

Standard Oil Company of New Jersey. *Ships of the Esso Fleet in World War II.* New York: Standard Oil Company, 1946.

Stanford Law Review. "Under Two Flags: Foreign Registry of American Merchantmen." *Stanford Law Review* 5 (1953): 797.

Stettinius. See Herring; see also Johnson, Walter.

Stettinius, E. R., Jr. *Lend-Lease, Weapon for Victory.* New York: Macmillan, 1944.

Stevenson, William. *A Man Called Intrepid: The Secret War.* New York: Harcourt Brace Jovanovich, 1976.

Stockton, C. H. "The International Naval Conference of London, 1908–1909." *American Journal of International Law* 3 (1909): 596.

Stone W. T. "Will Neutrality Keep Us out of War?" *Foreign Policy Reports*, 1 October 1939.

Sturmey, S. G. *Some Aspects of Ocean Liner Economics*. Manchester: Manchester Statistical Society, 1964.

Sun Oil Company. *The World Tanker Fleet* (annual).

Surveyor. "The First Energy Crisis: Tanker Technology Developed Quickly to Satisfy WWII Needs." *Surveyor*, February 1975.

Sweeney, J. "Oil Pollution of the Oceans." *Fordham Law Review* 37 (1968): 155.

———. "Admiralty Law: Oil Pollution and the Oceans." *American Trial Lawyers' Law Journal* 33 (1970): 289.

Syfert, Dwight. "The Liberian Coasting Trade, 1822–1900." *Journal of African History* 18 (1977): 217.

Tearle, W. J. "Oil Pollution from Shipping: The International Response." *University of Queensland Law Journal* 7 (1971): 303.

Thomas, Hugh. *The Spanish Civil War*. New York: Harper, 1961, 1977.

Thorndike, Joseph L. "Cap Reiber." *Life*, 1 July 1940.

Townsend, E. Reginald. *President Tubman of Liberia Speaks*. London: Consolidated Publishing Co., 1959.

Trefousse, Hans. *Germany and American Neutrality, 1939–1941*. New York: Octagon, 1951.

Truman, Harry S. *Memoirs*, 2 vols. Garden City, N.Y.: Doubleday, 1955, 1956.

Tucker, E. S. "Keeping the Seas Clean." *Petroleum Economist* 45 (1978): 103.

United Nations, General Assembly. "Resolution on the Prevention of Marine Pollution." *International Legal Materials* 9 (1970): 424.

United Nations, Secretariat. *Laws Concerning the Nationality of Ships*. UN Legislative Series, 1955.

United States, Congress, House, Committee on Merchant Marine and Fisheries. *Hearings on HR 8361*. 71st Cong., 1930.

United States, Congress, House, Committee on Merchant Marine and Fisheries. *Hearings on HR 3419*. 81st Cong., 1949.

United States, Congress, House, Committee on Merchant Marine and Fisheries, Subcommittee on Merchant Marine and Fisheries. *Study of Vessel Transfer, Trade-in and Reserve Fleet Policies*. 85th Cong., 1957.

United States, Congress, House, Committee on Merchant Marine and Fisheries, Special Subcommittee on Merchant Marine. *Study of Trade-out and Build Activities of the Onassis Companies* (Report 1688). 85th Cong., 1958.

United States, Congress, House, Committee on Merchant Marine and Fisheries, Subcommittee on Merchant Marine and Fisheries. *Hearings on HR 6601, 7601*. 86th Cong., 1959.

United States, Congress, House, Committee on Merchant Marine and Fisheries, Subcommittee on Merchant Marine. *Energy Transportation Security Act of 1974 (HR 8193)*. 93d Cong., 1974.

United States, Congress, House, Committee on Merchant Marine and Fisheries, Subcommittee on Merchant Marine. *Energy Transportation Security Act of 1977 (HR 1037)*. 95th Cong., 1977.

United States, Congress, House, Committee on Merchant Marine and Fisheries. *New Panama Canal Treaty Hearings*. 95th Cong., 1977.

United States, Congress, Senate, Special Committee Investigating the Munitions Industry ("Nye Committee"), 73d Cong., 1934.

United States, Congress, Senate, Committee on Interstate and Foreign Commerce, Subcommittee on Marine and Maritime Affairs. *Investigation: Transfers of Ships to Foreign Registry.* 81st Cong., 1949.

United States, Congress, Senate, Committee on Interstate and Foreign Commerce. *Hearings on S. 3823.* 81st Cong., 1950.

United States, Congress, Senate, Committee on Interstate and Foreign Commerce. *Merchant Marine Study and Investigation.* 81st Cong., 1950.

United States, Congress, Senate, Committee on Government Operations, Permanent Subcommittee of Investigation. *Hearings on Sale of Government-Owned Vessels.* 82d Cong., 1952.

United States, Congress, Senate, Committee on Interstate and Foreign Commerce, Subcommittee on Commerce. *Investigation of Federal Maritime Administration, Transfer to Foreign Flag, S. 173.* 83d Cong., 1954.

United States, Congress, Senate, Committee on Interstate and Foreign Commerce, Subcommittee on Merchant Marine and Fisheries. *Hearings on Ship Transfers.* 85th Cong., 1957.

United States, Congress, Senate, Committee on Commerce, Subcommittee of the Subcommittee on Communications. *Final Report, Pursuant to S. 395.* 86th Cong., 1961.

United States, Congress, Senate, Committee on Appropriations. *Coast Guard Resource Needs for Responding to Oil Spills, Fiscal Year 1979.* 95th Cong., 1979.

United States, Department of Commerce, Maritime Administration. *Ships Registered Under the Liberian, Panamanian and Honduran Flags Deemed by the Navy Department to be Under United States Effective Control.* Washington: U.S. Department of Commerce, Maritime Administration, 1968.

United States, Department of Commerce, Maritime Administration, Office of Subsidy Administration, Division of Trade Studies and Statistics. *Foreign Flag Merchant Ships Owned by U.S. Parent Companies as of June 30, 1974.* Superintendent of Documents, 1975.

United States, Department of Commerce, Maritime Administration, Office of Technology Assessment. *Oil Transportation by Tankers: An Analysis of Marine Pollution and Safety Measures.* Washington: U.S. Government Printing Office, 1975.

United States, Department of Commerce, Maritime Administration. *Shipboard Guide to Pollution-Free Operations.* Washington: U.S. Department of Commerce, Maritime Administration, 1976.

United States, Department of Commerce, Maritime Administration, Office of Policy and Plans. *The Maritime Aids of the Six Maritime Nations.* Washington: Government Printing Office, 1977.

United States, Department of Commerce, Maritime Administration. *Foreign Flag Merchant Ships Owned by U.S. Parent Companies, as of December 31, 1976.* Washington: Government Printing Office, 1978.

United States, Department of State. "United States and Liberia Sign Point Four Agreement." *United States State Department Bulletin,* January 1951.

United States, Department of State. *Foreign Relations of the United States.* Volumes as cited in text notes.

United States, Department of Transportation, United States Coast Guard. *Background Summary Regarding the International Conference on Tanker Safety and Pollution Prevention Held in London, England, 5–17 February 1978.* Washington: Coast Guard, 1978.

United States, Department of Transportation, United States Coast Guard. *Final Regulatory Analysis and Environmental Impact Statement, Regulations to Implement the Results of the International Conference on Tanker Safety and Pollution.* Washington: Coast Guard, 1979.

United States, War Shipping Administration. *Comparative Analysis of Union Agreements of General Agents of the War Shipping Administration, Covering Unlicensed Personnel on Dry Cargo Vessels as of October 1, 1945.* Washington: 1946(?).

United States, War Shipping Administration. *United States Merchant Marine at War: Report of the War Shipping Administration to the President.* Washington: War Shipping Administration, 1946.

Valentine, G. D. "The Declaration of London." *Juridical Review* 23 (1911–12): 1.

Vandenberg, Arthur, Jr. *The Private Papers of Senator Vandenberg.* 1952. Reprint. Westport, Conn.: Greenwood, 1974.

Van Panhuys, H. F. "Genuine Link Doctrine and Flags of Convenience." *American Journal of International Law* 62 (1968): 942.

Vernon, Raymond. *Sovereignty at Bay: The Multinational Spread of United States Enterprises.* New York: Basic Books, 1971.

Watts, A. D. "The Protection of Merchant Ships." *British Yearbook of International Law* 33 (1957): 52.

Wilbur, Curtis D. "Commerce and the Flag." *United States Naval Institute Proceedings* 53 (October 1927): 1049.

Wilcox, Clair. "Merchant Marine." *Fortune,* November–December 1944.

Wilkins, Mira. *The Maturing of Multinational Enterprise: American Business Abroad from 1914 to 1970.* Cambridge, Mass.: Harvard University Press, 1974.

Williams, William Appleman. *The Tragedy of American Diplomacy.* Cleveland: World Publishing Company, 1959. Reprint. New York: Dell, 1962.

Willoughby, Malcolm Francis. *Rum War at Sea.* Washington: Government Printing Office, 1964.

Wilson, Charles M. *Empire in Green and Gold.* 1947. Reprint. New York: Greenwood, 1968.

Wilson, R. R. "Non Belligerency in Relation to the Terminology of Neutrality." *American Journal of International Law* 35 (1941): 121.

Winslow, Ron. *Hard Aground: The Story of the Argo Merchant Oil Spill.* New York: Norton, 1978.

Wirsing, Robert G. *International Relations and the Future of Ocean Space.* Columbia, S.C.: University of South Carolina Press, 1974.

Wiswall, Frank L. "The ILO at Sea." *Cornell International Law Journal* 3 (1970): 153.

Wittig, Edith. "Tanker Fleets and Flags of Convenience: Advantages, Problems and Dangers." *Texas International Law Journal,* Winter 1979.

Woolsey, C. H. "New Treaties between the United States and Panama." *American Journal of International Law* 31 (1937): 297.

———. "The Taking of Foreign Ships in American Ports." *American Journal of International Law* 35 (1941): 497.

Wreh, Tuan. *Statutes and Cases on Liberian Maritime Law.* Monrovia, 1975.

Wulf, Norman A. "Contiguous Zones for Pollution Control." *Journal of Maritime Law and Commerce* 3 (1972): 537.

Zannetos, Zenon S. "Some Problems and Prospects for Marine Transportation of Oil in the 1970s." Paper delivered at Alfred Sloan School of Management, Massachusetts Institute of Technology, Cambridge, March 1973.

————. *Theory of Oil Tankship Rates: An Economic Analysis of Tankship Operations.* Cambridge, Mass.: MIT Press, 1966.

Zeis, Paul M. *American Shipping Policy.* Princeton, N.J.: Princeton University Press, 1938.

Zumwalt, Elmo R. *On Watch: A Memoir.* New York: Quadrangle, 1976.

Index

Hull, Cordell (*cont.*)
Panamanian ships, 91; on Arias over-
throw, 95–96; on World War II use of
Panamanian registry, 105–6
Hunzedal, H. V., 63
Hurley, Edward, 4

I. C. White, 94
Ida, 10, 11–12
I. G. Farben, 226 n.28
Ignacia Aguado, 227 n.1
Ilona, 63
Import Quotas. *See* Energy Transportation
Security Act
Incres, 166–68
Independent Tanker Owners' Association
(Intertanko), 183–84, 187
Intergovernmental Maritime Consultative
Organization (IMCO), 155–57, 179, 190
International Bureau of Radiotelegraphy,
32
International Convention for the Preven-
tion of Pollution from Ships (MARPOL-
73), 190–91
International Court of Justice, 154–55, 157,
211
International Labor Organization (ILO),
113, 134, 138–41, 240 n.15
International Maritime Workers Union
(IMWU), 159
International Transport Workers Federa-
tion (ITF), 112–13, 137–39, 141, 157–59
International Trust Company, 123, 127–
31, 183, 215, 238 n.52
Isonomia, 10, 11
Israel, 212
Italy, ships from, transferred to Panama,
89, 195

Jaeckel, Theodore, 13, 17
J. A. Mowinckle, 100
Janko, 88, 196
Japan: pay scale of, 11; use of Panamanian
flag by, 65, 87, 88–89; U.S. embargo of
scrap to, 80
Jenkins, J. Caldwell, 46
Jewish refugees, 64–66, 87–88
Johnson, Walter, 115
Johnston, Eric A., 119, 135
Joint Chiefs of Staff (JCS), 199–206, 208–9
Jones Act (1920), 3, 5, 160–62
Josiah Macy, 48–49, 68

Karachi, 101
Kellogg-Alfaro Treaty, 28–29, 36
Kendall, David, 164
Kennedy, John F., 165–68
Kennedy, Joseph, 43–44

Kenney, W. John, 201
Kepner, Charles, 46
Kimberly-Clark Corporation, 81
Klein, E. Stanley, 120–23, 130, 131
Koehler, John, 158
Kulukundis, Manuel, 59, 146–47, 227 n.27
Kupan Transport, 180
Kyriakides, N., 58

Labor: exploitation of, 12, 14, 17, 36, 68–
69, 105, 106–9, 139–41; protests of,
against flags of convenience, 14, 111–14,
134, 136–38, 152–53, 158–59. *See also*
National Maritime Union, Seafarers' International Union, International Transport Workers Federation
Ladimer, Irving, 112
LaFeber, Walter, 2
La Follette Seamen's Act (1915), 4, 12, 39
Lake Poularde, 178
Land, Emory: appointed Maritime Com-
mission, 43–44; on neutrality, 79; on
transfer United States Lines ships to
Panama, 80–81, 84–86; on arming
Panamanian ships, 90–93, 95; War Ship-
ping Administrator, 99, 102, 107, 194;
debate with State Department over use
Panamanian flag, 103, 108–9, 195; eva-
sion of neutrality, 200; postwar advocacy
of effective control, 206
Langer, William, 72
Lauritzen v. Larsen, 160, 168
Law of the Sea Conference (Geneva, 1958),
155
League of Nations, 28
Leahy, William, 198
Lebanon, 34
Lee, Robert C., 78
Lend-Lease Act, 87
Liberia: early maritime background, xviii;
ship registry system, origins, 115–33,
236 n.32, 237 n.37, n.39, 238 n.51; and
Panama, 116, 136; challenges to system,
149, 152–53, 179, 183–85; and IMCO,
155–57; treaty with U.S., 162; growth of
system, 171–76, 191, 239 n.59; and mari-
time disasters, 175–83; Maritime Com-
mission, 178; reform of system, 185; and
effective control, 201–6, 211–16
Liberia Company. *See* Stettinius, Edward
R., Jr.
Liberia Development Corporation, 131. *See
also* Stettinius, Edward R., Jr.
Lichtenstein, 154
Liesel, 64
Life (magazine), 135
Lincoln Land, 34
Lininger, Fred, 130–31

San Francisco Chronicle, 93
Sansinena, 178, 244 n.22
Santa Marta, 227 n.1
Saugstad, Jesse, 89, 92
Schaeffer, George, 129, 131
Seafarers' International Union (SIU), 108, 159, 169
Sea Level, 162
Sea power theory, 4, 36, 42, 198, 211. See also Mahan, Alfred T.
Sentfleben (ESSO officer, Poland), 51
Sessa, 91, 94, 96, 195, 232 n.56
Shantz, Harold, 63, 228 n.17
Shipmate, 208
Ship Sales Act (1946), 110–11, 146, 198–99
Siebert, Edwin L., 121
Singapore, 210
Skandinavia, 76
Smith, Blackwell, 120, 123, 124
Smuggling: 6–7; of liquor, 21–27; of weapons, refugees, 61–68, 227 n.19
Socdeco, 63
Sota y Aznar, 58
South, John Glover, 24, 27–31
Spain, 56–58, 62–64, 68, 77
Spanish-American War, 3
Standard Oil of California, 52
Standard Oil of New Jersey. See ESSO
Star and Herald, 11
Stark, Harold, 75
State Department. See United States State Department
Stettinius, Edward R., Jr., 115–16, 118–27, 131, 146, 201–3
Stone, Stuart, 25
Struma, 64–65, 196
Suez Canal, 171–72
Sullivan and Cromwell, 16–17, 18, 155
S. V. Harkness (Svithoid), 49, 76

Taboga, 21
Taft-Hartley Act, 142, 159–60
Taft, O., 67
Taylor, Frank, 78
Teitsworth, Charles, 149
Tepsdorf, C., 12–13
Texaco, 76
Thebes Shipping Company, 182, 185
Tinoco, Federico, 6
T. J. Williams, 94
Tolbert, William H. R., 212, 214, 215
Torrey Canyon, 175–82
Trans-Ocean Tankers Corporation, 180
Trippe, Juan, 130
Truitt, Max Orell, 79
Truman, Harry S, 111, 112, 115, 131, 142
Truslow, Francis Adams, 126–29, 238 n.51
Tubman, W.V.S., 204, 211–12

Tunica, 10
Typhoon (Colorado), 101

Union Oil, 176, 178, 243 n.3
United American Lines, 15–18
United Fruit Company: first transfer to Panama, 35; and ocean mail contract, 44–47, 54; at outbreak World War II, 89; Honduran registry, 132, 142; position on Panamanian registry, 138–39; and labor jurisdiction cases, 164–66, 169
United Nations Conference on Trade and Development, xxi
United States Lines, 78–87
United States Naval Institute Proceedings, 42, 206, 207
United States Navy, 42, 75, 116, 144, 206–11. See also Office of Naval Intelligence
United States Shipping Board: and 1920s shipping problems, 3–5; role in first transfer to Panama, 9–10; and Harriman ships, 14–18; opposition to transfers, 33–35, 37; Hoover's policy on, 39–41; powers to Maritime Commission, 43; approval transfer for diesel experimentation, 48–49. See also Maritime Commission
United States State Department, position on: liquor smuggling, 8–9, 20–27, 28–31; consular service to Panamanian flag, 13, 21, 32–33, 63–64, 66–67, 224 n.35, 228 n.20; Harriman vessels, 17; neutrality issues, 81–89; Arias overthrow, 95–97; Stettinius group authorship Liberian law, 124–29; Panama, late 1940s, 137–38; Panamanian and Liberian status in IMCO, 155; NLRB jurisdiction foreign-flag vessels, 162, 164–65; oil pollution reforms, 190. See also Neutrality legislation
Universe Leader, 244 n.22

Vancouver (Canada), 22, 25, 32–33
Vandenberg, Arthur, 115
Venezuela, 99–100, 203
Venizelos, Eleutherios, 64
Vernikos (shipping interests), 64–65
Versailles treaty, 9
Vestfold Corporation, 60–61
Vickery, H. L., 92
Viking, 34
Vikingen, Ltd., 59–60
Vistula, 48
Vogemann, Herman, 65–66
Vogtland, 66
Volstead Act, 15. See also Smuggling
Voluntary Tanker Pool, 201
Vos, Herman, 139

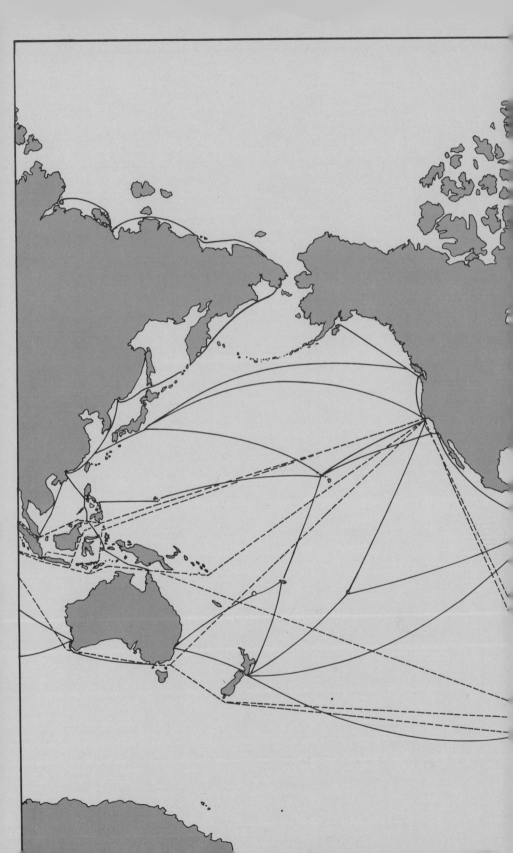